GROWING OLD IN CHRIST

GROWING OLD IN CHRIST

Edited by

Stanley Hauerwas
Carole Bailey Stoneking
Keith G. Meador
and
David Cloutier

WILLIAM B. EERDMANS PUBLISHING COMPANY
GRAND RAPIDS, MICHIGAN / CAMBRIDGE, U.K.

© 2003 Wm. B. Eerdmans Publishing Co.
All rights reserved

Wm. B. Eerdmans Publishing Co.
255 Jefferson Ave. S.E., Grand Rapids, Michigan 49503 /
P.O. Box 163, Cambridge CB3 9PU U.K.
www.eerdmans.com

Printed in the United States of America

08 07 06 05 04 03   7 6 5 4 3 2 1

ISBN 0-8028-4607-6

Contents

Part III: The Christian Practice of Growing Old

Introduction

CAROLE BAILEY STONEKING

A tale ascribed to the sage Dov Baer of Mezhirech tells of a certain Rabbi Leib who wandered over the earth, following the course of rivers, in order to redeem souls of the living and the dead. In the tale, Rabbi Leib explains to his followers his own earlier spiritual mission when he had set out to visit a famous sage. "I did not go to the Maggid in order to hear Torah from him," he said, "but to see how he unlaces his felt shoes and laces them up again."

The teachings of the Hasidic sages often took this form of indirect communication, shifting back and forth between the sacred (the words of Torah) and the mundane (shoelaces). The tales stretch the mind, requiring tolerance for ambiguity and incongruity. To spiritualize the mundane, "to hallow this life," is one goal of Jewish spirituality. Such ordinary actions as putting on and taking off clothing — tying and untying, covering and uncovering — become the parable of a way of living.

The editors of this volume felt that thinking about the living of a long life should be a path to wisdom, a path to thinking about a good life. And we were right, but in an unexpected fashion. The contributors to this volume have led us into sometimes humorous, sometimes poignant, always provocative conversation with a wonderful cast of fellow travelers, from Piers the Plowman to Delia Grinstead to Aelred of Rievaulx to St. Thomas Aquinas, a chorus of voices uncovered by the contributors who have themselves reinvigorated the ancient biblical tradition of using storytelling to explore truth.

The contributors have raised important questions: How does the story of Christ shape the stories we tell ourselves about our pasts and our future? How do we remember those stories? Does the purpose of life become clearer in old age? How are virtues such as deliberateness, reflective humor, patience, and generosity nurtured? How do we find common meanings across generational divides? What is the essence of a person? What does it mean to live a "full" life? What does it mean to die well? The answers to these questions are not charted out like a neat linear map to the end of our earthly lives; rather, they require a tolerance for ambiguity and incongruity. The answers spiritualize the mundane, "hallow this life," and bring us home.

This book is addressed to the aging — that is, to everyone. We hope that clergy and laity alike will find it both accessible and helpful. The essays integrate stories with systematic accounts, demonstrating that help and understanding come through serious intellectual engagement as well as through good moral examples. We have addressed this book to Christians in the hope that theological reflection might help them in living more faithful lives and in dying-into-life. We also hope, however, that this book might be of some help to non-Christians, that at the very least it might generate conversation and reflection on both the problems and the gifts of aging.

The book is organized into three parts. The essays in Part I, "Biblical and Historical Perspectives on Aging," focus on scriptural, early church, and medieval Christian perspectives on growing old. These essays treat not only the various descriptions of aging in the literature of those eras but also the broader theological themes that can inform our current practices and understanding of the elderly in Christian communities. In the first essay, Richard and Judith Hays reflect upon the witness of Scripture for the Christian practice of growing old. They survey the scattered references to aging characters found in the Bible and reflect on a Messiah who died young. Does Jesus' death in the prime of his life leave us with any christologically informed pattern for the Christian practice of growing old? Rowan Greer explains that since old age was attained only by the few rather than the many in the early church, it was viewed as a gift. He suggests that we, like those in the early church, should see the aged as representatives of the culmination of virtue and wisdom. David Aers reveals that in the Middle Ages the evils of old age were emphasized far more than its potential goods, but he also uncovers the voice of one medieval poet who offered a vision of growing old as a time of Christian exploration, exploration possible only within the sustaining community of the body of Christ, the church.

The essays in Part II, "Critical Perspectives on Modern Problems of Aging," examine modern views of aging, which often take the form of a fear of aging and of the aged; they also discuss the relation of such views to our political, economic, and social systems, as well as their implications for the elderly and society as a whole. The first essay in this part of the book is my own attempt to uncover modernity's dissociation of ideas from images and attitudes by focusing on the actual lives, in contrast to the cultural representations, of people who are growing older. In "Growing Old in a Therapeutic Culture," Keith Meador and Shaun Henson uncover the dangers of therapeutic optimism, which has been fed by the powers of modern medicine. They argue that in place of such optimism Christians ought resolutely to claim a narrative of hope grounded in the life, suffering, death, and resurrection of Jesus, a narrative that does not see aging as an evil that we are to fight. Patricia Beattie Jung investigates the differences between the young and the old as well as variability among the elderly themselves, and examines the differences that factors such as gender, race, and socioeconomic status make in one's experience of growing old. In "The Language of Death: Theology and Economics in Conflict," D. Stephen Long describes the way in which Christian discourse on dying well has been replaced by economists' talk of "scarce resources." In the final essay of this section Joel Shuman calls attention to the medicalization of death, to the way capitalism shapes us to believe that when we are no longer capable of producing or consuming we have no reason to live, and, perhaps most devastating, to the erosion of those tradition-bearing communities which, until quite recently, taught us how to die and how to care for the elderly and the dying. Shuman provides a transition to the last section of the book by sketching what the Christian alternative for growing old in our culture might look like.

Part III, "The Christian Practice of Growing Old," gathers constructive accounts of Christian practices that not only confront modern understandings of aging but also sustain the gift of a long life by providing meaning, solace, celebration, and challenge. In the first essay in this section, Stanley Hauerwas and Laura Yordy reflect on the peculiar challenge aging presents to friendship; they contend that friendships both among the elderly and between the elderly and the young are essential to the church, and they offer practical suggestions about how churches can approximate Aelred of Rievaulx's vision of a community of friendship. Susan and L. Gregory Jones's articulation of what it means to participate in worship helps us to move beyond notions that personhood is circumscribed by memory, mental activity, or the mind in isolation from other faculties. They invite us to see worship as a site for reclaiming the truth that all of us — from the very youngest to the very oldest — are creatures made in the image and likeness of God, destined for communion with God, and worthy of participation in the praise of God. In "The Virtues of Aging," Charles Pinches weaves personal stories as well as the stories of Homer into a serious reflection on what it means to speak of the virtues of aging. David Matzko McCarthy argues that those with longevity are often the best sources of wisdom about sustaining continuity through change, but not if they are socially isolated and segregated from the common life of the body of Christ. David Cloutier's essay provides a persuasive case for the inadmissibility of physician-assisted suicide for those who follow Christ, revealing the unique place of suffering and dependency in the Christian vision of the good life. The final essay of the book, M. Therese Lysaught's "Memory, Funerals, and the Communion of Saints," probes the question, "What might it mean, that our bonds with those who have died 'do not unravel'?" Offering a critique of common descriptions of the concept of memory, Lysaught suggests that funeral practices are an important reminder that those who have died remain members of the community. In resituating the dead within the communion of saints, such rituals resituate the living as well, and teach us to truly remember the elderly in our midst.

The editors are grateful to all of those who have helped in the writing of this book. The contributors have shared not only their time and talent but also their own stories, feelings, and thoughts. We offer our sincere thanks to each and every one. We are grateful, too, for the seniors in our lives who have shared their experiences of the flow of the generations and their insights into what it means and what it should mean to grow old and die "in Christ."

PART I

BIBLICAL AND HISTORICAL
PERSPECTIVES ON AGING

The Christian Practice of Growing Old: The Witness of Scripture

RICHARD B. HAYS *and* JUDITH C. HAYS

Introduction

In contrast to American culture's recent preoccupation with the problem of aging and care of older persons, the New Testament has surprisingly little to say on the topic. The relative silence of these texts may be explained, at least in part, by the very different social and cultural world in which the New Testament writers lived: fewer people lived to an advanced age,[1] and those who did were honored and esteemed within the community. Aging, therefore, was not seen by the early Christians as a "problem" to which some sort of religious so-

---

1. On life expectancy in the ancient Mediterranean world, see Tim G. Parkin, *Roman Demography and Society* (Baltimore: Johns Hopkins University Press, 1992). Parkin estimates that life expectancy at birth was about 25 years, due largely to high infant mortality rates, and that "in Roman society those over the age of 60 years represented some 5 to 10 percent of the total population" (p. 134). Roger Bagnall and Bruce Frier (*The Demography of Roman Egypt* [Cambridge: Cambridge University Press, 1994]) calculate that for Roman Egypt, female life expectancy at birth was between 20 and 25 years, but that females who survived to age 10 enjoyed a life expectancy ranging from 34.5 to 37.5 years, meaning that they would, on average, die between the ages of 44 and 47 (p. 90). See also Evelyne Patlagean, *Pauvreté économique et pauvreté social á Byzance, 4e-7e siecles* (Paris: Mouton, 1977), pp. 95-101. According to her figures, half of the populace died before reaching the age of 44. By way of comparison, in the United States life expectancy was 76.7 years for those born in 1998 (National Center for Health Statistics, *Health, United States 2000 with Adolescent Health Chartbook* [Hyattsville, Md.: 2000], p. 4). In addition, by the year 2000, 13 percent of the population of the United States had attained the age of 65 or older (Federal Interagency Forum on Aging Related Statistics [FIFARS], *Older Americans 2000: Key Indicators of Well-Being* [Hyattsville, Md.: FIFARS, 2000], p. 2). Girls who were 10 years old in 1998 could expect to live an average of 60.2 more years, and the median age of survivorship for the total U.S. population was 80 years (Centers for Disease Control: National Vital Statistics Report 48:18, pp. 2, 4).

lution was required. Consequently, the New Testament documents provide few answers to questions that may seem of urgent concern to us: how to forestall the physical appearance of advancing age; how to cover the costs of long-term care for the aged; how to promote the preferences of dying patients. By comparison to the New Testament, the Old Testament tells more stories about characters of great age — from Methuselah to David — but here again the cultural context within which aging is understood differs so dramatically from ours that the fit between our concerns and the concerns of the writers is rough. Does this mean, then, that the Bible is of limited usefulness for our theological reflection on the Christian practice of growing old? On the contrary, because the scriptural texts provide a different evaluative framework for understanding aging, they may cause us to pause and reframe our own reflections.

This chapter will focus on the New Testament material, but we must always remember that the church's Scripture includes the twofold canon of Old Testament and New Testament together. The New Testament texts belong to the longer story of God's dealing with Israel, as disclosed in the Old Testament. The New Testament writers narrate the continuation of that story and offer particular sets of lenses through which to interpret it. Consequently, our discussion of aging, while focusing on the New Testament, will keep the wider biblical perspective in view.

Our discussion is divided into four parts. We begin with lexical observations about the terms employed for "old" and "aging" in the New Testament and with some observations about their significance. Then we will survey the New Testament's portrayal of aging characters and offer theological reflections on the themes highlighted in these stories. The third section of the chapter will take up the striking fact that Jesus, the New Testament's paradigm for a life lived faithfully before God, was executed as a young man and never experienced advanced age. What is the significance of this fact for theological reflection about aging? Finally, we will suggest that the matter of greatest concern to the biblical writers was not aging as such but the *telos* toward which the aging process leads: mortality. A biblical perspective on growing old will cause us to focus on death as the end toward which we move — and yet as the last enemy confronted by God's redemptive power.

Biblical Terminology for Aging

In the New Testament we encounter several different terms that refer to aging or to persons of advanced age, though none of the terms appears frequently.

The word *presbytes* ("old man") appears three times; in two of these cases the term is offered as a self-description, once by Zechariah (Luke 1:18) and once by Paul (Philem. 9). The third occurrence of the term refers to "old men" in the church in Crete, to whom Paul's emissary Titus is to provide instruction (Titus 2:2). The equivalent feminine noun, *presbytis* ("old woman") appears in the same context (Titus 2:3), its only appearance in the New Testament. The closely related term *presbyteros* ("elder") is used with some frequency as a term for those who are recognized as community leaders in the synagogue (e.g., Matt. 21:23; Luke 7:3; Acts 25:15) or in the church (e.g., Acts 15:2; 1 Tim. 5:17; Titus 1:5; James 5:14). This usage presupposes that leadership is linked to seniority in the community. Sometimes, however, the term *presbyteros* — actually a comparative adjectival form, as the English translation of "elder" rightly suggests — refers to older people without reference to any office of leadership, as in Acts 2:17, 1 Timothy 5:1 (cf. also the feminine plural form *presbyteras* in 1 Tim. 5:2), and perhaps 1 Peter 5:5.

The noun *geron* ("old man," whence our English word "gerontology") turns up only once, in Nicodemus' question to Jesus (John 3:4). Related terms are *geras* ("old age": Luke 1:36) and the verb *gerasko* ("grow old": John 21:18; Heb. 8:13). This term appears to refer simply to chronological age without carrying any of the connotations of dignity that attach to *presbytes/ presbyteroi*.

Finally, the adjective *palaios* (from which words such as "paleontology" are derived) means "ancient, having been in existence for a long time," and it often carries the "connotation of being antiquated or outworn."[2] It can refer to an old, torn garment or old, brittle wineskins (Mark 2:21-22 and parallels), to the old leaven that is discarded in preparation for Passover (1 Cor. 5:7), to the "old covenant" read in the synagogue (2 Cor. 3:14; cf. Rom. 7:6), or, figuratively, to the old unregenerate self now put to death (Rom. 6:6) or removed like an outworn garment and replaced by a new identity in Christ (Eph. 4:22; Col. 3:9). Less frequently in New Testament usage, *palaios* refers to a teaching that is valuable and venerable because of its age (Matt. 13:52; 1 John 2:7). Significantly, the term *palaios* is never used in a literal sense to describe a person of advanced age. Unfortunately, because the single English word "old" is used to translate this term as well as the word families linked to *presbytes* and *geron*, the pejorative connotations of *palaios* can bleed over and cause English readers to assign inappropriately negative associations to the other terms discussed above.

---

2. F. W. Danker, *A Greek-English Lexicon of the New Testament and Other Early Christian Literature,* third ed. (Chicago: University of Chicago Press, 2000), p. 751.

Older Characters in the New Testament

Older characters play a significant role in the opening chapters of Luke's Gospel. The first characters who appear on stage in Luke's story are the priest Zechariah and his wife Elizabeth, who were both "advanced in years" (Luke 1:7). Although they were both "righteous before God, living blamelessly according to all the commandments and regulations of the Lord," they remained, to their dismay, childless (1:6-7). When the angel Gabriel appears to Zechariah in the Temple and promises that Elizabeth will bear a son named John who is to play the role of Elijah in calling Israel to repentance (1:13-17), we hear echoes of the Old Testament stories of Abraham and Sarah (Gen. 18:1-15; 21:1-7) and of Hannah and her husband Elkanah (1 Sam. 1:1-20). In these stories, the surprising grace of God is made manifest through the promise and birth of a child to a previously barren couple. The parallel to the Abraham-Sarah story is especially strong because of the advanced age of the pair to whom the promise is made. The motif of surprising fruitfulness in old age highlights the power and freedom of God: "Is anything too hard for the Lord?" (Gen. 18:14; cf. Luke 1:37).

Nonetheless, like Sarah, who greeted the divine promise with skeptical laughter, Zechariah finds the promise incredible; consequently, Gabriel strikes him temporarily speechless (Luke 1:18-23). Almost immediately, however, Luke also narrates the fulfillment of the promised good news: "After these days, his wife Elizabeth conceived" (1:24). As the plot unfolds, we find a continuing emphasis on the advanced age of the new parents. In Gabriel's annunciation speech to Mary, he discloses to her that "your relative Elizabeth in her old age has also conceived a son" (1:36).

Despite Zechariah's initial doubts, both he and Elizabeth become prophets who discern the new thing that God is doing. They are the first two figures in Luke's story who are said to be "filled with the Holy Spirit" (1:41, 67). Elizabeth pronounces Mary "blessed among women" and describes her prophetically as "the mother of my Lord," thereby becoming the first to ascribe the title *kyrios* to Jesus (1:42-43). Zechariah, in turn, finds his tongue loosed after the birth of John and utters a prophecy that summarizes the epic sweep of the biblical narrative and declares that God's promises to redeem Israel are now being brought to fulfillment (1:67-79). Thus, in Luke's carefully structured narrative, the older figures Elizabeth and Zechariah become both the instruments of God's purpose and — alongside Mary — the first interpreters of God's saving acts.

As Luke's story of the birth and infancy of Jesus continues, we encounter two more aged characters who serve as prophetic voices: Simeon and Anna become the prophetic chorus welcoming the child Jesus on the occasion of his purification in the Temple (Luke 2:22-38). The old man Simeon, who has long been hoping for "the consolation of Israel" (i.e., its deliverance from oppression), has been promised by the Holy Spirit that he will not die before he has seen the Lord's Messiah. Upon seeing the infant Jesus, he recognizes him as God's chosen one and movingly declares,

> Master, now you are dismissing your servant in peace,
>   according to your word;
> for my eyes have seen your salvation,
>   which you have prepared in the presence of all peoples,
> a light for revelation to the Gentiles
>   and for glory to your people Israel. (Luke 2:29-32)

Furthermore, speaking under the guidance of the Spirit, he intones to Mary a dark prophecy of the Passion, foretelling both her own suffering and the role of her child Jesus as a polarizing sign "for the falling and the rising of many in Israel" (Luke 2:34). Similarly, Anna — an eighty-four-year-old prophetess who frequents the Temple to worship and pray night and day — recognizes Jesus, gives thanks to God, and declares the news about him "to all who were looking for the redemption of Jerusalem" (2:38).

Thus, Luke's narrative provides a matched pair of older male and female witnesses prefiguring Jesus' messianic vocation and the conflict that his mission will engender. The advanced age of Simeon and Anna signifies their time-tested wisdom, while at the same time symbolizing Israel's long-suffering expectation of deliverance. These two aged figures also suggest that radical openness to the redeeming power of God may be found among elders — perhaps particularly there.

In John's Gospel, we encounter an aged character who exemplifies a more ambiguous reception within Israel for Jesus. Nicodemus, a "ruler of the Jews," seeks out Jesus by night to question him (John 3:1-21). We are not told his age, but his response to Jesus' mysterious declaration about the necessity of being born again suggests that he may be well advanced in years: "How can a man be born *when he is old?* Can he enter a second time into his mother's womb and be born?" (John 3:4; emphasis added). Jesus' answer indicates that Nicodemus should not marvel at this call to be born again, even in late life, because the new birth is the work of the Spirit, which blows freely where it will.

In this story, in contrast to the account of Simeon and Anna, age confers no special wisdom or insight. Indeed, Nicodemus' role as an established "teacher of Israel" seems to stand in the way of his comprehension of the word of God embodied in Jesus, and his coming "by night" associates him symbolically with those who "loved darkness rather than light because their deeds were evil" (John 3:19). Nicodemus fades out of the scene in John 3, and we are not told how he responds to Jesus' elusive challenge. His last recorded words express a bewildered skepticism: "How can this be?" (3:9). Yet, if we read this story in a canonical context, we may note the similarity between Nicodemus' response and the response of Mary to Gabriel's promise that she will bear a child who will become the new Davidic king: "How can this be, since I have no husband?" (Luke 1:34). Perhaps, then, Nicodemus' question is no more his final response than is Mary's. Indeed, two other references later in the story suggest that Nicodemus continues to be at least a secret believer in Jesus: he speaks up — albeit noncommitally — in defense of Jesus before the chief priests and Pharisees (John 7:45-52), and he joins Joseph of Arimathea in anointing the body of Jesus for burial (19:38-42).

The last chapter of John's Gospel, in its depictions of Peter and the Beloved Disciple, offers evidence of some importance for a survey of aged characters in the New Testament. Here the risen Jesus prophesies Peter's eventual death as an old man: "Truly, truly, I say to you, when you were young, you girded yourself and walked where you would; but *when you are old*, you will stretch out your hands, and another will gird you and carry you where you do not wish to go" (John 21:18; emphasis added). This prophecy of martyrdom as an old man provokes Peter to ask about "the disciple whom Jesus loved." Jesus' evasive answer provides the occasion for the narrator to comment that, contrary to some rumors, Jesus had not predicted that the Beloved Disciple would not die (21:23). This authorial comment seems to presuppose a situation late in the first century when the Beloved Disciple, after a long life of bearing witness and serving as the source of community tradition (21:24), has in fact died. Thus, the story implies that both Peter and the Beloved Disciple, despite their different manners of death, continued into their old age as witnesses for the gospel and key leaders of the early Christian movement.

Turning to the Pauline Epistles, we find only a few passages dealing with aged characters. The most important of these is Paul's recounting in Romans 4 of the story of Abraham and Sarah. In the course of explicating the faith of Abraham, Paul highlights his advanced age: "He did not weaken in faith when he considered his own body, which was as good as dead because he was about a hundred years old, or when he considered the barrenness of Sarah's womb" (Rom. 4:19). Despite these seemingly hopeless circumstances, Abraham continued to trust "that God was able to do what he had promised," and his faith was reckoned to him as righteousness (4:21-22). Thus, Paul casts Abraham as an exemplar of faith, not merely for elders but for the whole world.

Paul makes one passing reference to himself as an "old man" who is now a "prisoner for Christ Jesus" (Philem. 9). This self-description may be intended to elicit sympathetic respect from the letter's addressees, whom he is seeking to persuade to deal mercifully with the slave Onesimus. Elsewhere, Paul's references to himself as the "father" of his converts serve a similar purpose of appealing for the respectful obedience due to an older parent (e.g., 1 Cor. 4:14-16; 2 Cor. 6:13; Gal. 4:19-20; 1 Thess. 2:11-12) — though the emphasis here is less on Paul's age than on his metaphorical "paternity" of his churches.

The respect due to older members of the community is emphasized in the Pastoral Epistles. See, for example, 1 Timothy 5:1: "Do not rebuke an older man, but exhort him as you would a father." Here we find also specific directives that the community should provide assistance to widows over the age of sixty, and that women recognized by the church as widows should devote their energies to prayer, hospitality, and service to the afflicted (1 Tim. 5:3-16). The letter to Titus adds that older women should be instructed "to be reverent in behavior, not to be slanderers or slaves to drink," and that they should train the younger women in their domestic duties, so that "the word of God may not be discredited" (Titus 2:3-5). The older men, on the other hand, are to be instructed, in a more general way, to be "temperate, serious, sensible, sound in faith, in love, and in steadfastness" (Titus 2:2). These unexceptional moral teachings for the elderly are part of a larger concern in the Pastorals that the church community be respectable in the eyes of the wider culture, but they offer little in the way of specifically Christian moral vision for growing old.

As we survey these scattered references to aging characters in the New Testament, can we make any general observations or discern any general themes?

First, the New Testament writers deem elders worthy of honor, respect, and special care. When elders are alone and in need, the church community is called to provide for their care, and those who fail to provide for their own older family members are harshly condemned: "they have denied the faith, and are worse than unbelievers" (1 Tim. 5:8). According to the Epistle of James, "religion that is pure and undefiled" devotes its attention to caring for widows and orphans (James 1:27). One of Jesus' sternest judgments against the scribes and Pharisees is directed against the casuistry they employed to abdicate responsibility for caring for parents (Mark 7:9-13). Even at the time of his crucifixion, Jesus showed concern for his mother Mary by commending her into the care of the Beloved Disciple, who then "took her into his own home" (John 19:26-27).

In turn, older persons bear a particular responsibility. They are to be paradigms of faith, role models exemplifying reverence and temperance (Titus 2:2-5). They are to exercise leadership in the community, especially in teaching and counseling. They may even find a special vocation to suffering, to face death, even martyrdom, without seeing the fulfillment of God's promises to his people. If so, their example of faith nonetheless continues beyond their deaths as a witness to later generations (Heb. 11).

This sort of exemplary faith is embodied by the older characters in Luke's infancy narrative and in Paul's account of Abraham and Sarah: they are well practiced in watchfulness for God. Precisely as people who have clung to God's promises over many years, they embody the virtues of long-suffering patience and trust in God's ultimate faithfulness. They also exemplify faith and hope, even when circumstances seem hopeless.

Finally, the older biblical characters signal the possibility of unanticipated fruitfulness in old age: Zechariah and Elizabeth, Abraham and Sarah, and perhaps even Nicodemus in John's story, demonstrate the possibility of change, new life, and the fruition of hopes at the end of the life span. Those who trust in God are not locked into the past — neither into traditional social roles nor into well-worn paths chosen earlier in life. Rather, they remain open to receive what God desires to give, open to the fresh, surprising working of God's Spirit. As in the prophecy of Joel, quoted by Peter in his Pentecost sermon, "Your young men shall see visions, and your old men shall dream dreams" (Acts 2:17, quoting Joel 2:28).[3] Unlike the old priest Eli (1 Sam. 3:1-9), the aged characters spotlighted in the New Testament remain open to hear the voice of God and to act on what they hear. They are the righteous people described in Psalm 92:

> The righteous flourish like the palm tree,
>   and grow like a cedar in Lebanon.
> They are planted in the house of the Lord;
>   they flourish in the courts of our God.
> In old age they still produce fruit;
>   they are always green and full of sap,
> showing that the Lord is upright;
>   he is my rock and there is no unrighteousness in him. (Ps. 92:12-15)

3. This verse is numbered as Joel 3:1 in the Hebrew text and in the Septuagint. Luke's citation of the passage in Acts 2:17 reverses the clauses, placing the climactic emphasis on the "old men" (presbyteroi).

The Scriptures are filled with stories of God's breaking into the individual lives of older persons to confer a particular gift or vocation.

Equally important, perhaps, are the things *not* said about older characters in the New Testament. Nowhere in the biblical canon are they pitied, patronized, or treated with condescension. Nowhere is growing old itself described as a problem. Nowhere are elders described as pitiable, irrelevant, or behind the curve, as inactive or unproductive. Nowhere are they, as in so many Western dramas and narratives, lampooned as comic figures. On the contrary, they are seen as the bearers of wisdom by virtue of their age. Death is treated as an enemy to be conquered by Christ at the eschaton (e.g., 1 Cor. 15:24-26), but it never seems to occur to the New Testament authors to characterize the aging process itself as an evil to be overcome. Thus, the New Testament offers us an alternative vision in which the modern, popular view of aging as a "problem" might appear puzzling and unhealthy.

Reflections on a Messiah Who Died Young

Jesus did not grow old. The church has looked to Jesus of Nazareth as the definitive model for true humanity, the model for a life lived faithfully. Yet he did not live into what we would normally consider "late life." Luke tells us that "Jesus was about thirty years old when he began his work" (Luke 3:23), and within the span of three years he had aroused such controversy that he was put to death by the Roman authorities. To be more precise, Jesus was probably born between 6-4 B.C.E., under the reign of Herod the Great (who died in 4 B.C.E.), and was probably executed in 30 C.E. under the Roman governor Pontius Pilate. By this reckoning, he would have been no more than thirty-six years old at the time of his death.[4] Thus, Jesus died in the prime of his life, without experiencing old age. Does this mean that we are left with no christologically informed pattern for the Christian practice of growing old? If so, what is the theological significance of this state of affairs?

First of all, the manner of Jesus' death stands as a permanent reminder that fidelity is more important than longevity. Length of years is a blessing (Prov. 16:31; 20:29), but we should not presume that we have a right to a long

---

4. On the complicated issue of establishing the precise dates of Jesus' birth and death, see John P. Meier, *A Marginal Jew: Rethinking the Historical Jesus*, Anchor Bible Reference Library (New York: Doubleday, 1991-2001), vol. 1, pp. 372-433. In John 8:57 Jesus' skeptical interlocutors say, "You are not yet fifty years old, and have you seen Abraham?" This does not mean that Jesus was approaching fifty: it is merely an approximate yardstick to indicate how outrageous they consider the assertion that Abraham saw Jesus' "day" and was glad.

life. God may call us to surrender our lives. The way of discipleship, as Jesus repeatedly taught his followers, leads to the cross (e.g, Mark 8:34-38; Luke 14:25-27). Jesus models for us a resolute trust in God that empowers us to act freely and to bear witness to the truth, even if such witness-bearing may lead to death. The book of Revelation extols the faithful martyrs who have conquered the great dragon Satan "by the blood of the Lamb and by the word of their testimony, for they did not cling to life even in the face of death" (Rev. 12:11). Thus, Christians are taught by the example of Jesus that we do not have to live in a cautious mode of self-protection, clinging to our lives desperately at all costs, making an idol of our own physical survival. We are free to let go of our lives when the time comes, because we believe that God will vindicate us in the end. (See also the final part of this chapter below, on death and resurrection.)

A corollary of this point is that, because we cannot necessarily count on a long life, we should live each moment of time in its fullness, whether we are nineteen or ninety. Jesus' remarkable teaching that we should not be anxious about our lives or about tomorrow (Matt. 6:25-34) is to be understood not only in light of Jesus' radical trust in God's righteousness but also within the context of the story of the Passion. Precisely because we cannot control tomorrow and cannot choose the time of our own death, we are to receive each day as a gift, looking to God for our daily bread and making sure that we seek first the kingdom of God rather than squandering our time and energy on secondary concerns.

Second, even though Jesus died young, his suffering both represents and redeems all human experience, all human suffering. As the Son of Man, he bears all human destiny in himself. In the course of articulating their understanding of the incarnation, early Christian theologians insisted that Jesus was not only truly God but also truly human, for only by taking on human nature fully could he redeem it fully. As Gregory Nazianzen formulated this conviction, "What is not assumed is not made whole, and what is joined to God is saved."[5] This means that Jesus' life and death are to be understood as paradigmatic for all human experience. It does not matter that Jesus was not female, not a Gentile, not highly educated, not aged. It does not matter, for in his suffering, death, and resurrection we are all mysteriously included; his experience absorbs ours and becomes the key to understanding our own experience. This is true whether we are male or female, African or Chinese, illiterate or learned, young or old. Therefore, the Christian practice of growing old requires us to learn the imaginative skill of employing the cross and

---

5. Gregory Nazianzen, Epistle 101 (Ad Cledonium), Patrologia Graeca 37: 181C-184A.

resurrection as the lens through which we view our own aging and dying. We learn to interpret the suffering that we experience — if in fact old age brings us suffering — as "always carrying in the body the dying *(nekrosis)* of Jesus, so that the life of Jesus may also be made visible in our bodies" (2 Cor. 4:10). Our goal, as Paul puts it, is "to know Christ and the power of his resurrection and the sharing *(koinonia)* of his sufferings, becoming like him in his death" (Phil. 3:10).

All of this runs contrary to the current widespread tendency to suppose that we can share deep solidarity only with those who participate precisely in our own particular experience of culture, race, class, gender, or adversity. The gospel teaches us another way: all of us are to understand our lives as grounded in the story of Jesus, and we find there a commonality that we could otherwise never have discerned. Thus, paradoxically, the elderly will find in the story of Jesus, who died in his mid thirties, a pattern that will continue to shape their own lives as they confront the challenges of growing old.

This pattern, as interpreted for us by the New Testament, is the pattern of self-giving for the sake of others. The Christian practice of growing old is shaped by the example of Jesus, who emptied himself and became obedient, even to the point of death, for our sake (see Phil. 2:1-13). Thus, Paul can write of himself:

> I have been crucified with Christ; and it is no longer I who live, but it is Christ who lives in me. And the life I now live in the flesh I live by the faithfulness of the Son of God, who loved me and gave himself for me. (Gal. 2:19b-20)[6]

Consequently, as we grow old, we should seek to discern how to give our lives for others. Old age is not a time simply to relax and play golf, nor is it a time only to reminiscence about the past. (Though relaxation and reminiscence surely have their rightful places in our lives.) Instead, in old age, as throughout our lives, we must continue to pursue the way of service, conforming our own lives to the self-giving pattern of Jesus. This christological pattern for the years of late life challenges and subverts many of the conventional models for aging that we see around us: old people as helpless, useless burdens on society, or old age as a time to sit back and reap the rewards we have earned through a lifetime of work. To understand late life in light of the pattern of a Messiah who died young is to embrace T. S. Eliot's counsel: "Old men ought

---

6. On this translation, see Richard B. Hays, *Galatians,* New Interpreter's Bible, vol. 11 (Nashville: Abingdon, 2000), pp. 242-45.

to be explorers"[7] — with the proviso that the territory we are exploring is the way of discipleship that Jesus has charted for us.

The Defeat of Death, the Last Enemy

While the Bible shows little concern with *aging* as a problem, *death* is another matter. The biblical writers have a sober and realistic view of death as a grim shadow cast over the world. The psalmist laments the brevity of life and the inevitability of mortality:

> For all our days pass away under your wrath;
>   our years come to an end like a sigh.
> The days of our life are seventy years,
>   or perhaps eighty, if we are strong;
> even then their span is only toil and trouble;
>   they are soon gone, and we fly away. (Ps. 90:9-10)

For the Old Testament writers, let it be said clearly, "flying away" does not mean the ascent of the soul to heaven. It is, rather, simply a description of the transient passing of human life, like a withered flower blown away by the wind (Ps. 103:15-16). If there is any thought of "life after death" in the Old Testament, it is primarily envisioned in terms of the image of going down to Sheol, the gloomy underworld realm of the departed. In the memorable imagery of Isaiah, death is "the shroud that is cast over all peoples, the sheet that is spread over all nations" (Isa. 25:7). Isaiah prophesies the day when God will destroy this shroud and "swallow up death forever" (Isa. 25:8), but that day remains, within the narrative world of the Old Testament, only a future hope.

The aversion to death is not found only in the Old Testament; if anything, it is even clearer in the New Testament that death is a great evil. In contrast to the serene detachment of Socrates facing his own death with imperturbable equanimity, Jesus prays in the Garden of Gethsemane in a state of agitation and grief as he contemplates his impending arrest and execution. He begs God to spare him from death (Mark 14:32-42). According to some manuscripts of Luke's Gospel, "In his anguish he prayed more earnestly, and his sweat became like great drops of blood falling down on the ground" (Luke 22:44). This point must be emphasized, because sentimental Christian piety sometimes lapses into a careless talk about death as a smooth passage into a

---

7. T. S. Eliot, "East Coker," in *The Complete Poems and Plays* (New York: Harcourt, Brace and World, 1962), p. 129.

better world. But nothing could be further from the perspective of the New Testament writers. Jesus weeps at the tomb of Lazarus (John 11:32-37). Paul characterizes death as "the last enemy," which remains to be destroyed by Christ in the eschatological future when all things will at last be made subject to God (1 Cor. 15:26-28). Thus, in a world that still does not see all things in subjection to Jesus (Heb. 2:8), the process of aging carries with it the fearful prospect of death.

The New Testament's answer to the problem of death is firm and consistent: God will overcome the power of death by the resurrection of the body at the last day. The resurrection of Jesus is both the first fruits of this final resurrection and the sign of the eschatological resurrection in which all Christ's people will share (1 Cor. 15:20-28). Thus, the hope of resurrection lies at the heart of the way in which Christians embody the practices of growing old. The resurrection shapes our understanding of aging in at least two decisive ways.

First, the doctrine of resurrection affirms God's unwavering fidelity to the creation, God's determination to redeem what he has made. For that reason, Gnostic indifference to the body is the farthest thing from Christian thought and practice. Christians, as Paul writes, groan in solidarity along with the created order awaiting redemption: "We know that the whole creation has been groaning in labor pains until now; and *not only the creation, but we ourselves,* who have the first fruits of the Spirit, groan inwardly while we wait for adoption, *the redemption of our bodies*" (Rom. 8:22-23; emphasis added). Note that those who have the Spirit long not for redemption *from* their bodies but rather for redemption *of* their bodies. This fundamental element of Christian doctrine gives rise to a wide range of practices that honor and care for the physical body, in life and in death.[8] We expect that the body will not be discarded but rather transformed in the resurrection. Therefore, life in the body continues to matter greatly as we grow old.

Second, because the resurrection of Jesus proclaims God's triumph over the power of death, we are set free from fear, no longer paralyzed or controlled by fear of aging and dying. This good news is movingly articulated by the Letter to the Hebrews:

Since, therefore, the children share flesh and blood, [Jesus] himself likewise shared the same things, so that through death he might de-

---

8. For an extended discussion of church sponsorship of establishments to shelter and feed the poor, and care for the sick, the aged, and the dying, from the fourth century to the present, see Guenter B. Risse, *Mending Bodies, Saving Souls: A History of Hospitals* (New York: Oxford University Press, 1999).

stroy the one who has the power of death, that is, the devil, *and free those who all their lives were held in slavery by the fear of death*. (Heb. 2:14-15; emphasis added)

As we grow old, we face death in and with Christ; therefore, while death remains a terrible enemy of human flourishing and of God's redemptive will for the world, we know that its "sting" has been taken away, as Paul declares in 1 Corinthians 15:55. We live no longer under slavery to fear. John Donne, the great seventeenth-century metaphysical poet, takes up Paul's taunt to Death, personified as a power that seeks to destroy us:

> Death be not proud, though some have called thee
> Mighty and dreadfull, for, thou art not soe,
> For, those, whom thou think'st, thou dost overthrow,
> Die not, poore death, nor yet canst thou kill mee.
> . . . .
> One short sleep past, wee wake eternally,
> And death shall be no more; death, thou shalt die.[9]

In such confidence inspired by the New Testament's testimony, we are set free from the paralysis that the fear of death produces in our culture: we need not deceive ourselves with costly amusements that distract us from the truth of our mortality and foster the illusion that we are immortal. Likewise we are set free from the frantic urgency to forestall death at all costs: we need not grasp at life or harness every medical technology at our disposal. We can look death in the face without fear, because we trust in the promise of resurrection. This means that the practice of growing old can be characterized by a sober confidence, no matter what trials and complications we face. As Christians, we are people trained to die.[10] We have been trained for this from our childhood by focusing, week in and week out, on the story of the cross and resurrection. We need not avert our eyes from our own death, for our identity is grounded in the crucified Messiah who has gone before us through death and resurrection. That is why Paul can encourage the Thessalonians not to be afraid of death's power to separate them from their loved ones:

> But we do not want you to be uninformed, brothers and sisters, about
> those who have died, so that you may not grieve as others do who have

9. John Donne, "Holy Sonnet X," in *The Complete Poetry and Selected Prose of John Donne*, ed. C. M. Coffin (New York: Modern Library, 1952), pp. 250-51.

10. Stanley Hauerwas, *A Community of Character: After Christendom*, 2nd ed. (Nashville: Abingdon, 1999), p. 43.

no hope. For since we believe that Jesus died and rose again, even so, through Jesus, God will bring with him those who have died. . . . Therefore encourage one another with these words. (1 Thess. 4:13-14, 18)

Conclusion

In light of this survey of biblical visions of old age, what can we say about how Scripture might inform our own understanding of aging? We conclude this chapter by offering a few reflections on the Christian practice of growing old, as it is shaped by the witness of Scripture.

The weight of the biblical witness is on the side of similarity rather than difference between aged and younger Christians. All followers of Jesus are to practice watchful waiting on God across the span of their years. At its heart, watchful waiting includes regular participation in corporate worship. The recitation of the historic creeds, the hearing of the Word, and the cycle of the liturgical year provide constant rehearsal of the life story to which all Christians find their lives conformed. Through rehearsal, we come to experience the mystery of which Paul testifies: "it is no longer I who live, but it is Christ who lives in me" (Gal. 2:20).

Should Christians reach old age, the accumulation of waiting bestows upon them a wisdom about the kingdom of God to which younger Christians should attend closely and defer. The special responsibility of older Christians is to lead, to teach, to counsel, as their gifts allow and as opportunities arise. Should older Christians become physically incapable of caring for themselves and have no family to attend to their needs, the church is responsible for their care. Even in debilitation and illness, however, their ministry of example may intensify: they embody the way of the cross and gratefully receive the service of others.[11]

In late life, Christians remain subject to the possibility that God will act decisively in history and in their lives in such a way as to turn their lives upside down. They may be called to a new ministry. They may receive new revelation. They may see the fulfillment of a long-awaited hope. In this they do not differ from younger Christians.

Finally, in old age as in youth, Christians are to take the Lord Jesus Christ as the model for their daily lives and interactions with others. When facing death, as they are more likely to do than are young Christians, elders with

---

11. On these themes see Audrey West, "Whether by Life or by Death: Friendship in a Pauline Ethic of Death and Dying," chap. 3 (Ph.D. diss., Duke University, 2001).

long practice of self-sacrifice and loving obedience to Jesus may repudiate fear and embrace hope more gracefully than those less practiced. Having long remembered and rehearsed the Passion of Jesus, they face death with the expectation that their story, like his, will continue in the life of the resurrection. But their confidence is not a natural fruit or reward of age itself; rather, it is a consequence of practice. Therefore, the Christian practice of growing old is a lifelong habit of believing God's witness in the Scriptures and acting on it, for as long as God gives life.

Special Gift and Special Burden:
Views of Old Age in the Early Church

ROWAN A. GREER

There are obvious risks in trying to understand how the early church regarded old age and how Christians treated the elderly. Part of the difficulty lies in the fragmentary character of the evidence and in the simple fact that statistical estimates can be no more than educated guesses. We cannot be certain about life expectancy or about the proportion of the total population in the Roman Empire that might be regarded as elderly. Moreover, we cannot suppose that Christian attitudes and approaches to old age were uniform either across time or geographically. More important than these difficulties, however, is our tendency to notice in the literary evidence what correlates with our own questions. For us old age is a problem most people will face. As a consequence, the social, economic, and moral aspects of old age loom large as issues with which we must deal.

What I wish to argue in what follows is that old age in the early church was special. In the ancient world the few and not the many attained old age. Partly for this reason we do not find any extended treatments of old age. There is no Christian parallel to Cicero's *De senectute*. We should not expect to find any full attempt to address old age as a central problem. On the other hand, there certainly were old people in antiquity; and there is no lack of literary evidence for attitudes toward them. Christian writers, I think, saw old age as both a gift and a burden. The gift is one of wisdom and virtue; the burden, physical and mental debility, but also vices peculiar to the elderly. Let me begin by calling attention to a number of texts that address the question of the length of life.

How Long Is Life? How Old Is "Old"?

Two passages in Scripture have the possibility of suggesting how long human life should be. Before the flood and, apparently, after the "sons of God" took the "daughters of men" as wives the Lord said, "My spirit shall not abide in man for ever, for he is flesh, but his days shall be a hundred and twenty years" (Gen. 6:3). The other verse is Psalm 90:10: "The years of our life are threescore and ten, or even by reason of strength fourscore. . . ." Lactantius, early in the fourth century, understands Genesis 6:3 to agree with "competent authorities [who] report that men are accustomed to reach one hundred and twenty years."[1] Not only does this judgment fly in the face of experience, it also finds itself contradicted by the fact that a number of people after the flood lived longer than 120 years.

The exegetical problem is, of course, what looms largest in the minds of the church fathers. Indeed, Lactantius' understanding may well reflect his relative unfamiliarity with Scripture. The solution to the problem revolves around pointing out that Genesis 5:32 says that Noah was five hundred years old and by assuming that what God says in Genesis 6:3 is at the same time and so one hundred years before the flood. The 120 years are, therefore, not the span of human life but the time left to elapse before the flood.[2] Many of the texts that cite the verse from Genesis 6 ignore the 120 years altogether. What strikes many of the early interpreters is the idea that God's "spirit" is incompatible with "flesh." Here it becomes necessary to understand "flesh" as sinful humanity.[3]

Although Genesis 6:3 gives no true understanding of the length of life, we might suppose that the seventy or eighty years of Psalm 90:10 takes us to firmer ground. That at least was my hope, but I have been able to find only one reference to the verse as "David's limit of our age."[4] Interpretations tend

---

1. Lactantius, *Divine Institutes* 2.13, in *Ante-Nicene Fathers* (hereafter ANF), ed. A. Roberts and J. Donaldson (Buffalo: Christian Literature, 1885-1896), vol. 7, p. 63.

2. There are variations of interpretation. Julius Africanus argues that God is addressing those twenty years and older: "For the space of time meant was 100 years up to the flood in the case of the sinners of that time; for they were twenty years old" (ANF 6, p. 31). Augustine, however, takes Noah's 500 years as a round number that should be understood as 480. Thus, the 120 years are quite simply the time left until the flood (*City of God* 15.24).

3. See, for example, Origen, *De principiis* 1.3.7 and *Contra Celsum* 7.38; Ambrose, *Commentary on Luke* 6.94 and *De mysteriis* 10.

4. Gregory Nazianzen, *Oration 18: On the Death of His Father* 38, in *A Select Library of the Nicene and Post-Nicene Fathers of the Christian Church* (hereafter NPNF), ed. Philip Schaff et al. (Buffalo: Christian Literature, 1887-1894), second series, vol. 7, p. 267: "At last, after a life of almost a hundred years, exceeding David's limit of our age . . . he brought it to a close in a good

to ignore the time references and concentrate on the psalmist's theme of the vanity and transience of human life. Gregory of Nyssa, for example, focuses on the Septuagint version of the previous verse in the psalm: "Our years were exercised like a spider." Human life is a spider's web, easily brushed away. We weave our lives in "insubstantial pursuits"; honor, station, birth, wealth — all are "false conceits." The "toil and trouble" of which the psalm speaks belong to every age.[5]

It is difficult to escape the conclusion that the writers of the early church

---

old age." Four other texts treat the time references as not definitive. Eusebius in his commentary on the Psalms treats the seventy or eighty years as a support for Symmachus' translation of the end of verse 10, "Cut off we soon fly away," instead of the Septuagint's "Meekness has come upon us and we are chastened." The seventy or eighty years underline the transient character of human life (*Patrologia Graeca* [hereafter PG] 23.1137C). Hesychius of Jerusalem puzzles over the time references. The Septuagint version ("The days of our years *in them* are 70 years . . .") means for him that "in them" few attain the number of years mentioned. On the other hand, even though "many attain 100 years or more," anything beyond eighty refers to such extreme old age that those who survive are so close to dead as to make no difference (PG 55.757). Theodoret compares the verse to Genesis 47:9 (Jacob's 130 years are "few and evil") and says "there are some who surpass the time mentioned, but that happens only to the few. Here he teaches what is common and obtains for most." Just as David makes no mention of those who fail to attain seventy, so he makes no mention of those who remain till extreme old age (PG 80.1603BC). Augustine actually treats verse 5 of the psalm ("Their years are as things which are nothing worth . . .") as the recitation of "some law written in the secret wisdom of God, in which He has fixed a limit to the sinful life of mortals. . . ." The seventy or eighty years of verse 10 "appear to express the shortness and misery of this life." Those who reach seventy "are styled old men," and beyond eighty "their existence is laborious through multiplied sorrows." But, he says, old age often comes before seventy, and one can point to "wonderfully vigorous" octogenarians. Thus, the spiritual meaning of the verse must be preferred (*Expositions on the Psalms*, Psalm 90:6-9, NPNF first series, vol. 8, p. 442f.). None of these comments treat the figures seventy and eighty as normative for human life.

5. Gregory of Nyssa, *In inscriptiones psalmarum* 1.7. See also the allegorical interpretations of Clement of Alexandria and Hippolytus. Clement discusses Psalm 90:10 in the context of his interpretation of the commandment to keep holy the Sabbath. Periods of seven punctuate human life, and David's reference to eighty appears to refer to the eighth day of the resurrection (*Stromateis* 6.145.1; ANF 2, p. 514). Clement also gives a confused allegorical treatment of Genesis 6:3, where he follows Philo's *Quaestiones et solutions in Genesim* 1.91 (*Stromateis* 6.84.1; ANF 2, p. 499). Hippolytus argues that seventy and eighty refer to the fifteen "songs of degrees" (7 + 8), and that these songs begin after Psalm 120. Thus, he places our two texts together and treats them as mystical references to the way the psalter is arranged (*Commentary on Psalms*, fragment 1.4; ANF 5, p. 200). Augustine in his *Expositions on the Psalms* prefers the spiritual meaning. Seventy plus eighty is 150, which signifies the same as fifteen. The seven refers to the Old Testament and its observation of the Sabbath; eight, to the New Testament and the day of resurrection. There are fifteen steps in the Temple and fifteen "songs of degrees," etc. (NPNF first series, vol. 8, p. 443).

do not think that Scripture reveals to us the normal span of human life. In addition, the aged are the exception rather than the rule. A passage from Gregory Nazianzen's funeral oration for his father gives us a better idea of ancient assumptions about the length of life:

> At last after a life of almost a hundred years, exceeding David's limit of our age, forty-five of these, the average life of man, having been spent in the priesthood, he brought it to a close in a good old age.[6]

Let me note that the seventy or eighty years of Psalm 90 are a "limit" and not a norm. If forty-five years are the average, then few attain this limit. What explains Gregory's figure for the average age? Perhaps he has in mind the conventions of the ancient world that define "juniors" as those from seventeen till forty-six, and "seniors" as those forty-six and older. Moreover, at sixty it was customary to exempt people from certain obligations,[7] and we commonly find sixty as a designation for the beginning of old age.[8] Gregory Nazianzen speaks of Athanasius' death in his late seventies as one "in a good old age."[9] Palladius refers to Melania the Elder as "already an old woman of 60."[10]

If we turn to texts in which the writers refer to themselves as aged, we find ourselves on more slippery ground. The speech that John Chrysostom gives his widowed mother in *On the Priesthood* supplies an example. His mother is seeking to persuade John to stay with her and to delay his embrac-

---

6. Gregory Nazianzen, *Oration* 18.38 (NPNF second series, vol. 7, p. 267).

7. See Aulus Gellius, *Attic Nights* 2.15, 10.28, and 15.7 (see *The Attic Nights of Aulus Gellius,* trans. John C. Rolfe, Loeb Classical Library no. 195, 3 vols. [London: W. Heinemann, 1927-], vol. 1, p. 161; vol. 2, p. 293; vol. 3, pp. 77f.). The "climacteric" year, however, is sixty-three. Cf. J. P. V. D. Balsdon, *Life and Leisure in Ancient Rome* (London: The Bodley Head, 1969), pp. 169, 188f., 220. Rodney Stark in his *The Rise of Christianity: A Sociologist Reconsiders History* (Princeton, N.J.: Princeton University Press, 1996) discusses mortality rates in the Roman Empire. Epidemics in 165 and 251 may have destroyed at least a quarter of the population (p. 73). The practice of female infanticide and abortion contributed to depopulation and the surplus of men (save in the Christian church, where Stark argues that there were more women than men) (pp. 97, 117ff.). Stark concludes that life expectancy at birth was probably less than thirty years, though he argues that Christians had a better chance because they did not practice infanticide and abortion and seem to have cared for one another more effectively than pagans (pp. 155 and 189).

8. Cf. Plato, *Laws* 6.759d.

9. Gregory Nazianzen, *Oration 21: On the Great Athanasius* 37 (NPNF second series, vol. 7, p. 280).

10. Palladius, *The Lausiac History* 53, in *Ancient Christian Writers: The Works of the Fathers in Translation* (Mahwah, N.J.: Paulist, 1946-), vol. 34, p. 134. Hereafter *Ancient Christian Writers* will be cited as ACW.

ing of the monastic life. She pulls out all the stops and says, "The young indeed look forward to a distant old age, but we who have grown old have nothing but death to wait for."[11] Since she was widowed at the time of her son's birth when she was only twenty, she can scarcely be forty years old. Even by ancient standards forty seems not quite aged. Basil the Great, however, who probably died before he was fifty (in 379), speaks of himself as "burdened with old age."[12] More in line with what we should expect, Gregory of Nyssa, Paulinus of Nola, and Prudentius all refer to themselves as old in their fifties.[13] At fifty Prudentius says that the "end is close upon me, and by now what God is adding to my days is on the border of old age." He may be thinking of sixty as the operative age. Paulinus of Nola jests that both he and Turcius are "fathers," he because of age and Turcius because he has fathered a child.

Paulinus hints that age may not be the most important consideration in evaluating human life. Augustine makes the point explicit by arguing that death is our common lot:

> I am certain of this, that no one has died who was not going to die at some time, and the end of life reduces the longest life to the same condition as the shortest. When something has once ceased to exist, there is no more question of better or worse, longer or shorter. What does it matter by what kind of death life is brought to an end?[14]

Length of life does not matter because not everyone can expect to live till old age. Old age and death have no clear correlation as they do for us.[15] As I have implied, this appears to me part of the reason the early Christians do not

---

11. John Chrysostom, *On the Priesthood* 1.5 (NPNF first series, vol. 9, p. 34). See *Letter to a Young Widow* 2 (NPNF first series, vol. 9, p. 122): "I told him [Libanius] that she [my mother] was forty years of age of which twenty had elapsed since she lost my father. . . ."

12. Basil the Great, Letter 277, in *Saint Basil, the Letters,* trans. Roy J. Defarrari, 4 vols., Loeb Classical Library no. 190 (London: W. Heinemann, 1926-34), vol. 4; cf. Letters 30, 272.

13. Gregory of Nyssa, *Life of Moses,* in Classics of Western Spirituality (New York: Paulist, 1978), p. 29; *Contra Eunomium* 2.605 (NPNF second series, vol. 5, p. 311); *Refutatio Confessionis Eunomii* 208 (NPNF second series, vol. 5, p. 132); *De inf. quae* (PG 46.161B). Paulinus of Nola, Poem 21.288 (ACW 40, p. 182). The poems of Prudentius can be found in *Prudentius,* trans. H. J. Thomson, Loeb Classical Library no. 387 (Cambridge: Harvard University Press, 1949-53), vol. 1, p. 3.

14. Augustine, *City of God* 1.11.

15. Cf. Ronald Blythe, *The View in Winter: Reflections on Old Age* (Harmondsworth: Penguin Books, 1980), p. 4: "Another contrast between old age then and old age now is that we place dying in what we take to be its logical position, which is at the close of a long life, whereas our ancestors accepted the futility of placing it in any position at all."

make a central problem of old age. As Ambrose says: "[e]very age is perfect in Christ. Every age is full of God."[16] The young die as well as the old.

Basil the Great writes to console the widow of Arinthaeus the General and does so by saying her husband has "come to the end brilliantly, not bent by old age, not deprived of any of his distinctions, great in the present life and great in the life to come."[17] Gregory Nazianzen's funeral oration speaks of his sister Gorgonia as "full not of the days of man." We can be moved by his description of their "aged mother bent over her, with her soul convulsed with envy of her departure." Gregory's panegyric on his brother Caesarius, who died when he was thirty-nine, dismisses the importance of the fact that Caesarius has "outstripped us." Since we shall all be "reduced to the same dust," it makes no difference whether we precede or follow others "to the tomb."[18] The letters by which Synesius of Cyrene, in his early forties, laments the deaths of his children do not resort to such easy consolations.[19]

If one context into which we must place early Christian attitudes to old age is the absence of any tight correlation between old age and death, another and more important context is the Christian hope. I would argue that early Christianity, while certainly a way of life and certainly concerned with this world, was nonetheless oriented to Christian destiny in the age to come. The emphasis is upon Christ as the victor over death and upon the hope of the resurrection that victory guaranteed. According to Origen, when Scripture refers to Joshua as "old and well advanced in years" (Josh. 23:1), it means that he was spiritually mature and not merely that he was old. Origen continues his homily by meditating on the rest that Joshua gave the people and upon its typological fulfillment in Christ.[20]

Of course, many accused Origen of over-spiritualizing and so of implicitly denying the resurrection hope. Yet even this reaction underlines the centrality of the resurrection for the early church. Even the pagan satirist Lucian, who treats the Christians as foolish simpletons, notes that their two chief follies are their community solidarity and their belief that "they will live for ever."[21] The

16. Ambrose, Letter 17.15 (NPNF second series, vol. 10, p. 413). Ambrose is writing to the child emperor Valentinian II, and so his remarks are only indirectly relevant to old age. Moreover, what he says looks very much like a *captatio benevolentiae*.

17. Basil, Letter 269, in *Saint Basil*, vol. 4, p. 139.

18. Gregory Nazianzen, *Oration 8: On His Sister Gorgonia* 21-22 (NPNF second series, vol. 7, p. 244); *Oration 7: On His Brother Caesarius* 18, 24 (NPNF second series, vol. 7, pp. 235 and 238).

19. Synesius of Cyrene, Letters 152, 153, 154.

20. Origen, *Homily 16 on Joshua* (no. 71 in the *Sources chrétiennes* series, pp. 358ff.).

21. Lucian, *The Passing of Peregrinus* 11-13, in *Lucian*, trans. A. M. Harmon, Loeb Classical Library no. 302 (London: W. Heinemann, 1913-67), vol. 5, pp. 13f.

two "follies" seem to me related; it is the resurrection hope that constitutes the Christian community. In general we can construe the catacomb art in this fashion. Many of the scenes depicted in the frescoes are stories of deliverance — Noah from the flood, Jonah from the whale, Israel from Egypt by crossing the Red Sea, Daniel from the lions' den, the Three Children from the burning fiery furnace. The art is funerary, and so we are to think of the deliverance from death itself. At the same time, some of the stories are types of Christian baptism. Thus, another form of deliverance is incorporation into the Christian community. We might even think of baptism as the ritual dying and rising with Christ that finds its actualization in death and resurrection.[22] The church remembered its martyrs on the day of their death, since that was the point at which they entered into the mystery of death and resurrection.

Old age or the failure to attain it pale in significance when placed in the context of the resurrection hope. Indeed, Augustine's defense of the resurrection of the body includes the problem of how the aged will be raised, but he is more concerned with other questions: How can an earthly body exist in heaven? Will abortions be raised? What about our hair and nail clippings? What about cannibalism? His key biblical text is Ephesians 4:13: "until we all attain . . . the stature of the full maturity of Christ." Thus,

> each person will be given the stature which he had in his prime, even though he was an old man when he died, or, if he died before maturity, the stature he would have attained. . . . [I]f the words [of Eph. 4:13] refer to the bodily resurrection, we must take them to mean that the bodies of the dead will rise neither younger nor older than Christ. They will be of the same age, the same prime of life, which Christ, as we know had reached. For the most learned authorities of this world define the age of human maturity as being about thirty years; they say that after that period of life a man begins to go downhill towards middle age and senility.[23]

Old age, an issue for some in this life, is a matter of indifference when seen from the larger perspective of the resurrection. Nevertheless, in the short run old age does matter. And so, let me turn to old age as a gift and as a burden.

---

22. Romans 6 interprets baptism as dying and rising with Christ. Cf. Colossians 2:12. Ignatius of Antioch regards his martyrdom as a dying and rising with Christ and the actualization of his baptism (see, e.g., Romans 2, 4, 6). I should note that this was not the only way baptism was understood.

23. Augustine, *City of God* 22.15.

The Gift of Virtue and Wisdom

Ambrose can speak of "the honour of old age" and can say that "seriousness is the true grace of an old man."[24] He is almost certainly speaking of those who have grown old and venerable in virtue, like Polycarp, who said as he was martyred that he had served Christ for eighty-six years.[25] Paulinus of Nola, whose conversion was gradual, like a slow awakening from sleep, and who slowly divested himself of his great wealth to serve the shrine of St. Felix in Nola, calls this aging in virtue a renewal of youth. He was probably about fifty years old when he wrote,

> As you know, Sanctus, my blessed brother, for a long time I wallowed in this world and grew old amongst my enemies. I pray that I have grown old towards them, so that now in retirement, having abandoned the broad road, I may have *my youth renewed like an eagle's* (Ps 102:5) in Christ, so I may be stripped of the old man's debility and *put on the new man who is created according to God* (Eph 4:24).[26]

The virtues of old age are, in one sense, virtues common to all; but they demand special admiration when they have been cultivated throughout a long life.

Continence is one of the virtues associated with old age. We often find the idea that old age carries with it the extinction of lust. Paulinus commends Apronius because he is "a boy in years but old towards the motions of the flesh."[27] Gregory Nazianzen asks the elderly who delay baptism, "why do you fear youthful passions in deep old age and at your last breath?"[28] Basil the Great explains his decision to forbid one of his priests from living with a *subintroducta,* a spiritual sister, in a way that reflects this assumption:

> You should, therefore, have been the more ready to comply with my demand in proportion as you profess to be free from all carnal passion.

24. Ambrose, *On Belief in the Resurrection* 2.124 (NPNF second series, vol. 10, p. 195) and *On the Duties of the Clergy* 1.17.65 (NPNF second series, vol. 10, p. 12).

25. *Martyrdom of Polycarp* 9.

26. Paulinus of Nola, Letter 40.6 (ACW 2, p. 207). The letter is to be dated at the earliest in 398, and Paulinus was born about 353.

27. Paulinus of Nola, Poem 21.198 (ACW 40, p. 179).

28. Gregory Nazianzen, *Oration on Holy Baptism* 17 (NPNF second series, vol. 7, p. 365). The correlative assumption is that "youth is wild." See John Chrysostom, *Homily 9 on 1 Timothy* (NPNF first series, vol. 13, p. 436); cf. *Homily 5 on 1 Thessalonians* (NPNF first series, vol. 13, pp. 346f.), where he recommends early marriage as a remedy for fornication. See also Augustine, *Confessions* 1.11, 2.2.

> For I neither believe that a man of seventy years is living with a woman for the gratification of his passions, nor have we reached our present decision on the ground that any outrageous act has been committed, but because we have been taught by the apostle not to put a stumbling-block or a scandal in our brother's way (Rom. 14:13).[29]

More positively, Basil can regard an old monk as a safeguard against immoral relations between young monks, and Ambrose insists that older clergy accompany the younger clergy if they must visit the houses of widows or virgins.[30]

The virtue of sexual continence, supposedly easy in the elderly, is not the only one we find commended.[31] John Cassian suggests that humility in the aged is a great virtue, since it represents the overcoming of pride and vainglory, vices that can be associated with old age. Abba Pinufius, "held in honour and respect by all men out of reverence either for his life or for his age or for his priesthood," leaves his monastery because this reverence interferes with his practice of humility. He goes to the strictest monastery in the Thebaid anonymously, where he is finally admitted out of compassion and given the lowly task of a gardener. He is, of course, at length recognized and is honored for his exemplary humility.[32] We can argue, I think, that this understanding of the virtue of the elderly is peculiarly Christian.

Perhaps the most moving description of the virtue and wisdom of the aged is one given by Paulinus of Pella in his autobiographical poem. The story he tells is of someone brought up in wealth and peace, highly educated and civilized. But when he was thirty years old in 406 his father died, and the barbarians crossed the Rhine. They sacked Bordeaux, and Paulinus lost most of his property. The rest of his story is one of hardship and tragedy; yet at the age of eighty-three he titles his poem *The Thanksgiving*. This is because "while reasonably chastening me with continual misfortunes, he [God] has clearly taught me that I ought neither to love too earnestly present prosperity

---

29. Basil, Letter 55, in *Saint Basil*, vol. 1, p. 349.

30. Basil, *De renuntiatione saeculi* 207B, in *The Ascetic Works of Saint Basil*, by W. K. L. Clarke (London: SPCK, 1925), p. 66; Ambrose, *On the Duties of the Clergy* 1.20.87 (NPNF second series, vol. 10, p. 15).

31. Cf. John Chrysostom, *Homily 49 on Matthew* 8 (NPNF first series, vol. 10, p. 309): "For this in fact is the marvelous thing, when temperance shines forth in youth, since he surely that is temperate in old age cannot have a great reward, having in perfection the security from his age." Similarly, when Ambrose tells the story of Lawrence's martyrdom, he has Bishop Xystus say, "We as old men have to undergo an easier fight; a more glorious triumph over the tyrant awaits thee, a young man" (*On the Duties of the Clergy* 1.41.215 [NPNF second series, vol. 10, p. 35]).

32. John Cassian, *Institutes* 4.30 (NPNF second series, vol. 11, p. 229). Cf. *Institutes* 4.2 and *Conferences* 19.2 (NPNF second series, vol. 11, pp. 219 and 490).

which I knew I might lose, nor to be greatly dismayed by adversities wherein I had found that his mercies could succour me." By saying this Paulinus means something more than a stoic acceptance of fate. He later says that "with perception improving with old age I recognize that to my profit they were withdrawn from me, that by the loss of earthly and failing riches I might learn to seek rather those which will endure for ever." The poem ends with his prayer that Christ will dispel his doubts and fears "by the sure confidence that alike while I am in this mortal body I am thine, since all is thine, and that when released from it I shall be in some part of thy body."[33] He sees his involvement in this world from the perspective of eternity.[34]

Virtue and wisdom, then, cannot finally be separated. At a theoretical level most of the writers of the early church were Christian Platonists who assumed the identity of knowledge and virtue, since to know the good is to do the good. But in a more commonsense way they also realized the importance of the union of precept and example. John Cassian tells the story of old Abba John. On his deathbed the brethren ask him for his final words as a legacy to help them toward perfection. The old man "sighed and said, 'I never did my own will, nor taught any one what I had not first done myself.'"[35] Ambrose also underlines the importance of the witness, guidance, and counsel the old can give the young. His examples include Moses and Joshua; Abraham and Lot; Elijah and Elisha; Barnabas and Mark; Paul and Silas, Timothy, and Titus; and Peter and John.[36] Basil the Great exhorts the brethren to "go to old men difficult of access, who anoint with their maxims the young men for deeds of virtue. . . ."[37]

The authority of the elderly for teaching and discipline finds constant attention in our sources. Basil rebukes the young deacon Glycerius for "scorn-

33. Paulinus of Pella, *Eucharisticus,* preface 3, lines 439ff., lines 612ff., in *Ausonius,* trans. H. G. Evelyn White, Loeb Classical Library no. 115 (London: W. Heinemann, 1919-21), vol. 2, pp. 307, 339, 351.

34. Cf. John Gardner's novel *The Resurrection.* The hero, James Chandler, facing his death by the quick kind of leukemia, writes in his journal: "More than 'in the world but not of the world' (he wrote). More than Platonic. The wisdom of old people when, as sometimes happens, old people chance to become wise. To whom the death of a child is tragic but tolerable, as it is not to us. In whom no trace of self-pity remains. Who are not overly grieved by tragedy in life, and not because they have no commitment, no interest in the central figure of the tragedy, but because, having loved repeatedly, having survived by the skin of their teeth many times, just as those who love them will, despite their own wish, they can give of themselves unstintingly, fully prepared to pay back all they have spent. To see life's beauty whole implies at once the ardent desire to look and the necessity of backing off" (Ballantine paperback, p. 204).

35. John Cassian, *Institutes* 5.28 (NPNF second series, vol. 11, p. 243).

36. Ambrose, *On the Duties of the Clergy* 2.20.97-101 (NPNF second series, vol. 10, pp. 58f.).

37. Basil, *De renuntiatione saeculi* 207D, in *Ascetic Works,* by Clarke, p. 67.

ing his own presbyter, a man who is venerated for both his conduct and his age."[38] Both Gregory Nazianzen and John Chrysostom in their treatments of the priesthood wrestle with the question of age. Both regard their youth as an obstacle to ordination, yet both see the necessity of exceptions to the rule.[39] Similarly, the abbas in the monasteries often have authority because of their long and virtuous lives.[40] More generally, Cyprian of Carthage in the third century exhorts his readers to serve God and to give alms as follows:

> Be rather such a father to your children as was Tobias. Give useful and saving precepts to your pledges, such as he gave to his son: command your children what he also commanded his son. . . . (Tobit 14:10f., 4:5-11).[41]

It would be difficult to argue that teachers and authorities in the church were always literally elders, but it is common to find younger leaders described as old in wisdom if not in age.[42]

If the authority of the aged in teaching and discipline stems primarily from their virtue, it is also based upon their experience. Basil introduces his advice to young men regarding how to profit from pagan literature by saying,

> For the fact that I have reached this age, and have already been trained through many experiences, and indeed also have shared sufficiently in

38. Basil, Letter 169, in *Saint Basil*, vol. 2, p. 441. See also Letter 170 on the same subject. Glycerius neglected his work, surrounded himself with virgins, and had the presumption to call himself patriarch. Basil speaks of his own rebuke as a fatherly one. Cf. Letter 278, where he speaks of the propriety of a young man visiting an old one (vol. 4, p. 165).

39. See Gregory Nazianzen, *Oration* 2.47, 73 (NPNF second series, vol. 7, pp. 214 and 220). In section 73 he cites Ecclesiastes 10:16: "Woe to thee, O city, whose king is a child." Cf. Basil, Letter 61, where the same biblical verse is cited in reference to the governor of Libya. Gregory also treats the moral of Christ's baptism to mean that we are "[t]o purify ourselves first; to be lowly minded; and to preach only in maturity both of spiritual and bodily stature. . . . dost thou before thy beard has grown presume to teach the aged?" (*Oration on the Holy Lights* 14 [NPNF second series, vol. 7, p. 357]). John Chrysostom persuades his friend Basil that he, Basil, is an exception to the rule that the young ought not be ordained (*On the Priesthood* 1.7, 2.8, 3.15, 6.12 [NPNF first series, vol. 9, pp. 36, 44, 53, 81f.]).

40. See, for example, John Cassian, *Institutes* 11.17 and *Conferences* 18.3 (NPNF second series, vol. 11, pp. 279 and 480).

41. Cyprian, *On Works and Alms* 20 (ANF 5, p. 481).

42. For example, John Chrysostom tells his friend Basil, "you will speedily teach them [those who object to his youth and inexperience] by your acts that understanding is not to be estimated by age, and the grey head is not to be the test of an elder — that the young man ought not to be absolutely excluded from the ministry, but only the novice; and the difference between the two is great" (*On the Priesthood* 2.8 [NPNF first series, vol. 9, p. 44]).

the all-teaching vicissitude of both good and evil fortune, has made me conversant with human affairs, so that I can indicate the safest road, as it were, to those who are just entering upon life.[43]

Similarly, John Cassian explains that it is customary in the monasteries for the older monks to give instruction and spiritual direction to "the younger brethren." His emphasis is upon precepts that will assist the young to deal with their sins and their temptations. And he justifies this custom on the basis of the fact that

they have had experience of numberless falls and the ruin of all sorts of people. And often recognizing in ourselves many of these things, when the elders explained and showed them, as men who were themselves disquieted by the same passions, we were cured without any shame or confusion on our part. . . .[44]

It is not merely long persistence in virtue that gives the old authority, it is also the fact that they have themselves struggled, sometimes unsuccessfully, for the virtue that is the true basis of their authority.

One final theme we find is the appeal to the old as bearers of the tradition. Irenaeus speaks of his youth in "Polycarp's hall" and of the indelible impression made upon him by the old bishop of Smyrna. Polycarp, in turn, told of his teacher and master, John the Apostle. Through memory and personal association Irenaeus traces his message back to an eyewitness of the resurrection.[45] Similarly, Basil defends his orthodoxy to the people of Neocaesarea by appealing to the teaching of his grandmother, Macrina,

by whom we were taught the sayings of the most blessed Gregory [the Wonderworker] (as many as she herself retained, preserved to her time in unbroken memory), and who moulded and formed us while still young in the doctrines of piety.[46]

In his old age Augustine sees the importance of this chain of memory by seeking to make provision for his successor as bishop. Old age has nothing further to look forward to in this life. No one knows "how long old age may . . . be

---

43. Basil, "To Young Men On How They Might Profit from Pagan Literature," in *Saint Basil*, vol. 4, p. 379.

44. John Cassian, *Institutes* 7.13 (NPNF second series, vol. 11, p. 252).

45. See the citation from Irenaeus in Eusebius, *Ecclesiastical History* 5.20.5-8, trans. Kirsopp Lake, Loeb Classical Library no. 153 (London: W. Heinemann, 1926-32), vol. 1, pp. 469ff.

46. Basil, Letter 204, in *Saint Basil*, vol. 3, p. 169.

prolonged . . . but it is certain that no other age destined to take its place lies beyond." For this reason he designates Eraclius as his successor.[47]

Widows

While it is clear that in late antiquity not all widows were elderly, widowhood and old age are closely associated in the early church for the simple reason that 1 Timothy 5:9 establishes as one of the qualifications of "enrolled" widows that they be at least sixty years old. This scriptural requirement often seems problematic to the church fathers. Ambrose, in his treatise *Concerning Widows*, attempts to resolve the puzzle by saying that it is "[n]ot that old age alone makes the widow, but that the merits of the widow are the duties of old age." Besides, "youth is prone to fall because the heat of various desires is inflamed by the warmth of glowing youth. . . ." Nevertheless, says Ambrose, "I do not think that he [Paul] thought that the younger should be excluded from the devotion of widowhood."[48] Ambrose's somewhat confused discussion seems to me to reflect the tension between the scriptural age requirement and the fact that younger widows were apparently "enrolled."[49]

Another ambiguity revolves around whether widows were enrolled so as to be recipients of church funds or were constituted as an order of ministry in the church. It seems best to argue that these purposes need not exclude one another and to recognize that different practices must have obtained in different places at different times. Both the Old Testament and the New urge the care of widows and orphans, and there can be no doubt that the church provided for widows. Could the age requirement of 1 Timothy reflect an assumption that younger widows might remarry? Ambrose does not think so, since he argues that the "persecutors of the faith" were "persecutors of widowhood."[50] Presumably he is thinking of the Emperor Augustus' legislation requiring widows under fifty years old to be remarried within a year of their husbands' deaths.[51]

---

47. Augustine, Letter 213 (NPNF first series, vol. 1, p. 569).

48. Ambrose, *Concerning Widows* 2.9 and 2.12 (NPNF second series, vol. 10, pp. 392 and 393). Ambrose's treatise describes widowhood as a Christian and spiritual ideal; he discusses biblical widows like Anna, Naomi, Judith, and Deborah, treating them as models.

49. See Basil, Letter 199, in *Saint Basil*, vol. 3, p. 117. Basil seeks to impose the age requirement but recognizes that it has sometimes been violated.

50. Ambrose, *Concerning Widows* 14.85 (NPNF second series, vol. 10, p. 406).

51. Augustus issued the Lex Julia in 18 BCE and the Lex Papia Poppaea in 9 CE. Cf. Bonnie Bowman Thurston, *The Widows: A Women's Ministry in the Early Church* (Minneapolis: Fortress Press, 1989), p. 16.

But his view reflects his understanding of widows as more than the recipients of charity and as in some sense the equivalent of virgins.[52]

It would seem the case that "enrolled" or "appointed" widows were often the "altar of God" not only because they received the offerings of the church but also because their special task was to offer constant prayer to God.[53] As an order in the church the enrolled widows seem sometimes to have had a special ministry correlative with that of the virgins. Perhaps this is why Ignatius can refer to "the virgins called widows."[54] And this may explain why younger widows were sometimes enrolled and why the *Didascalia* reduces the age for enrollment to fifty years. From very early times in many places enrolled widows must have been an "order" in the church. Even though Hippolytus early in the third century insists that widows do not receive ordination (the laying on of hands), it may well be the case that certain churches did ordain widows.

This possibility correlates with another confusion, that of widows with deaconesses. The *Apostolic Church Order* speaks of three kinds of widows, the third of which fulfills the same tasks as the male deacons. The *Apostolic Constitutions* specifies that deaconesses are to be chosen from the widows and to be ordained with the laying on of hands. Theodore of Mopsuestia understands 1 Timothy 3:11 ("The women likewise must be serious . . .") to refer to female deacons. Both the context of the biblical verse, which deals with the qualifications of deacons, and the practice of his own church make this interpretation an obvious one. Theodore also notes in his comment on 1 Timothy 5:9 that it is mistaken to apply the sixty-year age requirement for widows to deaconesses.[55] By the end of the fourth century the church in the East differed from that in the West. In the East we find ordained deaconesses; in the West the persistence of the order of enrolled widows. The main point to make for my purposes is that aged widows often had a special function and ministry.

---

52. Cf. Peter Brown, *The Body and Society: Men, Women, and Sexual Renunciation in Early Christianity* (New York: Columbia University Press, 1988), pp. 147ff.

53. See Roger Gryson, *The Ministry of Women in the Early Church* (Collegeville, Minn.: Liturgical Press, 1976), p. 13. He argues that the two meanings need not exclude one another. See also Carolyn Osiek, "The Widow as Altar: The Rise and Fall of a Symbol," *The Second Century* 3, no. 3. (1983): 159-69. Professor Osiek has collected all the references to and examined the various functions of the metaphor.

54. Ignatius, *Smyrnaeans* 13.1.

55. H. B. Swete, *Theodore of Mopsuestia on the Minor Epistles of S. Paul* (Cambridge: Cambridge University Press, 1882), vol. 2, pp. 128, 155ff. Note 11 on p. 128 includes Pelagius' recognition that there were deaconesses in the East. Note 12 on p. 158 is also useful. For fuller discussion see Gryson, *The Ministry of Women in the Early Church*, whose discussion I am following.

The Vices and the Burden of Old Age

Although it can be no more than my impression, it would seem to be the case that our sources underline the honor and importance of the aged in example and precept. Nevertheless, there is also a clear recognition that the ideal does not always obtain. The virtues of old age ought to be the crown of a lifelong quest;[56] nevertheless, there are vices that can be specially associated with the elderly. The old can, for example, be garrulous.[57] In the sayings of the desert fathers we meet an old man who says,

> When first we used to meet each other in the assembly and talk of what was helpful to our souls, we became ever more withdrawn from the things of sense, and mounted to the heavenly places. But now we meet, and spend our time in gossip, and each drags the other downwards.[58]

There may be some relation of this observation to the recognition that old people sometimes rest on their laurels and become slothful. Most old men, says Abba Moses according to John Cassian, "pass their old age in a luke-warmness . . . and in sloth, and so obtain authority not from the ripeness of their character but simply from the number of their years."[59]

Clement of Alexandria attacks the vanity of the old, who "like serpents" think they can "divest themselves of the old age of their head by painting and renovating themselves." No matter what they do, they cannot escape wrinkles and death. The attempt to appear young when old is a repudiation of the true honor of old age.[60] More serious is the vanity of pride, and there are a number of texts that treat vainglory and pride as the peculiar vices of the aged. In speaking of vainglory John Cassian says,

> For all other vices, as we said above, are sometimes diminished by the lapse of time, and disappear: to this one length of life, unless it is supported by skilful diligence and prudent discretion, is no hindrance, but actually supplies it with new fuel for vanity.[61]

---

56. Cf. John Chrysostom, *Homily 81.5 on Matthew* (NPNF first series, vol. 10, p. 490). Without virtue we come "to old age as to a hold full of bilgewater." Shipwreck is the consequence.

57. Cf. Clement of Alexandria, *The Instructor* 2.8 (ANF 2, p. 252). Macrobius in his *Saturnalia* says "the old are habitually talkative" (7.2.14). He also notes that old men are often drunk (7.6.11 and 7.6.15ff.).

58. *The Sayings of the Fathers* 105, in *Western Asceticism*, ed. Owen Chadwick, Library of Christian Classics vol. 12 (Philadelphia: Westminster, 1958), p. 129.

59. John Cassian, *Conferences* 2.13 (NPNF second series, vol. 11, p. 314).

60. Clement of Alexandria, *The Instructor* 3.3; cf. 3.11 (ANF 2, pp. 275 and 285).

61. John Cassian, *Institutes* 11.8 (NPNF second series, vol. 11, p. 277).

Pride can sometimes take the form of refusing to receive instruction. Old dogs dislike learning new tricks. There are several stories of this kind in the Pachomian literature. In one of them some old monks refuse to listen to the young monk Theodore's instruction, walk out of the assembly, and complain to Pachomius: "you have made a boy teacher of us, a large group of old men and of other brothers." Pachomius, who seems constantly to have faced rebellion in the ranks, groans and says that "pride is the mother of all evils."[62]

A story told by John Cassian and found elsewhere is the most striking indictment of pride in the elderly. A young monk, troubled by "the spirit of fornication," seeks counsel from an old monk, who responds with a rigidity that drives the young monk to despair and to the decision to return to his village and take a wife. On his way Abba Apollos meets the young man, hears his story, and seeks to reassure him by saying that "he himself was daily tried by the same pricks of desire and lust." Abba Apollos succeeds in delaying the young man's return to the world and prays that God will turn the assault upon the young man's aged advisor, "that he may learn to condescend to the weakness of sufferers, and to sympathize even in old age with the frailties of youth." The demon of lust obliges, the story ends happily, and the old man learns his lesson.[63]

The burdens of old age are perhaps more obvious than its vices. It is not difficult to find references to physical debility. In the monastic literature the old are often ranked with children and the sick, who are freed from extreme rigor in fasting.[64] Sometimes references to the debility of the aged occur in the context of stories about people who overcome the physical constraints of old age. Theodoret of Cyrus tells of Eusebius of Asikha:

> When he reached extreme old age, such that he lost most of his teeth, he changed neither his food nor his lodging. Frozen in winter and

---

62. *Paralipomena from the Life of Holy Pachomius* 1.1, in *Pachomian Koinonia*, vol. 2, trans. Armand Veilleux, Cistercian Studies no. 46 (Kalamazoo: Cistercian Publications, 1981), pp. 19ff. Cf. *The Bohairic Life of Pachomius* 68-69, in *Pachomian Koinonia*, vol. 1, trans. Armand Veilleux, Cistercian Studies no. 45 (Kalamazoo: Cistercian Publications, 1980), pp. 89ff.

63. John Cassian, *Conferences* 2.13 (NPNF second series, vol. 11, pp. 313ff.). Cf. *The Sayings of the Fathers* 4, in *Western Asceticism*, ed. Chadwick, pp. 60ff.

64. See John Cassian, *Institutes* 5.5, *Conferences* 2.22 (NPNF second series, vol. 11, pp. 235 and 317); *The Rules of Saint Pachomius* 5 (*Pachomian Koinonia*, vol. 2, p. 143); *Rule of St. Benedict* 37, cf. 66 (*Western Asceticism*, pp. 316 and 334). Benedict follows *The Rule of the Master* in ranking the aged with the sick and children, and he also follows his source in assigning old men as porters for the monastery, who eat with the abbot (*The Rule of the Master* 28.26, 50.78, 53.4, 53.52, 84.1, 95, trans. L. Eberle [Kalamazoo: Cistercian Publications, 1977], pp. 188, 213, 214f., 218, 250, 283f.) Characteristically, Benedict makes the additional provision that one of the younger monks can be assigned to the aged porter if he needs help (Rule 66, p. 334).

burnt in summer, he bore with endurance the contrasting temperatures of the air, his face shriveled up and all the limbs of his body wasted away.[65]

Despite this condition Eusebius was able to perform a feat of climbing that enabled him to escape the many people seeking his blessing. In some contrast to this story John Cassian tells of Abba Chaeremon, who at more than a hundred years is so bent with age that he could only crawl and who laments the fact that "the feebleness of age has relaxed my former strictness, as it has also destroyed my confidence in speaking."[66]

Abba Chaeremon's second complaint reflects another of old age's burdens, the loss of memory and of mental ability. Clement of Alexandria calls his *Stromateis* "my memoranda . . . stored up against old age, as a remedy against forgetfulness."[67] Ausonius speaks of "my scarce-remembering age" and notes that "old men are twice children."[68] Gregory Nazianzen, who in his early fifties resigned the See of Constantinople, sums up the burden of old age as follows:

> Give me respite from my long labours. . . . behold, I pray you, the condition of this body, so drained by time, by disease, by toil. What need have you of a timid and unmanly old man, who is, so to speak, dying day by day, not only in body, but even in powers of mind. . . .[69]

We find old age understood in an ambiguous or even contradictory fashion. On the one hand, it represents the culmination of a life of virtue and wisdom; and as such it is a great gift to the Christian community. On the other hand, it is often a time of physical and mental weakness. This may be a theoretical contradiction, but it is scarcely one from the perspective of the realities of human life.

The weakness of the aged means that they are sometimes unable to care

---

65. *A History of the Monks in Syria* 18.1, trans. R. M. Price (Kalamazoo: Cistercian Publications, 1985), pp. 126f.

66. John Cassian, *Conferences* 11.4 (NPNF second series, vol. 11, p. 416). Examples could be multiplied. In contrast, Athanasius (*Life of Antony* 93) says that Antony at nearly 105 was unaffected by old age save that his teeth "simply had been worn to the gums." This may say more about Athanasius' ideal of the mind governing the body than about the truth of the matter. The physical limitations of old age sometimes are thought to disqualify elders from the ascetical life. See Palladius, *Lausiac History* 18.13-16 and 22.2-8 (ACW 34, pp. 62f. and 77ff.).

67. Clement of Alexandria, *Stromateis* 1.1 (ANF 2, p. 301).

68. Ausonius, Epistles 22 and 8, in *Ausonius,* trans. White, vol. 2, pp. 79 and 27.

69. Gregory Nazianzen, *Oration* 42.20 (NPNF second series, vol. 7, p. 392).

for themselves. Children have the obligation to support their aged parents. Gregory Nazianzen describes his own efforts to care for his aged parents, and Basil the Great asks Amphilochius to secure from his aged father permission to leave him for a brief time in order to pay Basil a visit.[70] John Chrysostom's widowed mother, though she is not old, implores her son to remain faithful to his obligation to care for her.[71] We also find young monks in the monasteries who are charged with the care of a particular aged monk who needs support.[72] Basil refers to the custom of dispensing the aged from their civic obligations, and in one case he pleads with the governor of Cappadocia not to enroll a four-year-old boy as a senator so that his grandfather will not lose his dispensation.[73] Clement of Alexandria castigates the wealthy who "overlook the chaste widow, who is of far higher value than a Melitaean pup, and look askance at a just old man, who is lovelier in my estimation than a monster purchased for money." People take better care of their pets than of widows, orphans, and the aged.[74] The duty to support the aged, then, is one that belongs not only to their children but also to every Christian.

Concluding Reflections

The question whether and how we can learn from history, of course, raises complicated theoretical questions I can make no claim to answer. There is a vast difference between old age in the ancient church and old age for us.[75] Nevertheless, old age is a perennial human challenge; and some of the attitudes taken toward it by ancient Christians at least resonate with some of my own attitudes. It seems important to me, perhaps because I have myself entered old age, to see it as one's completion of life and as a gift.[76] The old have

70. Gregory Nazianzen, *Oration 2.103* (NPNF second series, vol. 7, p. 225). Basil, Letter 150, in *Saint Basil*, vol. 2, p. 371. Ambrose recommends care of parents and of widows in *On the Duties of the Clergy* 1.33.170 and 2.29.144 (NPNF second series, vol. 10, pp. 29 and 65).

71. John Chrysostom, *On the Priesthood* 1.5 (NPNF first series, vol. 9, p. 34).

72. Dorotheos of Gaza, *Discourse on the Fear of God*, trans. E. P. Wheeler, Cistercian Studies no. 33 (Kalamazoo: Cistercian Publications, 1977), pp. 117f. Meno of Nikiou, *The Life of Isaac of Alexandria*, trans. D. N. Bell, Cistercian Studies no. 107 (Kalamazoo: Cistercian Publications, 1988), pp. 51f.

73. Basil, Letters 84 and 104, in *Saint Basil*, vol. 2, pp. 107ff., 197.

74. Clement of Alexandria, *The Instructor* 3.4 (ANF 2, p. 279). For the care of the aged see also Barnabas 20 in *The Apostolic Fathers*, trans. Kirsopp Lake, Loeb Classical Library no. 24 (London: W. Heinemann, 1917-19), vol. 1, p. 407, and Tertullian, *Apology* 39 (ANF 3, p. 46).

75. Cf. Blythe, *The View in Winter*, p. 4 (for relevant quotation, see note 15 above).

76. Cf. Blythe, *View in Winter*, p. 237: "life for him [Charles de Montalembert] was pro-

long memories and much experience. They sometimes fashion memory and experience into wisdom, a wisdom they can impart to those younger than they and one that can be the source of a detached caring that can benefit others without imposing the cost often exacted by a younger and more egotistical ambition. The old can teach us to see ourselves not as isolated individuals but as part of a long human procession that reaches far into the past. Perhaps most important from a Christian perspective, the old can sometimes see beyond the world of our experience to the Christian's destiny. If Augustine is correct in construing the Christian life as a long convalescence with the cure reserved for the age to come, the old are closer to that cure and can give us hope.

Discerning and accepting the gift of old age, then, may be more important than caring for the aged. Or one could put the point another way: the best care we can give the aged is, when possible, to use their gifts and to love them for what they can give. This means trying to avoid segregating the aged or at least seeking to mitigate that isolation as much as we can. We can strive to enable the aged to keep on serving, to be needed. There are obvious limits to the idealistic aims I am suggesting, and more often than not there comes a time when the aged become only a burden to themselves and to others.[77] But we can at least strive to avoid deciding prematurely that the gift has gone and only the burden remains.

---

longed without being saddened." See also p. 238: The Cowley Fathers are a community that "tries to look at life as a natural entity, whatever its length."

77. Cf. Blythe, *View in Winter*, pp. 22f.: "Just as the old should be convinced that, whatever happens during senescence, they will never suffer exclusion, so they should understand that age does not exempt them from being despicable."

The Christian Practice of Growing Old
in the Middle Ages

DAVID AERS

This essay concludes with extended reflections on a profound treatment of aging and the role of the church found in an English poem of the later Middle Ages, but it begins by illustrating conventional approaches to old age. Medieval encyclopedias were designed to convey received knowledge about everything, and I set out from one of these. *De Proprietatibus Rerum* was an extremely popular compilation written in the thirteenth century and translated into English by John Trevisa in the late fourteenth century.[1] The sixth book of *On the Properties of Things* includes one of the numerous schemes used to organize the processes of human life into stages. Bartholomaeus classifies them as follows: (1) "the firste childehode" (the first seven months of life); (2) "anothir childehode" (up to fourteen); (3) "the age of yonge striplynge" (up to twenty-one or twenty-eight or thirty or thirty-five);[2] (4) "middil age" (up to forty-five or fifty); (5) and (6) are two stages of old age, "elde," which involves "failynge of wittes," culminating in madness; (7) the final stage is "the ende of age and of life."[3]

---

1. *On the Properties of Things*, John Trevisa's translation of Bartholomaeus Anglicus, *De Proprietatibus Rerum*, ed. M. C. Seymour (Oxford: Clarendon Press, 1975). In quoting I modernize lettering but not spelling. On the treatment of age in Bartholomaeus see the following, all three being indispensable studies of the present subject: J. A. Burrow, *The Ages of Man* (Oxford: Clarendon Press, 1988), pp. 88-89; Mary Dove, *The Perfect Age of Man's Life* (Cambridge: Cambridge University Press, 1986); Elizabeth Sears, *The Ages of Man: Medieval Interpretations of the Life Cycle* (Princeton: Princeton University Press, 1986), pp. 127-28. Unless otherwise specified, I quote the Bible from *The Jerusalem Bible* (London: Darton, Longman, and Todd, 1966).

2. On the "difficulty" here, of "harmonizing" different traditions, see Burrow, *The Ages*, pp. 88-89.

3. The seven stages are quoted from *Properties*, bk. 6, pp. 291-92.

This model of aging assumes man as the norm, an assumption pervasive in medieval culture.[4] Following Aristotle, the writer observes that "a man is as it were fourme and schape, and womman as it were pacient and suffringe."[5] The time of "elde" is viewed with ambivalence. Although a period of great suffering, it is also, potentially, one of great goods. The latter are said to be freedom from tyrannical rulers, the end of lust, and the beginning of spiritual joys. Against these potential goods, however, the encyclopedist sets a catalogue of the evils of age which involve the whole person.[6] Weakness, many discomforts, sickness, sorrows, the destruction of the body, these are described in some detail, while we are also told that "Alle men dispisen the olde man and ben hevy and wery of him."[7] This hint of gerontophobia together with an approach that lays far greater stress on the many evils of old age than on the potential goods is characteristic of late medieval writing on old age.[8] There seems to be a marked shift from Augustine's analogy between the sixth age of life and the sixth age of the world, the period initiated by the incarnation and lasting to the world's end: while the "exterior" man is ruined, the "inner" may be renewed day by day.[9] Here the reader's attention is shifted from the disintegrating body

4. For an excellent recent introduction to this vast subject, see R. H. Bloch, *Medieval Misogyny and the Invention of Western Romantic Love* (Chicago: University of Chicago Press, 1991); this should be read with the very different focus on works of social history by Judith Bennett, "Medieval Women, Modern Women," in *Culture and History 1350-1600*, ed. David Aers (London: Harvester, 1992), chap. 5; on the major role and content of medical discourse see the outstanding studies of Joan Cadden, *The Meanings of Sex Difference in the Middle Ages: Medicine, Science and Culture* (Cambridge: Cambridge University Press, 1993), and Danielle Jacquart and Claude Thomasset, *Sexuality and Medicine in the Middle Ages* (Philadelphia: University of Pennsylvania Press, 1990). For commentary on the treatment of the "old female body" and its poison, see Shulamith Shahar, "The Old Body in Medieval Culture," chap. 8 in *Framing Medieval Bodies*, ed. Sarah Kay and Miri Rubin (Manchester: Manchester University Press, 1994), pp. 161-62, and her survey, *Growing Old in the Middle Ages* (London: Routledge, 1997), chap. 2.

5. *Properties*, p. 306: on the "maiden childe and a wench" see VI.2; on motherhood, VI.7; and on particular states of masculinity, VI.5, 12-14, 18.

6. Cartesian dualism is alien to medieval thought about human identities: for a current stimulating essay on the popularity of academic essays and books about "the body," see Caroline Bynum, "Why All the Fuss about the Body? A Medievalist's Perspective," *Critical Inquiry* 22 (1995): 1-33. Relevant to the parenthetical remarks here are Jacquart and Thomasset, *Sexuality and Medicine*; Cadden, *The Meanings of Sex Difference*; and Caroline W. Bynum, *Holy Feast and Holy Fast* (Berkeley: University of California Press, 1987), and her *Fragmentation and Redemption* (New York: Zone, 1991).

7. *Properties*, pp. 292-93.

8. For a concise illustration of this, see Alicia K. Nitecki, "Figures of Old Age in Fourteenth-Century English Literature," in *Aging and the Aged in Medieval Europe*, ed. Michael M. Sheehan (Toronto: Pontifical Institute of Mediaeval Studies, 1990), pp. 107-16.

9. See Augustine, *De Diversis Quaestionibus LXXXIII*, I.58 (*Patrologia Latina* [ed. J. P. Migne,

to the "spiritual ages" of development within a distinctively Christian vision of history and individual life, both oriented toward the seventh day and the joyful peace of the city of God.[10] But in much late medieval writing about old age this vision, in practice, seems to be sidelined, despite the massive influence of Augustine's works and Augustinian exegesis of the six water pots at the marriage in Cana (John 2.1-10), allegorical exegesis that turned these vessels into a figure of the six ages of man and the six ages of the world.[11]

Lotario dei Segni, the future Pope Innocent III, wrote a work on the miseries of being human (De miseria condicionis humane[12]) which includes an account of old age that typifies late medieval representations.[13] Old age is treated as the culmination of the repulsive miseries that characterize our condition. Death is a relief from a life that has actually been no more than a long process of dying. Not only does the body disintegrate in excruciating pain (teeth rot, eyes mist over, ears become deaf, heart weakens, and so on), but the person's moral dispositions correspondingly degenerate. The aged become prickly, unforgiving, grasping, avaricious, quarrelsome, depressed, garrulous, bad listeners, nostalgic, and overwhelmed with anxiety. The official aim of such texts is to detach their readers from a world that is transient, full of suffering, packed with impediments to spiritual life — a deceptive, powerful vanity.[14] A late medieval lyric on aging suggests that the young should learn from the catastrophic losses of old age that worldly bliss is "but thinge of vanyte" which makes people lose their way.[15] Focusing on the old person's

---

Paris, 1844-65] 40.43; see also Augustine, De Genesi contra Manichaeus I.23-24 (Patrologia Latina 34.190-93) and De Vera Religione, 26.48-49 (Patrologia Latina 34.143-44).

10. See the clear outlines and references in Burrow, The Ages, pp. 80-83, 89, 91n.96; Dove, Perfect Age, pp. 48-51; and Sears, The Ages of Man, pp. 55-58.

11. On the water vessels and John 2:1-10 see Burrow, The Ages, pp. 90-92 (with references in n. 96 and n. 97), and Sears, The Ages of Man, pp. 69-79 (with figures 18-19).

12. Lotario dei Segni, De miseria condicionis humane, ed. and trans. R. E. Lewis (Athens, Ga.: Chaucer Library, 1978).

13. In his discussion of the decisive influence of Isidore of Seville's Etymologorum sive Originum Libra XX on the encyclopedic and late medieval traditions of representing old age, John Burrow notes that "Isidore entirely dispensed with the Biblical matrix which shaped Augustine's account" of the ages of the world and human life, observing that "the result could as well be the work of a pagan grammarian as a Christian writer. But it made an excellent entry for an encyclopaedia" (The Ages, p. 83; see pp. 82-88). Even a Christian encyclopedia?

14. See especially 1.10 in De miseria, but passim; for a characteristic late medieval vernacular version, see Eustaches Deschamps, "De la fragilite humaine," in Oeuvres Completes, ed. Le Marquis de Queux de Sainte-Hilaire, vol. 2 (Paris: Didot, 1880), pp. 242-69.

15. "From the tyme," pp. 233-36 in Religious Lyrics of the XVth Century, ed. Carleton Brown (Oxford: Clarendon Press, 1962); see also "As I wente one my playing," pp. 230-33. I have modernized letters.

mourning, readers are customarily reminded that life is but a "cheyr feyree [cheery fair]" from which they must depart, praying for a mansion in paradise to the one who shed his blood "for my redempcion."[16]

Despite the final turn to Christ in some of this writing, by no means in all, it is true to say that old age is customarily treated with "horror and repugnance"; in the case of women's old age the horror is often compounded with an anxiety about female sexuality and its danger to men.[17] This gendered twist to conventional attitudes could be rationalized by current theories about menstrual blood which was considered "impure, harmful and possessing destructive power": in old age women became "incapable of eliminating the superfluous matter" from their bodies, and so even more dangerous. Discussing these views, Shulamith Shahar quotes from *De Secretis Mulierum* [*On Women's Secrets*]: "the retention of menses engenders many evil humours. The women being old have almost no natural heat left to consume and control this matter, especially poor women who live on nothing but coarse meat. . . . These women are more venomous than the others."[18] Christians grew old in a culture pervaded by a mixture of normative misogyny and repugnance at old age. One can glimpse how such a mixture could make its contribution to the mass killings of "witches" (mostly women, and predominantly older women) by Christians in late medieval and early modern Europe.[19] This may seem far removed from Augustine's treatment of human ages in *De Vera Religione* and elsewhere, and it may be tempting to deny that it is in any sense distinctively Christian. Nevertheless, such perceptions were widely held by Christians, one aspect of the form Christianity took in that historical world.

Writers whose concerns were perhaps more obviously pastoral, however, did certainly present old age as a final opportunity, an opportunity for penitence and conversion. A commonplace example of this approach is offered by a poem in a Carthusian manuscript, "Of the seven ages." Each age, with its il-

---

16. Here see *Religious Lyrics*, pp. 230-33 ("As I wente") and 236-37 ("Ffare well"); the whole sequence of poems on pp. 230-58 is relevant, all being excellent examples of conventional perspectives.

17. Nitecki, "Figures of Old Age," p. 108; see pp. 111-12 and references there.

18. Shahar, "The Old Body," p. 163.

19. On this appalling history there is now a vast literature. Works I have found especially relevant here are the following: Diane Purkiss, *The Witch in History* (London: Routledge, 1996); S. Clark, "Inversion, Misrule, and the Meaning of Witchcraft," *Past and Present* 87 (1980): 98-127; C. Larner, *Enemies of God: The Witch-Hunt in Scotland* (Baltimore: Johns Hopkins University Press, 1981); A. Macfarlane, *Witchcraft in Tudor and Stuart England* (New York: Harper and Row, 1970).

lustrative drawing, is staged as a conflict between the soul's good angel and the devil's temptations. In the sixth age, the angel tells the old man that good prayers will alleviate pain and save his soul, while the fiend tells him to defer, to leave amendment until his sins have forsaken him. (The manuscript's illustration shows an old man walking with a crutch in his left hand and a rosary in his right.) In the seventh age the old man bestows his goods in charity, amends his life, cries for mercy and grace to God, and does whatever "goode werkes" he can. In this way, the poem declares, the fiend is finally defeated. (Here the illustration shows the old man in bed, the angel drawing out the small figure of the soul through the mouth and the hairy devil, with horns, green webbed wings, tail, and webbed feet with claws, lamenting his loss.)[20] The message is that the miseries of old age offer a period of penitence in which God's mercy will be available to all who respond in "goode werkes" (see Matt. 25:31-40) and seek amendment of life. We see the same commonplaces deployed in the popular "Testament" written by John Lydgate, a prolific writer from the Benedictine abbey of St. Edmund's in Bury.[21] He was ordained priest in 1397 and died in 1449. The poem presents the monk's old age as the closure of a "perilous dredfull pilgrimage," a journey full of traps and brigands. Fallen into old age and infirmity his vocation is now to "Crye unto Iesu for my synfull outrage." Age calls him to his grave and demands a "rekenyng" of his lifetime. Only Jesus can save him from the devil's knowledge of his past. Old age is chiefly viewed as death's "chief marynere [mariner]." Its tissue of feebleness, sickness, melancholy, and physical, mental, and spiritual pains is designed to provoke remembrance of supposedly "myspent tyme," which Lydgate conjures out of familiar stereotypes of wild young men and hypocritical, lazy monks. Here and elsewhere, old age, at its very best, is seen as a penitential period fixated on past sins and the rendering of accounts at approaching death, accounts that only the generous mercy of Christ or the Virgin Mary could make good against the devil's strong claims.

This version of the Christian practice of growing old is clearly expressed in a treatise on the seven capital sins and their remedial virtues written by a fourteenth-century English Franciscan. The text is a handbook for preachers

---

20. British Library, MS Add 37049, ff28v-29; the poem is printed and discussed by A. Nelson, "'Of the Seven Ages': An Unknown Analogue of *The Castle of Perseverance*," *Comparative Drama* 8 (1974): 125-38, see 126-32; the fifteenth-century play discussed on pp. 132-36 is certainly relevant to the present chapter, from which only limits of space exclude it.

21. For the poem, see *The Minor Poems of John Lydgate: Part One*, ed. H. N. MacCracken (EETS [Early English Text Society], ES 107, 1911, 1962), pp. 329-62, especially lines 194-270, 608-753. The best study of Lydgate remains Derek Pearsall, *John Lydgate* (London: Routledge, 1970); here the *Testament* is discussed on pp. 294-96.

known as *Fasciculus Morum*. It likens human life to a penny consisting of four ages — childhood, youth, manhood, and old age:

> But often a man's first three ages are spent in vain enterprises. Yet if he eagerly provides for himself in his fourth and last age and recovers the things he has lost and becomes rich in good manners [in moribus bonis], he is rightly worthy of praise, for the prize is not promised to those who begin a life of penance, but rather to those who firmly persevere in it; for it is written: "he that perseveres unto the end shall be saved [Matt. 10:22]."

Humble penance overcomes "the Invincible" and turns "the awesome judge" into a "loving father."[22] The fourth part of the penny, old age, is especially well suited to encourage penance and preparation for the judgment encountered in death. Here, perhaps, a distinctively Christian understanding of the creature's situation works against the culture's gerontophobia to reinforce the virtues of hope and faith in the reconciliation with God and with our neighbors achieved by Christ ("God's love for us was revealed when God sent into the world his only Son so that we could have life through him; this is the love I mean," 1 John 4:9-10). The transforming power of this reconciliation is conditional upon the subject's commitment to penance, bodily and spiritual. Ideally penitence, including formal confession to a priest, should be done at the time the person sins, certainly "while he is healthy and strong, not sick and weak." The author of *Fasciculus Morum* observes that according to Augustine, "'If you repent when you can no longer sin, your sins leave you, not you them.' The second kind is not as suitable, for it is done at the end of one's life when one's strength may not suffice for doing penance." Nevertheless, as we have noted, the state of old age provides ample material for penitential afflictions. If these are received appropriately, "the effect of penitence is that through it man is absolved from his sins, restored to the church, reconciled with Christ, enriched with spiritual gifts, and from being a child of the devil made a child of God."[23]

Medieval devotion was centered on a particular version of Christ's hu-

---

22. *Fasciculus Morum: A Fourteenth-Century Preacher's Handbook*, ed. and trans. Siegfried Wenzel (University Park, Pa.: Pennsylvania State University Press, 1989), p. 431 (from V.6, on penance in general).

23. *Fasciculus Morum*, pp. 429, 433; on penance see pp. 428-517; on confession see especially pp. 254-57, 468-97. On the sacrament of penance and the medieval confessional see T. N. Tentler, *Sin and Confession on the Eve of the Reformation* (Princeton: Princeton University Press, 1977); Pierre J. Payer, *The Bridling of Desire* (Toronto: University of Toronto Press, 1993); Anne Hudson, *The Premature Reformation* (Oxford: Oxford University Press, 1988), pp. 294-99.

manity (concentrated on infancy and Passion narratives) together with an ideal of "imitation" which could lead to extremely physical enactment of identification.[24] Yet Christ died in what was considered the "perfect age" of man's life.[25] He chose not to grow old but to be crucified in the prime of human life. According to St. Thomas Aquinas he did so because it would not be suitable for him to display the diminishing natural powers intrinsic to old age (a somewhat peculiar argument in the face of the crucifixion and texts such as Philippians 2:5-11) and because dying in the perfect age ("in juvenali aetate") he rose in it, disclosing the form of those resurrected into the plenitude of Christ.[26] He who embodied all the virtues in their supernatural perfection did not offer a specific model, a specific narrative, for the aging to "imitate." Dante's attempt (in *Il Convivio*) to imagine an ideal old age in connection with Jesus seems rare. Like St. Thomas, Dante argued that Christ chose to die at the "high point" of human life because "it was not fitting that his divinity should be present in something that was in decline." Had Christ not been crucified when he was, Dante speculated, he would have lived to his eighty-first year (like Plato). At that age "he would have exchanged the mortal body for the eternal."[27] Lacking Jesus as a realized model for old age, Dante constructs one for the "noble" soul. Virtuous old age is "prudent and just and generous," fulfilling the "social" and governmental duties required of Aristotelian man. It will also include helping the poor and needy.[28] In extreme old age "the noble soul . . . returns to God, as to the port from which it departed when it came to set sail on the sea of this life." The pilgrimage is envisaged in very different terms to Lydgate's terrifying journey, "for it was direct and

24. As an introduction to this massive subject, so central to the study of medieval Christianity, see the following: J. Marrow, *Passion Iconography in Northern European Art of the Late Middle Ages and Early Renaissance* (Kortrijk: Ghemmert, 1979); Sarah Beckwith, *Christ's Body* (London: Routledge, 1993); Miri Rubin, *Corpus Christi* (Cambridge: Cambridge University Press, 1991); T. Bestul, *Texts of the Passion* (Philadelphia: University of Pennsylvania Press, 1996); David Aers and Lynn Staley, *The Powers of the Holy* (University Park, Pa.: Pennsylvania State University Press, 1996), chap. 1; Caroline W. Bynum, *Holy Feast*.

25. Here the major study is Mary Dove, *Perfect Age*.

26. In my references to St. Thomas's *Summa Theologiae*, I use *Summa Theologica* (Rome: Forzani and Sodalis, 1894): here I quote from III.46.9 ad 4, with Ephesians 4:13. See too Augustine, *The City of God* XXII.15, trans. H. Bettenson (London: Penguin, 1984), here pp. 1055-56; Dove, *Perfect Age*, pp. 47-48; Burrow, *The Ages*, p. 143. On the resurrection of the body in medieval thought, see the magnificent study by Caroline Bynum, *The Resurrected Body* (New York: Columbia University Press, 1995).

27. Dante, *Il Convivio*, trans. C. Ryan, *The Banquet* (Saratoga: Anma, 1989), quoting from IV.23 (p. 183) and IV.24 (p. 184). On Dante's *Convivio* in this context, see Sears, *The Ages of Man*, pp. 103-7, and Burrow, *The Ages*, pp. 32-36, 118-20.

28. Dante, *Banquet* IV.27 (pp. 192-95); Aristotle is invoked at IV.27.3 and IV.27.5.

pleasant and untroubled by violent storm." Death is "natural" and the one approaching it "lowers his sails and enters it gently, guiding his ship slowly in." Setting aside worldly affairs that had still licitly concerned old age, in extreme old age we turn to God "with our whole mind and heart so that we may come into that port with the utmost gentleness and tranquility." Unlike the punitive and penitential norms exemplified earlier in this essay, Dante maintains that "our own nature" gives us this paradigm, "for in a truly natural death there is no pain, no bitterness whatever; rather just as a mature apple lightly and without violence detaches itself from its branch; so our soul without suffering departs from the body in which it has dwelt. That is why Aristotle says in *On Maturity and Old Age* that 'there is no sadness in a death that occurs in an old age.'"[29] The "noble" soul is welcomed by the citizens of the eternal city as the old person is dying, a vision enabled by "the soul's good actions" and "its practice of contemplation." Dante here invokes Cicero's *De Senectute*: "Listen to what Cicero says in the person of Cato the elder: 'I already seem to see our fathers, and I desire with all my heart to see them, whom I loved; and not only them, but even those of whom I only heard others speak.'"[30] Unlike the conventional approaches we have examined, Dante's ideal old person wholeheartedly "blesses the years gone by," viewing them as a successful merchant coming to the port with treasure and the resources to enjoy life in his city, blessing the journey he has made.[31] Cicero's Cato has provided Dante's model for virtuous old age and dying, filling in the gap left by Jesus. Indeed, Dante develops an allegory in which the return of the aged Marcia to her first husband, Cato, is interpreted as the soul's return to God: "What person on earth was more worthy than Cato to represent God?"[32]

This is an enchanting image of old and extreme old age. Set aside the Augustinian emphasis on the grimmest realities of fallen life. Set aside the specific narratives of Jesus in the Gospels. Set aside the political and religious powers that rejected him. Set aside the crucifixion and resurrection, the appearances to disciples who had abandoned him but whose calling and forgiveness he reaffirmed. Set aside all this and imagine Jesus and other "noble" souls growing gracefully old. Dante does this, against the grain of his culture, and constructs a model of Stoic virtues and their fruition. But, for a Christian writer, at some cost. The church seems to be irrelevant, an issue to which I shall return in discussing *Piers Plowman*. And the model seems very vulnera-

29. Dante, *Banquet* IV.28 (pp. 195-98).

30. Dante, *Banquet* IV.28.5-6 (p. 196); for Cicero's *De Senectute*, see *De Senectute, De Amicitia, De Divinatione*, ed. W. A. Falconer (Cambridge: Harvard University Press, 1979).

31. Dante, *Banquet* IV.28.11 and 12 (p. 197).

32. Dante, *Banquet* IV.28.13-15 (pp. 197-98).

ble to Augustine's arguments against the Stoics in *The City of God*. Augustine insisted on the fragility of the will's hold on virtue, the necessarily miserable, because fallen, state of our mortality, the inability of humans to love and delight in true righteousness without the help of divine grace, and the absolute need of a mortal but divine mediator to deliver us from self-destruction.[33] The Augustinian soul, unlike the "noble" soul of Dante's *II Convivio*, is burdened by its sin (the original cause of all suffering), while bodily death is normally a painful, anguished, and violent event, tearing apart that which God had joined so closely.[34] For Augustine, even death faithfully and patiently endured is the virtuous endurance of punishment.[35] He concedes that the Stoic model in which reason constantly orders the emotions in tranquil mastery is admirable, a state to be desired, but he emphasizes that "it does not belong to the present life." He quotes from 1 John 1.8, "If we say there is not sin in us, we are fooling ourselves, and we are remote from truth," and then he comments in these words: "And since this state of *apatheia* will not come until there is no sin in man, it will not come in the present life."[36] Christ's work has not made that kind of difference, and our necessarily social life remains enmeshed in darkness and mourning of loss upon loss.[37] Here at least medieval Christianity habitually remained closer to Augustine than to Dante's Ciceronian model. And is there anything about the world at the beginning of the twenty-first century that should make us find Augustine's vision unrecognizably alien? I do not think so.

But did anyone actually live long enough to grow old in the late Middle Ages, and if they did what kind of social circumstances did they experience? Life expectancy in this period was such that those who survived to around twenty could on average expect to live to around fifty. This being an average, many lived longer, and Joel Rosenthal's recent study of old age in medieval England emphasized "the ubiquity of the aged."[38] So they were not the invention of encyclopedists and moralists. As for the contexts, most people lived in villages and very small towns, their livelihood dependent on agricultural production and, in certain areas, on wool and cloth production, together with a wide

33. Augustine, *City of God* IX.4-5, 14-15, 17.
34. Augustine, *City of God* XIII.2-6, 15; XIV.3, 5-6.
35. Augustine, *City of God* XIII.6.
36. Augustine, *City of God* XIV.9.
37. Augustine, *City of God* XIX.5-8 (especially pp. 860, 862-63).
38. See J. T. Rosenthal, *Old Age in Medieval England* (Philadelphia: University of Pennsylvania Press, 1996); on life expectancy, p. 3 and p. 193n.7; on the presence of the aged, pp. 99-100, 115, 171, 173.

range of artisanal occupations. The standard family unit was a single generational nuclear one.[39]

Once the aged could not manage their own lands and tenements how did they survive? The answer is that they tended to make maintenance agreements. In this *contractual* agreement, the elderly surrendered their lands and resources in exchange for certain carefully stipulated benefits. These contracts were often not with the children of the old people, and Judith Bennett's study of women and households in the English countryside found that "social custom did not require children to care for aged parents and that some children, already established in independent households, saw no advantage to undertaking the care of an elderly parent."[40] Elaine Clark's research on East Anglian sources showed how the contractual arrangements depended on the economic strength of the elderly, and because such arrangements are still not habitually associated with the Middle Ages, it is worth giving a representative example. This early-fifteenth-century agreement comes from Wymondham, near Norwich (Norfolk):

> From William Hardyng and Agnes, his wife, to Richard Hardyng and Margaret, his wife, 2 acres, 3 rods of customary land and half a messuage from the tenement "retherys" with appurtenances in Norton. Conditions: food and drink, clothing, footwear and all other necessities; the new tenants to discharge all the old tenants' debts; the new tenants to cover all funeral expenses and to arrange for Masses to be celebrated in the church of Wymondham for the souls of William, Agnes and other benefactors. Entry fine [new tenants to lord of the manor] 10s.[41]

---

39. This sentence points to a substantial field of study; two decisive essays by J. Hajnal provide an essential introduction: "European Marriage Patterns in Perspective," in *Population in History*, ed. D. V. Glass and D. E. C. Eversley (London: Arnold, 1965), pp. 101-43, and "Two Kinds of Pre-Industrial Household Formation Systems," *Population and Development Review* 8 (1982): 449-94. I have found the following especially helpful in relation to the subject of this essay: Elaine Clark, "Some Aspects of Social Security in Medieval England," *Journal of Family History* 7 (1982): 307-20; Judith M. Bennett, *Women in the Medieval Countryside* (New York: Oxford University Press, 1987), pp. 7-8, 48-49, 59-64, 177-89; L. R. Poos, *A Rural Society after the Black Death* (Cambridge: Cambridge University Press, 1991), especially chaps. 1-4, 7-8; R. H. Hilton, *The English Peasantry in the Later Middle Ages* (Oxford: Oxford University Press, 1975), chaps. 2-3, 5-6; for examples of urban studies disclosing family organization, see David Nicholas, *The Domestic Life of a Medieval City . . . Ghent* (Lincoln, Neb.: University of Nebraska Press, 1985), especially pp. 4-12, and Heather Swanson, *Medieval Artisans* (London: Blackwell, 1989).

40. Bennett, *Women in the Medieval Countryside*, p. 62.

41. Clark, "Some Aspects of Social Security," p. 318.

In this conventional exchange we see the normalization of contractual relations in late medieval England. They permeate the care of the old, including their burial and, as this example illustrates, the care of their souls in purgatory. As Richard Smith recently observed, "The retirement or maintenance contract in its most straightforward form afforded the elderly the means to surrender the use of their lands and resources to family members (or indeed non-kin) in exchange for individually arranged benefits and annuities."[42] Smith found that after 1380 "cash annuities" paid by the young to the old became a common part of the agreement, and he noted how "arrangements were becoming less of a 'face-to-face' affair; the parties were less likely to coreside or to reside in premises within the messuage site as population pressures relaxed and unoccupied housing flooded onto the market." The contracts could be, and were, enforced by manorial courts.[43] Such arrangements for the elderly were also made "in towns and cities; in the mansions of the great; in abbots' lodgings, priests' houses, and bishops' palaces."[44] Old people whose resources did not enable any such contracting for social security became part of the "deserving" poor dependent on casual charity and the few hospitals and almshouses.[45] Their situation was utterly miserable.[46] What has changed here?

Before moving to the final part of this essay, I wish to acknowledge an aspect of medieval culture that may be as unexpected to modern people as the contractual arrangements for the old discussed above. The aspect I have in mind here belongs to a medical tradition and is powerfully articulated in a thirteenth-century work on delaying and impeding the effects of old age, *De Retardatione Accidentum Senectutis* by the Franciscan Roger Bacon.[47] He em-

---

42. Richard M. Smith, "The Manorial Court and the Elderly Tenant in Late Medieval England," in *Life, Death and the Elderly,* ed. Margaret Pelling and Richard M. Smith (London: Routledge, 1991), pp. 39-61.

43. Smith, "The Manorial Court," pp. 52, 53, 54-57.

44. Rosenthal, *Old Age,* p. 100; on the clergy see *Old Age,* pp. 111-12, and Nicholas Orme, "Suffering of the Clergy: Illness and Old Age in Exeter Diocese, 1300-1450," in *Life, Death and the Elderly,* ed. Pelling and Smith, pp. 62-73.

45. Rosenthal, *Old Age,* pp. 184-87; for examples of specific hospitals, see Robert S. Gottfried, *Bury St. Edmunds and the Urban Crisis: 1290-1539* (Princeton: Princeton University Press, 1982), pp. 192-204, and Miri Rubin, *Charity and Community in Medieval Cambridge* (Cambridge: Cambridge University Press, 1987), chap. 5.

46. The best introductions to medieval poverty remain Michel Mollat, *The Poor in the Middle Ages* (New Haven: Yale University Press, 1986), and Catharina Lis and Hugo Soly, *Poverty and Capitalism in Pre-Industrial Europe* (Hassocks: Harvester, 1979).

47. Roger Bacon, *De Retardatione Accidentum Senectutis,* ed. A. G. Little and E. Withington

phasized that the decline of old age, and even death itself, could be delayed. A scientific investigation of the causes of aging would enable the scientist to impede them. How? Through a combination of a disciplined, healthy regime and medicines that exploit the hidden forces of nature (vegetable, animal, and mineral). Bacon saw ways to stave off the marks of aging, such as gray hair, wrinkles, loss of sight, garrulity, anxiety, and weakness of body and mind (including disorders of imagination, memory, and reason). He proposed a regime involving features such as cleanness, controlled diets (including care over the food given to animals to be eaten), managed vomiting and laxatives, purification of the blood, and social pleasures and delights. It also involved medicines. Bacon described their preparation, their role, and their effects in his project. The goal of the regime was exemplified by a remarkable liquid found by an old peasant when his plough uncovered a container whose contents he drank: this turned the old person ("senex") into a man of thirty and made him live for an additional sixty years.[48] This example is not allegorized (so the plough is not read as the preacher's word, the liquid in the container not read as Christ's saving blood, and so on).

This strand within the Catholic cultures of the Middle Ages seems to share at least some hopes and perspectives with modern medical technologies and with capital investment and ideologies, perspectives that are quite extrinsic to distinctively Christian traditions. Given the existence of this strand, it is not surprising that works attempting to teach the "crafte of dyinge" should complain that Christians "now" defer "spirituall medycyne and remedy" for the soul's illnesses and set aside the "spirituall lech [physician]." Modern Christians, so the complaint goes, pursue "medicyns for the body" with much more faith and intensity than they apply known spiritual remedies. Even on the point of death contemporaries "will here nothinge of deth," preferring instead "a veyne and a false cherynge [cheering] and comfortyng and feyned behotynge [promising] of bodyly helth," trusting themselves to a medical regime of bodily medicines. The writer of this *ars moriendi* fears that in such faith we imperil our souls everlastingly.[49]

We will see Langland dramatizing the same concerns when we turn to *Piers Plowman,* and it is salutary to realize that certain attitudes toward medi-

---

(Oxford: British Society of Franciscan Studies, vol. 14, 1928); on this work see Dove, *Perfect Age,* pp. 42-43; Burrow, *The Ages,* pp. 25-26; Sears, *The Ages of Man,* pp. 100-102; Shahar, "The Old Body," pp. 173-74; and Agostino P. Bagliani, "Rajeunir au Moyen Age: Roger Bacon et le mythe de la propagation de la vie," *Revue médicale de la Suisse Romande* 106 (1986): 9-23.

48. Bacon, *De Retardatione,* pp. 45-46.

49. "The boke of the craft of dying" in *Yorkshire Writers,* ed. C. Horstman, 2 vols. (London: Sonneschein, 1896), pp. 406-20; here see p. 416. I have modernized letters.

cine which we may assume to be peculiarly post-Christian and modern were treated as serious and dangerous impulses *within* the Catholic culture of the Middle Ages. Unlike the medical text and the encyclopedic treatment of old age from which we began, *The boke of the craft of dying* is focused on Christ's works and devoted to cultivating a corresponding self-knowledge, faith, and prayerful recollection of the central Christian story of "the most fervent love" disclosed in the incarnation, life, "amorous dethe," and resurrection of Jesus.[50] In the *ars moriendi* old age does not have a special place. The emphasis was on cultivating dispositions and practices which would help the Christian toward a daily mindfulness of the major stories that disclosed her situation in this fragile life, stories that encourage the subject continually to give up the old self, corrupted by pursuing illusory desires, and continually to be renewed in the mind's spirit with God's creating force (Mark 1:14-15; Eph. 4:22-24; Col. 3:7-15).[51]

I complete this essay with reflections on the treatment of old age in one of the greatest of English poems, *Piers Plowman*. This visionary, allegorical, prophetic work exists in three, possibly four, versions written and rewritten from the 1360s to the late 1380s, or possibly later.[52] It uses an astonishing range of literary forms (prophetic challenge, sermon, scholastic disputation, satire, allegorical vision, penitential discourse, religious lyric, biblical exegesis, romance motifs, lives of Christ). The poet sets out to explore the state of the church and English communities after the Black Death, a period involving unprecedented social and ideological conflicts, including the great rising of 1381 and the emergence of the first English heresy (from 1401 those judged to be pertinacious Wycliffites, or Lollards, were burnt to death by the Catholic church in alliance with the Crown).[53] I have chosen to discuss one aspect of

50. "The boke," pp. 413-15, 418-19.

51. We are back in the company of Augustine's *De Vera Religione* (see n. 9).

52. In this essay all quotations of *Piers Plowman* are from *Piers Plowman: The B Version*, ed. G. Kane and E. T. Donaldson, revised ed. (London: Athlone, 1988); I have modernized letters. There is an excellent translation of this edition by E. T. Donaldson: *Piers Plowman*, ed. Elizabeth Kirk and Judith Anderson (New York: Norton, 1990). For the C version I use *Piers Plowman: The C-text*, ed. Derek Pearsall (London: Arnold, 1978). A good introduction to the poem is James Simpson, *Piers Plowman* (London: Longman, 1990).

53. A brief introduction to relevant aspects of the period, together with references for further study, is provided by David Aers, *Community, Gender, and Individual Identity: English Writing, 1360-1430* (London: Routledge, 1988), pp. 1-17. On Wycliffism and the ecclesiastical responses see P. McNiven, *Heresy and Politics in the Reign of Henry IV* (Woodbridge: Boydell, 1987), and N. Watson, "Censorship and Cultural Change in Late Medieval England," *Speculum* 70 (1995): 822-65.

this work not only because I would like everyone to read it, but because its treatment of aging raises some sharp questions in relation to medieval Christianity and its culture, questions that may still be pertinent to Christians.[54]

In the fifth passus of the B version of *Piers Plowman,* a crowd of penitent people set out in a search not for familiar shrines of familiar saints, like the famous one pursued by Chaucer's Canterbury pilgrims, but for a saint called Truth. After they have lost the way, help emerges not from those who might be most expected to offer it, the church's clergy, but from a lower-class layman, a plowman called Piers.[55] Later, much later, he will turn into a figure of Christ, becoming allegorically identified with Christ's humanity and with St. Peter, but here he is a contemporary lower-class layman, the best source of guidance at this stage of the journey. In the next passus he attempts to overcome the laborers' resistance to the wage freeze imposed by the dominant classes (in 1351) while maintaining a specifically Christian and traditional form of charity. Although this project proved to be impossible, the poet presents this plowman as a model of the virtues, cardinal and theological.[56] Yet, unlike Christ, he grows old (VI.83). His response is shaped by some of the norms we have surveyed: he will undertake penance and go on pilgrimage (a form of penance, in theory). In exemplary fashion he decides to get his will written and calmly recollects his obligations. Beginning with his faith in God's forgiveness at the final accounting he moves to consider his relations with the church. Piers will be buried in his parish church, a decision that is part of Langland's battle against the mendicant orders and what he sees as their destructive encroachment on relations in the local Christian community, the parish.[57] He recalls the past in a manner that is as far removed from the Stoic serenity of Dante's "noble" soul as it is from the guilt-driven, panicky conventions about a properly Christian old age that we have seen. His life is presented as one that has been utterly loyal to his local church (symbolized by prompt payment of tithes), and he notes that this

54. My reflections on Langland's treatment of old age have emerged in dialogue with two fine treatments of the topic: John Burrow, "Langland's *Nel Mezzo del Cammin,*" in *Medieval Studies,* ed. P. L. Heyworth (Oxford: Oxford University Press, 1981), pp. 21-41, and Dove, *Perfect Age,* chaps. 11 and 12.

55. The Catholic church in England was soon (1409) to pass legislation to deter laymen from discussing and exploring theology; see Watson, "Censorship and Cultural Change."

56. On this sequence and the problems the poet addresses, and is addressed by, see Aers, *Community, Gender, and Individual Identity,* chap. 1.

57. On Langland and the friars, see P. Szittya, *The Antifraternal Tradition in Medieval Literature* (Princeton: Princeton University Press, 1986), chap. 7, and Wendy Scase, *Piers Plowman and the New Anticlericalism* (Cambridge: Cambridge University Press, 1989).

church is now obligated to remember him in its prayers, as it remembers all Christians (VI.85-95).

The poet's model of good aging thus focuses on the role of the local community of the faithful, past, present, and future, a parish whose networks are sustained by lives like Piers's, ones that link the living and the dead.[58] It helps us identify what seems a surprising lack of attention to these relationships in much conventional medieval writing about old age. The causes and possible consequences of such a lack are certainly worth investigating, but here it suffices merely to draw attention to the issue. Piers bequeaths to his wife all that he has earned "with truth" and wants this shared among his children. He recalls that he has been a prompt payer of debts and that none are outstanding. He commits all remaining resources, including his life, to working worshipfully for Truth (God) in his own community, for the sake of the poor (VI.96-104). In this model of Christian aging in a Christian community Piers moves toward a good end without any of the punitive repugnance which was a commonplace part of the tradition Langland received. The plowman is "neither menaced nor disoriented by *elde*," remaining committed to "fruitful actions" in his community. This makes a striking contrast to Chaucer's Reeve, a brilliant figuration of an embittered and sexually obsessed old age in which texts like Innocent III's *De Miseria* are used to fuel contempt and hatred.[59]

It is in the light of Piers's aging that Langland's readers are called to reflect upon both the realities they know and the ensuing visions of aging in *Piers Plowman*. The poet figures himself as Will (both the soul's rational appetite and William Langland) and the poem is, among many other things, the quest of Will to find the answer to one of his initial questions to the Holy Church who has since disappeared: How may I save my soul (I:84)? By the eleventh passus Will has gone through social, political, and theological explorations that have resulted in him yielding up moral questions in a despair which first manifests itself as fideism (X.454-81) and then as libertine hedonism (XI.6-58). The temptation here is to wander through life as a supposedly autonomous being in a world of supposedly autonomous individuals where

58. On the parish and its forms of Christianity, see E. Duffy, *The Stripping of the Altars* (New Haven: Yale University Press, 1992); this is an immensely informative and often moving study, but its homogenization of the medieval past and its idealizing nostalgia should not be overlooked; see David Aers, "Altars of Power," *Literature and History* 3 (1994): 90-105.

59. On Piers here, I quote from Dove, *Perfect Age*, p. 124; for Chaucer's Reeve, see *The Canterbury Tales* I.3855-920, in *The Riverside Chaucer*, ed. Larry D. Benson, third ed. (Boston: Houghton Mifflin, 1987), and on this V. A. Kolve's commentary in *Chaucer and the Imagery of Narrative* (London: Arnold, 1984), chap. 5.

whatever one encounters must be there simply to gratify the nomad's insatiable fantasies and desires.[60]

Suddenly into this scene of narcissistic gratifications (the whole world is presented as a "mirror," XI.9, 20) a figure called "Elde" appears: Old Age, with a "heavy" look. He warns that the goods of Fortune are illusory and that to attach one's desires to them will have catastrophic consequences (XI.27-33, 44-45). This admonition is dismissed by Recklessness, who reassures Will that age is best ignored. Will is persuaded to go on as he has been doing (XI.34-58; 1 John 2:16). The poet implies that this decision is facilitated by the practices of the mendicant orders, who undermine the sacrament of penance and the local bonds within which restitution should be made, turning the sacrament into a commodity to be exchanged on a market (XI.53-58, picking up the dazzling example at III.35-63). Unlike Piers, Will seems to have abandoned his parish church, making an agreement to be buried in the mendicants' church.

But as the goods of Fortune leave Will, and as the years slide past, he finds himself "into Elde" (XI.59-62). He now decides that he wishes to be buried in his parish church, his Conscience telling him that a Christian should be buried in the church where she or he was baptized, a view that recalls the kind of commitment to a particular community that the poet had imagined in Piers (XI.63-67). The mobile friars, deprived of the economic benefits they had anticipated, reject Will and his views, provoking a fierce and conventional polemic against mendicant orders (XI.68-106). The problems of aging seem to be displaced, even when Will encounters the threatening parable of the eschatological supper to which many are called but few chosen (XI.107-36 Matt. 22:1-14). The text makes Will tremble and dispute with himself whether he is chosen or not, and while this disputation takes many enthralling paths, the issue of Will's aging returns. In passus twelve Will meets his own Ymaginatif (the image-forming power of the soul) and is confronted with his continual resistance to living with mindfulness of his "ende" — both death and, potentially, his true end in the divine vision. Ymaginatif complains that this denial has gone on for forty-five years while he has tried to persuade Will to recall his past "wantownesse" and to amend his life now, in "myddel age," lest in "olde elde" he lack the power to endure poverty and penance. The speaker cites another eschatological parable warning that it may not be in the first watch (youth) that the master (judgment) returns, or in the second (middle age), but that the servant must be ready since the Son of Man will certainly

---

60. Besides XI.6-58, see the depiction of this way of relating to others in the domain of work, XIII.354-98; and V.188-278, on the vice of covetousness.

come at an unpredicted hour (XII.9a; Luke 12:35-48).[61] Now although the second watch is past, Will continues to meddle with making poetry when he could be praying. Are there not enough books on ethics already written, enough preachers to expound the virtues (XII.10-19)?

Here the poet puts forward the standard view that moving into old age is a moment of great danger and great potential.[62] Had Will lived like Piers he would have cultivated dispositions that might have enabled a more calmly ordered and consistent path between the unfolding stages of the story that tells and simultaneously shapes a life. But, as we have seen, he had not, and it is Will, the figure of the poet, who will be recognized by most readers as their representative. Now he is being summoned, yet once more, to amendment of life, perhaps to the kind of neo-Franciscan conversion Piers eventually decided to make in the face of intractable contradictions in his social project.[63] Certainly he is being called to a life devoted exclusively to the liturgy and prayer, to abandon his searching explorations (he has already abandoned, or been abandoned by, his compulsive hedonism). Will acknowledges the force of this response to his aging, but he observes that he has not found the answers to his own most pressing questions about the good life in all the books and preaching Ymaginatif has invoked: had he done so he would go to "holi chirche" and there spend the rest of his life in prayer (XII.20-28). So the search will go on, whatever the age of the body, whatever the watch of the night, whatever the ambiguities of motive, and whatever the risks.

Here it seems Will is vindicated by the poet and the extraordinary poem we have is one of the consequences of such a decision. Yet Langland has to go *against* the grain of standard teaching about aging and old age, forcefully represented by Ymaginatif. As we have seen, conventional treatments are dominated by understanding this stage of life as one that should be given to recollection of past sin, penitential acts, and continued pleading for mercy (from Christ and the Virgin) to mitigate the horrors of purgatory and to avoid the catastrophe that is hell. The last thing imagined about old age was that it might, licitly, be a time of exploration. But for Will, the figure of the poet, this is what it will be, continuing explorations into "What were dowel [Do-Well] and dobet [Do-Better] and dobest [Do-Best] at the laste" (XII.26), in the

---

61. On the use of Luke 12:35-48, see Burrow, "Langland's *Nel Mezzo Del Cammin*," pp. 21-28; and T. Turville-Petre, "The Ages of Man in the *Parliament of the Three Ages*," *Medium Aevum* 46 (1977): 66-76, see 67-68.

62. See Burrow, "Langland's *Nel Mezzo Del Cammin*," pp. 35, 41; compare Dove, *Perfect Age*, pp. 106-7.

63. See VII.115-35; on this conversion, see Aers, *Community, Gender, and Individual Identity*, pp. 53-55.

complex England of the late fourteenth century and in the elusive puzzling lights of Christian traditions. The poet's move here might seem nearer a passage in T. S. Eliot's *Four Quartets* than to the medieval materials I have been considering:

> Old men ought to be explorers . . .
> For a further union, a deeper communion
> Through the dark cold and the empty desolation,
> The wave cry, the wind cry, the vast waters
> Of the petrel and the porpoise. In my end is my beginning.[64]

But it would be inappropriate and thoroughly misleading to make my end here, pulling Langland's explorations into Eliot's haunting lines. Instead I shall move to the final passus of *Piers Plowman*, skipping over eight passus which include profound and dazzling engagements with salvation history and the life and work of Christ, who turns out to be the key and heart of the poem's allegory, ethics, and politics.

The basic context for the passage I am now considering needs to be summarized: the poem's major explorations have been fulfilled in passus fifteen to nineteen, vindicating Will's refusal to accept Ymaginatif's conventional view of old age. After the harrowing of hell, the resurrection, the ascension, and Pentecost, we witness the Holy Spirit founding Christian communities with Piers now as St. Peter and a critical mirror to the contemporary papacy, which produced two warring popes from 1378. This sequence is Langland's utopia. It represents his vision of the church informed by the Holy Spirit, together with the relations of such a church to its social world, but then remorselessly shows the destruction of this church by practices that are plainly identifiable as historically present. What does Langland see as the forces that turn a divine gift into an absent utopia? His answer can be summarized: (1) human life and the traditional virtues are transformed to sustain communities in which markets, market values, and individual profit are paramount goods; and (2) the church is *assimilated* to the practices and values of this world. For Langland the fate of the sacrament of penance in his culture, which we have encountered above, is the crucial symptom of this assimilation: the fate is commodification and privatization.

But what has this got to do with the Christian practice of growing old in the Middle Ages? Everything, as it turns out, and as this essay should have prepared us to see. For Will (like the reader and the poet) is not aging in the

---

64. T. S. Eliot, "East Coker," part 5, from *The Complete Poems and Plays of T. S. Eliot* (London: Faber, 1973), pp. 182-83.

community of the faithful, which is envisaged as the early church under the guidance of the Holy Spirit, Piers, and an enlightened Conscience (XIX.182-390). He is growing old in a community of the kind I have just described, a figuration of the poet's society, one in which individual profit and the free choice of autonomous individuals form Christian practice. For example, the poet shows the incredulity and contempt with which Conscience is rejected when he teaches that Christians can only receive the body of Christ in the Eucharist if they have committed themselves to the sacrament of penance. Such a commitment entails the restitution of whatever is owed to others, including mutual forgiveness, a requisite for restoring the broken bonds of love in the community (XIX.383-402, 410-23, 451-81). Such demands, the poet suggests, seem an unrealistic and obnoxious challenge to modern cultural practices (XIX.391-476, XX.80-174).

The closing vision takes us back to Holy Church's observations in the first passus of the poem: people are busily pursuing the "worship" they can find in "the maze" of their world, apparently resisting stories of any other heaven than this (I.5-9). In this context old age is met by appeal to a secularized medical tradition, one nicely displayed by Bacon's *De Retardatione*. Life, threatened by Elde, flies to a thoroughly commodified medicine and buys with abundant gold remedies that make him rejoice. He believes that "lechecraft" can impede Elde and drive away Death with the drugs prescribed by the highly paid physician (XX.169-74). This is just the response we saw the *ars moriendi* resisting, and the poet dramatizes its desperate inadequacy by having Elde attack a physician who falls into a palsy and then dies (XX.175-77). But aging Life responds to these events with a yet more manic desire for "revel," the way of living Will had experienced in passus eleven. Here Langland turns the narrative to involve Will directly. Elde attacks Will fiercely, making him bald, deaf, toothless, lame, and impotent (XX.178-98). Death draws near and Will trembles with fear. What is to be done?

The answer comes from Kynde (a term for God and for the nature created by God), and it is one of the reasons we could not end this essay with the quotation from Eliot's "East Coker." Kynde tells Will that he must place himself *in the church*, "wend into unitee," and learn "som craft" until he is sent for. Will has consistently resisted practicing approved occupations and he asks "what craft" he is now to learn. The answer is that learning to love suffices. As for Will's skeptical question about bodily survival in the practice of this "craft," Kynde reiterates the evangelical, Franciscan line that has become so prominent in *Piers Plowman*: if you love loyally you will never lack clothing or worldly food (XX.201-11; Matt. 6:24-34). Kynde's demand is that Will set aside anxiety and trust himself to the evangelical path proclaimed by Jesus and followed by Piers. It seems that this way is the way for all stages of a Christian's life: it is, for Langland, constitutive of discipleship.[65]

In his suffering Will obediently tries to follow Kynde's commands, relying on belonging to the church, the community within which he will once more and always be learning to love, to set aside corrosive natural anxieties, and to receive "breed yblessed," the bread of life (XX.212-15; XIX.383-90). Langland's focus on the church, on faith in the evangelical precepts against anxiety, on learning to love, and on participation in the body of Christ seems, perhaps surprisingly, far from common in the treatments of old age in this period. His vision, grounded in the poem's christocentric disclosures from the fifteenth to the nineteenth passus, is quite distinct from any kind of stoicism. His emphasis is that a Christian practice of growing old demands complete commitment to a particular community of the church. Only there, he maintains, will we find the resources for growing old with faith in God's forgiving acceptance decisively revealed in Christ's life, death, and resurrection. The poet hears Christ himself declare that he, the lord of life, died to provide the drink of love for human souls to whom he has become brother (XVIII.365-409). As kin to humanity he proclaims his will to help humans in their neediness, "For I wer an unkynde kyng but I my kynde helpe" (XVIII.398). But to participate in this gift, we recall, Will must go into the barn of unity, "holy chirche" (XIX.317-34, XX.204).

The barn, however, turns out to be under siege by the seven capital sins and the forces of Antichrist (XX.212-16). This situation is only to be expected and, in Langland's view, even welcome in that the church should certainly not become "the world." Will, after all, has been sent by Kynde from "the world" to the barn of unity. Yet what now unfolds is a recapitulation of the church's assimilation by the world which the poet had explored and criticized so tenaciously throughout *Piers Plowman*.[66] Conscience responds to contemporary pressures and courtesies by agreeing to set aside the divinely warranted view (according to Langland) that Christ's forgiveness and grace do not simply abolish the order of justice in Christian communities: we recall that participation in Christ's body entailed restitution of broken bonds (XX.306-31; compare XIX.383-408). The enactment of Conscience's well-intentioned accom-

---

65. Mary Dove complains that Will is mistaken here since "even on the threshold of death, Will cannot sustain a sense of crisis or an awareness of the memento mori implicit in the series of the ages" (*Perfect Age,* p. 107). But it seems to me that Langland's point here is to show Will, instructed by Kynde, grasping the primacy of the evangelical demands that I have just recalled, a primacy for all ages and all seasons. So Langland is working *against* the version of *special* "crisis" fostered by both the conventional materials and our natural fears.

66. See especially Prologue, III, XV, and the conclusion being discussed here.

modations entails letting the besieging army, led by mendicant confessors, into the church (XX.355-79).

The consequences of this move are catastrophic. The sacrament of penance is once more commodified and assimilated to a network of worldly consolations; the decision to collude with normative practices of contemporary society de-Christianizes the church. The latter becomes an enchanted domain in which the sacraments actually contribute to dreams and illusions. The clergy produce an opiate that comfortingly removes all sense that there is a need for repentance and conversion (XX.371-80). Yet this is the community that Will has been told to join, now indistinguishable from the world. Doubtless Will and readers can recall the earlier invocation of Luke 12:38: "*Si non in prima vigilia nec in secunda &c.* [If not in the first watch nor in the second, etc.]/Amende thee while thow myght; thow has ben warned ofte" (XII.9a-10).

How does the aged Will amend when the community that bestows the crucial sacraments and sustains distinctively Christian virtues has taken the paths of illusion and enchantment? Langland's response to this perilous situation is startling. He has Conscience set out as a pilgrim from the drugged church, searching for Piers the Plowman (with all he symbolizes) and crying out for Grace (XX.380-86). The quest for the reformation of the church entails, at this point, leaving it. This is an astonishing move for a Catholic poet to make, and it is one whose consequences he did not, probably could not, pursue. Certainly it is a move made with absolutely no sense that this is some kind of triumphalist liberation of the individual Christian from the superfluous disciplines of traditional Catholicism. It leaves the aged Will in an excruciatingly dangerous, difficult situation.

The poet's remorselessly social theology, taking human embodiment with utter seriousness, has left us in no doubt that any Christian practice of growing old, one in which distinctively Christian virtues can flourish, needs the sustaining community founded by Christ, the Holy Spirit, and Piers the Plowman. If the old things are passed away, if all things are made new and in Christ new creatures are formed (2 Cor. 5:17), still these creatures need the barn of living stones, the city in which they "lerne to love" (XX.208), to learn the kindness that Kynde demands (XVII.198-356) and to receive the sacraments. What else, after all, can it mean for human beings to be incorporated, here and now, into the body of Christ? As James McClendon has argued,

> the forms of ongoing community (its structures of common life, its rules of admission and maintenance, its sacraments or salvific signs) must be birth canals of transformation as well as matrices of formation. . . . Christian journey cannot neglect the search for forms of com-

munity that will nurture both formation and transformation. One cannot ask about spirituality without also asking about the social and structural shape of the church.[67]

This is a thoroughly Langlandian understanding of "Christian journey." Perhaps the fourteenth-century writer's meditations on growing old, which are inseparable from his meditations on the church, perhaps even the very force of his exploratory questions, may prove to be a powerful resource for thinking today about "the Christian practice of growing old."

67. James McClendon, *Systematic Theology*, vol. 2: *Doctrine* (Nashville: Abingdon Press, 1994), p. 136.

PART II

CRITICAL PERSPECTIVES ON
MODERN PROBLEMS OF AGING

Modernity: The Social Construction of Aging

CAROLE BAILEY STONEKING

Prologue

In a poem entitled "Becoming Sixty," Ruth Jacobs acknowledges her "terror and anger at coming into sixty." Her lament is delivered in a biting image: "would I give birth only to my old age?" Some years later Jacobs's feelings of anger and fear give way, at least partly, to peace of mind, and she begins to count "the gifts that sixty gave." "A book," she writes, "flowed from my life to those who needed it."[1] We need it.

All of the authors in this volume are attempting to reflect from peculiarly Christian perspectives upon the gift of years. These are the reflections of Christians living in a society that has shown little understanding of growing old, and valued it even less. These essays have made me think — about letting go of youth, about support systems and adequate health care, about respect and consideration, about friendship, about who defines the way we view reality, and about hope. I have been assigned the task of reflecting upon modernity's construction of aging. But be forewarned: I'd also like to say something about aging in the context of hope — *hope's* constructions, if you will. I imagine the context of hope to make a difference, not only in the way aging is valued but in how that value is articulated, how it is uncovered. I have discovered that most of the literature about aging is written in the language of the academy: professional idiom, sophisticated, complicated, designed to drive away those not informed by the same grammar. If my language seems more like impatient speech than systematic exposition, so be it.

---

1. Ruth Harris Jacobs, "Becoming Sixty," in *When I Am an Old Woman,* ed. Sandra Martz (Watsonville, Calif.: Papier-Mache Press, 1991), p. 125.

While I am not yet "coming into sixty," I am coming into midlife, and Jacobs's question, of what she will give birth to, speaks to me with immediacy. I need the book her life writes. My realities include growing a family, growing a career, and attempting to calm growing fears, fears that come from that raw life outside of professional idiom — the sort of fears that I imagine propelled Anne Tyler's character Delia, from her book *Ladder of Years*,[2] to walk away from her life, unencumbered with her past.

Why do we more often fear the gift of years than revere it? Is it because we fear encumberment? Indeed, the years do eventually encumber us with wrinkles, sags, gray hair: the pages upon which our complicated histories are written — peculiar, distinctive, complicated histories. Suddenly, the mirror confronts us with the ambiguity of the gift of our years, our mortality, our histories coming to a close. Driven to complete our lives through our own powers, we in our peculiarly modern fantasy try to solve life's enigmas through our own wisdom. Nomads in at once the realm of freedom and of fate, we seem to be fated to wage an illusory battle to emancipate ourselves from our years. The years, as one modern poet writes, are "thugs"; they "don't serve their time, they're runaways."[3] The years, our particular years, literally the chronological measures of our lives, our histories, are a problem in a modern society marked by an insatiable but clearly contradictory hunger — namely, that most want at the same time to have the freedom offered by historicism and the consolation of a nonhistorical past. And all of this is Delia's story.

In *Ladder of Years*, Anne Tyler weaves the story of Delia Grinstead, a forty-year-old woman, the mother of three almost-grown children, who, by coincidence or accident or both, walks away from her life. She hitches a ride to a strange new town, rents a stark room, and begins to invent a new life, an unencumbered life, a life that doesn't "spill over." As "Ms. Grinstead," Delia tries to fashion an impersonal and independent existence. But inevitably the world crowds in. New friends and new responsibilities unintentionally accumulate — from a stray cat who craves a home to a sad, deserted husband and his little boy. Through the husband and boy, Delia is introduced to an older (if not wiser) character, Nat. It is Nat who unwittingly cracks a window upon one of the painful ironies of this tale.

Delia and the little boy regularly visit Nat in a retirement home, Senior City. On Delia's first visit Nat explains that Senior City is organized

---

2. Anne Tyler, *Ladder of Years* (New York: A. A. Knopf, 1995). Page numbers for references to *Ladder of Years* will be given parenthetically in the text.

3. Mura Dehn, "The Thugs," in *When I Am an Old Woman*, ed. Martz, p. 176.

like files in a filing cabinet. . . . We're organized on the vertical. Feebler we get, higher up we live. Floor below this one is the hale-and-hearty. Some people there go to work still, or clip coupons or whatever it is they do; use the golf course and the Ping-Pong tables, travel south for Christmas. This floor is for the moderately, er, challenged. Those of us who need wheelchair-height counters or perhaps a little help coping. Fourth floor is total care. Nurses, beds with railings. . . . Everybody hopes to die before they're sent to Four. (p. 193)

Nat gives voice to the pathos of aging in a society devoted to the limitless pursuit of independence, health, and success. While he applauds Senior City in theory ("it's certainly preferable to burdening your children"), still he muses, "something about the whole setup strikes me as uncomfortably, shall we say, symbolic. See, I've always pictured life as one of those ladders you find on playground sliding boards — a sort of ladder of years where you climb higher and higher, and then, oops!, you fall over the edge and others move up behind you. I keep asking myself: couldn't Thelma have found us a place with a few more levels to it?" (p. 194).

It is at least in part his desire to back down the ladder of years that leads the septuagenarian Nat to marry a woman in her thirties and father a child. Nat is elated at the birth of his son, but his elation ends in tears. Three weeks later, a frail Nat confesses to Delia, "It's a time trip . . . just a crazy, half-baked scheme to travel backwards and live everything all over again." Delia, whose own time trip has finally brought her back home, realizes that, unlike Nat's, hers has quite accidentally been a time trip that worked. "What else would you call it when she'd ended up back where she'd started, home with Sam [her husband] for good? When the people she had left behind had actually traveled further, in some ways?"

After her return home, Delia thinks back on her sudden departure. In the midst of a family vacation, she had quarreled with her husband. He had walked away before it was resolved, she had impulsively stamped off down the beach. When she looked back she had seen her children sitting up on their blanket, stationed some distance away from her own umbrella; Sam was standing off to the side. At the time it had struck her that it didn't seem like anyone was speaking, for the children faced the horizon and Sam was studying his watch. Abruptly she had veered away. But

now she saw that June beach scene differently. Her three children, she saw, had been staring at the horizon with the alert, tensed stillness of explorers at the ocean's edge, poised to begin their journeys. And

Delia, shading her eyes in the distance, had been trying to understand why they were leaving.

Where they were going without her.

How to say goodbye. (p. 326)

Delia's journey echoes a pervasive theme in ancient literature. Folk tales,
poetry, drama, fiction, art, and religious teaching tell of male heroes who set
out from safe but constricting origins, undergo a series of adventures that
transform them, and eventually reach or fail to reach a goal, prize, or spiritual
home. The stories of Gilgamesh, Job, Odysseus, and Aeneas reflect the power
of this metaphor in antiquity, when poets first articulated the two major
shapes of the journey: circular progression toward the renewal or restoration
of the traveler, achieved through a homecoming; and linear progression from
a situation of social or intellectual disorder to one of order.[4] And yet Delia's
story may be strikingly different. It may be that her story spirals rather than
circles; its virtue may be that it has no one point to make, no fixed point upon
a line, even while it is pointed. A fixed course, after all, will lead to a fixed
point, in a circle or on a line. But a spiral deepens images and at the same time
lifts them up. Having no fixed course, Delia's journey is itself heuristic, revealing that for each of us aging may be perceived as erratic, errant, in error, because we imagine we have missed the mark.

What the Mark Misses

If, for now, we use the term *aging* to apply broadly to the second half of life, if
we use it not to focus on a particular age group or on chronological age but
on the overall process and experience of growing old, then Delia's story is
about aging. And her quest — a quest to find meaning in the second half of
life — is a common one. Delia wants to mimic the secular, scientific, and individualist tendencies of the modern world by removing aging from its ambiguous place in life's journey. She wants to rationalize it, give it order — if
she can. But she can't. Though she doesn't articulate it, Delia seems to set out
imagining her journey as a linear progression, but by the end of her story she
seems to have come full circle. Is her journey, then, a simple return?

Though Delia's journey may not be linear, neither is it best described as

4. See William Bridges, "The Odyssey and the Myth of the Homeward Journey," in *Consciousness and Creativity*, ed. John-Raphael Staude (Berkeley: Pan/Proteus Books, 1977), pp. 99-
112; and George Roppen and Richard Sommer, *Strangers and Pilgrims* (Bergen: Norwegian Uni-
versities Press, 1964), pp. 18-20.

circular. Casting Delia's journey into the mode of a circle flattens the text of this ordinary woman's story. It buries the identity she discovers in the context of connectedness, with all its vexing, joyous, ambivalent delights. Delia's journey is comedic, generous, and humane because of its innocence, its realness, its connectedness. The book her life writes allows the reader to relax and feel secure in the narrative while it subtly probes moral and spiritual motifs: family and generational relations, gender, and attitudes toward aging. Unlike much of the scholarly literature on aging, it tells a story about the experience of aging, a story that leaves out neither emotion nor intellect, a story that keeps together the orderedness of words and the disorder of feeling, a story that attends to the everyday, pointing out that our moral commitments are in fact more profound than our customary descriptions depict. Significantly, Delia's story may point to what matters in a way that matters.

Unfortunately, however, our culture is not much interested in different ways of speaking; nor does it seem to recognize the confusion generated by its own failure to struggle with old questions about why we grow old, how we ought to grow old, or what it means to grow old, much less new questions about how these issues overlap with family, generational relations, and gender. Like other aspects of our biological and social existence, aging has been brought under the dominion of scientific management, which is primarily interested in *how* we age in order to explain and control the aging process. Thus blinded with science, we need the book Delia's life writes. She may not offer us an orthodox theory of aging, certainly no systematic exposition. Instead, she offers the text of her rather ordinary life, intensely personal, firsthand, eager, impatient; she gives voice to things that matter in a way that matters. It is a beginning.

It is a beginning of what will no doubt be an arduous, sobering, at times frustrating, and always difficult task, the exposure of needed repair, the calling of deep cultural assumptions radically into question. Indeed, in the last fifteen years the scholars who have studied issues involved in aging have taken their basic orientation not from the text of lived lives but from the social and biomedical sciences; most scholars, in other words, have viewed aging as an engineering problem to be solved or at least ameliorated. Even theologians who have focused on aging have often focused on aging as simply a matter of social policy: unemployment, poverty, disease, health care, retirement, and pensions. But Christian theology should have something more to offer. From a theological perspective the so-called "problem of aging" goes hand in hand with the cultural and symbolic impoverishment that has beset the last half of life since the late nineteenth century.

Impoverishment; or, Why Delia "Takes Leave"

Particular stories expose the truth that understanding aging is not just a matter of making generalizations about the status of old age, attitudes toward aging or the elderly, class and gender differences, or treatment of the poor or frail old. These are, to be sure, important issues. But these issues will not be resolved through modernity's traditional dissociation of ideas, images, and attitudes from the "facts" of aging — an epistemological stance that denies that the experience and cultural representation of human aging helps to constitute its reality.[5] This dissociation makes aging an abstraction and places us a comfortable distance away. It treats ideas, beliefs, and feelings about aging as if they were merely subjective reactions to an objective reality. This dissociation impedes a richer understanding of growing old. When internalized, it feeds a kind of false consciousness, a separation of body and self that is common in our culture.

By focusing solely on the abstract "problem of aging," apart from the actual lives and cultural representations of people growing older, the scientific management of aging also denies our universal participation and solidarity in this most human experience. By elevating scientific meanings of aging, by allowing them to dominate public discourse (and much else), we deny ourselves a critical vision, a larger story, within which one's experience makes sense. Christians have such a story. But unless there exists an essential and creative tension between, on the one hand, the empirical facts of aging and the meaning systems of science and medicine, and, on the other, the story of Christ and the ideals, images, and social practices that conceptualize and represent the end of human life, growing old will never be more than the dreary denouement of an individual's life drama.

Indeed, contemporary quests for meaning in the second half of life, quests such as Delia's, presuppose the decline of older, theological meanings, and the growing dominance of the mythology of scientific management. There is no denying that in the last fifty years the central goal of the modern scientific enterprise — the conquest of premature death from acute disease and the prolongation of healthy, vigorous life — has become a realistic expectation, if not for most people, then at least for white, middle-class Westerners. Ironically, however, the very success of this enterprise has also created a new

---

5. This traditional positivist approach has been increasingly challenged in recent years. See, for example, Ronald J. Manheimer, "The Narrative Quest in Humanistic Gerontology," *Journal of Aging Studies* 3, no. 3 (Fall 1989): 231-52; James E. Birren and Vern L. Benston, eds., *Emergent Theories of Aging* (New York: Springer, 1988), esp. chaps. 1 (Harry R. Moody), 2 (Gary M. Kenyon), and 11 (Gary T. Reker and Paul T. P. Wong).

fate for the developed world: most middle-class, white Americans will live well into the "long, late afternoon of life" and suffer from chronic disease before they die. Much of the peculiar pathos of aging in American culture derives from a denial of this new fate.

Indeed, since the mid-nineteenth century, not only scientists and scholars but all Americans have come to view aging not as a fated aspect of our individual and social existence but as one of life's problems to be solved through willpower, aided by science, technology, and expertise. According to this view, the road to a better future has been paved with the methodology of positivist science, which assumes that we know more about all aspects of aging than our historical predecessors, and certainly that the scholars know more about aging than an ordinary woman like Delia can say or know within the context of her connectedness, the context of her years.

Modern scholars of aging believe that an accumulation of empirical facts will someday produce total understanding of the natural and social worlds, allowing us to grow old without disease, suffering, conflict, or mystery. The problem with this mythology of scientific management is not that it is altogether false, but that it is only half true. The scientific management of aging fundamentally misconstrues the "problem" of aging. As T. S. Eliot once remarked, there are two kinds of problems in life. One kind requires the question, What are we going to do about it? The other calls for different questions: What does it mean? How does one relate to it?[6] The first kind of problem is like a puzzle that can be solved (though aging is more accurately ameliorated than solved) with appropriate technical resources and pragmatic responses. The second kind of problem poses a deeper range of challenges, which no particular policy, strategy, or technique will overcome. Of course, shaping one's vision according to the Christian story will not remove the challenges of aging, but it holds the possibility of helping us to understand, accept, and imaginatively transform the unmanageable, ambiguous aspects of our existence.

Ruth Jacobs's poem cited at the beginning of this essay, describing her "terror and anger at coming into sixty," reflects our culture's intractable hostility to physical decline, imposed with particular vengeance on older women.[7] The shame and revulsion at their own aging bodies, the biting question, "what will I give birth to?" reflects our culture's attitudes toward both women and aging. Should we then be surprised when women in their fifties

---

6. Cited by William F. May, "The Virtues and Vices of the Elderly," in *What Does It Mean to Grow Old?* ed. Thomas R. Cole and Sally A. Gadow (Durham: Duke University Press, 1986).

7. See Susan Sontag, "The Double Standard of Aging," in *Psychology of Women: Selected Readings*, ed. Juanita H. Williams (New York: Norton, 1979).

and sixties seek out fertility treatment? They merely mirror a society that has encouraged them to think of growing old not as a part of the human condition but as a solvable problem; they mirror a society that encourages them to view bearing and parenting children not as a gift (and an ambiguous one at that) but as an individual right. They mirror a society that detaches persons from their own histories, from the meaningful performance of aging within our bodies; their alienation, their desperation serve only the political economy in which we live.[8]

When and how did we become encumbered with such sensibilities? Thomas R. Cole, who has attempted to trace the cultural history of aging in America, marks a profound shift in the late eighteenth century.[9] Benjamin Franklin articulated the new scientific approach: "The rapid progress *true* science now makes," he wrote in 1780, "occasions my regretting sometimes that I was born so soon. It is impossible to imagine the height to which may be carried . . . the power of man over matter. . . . All disease may by sure means be prevented or cured, not excepting that of old age, and our lives lengthened at pleasure."[10] Franklin and other Enlightenment figures foreshadow the modern movement away from understanding aging in the context of moral and spiritual commitments, in the context of connectedness, and toward understanding it primarily as a scientific problem amenable to technical solution. Why strive to see the moral and spiritual possibilities of aging when, given enough basic research and medical intervention, we can eliminate (or at least manage) physical decline? The modern shift cannot contain and does not allow the paradoxes of later life: aging is a source of wisdom *and* suffering, spiritual growth *and* physical decline, honor *and* vulnerability.

Nineteenth-century Protestantism, itself committed to scientific progress (coupled with a growing commitment to Victorian morality), could not stem the tide. Indeed, rather than stem the tide, the dominant culture of middle-class Protestantism fed it with a rigid polarity of positive and negative stereotypes in the place of the ambiguities and contingencies of aging, a legacy that extends far into the twentieth century. While the Puritans had urged early American believers to seek spiritual strength and personal growth by accept-

8. See Joel J. Shuman, "Beyond Bioethics: Caring for Christ's Body" (Ph.D. diss., Duke University, 1998), for a compelling critique of scientific and philosophical positivism's claims to possess the only complete and accurate knowledge of the human body.

9. Thomas R. Cole, *The Journey of Life: A Cultural History of Aging in America* (Cambridge: Cambridge University Press, 1992). See also David Troyansky, *Old Age in the Old Regime* (Ithaca, N.Y.: Cornell University Press, 1989), esp. chaps 3-5.

10. Cited in Gerald J. Gruman, "A History of Ideas about the Prolongation of Life," *Transactions of the American Philosophical Society,* n.s., 56, part 9 (1966): 74.

ing frailty and decay as inevitable aspects of flawed human existence, the dominant Protestant culture of the nineteenth century, impelled by their perfectionism in physical and spiritual matters and their belief in the power of the individual will, dichotomized and rationalized experience in order to control it. These pressures to master old age, rather than accept it, generated a rigid dualism: anyone who lived a life of hard work, faith, and self-discipline could preserve health and independence into a ripe old age, which would be followed by a quick, painless, natural death; only the shiftless, faithless, and promiscuous were doomed to premature death or a miserable old age.

The pathos of the second half of life is intensified by the cultural hegemony of modern science and the bankruptcy of Protestantism, the encumbrances of a society devoted to the limitless pursuit of individual health and wealth, a culture relentlessly hostile toward decay and dependency. We cannot understand or relieve the pathos of aging in contemporary American society by attempting to unencumber ourselves of one another, by attempting to remove all disorder, by attempting to redefine our very selves or to solve, through our own devices, the enigmas of our individual histories. We cannot "manage" the second half of life in this way, through the uncritical pursuit of our own liberal individualism.

Delia's story uncovers these truths while also uncovering and subtly probing the social location of our culture's ideals and images; her story is strikingly different from that of the heroes of ancient literature in part because she is a woman. Her "situations" are utterly earthbound, implicated in connectedness yet also steeped in peculiar, culturally defined relationships of power and authority. Thus she is both attracted to and repulsed by a help-wanted ad put in the paper by a single father seeking a "live-in woman" for his twelve-year-old son, someone to wake the boy, serve him breakfast, help him with his homework, take him to the doctor, show enthusiasm for his videogames and war novels, and so on, as well as clean and cook.

> Delia clucked. The nerve of the man! Some people wanted the moon. She rattled the paper impatiently and refolded it. You can't expect a mere hireling to serve as a genuine mother, which was really what he was asking.
>
> She rose and placed the *Bugle* in the trash basket. So much for that.
>
> Crossing West Street, she glanced toward the shops — Debbi's and the dime store and the florist. How about a job in sales? No, she was too quiet-natured. As for waitressing, she used to forget her own family's dessert orders in the time it took to walk to the kitchen. And she

knew from her talks with Mrs. Lincoln at the library that the town was having to struggle to support even one librarian.

Actually, she reflected, passing the sterile white blinds of the Fingernail Clinic, a hireling would in some ways be *better* than a mother — less emotionally ensnared, less likely to cause damage. Certainly less likely to suffer damage herself. When the employer's child was unhappy it would never occur to the live-in woman to feel personally responsible.

She turned into Value Vision and took another *Bugle* from the stack just inside the door. (p. 160)

Middle-class, masculine ideals have a powerful hold upon us, not only as cognitive abstractions but as ritualized elements of individual and social life. Delia's taking leave is a struggle to go on when she doesn't know where she is.

Returning

Ultimately, Delia's journey brings her spiraling home. But is her coming home a restoration of the status quo, a simple return, a successful navigation of that dreaded whirlpool, the midlife crisis? Or does she come home not just a survivor of a midlife crisis but somehow wiser for her journey? Fortune brings her some measure of self-acceptance; it brings her some understanding of the inevitability of generational conflict — conflict guaranteed by the tensions that arise because each generation is destined to rise, decline, and die, to be replaced by a new generation. She uncovers something of value in her own "spilling over," in spite of its disorderliness. She is lucky. Therein lies the fragility of her story. Will luck foster her imagination? Will "home" again be perverted into a prison? What of the remainder of her journey, her next steps in time?

Steps in Time

In contemporary society, we are accustomed to the notion that a precise chronological age marks the transition from one stage of life to another.[11] Children begin kindergarten at age five; college begins at age eighteen; retire-

11. Howard P. Chudacoff, *How Old Are You? Age Consciousness in American Culture* (Princeton, N.J.: Princeton University Press, 1989).

ment at age sixty or sixty-five. Our awareness of chronological age is part of a more basic historical development: the emergence of the modern "life course." Understood as a pattern of rules, expectations, and events ordering activities over a lifetime, the life course of Western society has become an important institution in its own right since the eighteenth century. In an increasingly rationalized, urban, industrial society, chronological age ironically came to function as a uniform criterion for sequencing the multiple roles and responsibilities that individuals assumed over a lifetime, even as it also prescribes the crisis individuals experience at the beginning of the second half of life. How did we become so captive to the peculiarly modern, peculiarly uniform image of the Ladder of Years? What felled the older, much more animate image of the tree of life, or stilled the moving image of the wheel of life? What can we learn from the history of modernity's construction of aging? Indeed, tracing this history reveals much about the modern experience of aging.

Beginning in the late eighteenth century, the structure of the modern life course was constructed according to changes in demography.[12] Family life, as all of life, began to reflect age-stratified systems of public rights and duties. As the experience of a modern family cycle (end of school, first job, marriage, children, survival of both partners to at least age fifty-five, "empty nest," widowhood) became increasingly uniform, the boundaries drawn around participation in public life were tightened. Chronologically triggered public pension systems marked the beginning of retirement and the end of one's participation in the adult world, the cultural definition of full humanity. Age-at-death was also transformed from a pattern of relative randomness to one of predictability; as average life expectancy rose dramatically, death began to occur primarily in old age, not at varied points in the life cycle as had been the case in the past. As a result, fear of aging and fear of death merged. Modern society has now become a fully age-segregated society in which most of the aged do not occupy a vital role. It is no doubt a society that supports a burgeoning aging industry, but one that does not otherwise value the aging of the mind, body, and spirit. It not only offers no moral endorsement or meaning to growing older, it fears growing old (identifying aging with loneliness, obsolescence, and death). The emergence of this new cognitive map of the life course is in fact documented in the images of artists. Old motifs like the tree of life, the wheel of life, and the wheel of fortune were eventually replaced

12. Aage B. Sorenson, Franz E. Weinert, and Lonnie R. Sherrod, eds., *Human Development and the Life Course* (Hillsdale, N.J.: Lawrence Erlbaum, 1986), see esp. chap. 3; also H. P. Chudacoff and T. K. Hareven, "From Empty Nest to Family Dissolution: Life Course Transitions into Old Age," *Journal of Social History* 4 (1979): 69-83.

with rising and falling staircases, pyramids, and now ladders and slides, even waterfalls.[13] What steps brought us here and what did we lose along the way?

Combing the Beach for Fragments

A beautiful example of the ages of life arranged around the wheel of life survives in a fourteenth-century Psalter that belonged to Robert de Lisle of Yorkshire. The Psalter depicts Christ at the center, governing the wheel on which the fate of humans revolves. Radiating from the center are eight medallions illuminating four ages of life; two medallions — a coffin and a tomb — emphasize the natural end of life. The image conveys a sense of eternal turning, as a human life progresses from season to season until death breaks the cycle, opening the passage to eternal life. Significantly, each age is equidistant from God, stressing their subordinate but equal status. The inscription around the central Christ medallion reads *Cunta simul cerna totum racione guberno* (I perceive all ages at once, I rule all with reason). In redeeming human life from its natural cycle, this Christ-centered vision subordinates seasonal time to sacred time. Earthly time becomes a mere shadow of eternity.[14] And significantly, since no individual, regardless of age, can attain the transcendent stature of Christ, no one can ever consider herself or himself a fully completed person. This biblical ideal of adulthood affirms that all ages of life are equal in God's eyes. We are all as little children. A wise old woman or man is still somehow young, retaining a child's capacity for growth. Such is the hope of eternal time.

13. The most striking contemporary resymbolization of the ages and journey of life is Jasper John's popular series of paintings, *The Seasons* (1986-1987). John's four ages are represented by the four seasons and by an arm that moves around a clock-like circle. The symbols of his journey are taken from a little-known Picasso, *Minotaur Moving His House* (1936), in which the Minotaur pulls a cart containing all of his possessions (his encumbrances) — his individual experience. A clue to understanding the paintings is provided in the Minotaur myth, in which Theseus received a thread from Ariadne with which to retrace his steps so that he might find his way out of the maze guarded by the Minotaur. In John's series, the artifacts and influences represented on each canvas make up the artist's thread to his individual past. A ladder and rope tying these artifacts to the cart appear throughout the series, as do the stars (also borrowed from Picasso) that once guided ancient travelers. For a detailed analysis of *The Seaons* see Thomas R. Cole and Dale L. Meyer, "Aging, Metaphor, and Meaning: A View from Cultural History," in *Aging and Metaphor in Science and the Humanities*, ed. Gary Kenyon, Jans Schroots, and James Birren (New York: Springer, 1991), pp. 57-82.

14. Cole, *Journey of Life*; see also Emile Male, *The Gothic Image* (New York: Harper Torchbooks, 1958), p. 56.

Cultural historian Thomas R. Cole writes insightfully on the concepts of time and the life cycle. Up until the time of the early Middle Ages, he notes,

> An individual life cycle corresponded to the cycle of the seasons, of day and night. Seasonal and diurnal time, in turn, were part of the world's time, which began with Creation and would end with the Apocalypse. Ultimately, all time belonged to God. It was, therefore, not for sale, nor was it precisely divided into linear segments.[15]

In the early medieval countryside, only the bells of the monastery or parish church would have broken the natural rhythms of daily life. But soon changing ways of life changed such understandings of time as well.

> Gradually, however, this serene, otherworldly image of time and lifetime was eroding. In the new cities of the late Middle Ages, merchants and artisans became aware that the orderly conduct of business required more exact measurement of time. Churches and town halls installed mechanical clocks to ring the hours. Out of this awareness grew the modern notion that time was a precious commodity, to be used before it fled. In the confusion and bustle of urban life, artistic symbols of time merged with those of death, decay, and destruction.[16]

And yet, despite the growing governance of earthly time over common sensibilities, the favoring of secular power, and the emphasis on productivity, all characteristic of the late Middle Ages, aging still implied an (uncertain) journey to eternal life. The rising and falling staircase image, popular during this period, captured a complex message of the ages of life, juxtaposing the swiftness of time and the power of death with the wish for an orderly, long, *productive* life. The staircase image attempted to span the uncertainty, ambiguity, and helplessness of life. It depicted a developing middle class's struggle for success, as well as its fear of falling into social decline and eternal punishment.[17] It is a motif not unrelated to idiomatic language still used in English today, e.g., "going downhill," "slipping fast."

In the New World, the Puritans brought with them these Protestant ideas about aging along with a moral vision anchored in an ethic of constancy, an ethic characterized by relentless sobriety, self-control, and emotional steadi-

---

15. Cole, *Journey of Life,* p. 16.

16. Cole, *Journey of Life,* p. 16.

17. Cole, *Journey of Life;* See also P. Joerissen, "Die Lebensalter des Menschen — Bildprogramm und Bildform in Jahrhundert der Reformation," in *Die Lebenstreppe, Bilder der menschlichen Lebensalter,* Kommission bei R. Habelt (Bonn: Rheinland-Verlag, 1983), p. 44.

ness. The Puritans exactingly prescribed appropriate experience and behavior according to one's age of life; one proceeded along a well-marked road to salvation through careful self-examination and assessment of one's place. Aging Puritans were encouraged to clarify their souls by reviewing the past and searching for signs of election that might ease doubt and renew feelings of assurance. Thus a pilgrim's progress depended as much on looking backward as on looking ahead.

Indeed, life's pilgrimage became a predominant image. Puritanism surrounded the journey of the aging pilgrim with social conventions, beliefs, and symbols that esteemed the end of life. By restricting church membership to those old enough to examine themselves, by extending the conversion process, by emphasizing sanctification through experience and reflection, by often seating the oldest members of the congregation in front, and by prescribing veneration, the Puritans infused aging with a wealth of social and religious meaning. They encouraged even the oldest individual to cherish each moment of life while preparing to relinquish it. Living on the edge of uncertainty about both their earthly and their eternal fate, Puritans of all ages faced death "with an intensity virtually unknown in modern American life."[18]

It should come as no surprise, then, that John Bunyan's transformation of these themes into the religious folk epic *Pilgrim's Progress*[19] is Puritanism's most influential and enduring piece of literature. Interestingly, it depicts the archetypal male journey as one of middle age and the archetypal female journey as one that extends from young adulthood to old age. In Part One, the middle-aged Christian completes his journey within weeks — a far cry from Oedipus' decades of wandering or from medieval pilgrims' long years of searching. On the other hand, Christiana begins her journey in Part Two as a young mother and completes it as an "aged matron." Although she remains bound by conventions of female subordination, Christiana experiences the culmination of her spiritual quest in old age.

In Christian's midlife journey, Bunyan brilliantly fuses the pilgrimage motif with the spiritual stages of Puritan orthodoxy. He adapts the ballads and adventure stories that he loved as a child to the medieval figure of the

---

18. David E. Stannard, *The Puritan Way of Death* (New York: Oxford University Press, 1977), p. ix. See also Michael Walzer, *The Revolution of the Saints* (New York: Atheneum, 1968); Daniel B. Shea Jr., *Spiritual Autobiography in Early America* (Princeton, N.J.: Princeton University Press, 1968); Patricia Caldwell, *The Puritan Conversion Narrative: The Beginnings of American Expression* (New York: Cambridge University Press, 1983).

19. John Bunyan, *Pilgrim's Progress*, ed. Roger Sharrock (Harmondsworth, England: Penguin, 1965 [1684]), Part II.

lonely wayfaring man who sets out on a journey for truth. An ordinary man, a peasant folk hero, Christian is driven from the City of Destruction by his desperate need for a righteousness not his own, making more telling his dramatic encounter with Ignorance, a brash young man who suffers from the ultimate error of believing that he can effect his own salvation. Christian's journey reveals the difficulty of achieving a genuine belief that is nevertheless a gift from God. Notice, however, that it is a gift that comes midlife.

Christiana's journey, published as Part Two six years after the initial appearance of Part One, has never been as prominent in Anglo-American culture, yet it contains insights about aging that are notably absent in Part One. Significantly, Christiana's story shifts the focus from the individual to the community, leaving behind the individual's terror and desperation in order to attend to suffering and love in the context of Christian relationships. For example, in Part One, Christian suddenly leaves his wife Christiana and their children, setting out alone and in great distress. His journey runs its course within a few brutal weeks or months through a lonely and hostile landscape. Christiana, on the other hand, takes time to pack before embarking with her four sons and her neighbor Mercy. Her journey takes place over many years, during which time she ages.

It seems almost too obvious to point out that the separate paths of Christian and Christiana are laid out by the social conventions of gender; even though Bunyan's decision to write about Christiana can be contrasted with classical and medieval writers who restricted their reflections upon the journey of life to men only, Bunyan does not break with tradition in his presentation of chastity as the primary female virtue and sexual misconduct as the characteristic female sin. Ultimately feminine chastity, Christiana, is even replaced by male perfection, as Stand-fast becomes the most perfect bride of Christ. Since patriarchal portrayals of female frailty and subordination have been well documented by liberal feminist scholars, it is more intriguing at this point to note that Bunyan's treatment of Christiana is in at least one other significant way more traditional than his treatment of Christian. In medieval versions, the male hero's journey through the stages of the spirit took him through the stages of life as well. A faithful journey also meant enduring the ravages of time and the body's vicissitudes. Yet it is Christiana whose body ages; it is Christiana whose aging body remains the symbol of earthly imperfection; it is Christiana of whose death we are told, a death that takes place in the warmth and security of a Christian community.

It is Christiana whose growth in the spirit is inextricably linked to the gift of years, but it is the segregation of spiritual growth from physical aging embedded in Christian's story that became the dominant story of Protestant

America. It is Christian's story which folds neatly into secular priorities of middle-aged, male self-control, the same story that held captive Delia's imagination, the same story that intensifies fears of decay, dependence, and decline.

In Victorian America, when *Pilgrim's Progress* (Part One) reached the height of its influence, Christian became a model for the view that men, given enough faith and willpower, could somehow triumph over time and transcend its effects on the body. Although medieval culture subordinated the ages of life in the interests of Christian eternity, and although the Puritans resisted, somewhat, the priorities of worldly success and social usefulness, Victorian culture reversed these priorities for the sake of productivity, progress, and health. The religious and artistic traditions that would redeem the last half of life were tamed and assimilated to the quest for the normal life course mapped out by the gods of human sovereignty. In other words, when nineteenth-century evangelicals reinterpreted their religious heritage to accord with liberal capitalist values, they revised traditional Reformed ideas about aging, death, and the giftedness of life. The harsh truths of poverty, sickness, and suffering in old age were concealed, and death was romanticized as a quiet, painless, and disease-free event. Such sentimental images served to mask the devaluation of aging, the fear of decline and dependency, and hostility toward elders just as surely as romantic images of childhood, family life, and motherhood masked liberalism's hostility toward women and children.

Thomas Cole, the nineteenth-century American artist, immortalized this idealized version of life's orderly course in a series of four paintings known as *The Voyage of Life.* Commissioned in 1839 by evangelical banker Samuel Ward, *The Voyage of Life* was conceived as an American version of *Pilgrim's Progress.* Cole designed a visual sermon-poem that would treat in an allegorical and theological way what he called the "stream of life," Cole choosing a river to carry his cargo of messages and motifs.

In *Childhood,* a laughing infant emerges from a womblike cave onto the river of life, the sunrise bathing a lush spring landscape, a guardian angel steering the boat through the narrow riverbanks. In *Youth,* the most popular painting in the series, a young man has confidently assumed the tiller and assumes control of his own destiny, the lofty trees, blooming plants, clear stream, towering mountains, and midday summer sky all suggesting unbounded possibility. What the youth does not see, however, is the sudden turn in the distance, and the descent of the beautiful stream over a rocky ravine, a waterfall.[20] In *Manhood,* the raging river bears the voyager's boat over

20. The continued popularity of *Youth* leads one to wonder if Cole's message of youthful

rapids on a dark autumn evening. Hovering demons, representing suicide, intemperance, and murder, lurk in the dark clouds above. His tiller broken, the bearded man must navigate around the troubled waters with the aid of moral discipline, faith, and providence, all the while unaware that his guardian angel watches over him in the sky. In *Old Age,* a white-bearded, bald old man arrives on a winter midnight at the place where the river of life empties into the ocean of eternity. There is now not only no helm but no greenery; only black clouds and a dark ocean lie ahead. For the first time the guardian angel is visible to the voyager, pointing toward a golden city of lights. Old age, beyond the storms of life, is, for all practical purposes, dead to this world and only waits to ascend into heaven.[21]

In the ages-of-life motif, Cole collapses all the cares, trials, and dangers of life in the turbulence of *Manhood.* The solitary, middle-aged voyager must make personal decisions that will determine whether bends in the river are successfully passed, and yet his only real hope, as he cannot steer his own craft, lies in faith and dependence on God. Significantly, the dark foreground of the last two canvasses is offset by the placement of the voyager's guardian angel in each painting. The message: all is well despite unexpected rocks and turns in the river of life. The reward for faith is survival — a peaceful and passive old age, followed by beatific death and celestial afterlife. But in eliminating the full force of life's uncertainties, illusions, and anxieties, Cole also empties old age of many of its possibilities: the old man's survival does not bring with it the possibilities of deeper insights, knowledge, or wisdom, possibilities of growth — only the right to rest.

The realities of sickness and physical decline were assigned negative meaning as images of old age were bifurcated into an ideal old age tinged with

---

illusions has yet been received. Interestingly, the Institute for American Values recently released "A Report to the Nation from the Council on Civil Society," formally titled "A Call to Civil Society: Why Democracy Needs Moral Truths." On the cover of this report, a joint project of the Institute and the University of Chicago Divinity School, was a reproduction of *The Voyage of Life: Youth,* by Thomas Cole.

21. See E. P. Richardson, *A Short History of Painting in America* (New York: Crowell, 1956), p. 128. See also Louis L. Nobel, *The Life and Works of Thomas Cole,* ed. Elliot S. Vessell (Cambridge, Mass.: Harvard University Press, 1964); Joy Kasson, "The Voyage of Life: Thomas Cole and Romantic Disillusionment," *American Quarterly,* no. 27 (March 1975): 42-56. Cole's own descriptions of each age are included in Gorham D. Abbott's introduction to *The Voyage of Life: A Series of Allegorical Pictures* (Philadelphia: H. Cowperthwait, 1856), p. 3. The original series hangs today in the Munson-Williams-Proctor Institute in Utica, New York. A second set, which Cole executed from memory when Ward's heirs refused to permit the public exhibition of the paintings, was rediscovered in the Bethesda Hospital Chapel in 1962. In 1971 this second set was removed to the National Gallery of Art, where it hangs today.

passivity and nostalgia, and a miserable old age, God's punishment for disobedience. According to the Romantics, old age reaps what was sown in youth and manhood. Thus whereas the Puritans considered disease and suffering to be ineradicable, Romantics, reformers, and revivalists increasingly did not consider these experiences a necessary or even normal part of life. Their ideals of self-control and perfect health were matched by a negative mirror image, the old sinner suffering in a corrupt body. Whereas the Puritans stressed that piety and faith strengthened the aged to face their final trials, fulfill final obligations, and prepare for eternal life, the Romantics articulated no social obligation or usefulness for the aged. Their published sermons contain a great deal of advice about preparing for old age but almost no advice for the aged themselves. They assumed that preparing for old age was equivalent to preparing for death — the spiritual and social significance of both now hidden in a private, painless, secure, and *orderly* transition to the next world.[22]

By the late nineteenth century, the evangelical alliance with bourgeois individualism, humanitarianism, and progress celebrated the goals of the first half of life: education, expansion, efficiency, child rearing, and social utility. The second half of life increasingly appeared as nothing more than the diminution of one's capacity to achieve these goals, giving rise to the peculiarly modern lament which opened this essay, "would I give birth only to my old age?" Indeed, an image of the second half of life as literally barren of possibilities gives birth to modernity's attempts to "master" old age rather than yield to it, to eliminate rather than explore the final stage of life.

Rather than acknowledge human limits and the tension and contingency inherent in life's journey, modernity attempts "to contain the life experiences of the individual from birth to death by isolating them as a science."[23] By the late nineteenth century, thus, old age had come to represent an unacceptable obstacle to progress. While increasing longevity may have been, by a different measure, a sign of progress, the "curve of productivity" suggested to a leading physician of the time that society's "undue reverence" for old age was a "barbarian folly."[24] The frightening, uncontrollable aspects of a "bad" old age — previously assumed to be avoidable given enough moral strength — were increasingly pressed into a different mode by new social and economic forces. Anthony Trollope's satire *The Fixed Period* (1882) took up the shocking implications of these forces.

22. See for example, Henry Ward Beecher's "Old Age," in his *Forty-Eight Sermons* (London: Dickinson, 1870), pp. 236-43.

23. Burton Bledsein, *The Culture of Professionalism* (New York: Norton, 1977), p. 55.

24. George Miller Beard, *Legal Responsibility in Old Age* (New York: Russells, 1874), pp. 7, 9.

The Fixed Period

Trollope's futuristic novel is set in the late twentieth century on the imaginary island of Britannula, a republic that has recently gained independence from England and is considered the most progressive nation in the world. In their farsightedness, the young Britannulans agree on a novel solution to the problem of old people who outlive their usefulness and become a burden to themselves and society. According to the Fixed Period law, all citizens who reach sixty-seven years of age (the Fixed Period) are to be "deposited" in a special, honorary college known as Necropolis. For the benefit of the old and young, members of the college are to spend one year living in comfort, peaceful reflection, and social recognition before being peacefully chloroformed and cremated. In this manner, older people will avoid the "imbecility and weakness of human life when protracted beyond its fitting limits" and depart under "circumstances of honor and glory."[25]

When the first person on the island reaches the age of the Fixed Period, he not surprisingly claims to be one year younger than his actual age. Although old Mr. Crasweller had enthusiastically supported the Fixed Period in his youth, he now irrationally persists in seeing himself as the victim of a cruel law. President Neverbend's assurances that he will be a pioneer and hero leave Crasweller strangely unmoved. And despite increasing popular opposition, Neverbend continues to insist on the moral righteousness and social benevolence of the law. Thus he sets out to deposit Crasweller on the appointed day. In the end, Neverbend's plans are thwarted; he is "deposited" in jail, mourning that he must give up "our beneficent modern theory."[26]

Trollope's novel highlights the tendencies of a liberal modern society that has made chronological age a tool for regulating life and even more crucially for managing generational replacement in primary labor markets. If a certain number of years mark the limit of human productivity, rationality, and efficiency, then no one who has passed this fixed period should be allowed to hold office or control land or other forms of wealth. Trollope stripped the veil of sentimentalism from the verdict of rationalist, secular, capitalist culture: old age is irrelevant and burdensome.

While age discrimination and mandatory retirement are not only practiced by but in many ways legitimized by modernity, Trollope's imagination reaches even further, to the next rung. Over one hundred years ago he realized

---

25. Anthony Trollope, *The Fixed Period*, ed. R. H. Super (Ann Arbor: University of Michigan Press, 1990 [1882]), pp. 132, 142.

26. Trollope, *The Fixed Period*, p. 180.

our society's capacity to legitimize Jack Kervorkian; ironically, the futuristic *Fixed Period* is set in the year 1980, only a few years before Governor Richard D. Lamm of Colorado suggested that sick, old people had an obligation to "die and get out of the way."[27]

Trollope's Necropolis did what Kervorkian's logic would have us do: to dispose painlessly and efficiently of all people who have outlived their usefulness, while at the same time imbuing this ending of life with honor and distinction. What such a view marks is the collapse of that moral and religious frame which conceived life as a pilgrimage with a significance transcending and outlasting not only one's capacity for work but the span of any individual pilgrim's lifetime. What science would prolong in a society committed to material progress is in fact productivity (for women, literally re-productivity). Handed over to science, old age came to epitomize the previously unacknowledged though always inexorable barrier to the American dream of unlimited accumulation of health and wealth. As the founders of modern gerontology and geriatrics set about discovering the laws of normality and pathology as applied to senescence, they in effect completed the cultural shift from conceiving aging primarily as a mystery or as part of a spiritual journey to viewing it primarily as a scientific and technical problem. Concurrently, the course of life itself was "officially" institutionalized. Society launched the first mandatory retirement programs and built "rest homes" as scientists searched for a solution to the "problem of old age."[28] Medicalized and devalued, old age could be viewed only as an unwanted obstacle to modernity's dream of unlimited individual health and wealth. Provisions for the sick, frail, or dying elderly, though deeply instrumental, were cloaked to appear as "friendly gestures to the prisoners of [a] war against aging."[29] The aged were people left behind, like the frames of stolen pictures.

Aging (folded as it was into the fear of death) mocked modernity's doctrine of usefulness as measured by market productivity. In the fight against time, as historian Thomas R. Cole frames the issue, "old age emerged as the most poignant — and most loathsome — symbol of the decline of bourgeois self-reliance."[30] Moreover, the scientists and physicians who manned the

---

27. "Governor Lamm Asserts Elderly, If Very Ill, Have a Duty to Die," *New York Times*, 29 March 1984, p. A16.

28. Brian Gratton, *Urban Elders* (Philadelphia: Temple University Press, 1986). See also William Graebner, *A History of Retirement* (New Haven, Conn.: Yale University Press, 1980).

29. Henri Nouwen and Walter Gaffney, *Aging: The Fulfillment of Life* (Garden City, N.Y.: Doubleday, 1974), p. 17.

30. Thomas R. Cole, "Past Meridian: Aging and the Northern Middle Class, 1830-1930" (Ph.D. diss., University of Rochester, 1980), p. 125.

front lines rarely understood that as they gazed into the mirror of nature, they were seeing themselves. Hence the search for "normal" old age concealed its own class and gender dimensions as well as its role in relegating the aged to the margins of corporate industrial society.

Searching the past, the steps to the present, we uncover a lacuna, and if we're lucky we may be able to recognize that the modern project cannot correct or provide what is missing. If we're lucky, we may uncover the truth that modern images of aging are but continuations of cultural projects, of cultural privilege; we may discover, if we are lucky, a sense of what we have lost, of what we must listen for. But modernity trains us that salvation comes not through listening to stories but by doing. Our "doing" covers over a religious and spiritual vision of aging that is biographical as well as biological; our "doing" covers over the vision that aging is an experience to be lived meaningfully and not only a problem of health and disease. Is it any wonder that we as a society seem to have lost hope? The voices of modernity that would manage aging could not have anticipated the profound cultural confusion that arose from forgetting that aging has moral significance, a significance that calls for moral practices, a significance *born* of hope.

Midlife Midwife

The "midlife crisis" is but one product of that confusion, of hopelessness. The separation of work from the household, the expansion of wage labor, the accelerated pace of generational replacement, the fear of uselessness, of barrenness, of becoming an encumbrance to the advancing generation or of being cast away all combine to create a sense of urgency. The age of forty often marks the beginning of exhaustive if delusional attempts to seem younger, remain necessary, and circumvent the looming possibilities of displacement. Unfortunately, modernity, which prizes self-mastery, efficiency, and technical control, provides precious little nourishment for the seeds of such wisdom. In a society which leads us to believe that we are the exclusive authors of our own stories, of our own endings, the fragility of a "good old age" is indeed its susceptibility to luck.

Ironically, poignantly, even our attempts to debunk modern "myths" of old age sound the same cultural values that lead to the devaluing of the second half of life. The battle against ageism has accomplished much in relieving older people from outmoded cultural constraints, but ageism and its critics have much more in common than is generally realized. The movement to reform popular views of old age began among optimistic elders and their allies in gerontology, advertising, the media, labor, and business. The campaign against ageism enjoyed considerable success, particularly in expanding the range of choices for the middle-class elderly. But unfortunately, champions of the "new" old remained bound to the same false dichotomies and coercive standards of health that have historically plagued middle-class views. The same drive for accumulation of individual health and wealth, the same preoccupation with control of the body that gave rise to ageism in the nineteenth century, informed the attack on ageism. In repudiating the myths of dependence, decay, and disease, critics did not transcend the dualism of old age.

The critics of ageism simply replaced the old negative stereotype of the older person as conservative, unproductive, disengaged, inflexible, senile, poor, and sick with a more fashionable positive stereotype. Yet this positive stereotype, captured, for example, in advertisements featuring a sky-diving older woman or a jet-skiing older man, shows no more tolerance or respect for the intractable vicissitudes of aging than the old negative stereotype; old people now are (or should be) healthy, sexually active, engaged, productive, and self-reliant — in other words, young. While health and self-control had previously been understood as virtues reserved for the young, they were increasingly demanded of the old as well. In place of piety and divine grace, scientific knowledge and professional expertise are offered as the path to salvation; the meaning of aging still amounts to no more than the sum of its empirical parts. This view produces unrealistic optimism about aging which can only give way to exaggerated pessimism. It is a secularized version of the same type of dualism constructed by nineteenth-century evangelicals. Whether it is the pole of optimism or pessimism that holds sway, what these images lack, what we need, is not optimism, but hope.

Meanwhile, as the dark side of modernity's optimism, exaggerated pessimism, confronts limits on all sides, the war against aging has increasingly become a generational war. Critics of Social Security and Medicare blame the deteriorating condition of children and families on the "graying of the federal budget" (by the mid eighties, more than half of the federal domestic budget was being spent on the elderly). After 1985, this view was widely publicized by an advocacy group known as Americans for Generation Equity, which argued that society was displacing current costs onto future generations and ignoring its obligations to children and the unborn. The group traded on the increasingly powerful image of a greedy gerontocratic lobby, ruthless in its pursuit of hard-earned tax dollars to underwrite increasingly golden retirements.[31]

31. Sheila Kaplan, "The Generation Gap: The Politics of Generational Justice," *Common Cause* (March/April 1987): 13-15.

Until the early 1980s, the elderly had enjoyed a privileged status among welfare-state beneficiaries — built on the image of old people as poor, frail, and dependent.[32] But as the opposite image of aging was promoted through these new images of the healthy and active old folk, and as the generational equity campaign portrayed the elderly as politically powerful, selfish, and potentially dangerous, the dynamics of interest-group liberalism turned against the elderly. Old age emerged once again as a lightning rod for the storms of liberal capitalism and of middle-class identity. The personal anxieties about growing old of primarily middle-aged, white baby boomers merged with fears about declining fertility and the burden of an aging population, and merged with the fiscal and ideological crises of the welfare state, to create a specter of old age which completely obscures its possibilities. What the middle-aged baby boomer senses, even if she cannot articulate it, is that while the middle-class elderly have become healthier, more financially secure, and more politically potent, they nevertheless suffer from the cultural disenfranchisement imposed on old people in general. Having satisfied the social requirements of middle age and avoided or survived many previously fatal diseases, older people are often able to live ten or twenty years beyond gainful employment. But then what? Is there something special one is supposed to do, or not do? Is old age really the culmination of life? Or is it simply the anticlimax to be endured until medical science can abolish it?

Neither superficial optimism nor false pessimism can provide a response that does not destine us to live in fear of failure, for neither can accommodate the realities of decline and death. No matter how good our hygienic regimen or our medical care, our place on the biological continuum between normal aging and disease is only partly controllable. We are all vulnerable to chronic disease and death. This vulnerability defeats all efforts to write our own endings; our moral existence is inextricably timeful, and thus fragile. The wisdom of the gospel, however, is distinguished from both pessimism and optimism because it is derived from a source finally not subject to the contingencies of history, not subject, that is, to our own ability to create meaning. From a Christian perspective, individual as well as collective history remains morally ambiguous to the end. Hope takes the form of Christian eschatology; in other words, it moves beyond history. As subjects within God's time, Christians are taught that they are not subject to fortune in a manner that makes them impotent. Christians are children of hope.

Thus it is that Christians celebrate hope even as we struggle to resist the

---

32. Henry R. Moody, *Abundance of Life: Human Development Policies for an Aging Society* (New York: Columbia University Press, 1988), pp. 122-42.

seductiveness of optimism, the barrenness of pessimism. Hope requires such resistance: It requires that we face the unraveling of the knot that ties us to needing and wanting more for ourselves. It requires that we assemble reminders enabling us to recognize that self-deception is a permanent possibility. It requires that we attend to the disorderly text of our lives and learn to recognize moral commitments that are in fact more profound than our customary descriptions can suggest. And story is hope's midwife.

Back to the Story . . .

The work of writers such as Saul Bellow, Margaret Drabble, John Updike, and Anne Tyler has been dubbed by Margaret Morganroth Gullette a new genre, the "mid-life progress novel."[33] Although Gullette does not seem to note the historical resonance of the term *progress,* a character such as Delia arguably does not make linear progress; and more delicate still, neither must she be seen as simply traveling a circular course, as having arrived finally at the Mark. She is a middle-aged protagonist who, not unlike Tyler's other accidental tourist, spirals; a bewildered postmodern traveler, moving hesitantly — still uncertain of her direction, destiny, and self — toward home. Her fantastical dance with fate and mutability, her acceptance of mortality and finitude, her suffering and wisdom, all ancient themes, are but fragile gains, however, in a modern journey prompted by an impulse to move toward something — a unity of understanding, expiation of guilt, renewal of innocence, hope? Delia returns home with different criteria for sorting and unfolding messages, but without an explanation of "why." She returns home seeing her world in its surprising variety, its surprising sameness, its complexity and mysteriousness, its flawed and imperfect beauty; she sees what she cannot express except in a language and in forms more complex than theory, more allusive, more attentive to particulars. She returns home laden with the knowledge of her timefulness, her connectedness, with the challenge of how she ought say goodbye to her children. She returns home as to a threshold. Then too soon, much too soon, we are left with a challenge: how to say goodbye to her. We need the text her life writes. In fact, we need more of her life! Like the travels of Christian in *Pilgrim's Progress,* Delia's journey is too compact, it ends in the middle, as if she had simply completed a circle when she returned home, as if she had already arrived at her final destination, as if she has nothing left to do. We need more.

33. Margaret Morganroth Gullette, *Safe at Last in the Middle Years* (Berkeley: University of California Press, 1988).

We need Roxanna Slades,[34] Mattie Rigsbees,[35] and Annie Barbara Sorrells,[36] characters who continue to grow in wisdom as they age in years, who weave a collective past into the present, a personal past into a journey of hope. They offer no simple prescriptions, no romantic vision of a proper way to grow old, no promise that we will be unscathed by life's vicissitudes. But like Bunyan's Christiana they are reminders that each journey of life is lived in relation to others. We the gifted people are called "to give to others, so that when we leave this world we can be what we have given."[37] Death from this perspective can be made, as the death of Annie Barbara Sorrells demonstrates, into our final gift. "We belie it daily," wrote Florida Scott-Maxwell at age eighty-five, "but is it not possible that by living our lives we create something fit to add to the store from which we came? Our whole duty may be to clarify and increase what we are, to make our consciousness a finer quality. The effort of one's entire life would be needed . . . to return laden to our source."[38] How profound is our need for these voices of wisdom, for particular stories that may yet train us to understand "how the Christian story may fit over our lives."[39]

Children of Hope

We need the stories of Christianas; we need elder tales, stories of growing older, stories of transformation, self-transcendence, humility, and wisdom, not limited by a denial of physical decline and mortality. We need communities capable of hearing these stories, capable of viewing these time travelers not as fearfully alien old strangers but as pilgrims, children of hope, as ourselves. We need to revalue aging, to embrace the aging body as also a sacred space, to emphasize the spirituality of nurturing in all the ways that nurturing is both given and received throughout our lifetimes. Perhaps herein the irony lies: an aging woman's body and her earthly relationships, those very things that appeared to Bunyan as impediments, offer the ground for a recovery of spirituality in later life, the ground of practical wisdom.

34. Reynolds Price, *Roxanna Slade* (New York: Scribner, 1998).

35. Clyde Edgerton, *Walking Across Egypt* (Chapel Hill, N.C.: Algonquin Books, 1987).

36. Fred Chappell, *Farewell, I'm Bound to Leave You* (New York: Picador, 1996).

37. Nouwen and Gaffney, *Aging: The Fulfillment*, p. 13.

38. Florida Scott-Maxwell, *The Measure of My Days* (New York: A. A. Knopf, 1968), p. 40.

39. Stanley Hauerwas, "A Tale of Two Stories: On Being Christian and a Texan," in *Christian Existence Today: Essays on Church, World, and Living Today* (Durham, N.C.: Labyrinth Press, 1988), p. 29.

We need the books that flow from lived lives; in particular, Christians need the elder tales of elder Christians, peculiarly hope-filled tales, tales of the gift(s) of years. It is the text of lived lives that assembles for us quite literally bodies. Reinstating moral agents as concrete selves, embodied selves, reasserts the *inter*subjective nature of morality, thus redefining the second half of life as a moral category, not primarily a biological or psychological one. After all, Delia's story reveals that it is in the spiral of highly charged intimate relationships persisting over time that the possibilities for understanding are the greatest and the greatest understanding is possible. She discovers this, however, only because she is lucky. And that isn't enough.

Certainly her story, like all good stories, will require many tellings, and certainly the telling of her story will intersect in different ways with the grammar of the reader and the reader's tradition. Mired as we are in the modern tradition, captive to its images of aging, chained to its charting of life's course, it is too tempting to imagine Delia's arrival back home as the elusive Mark, the end of ambivalence. That would be something other than lucky — tragic comes to mind — for to imagine that Delia's journey has for all practical purposes come full circle, to an end rather than a threshold, is to sacrifice the still missing text of this ordinary woman's life.

But imagine Delia's story intersecting with a tradition that doesn't presume all moral ambivalence will one day end, or even that it should. Christians are gifted with such a tradition. We need not be so dependent upon luck if we attend to *the* story in which we imagine all our stories are embedded. We did not learn to "know" God any other way than through the story. Story is the way in. Endowing the relationships of elders, in particular their relationship to the Christian community, with moral significance and linking personal interpretation with an overall narrative understanding, a Christ vision, involves a shift from determinate rules regarding the first or the second half of life to models of practical wisdom and the unity of life. Such a shift, for example, may inform the moral decision not to ask physicians to do more than physicians can or should do; or, at least, it may inform that decision insofar as it is we who are formed by hope, which requires that we be less abstracted from the wellsprings of our own thought and action.

Afterword

When I began my research for this essay I discovered that which no longer surprises me: a modern industry, the aging industry. Aging, its elimination, its management, and its pathology is a ubiquitous topic. The federal government, various foundations, and the church have poured hundreds of thousands of dollars into research projects on such matters as elder abuse, dementing diseases, chronic illness, Social Security, age discrimination, retirement communities, retirement planning, changing demographic patterns, inflationary pressures . . . there is no end in sight. What I could not find, however, was conceptual clarity and something approaching coherence in most thinking on aging and its relationship to a larger social and political framework; rarer still was genuine theological reflection on the notion of aging, that is to say, reflection that takes seriously the story of Jesus, the church's own normative (if not descriptive) tradition. Theological reflection should be formed by hope. It should be distinctive by virtue of its peculiar posture toward the world, its peculiar intersection with the stories of ordinary women and men, ordinary people like Delia; its grammar should not be structured on the principle of detachment but on the impulse of hospitality. This is the peculiar claim that Christians imagine denotes the truth of who we are, of why we are a people whose possibilities for caring, whose arc of action, whose hopefulness, loops around and around and around the Lord's table, moving back onto the human site, re-making, re-turning, re-membering us, without distortion, without sacrificing the text of any part of our lives.

Christians can offer alternative understandings of the moral significance of growing old exactly because the cross is not a symbol of the fragility of a virtuous life, it is not "just a story" but the ground of a reality that subsumes the stories we would tell; the cross of Jesus is the grace of God, it is the ground of our hope, and it is the promise of deliverance. Growing old in Christ is to come to the table laden.

> *They shall bear fruit even in old age;*
> *They shall be ever fresh and fragrant.*
> *They shall proclaim: the Lord is just.*
> *He is my Rock, in whom there is no flaw.*

Psalm 92:14-15

Growing Old in a Therapeutic Culture

KEITH G. MEADOR *and* SHAUN C. HENSON

One of the primary manifestations of modernity is the therapeutic culture of Western civilization. While there can be varied legitimate interpretations of the term *therapeutic,* some positive and some negative, we will focus on certain aspects of both medical and psychological therapeutic assumptions that are problematic for Christians growing older in the current cultural context. Whether this present age is called postmodernity, late modernity, or a time of uncertainty, the therapeutic legacy of modernity cannot be denied. The assumptions embedded within that legacy include both psychological and medical claims that form expectations of how we should live as well as how we should die. The excesses of medical therapeutic modernity have frequently perpetuated the self-deception that death can be avoided if we work hard enough and sufficiently trust our rational scientific abilities. The psychotherapeutic mindedness of the first half of the twentieth century evolved in the afterglow of high modernity and its convictions regarding an autonomous psychological self. Whether the goal is framed as self-actualization, the freeing of one's psychic structure from dependency conflicts, or the deliverance from externally binding contingencies, there is no question that the supremacy of self-determination and autonomous rationality has ascended to new heights of significance within our therapeutic culture.

Philip Rieff, a sociologist, assessed the far-reaching consequences of this ascendance in his now-classic *The Triumph of the Therapeutic.*[1] Rieff exposed a distressing process by which we had grown to replace the traditional idea of the preeminence of God with nothing more than a personalized, manipulable

1. Philip Rieff, *The Triumph of the Therapeutic: Uses of Faith After Freud* (New York: Harper and Row, 1966).

sense of well-being. He observed that our story had become one in which we all wanted to "feel good," even if at the expense of any other preceding value or ethic. It was this pervasive change — the concrete emergence of a "psychological" human being marked by a self-deceptive sense of happiness as the *deus ex machina* of life — that Rieff called "the triumph of the therapeutic." We have taken a headlong fall "toward an anti-creedal analytic attitude,"[2] a course by which, according to Rieff, we have specifically left behind any sense of Christian culture, trading it in for little more than this quest for a protracted feeling that we are "okay." Into this new governing motif we *then* appropriate what we personally deem to be a suitable spirituality such as Christianity — provided, of course, that it does not upset our general sense of well-being.[3] Even a cursory reading of theology emerging from many sectors in the Western church is indicative of the fact that we, too, have been charmed into a maze of self-satisfaction, finding ourselves salted and enlightened by the world around us, rather than vice versa. The church has been, in fact, a central player in actually writing this story in which we are individual containers of a mind and self that needs therapy, rather than sinners in need of salvation.[4]

It is not news that modernity has been the womb within which such changes for church and society have developed and then sprung forth, leading to substantial cultural shifts. Many of these shifts have been swallowed whole and fully digested by the majority of us, Christian or not. Rieff's problem of the "therapeutic" embodies the effort by which our culture has sought to rid itself of moral expectations while fostering an ever growing assumption of personal prerogatives. Rieff comments that "Ours is the first cultural revolution fought to no other purpose than greater amplitude and richness of living itself. Is this not what is meant by the 'revolution of rising expectations'?"[5] Even as we enter a third millennium and stand at the edge of what

2. Rieff, *Triumph of the Therapeutic*, p. 7.

3. Rieff, *Triumph of the Therapeutic*, p. 13. In connection to Christianity, Jung, for example, a prominent psychotherapist and one of the chief architects of Rieff's therapeutic society, called for the "therapeutic release" *of myth components such as Jesus* from our collective unconscious mind, arguing that part of the very society-wide neurosis of modernity is the suppression of such myth images. In effect, if Jesus or orthodoxy no longer serve our "necessary" sense of well-being, we must rid ourselves of them. If our Jesus cannot serve to "release" us from our negative emotions, relationships, or very lives, then he must go, at least in exchange for a Jesus who "works" for us. It is in this way, even as a church in complicity with this type of trade-off, that we, too, have become part of the therapeutic culture, observations that are further explored as this essay progresses.

4. See E. Brooks Holifield, *A History of Pastoral Care in America: From Salvation to Self-Realization* (Nashville: Abingdon Press, 1983).

5. Rieff, *Triumph of the Therapeutic*, p. 241.

justly may be called postmodernity, we seem to have at least one foot still planted firmly in the former epoch — or, more specifically, at least in modernity's final death throes where the focus, brazenly, is all about *us,* perhaps even about how the entire world, its discoveries, and its God fit or do not fit into our own little personal cosmos.[6] Having made dramatic discoveries and developments of convenience and continuing to do so with unrivaled dispatch, we have concluded that the final chapter of betterment and good living is to be written not just about ourselves but very specifically about what we may call this "will to feel good."

For baby boomers and now Generation Xers, this cultural milieu has become part of our basic embedded assumptions. This is how we are, and we tend to think little of it. Living out our lives in such a therapeutic culture, however, leads us to an eventual inevitability: what does it mean to grow old in such a world?

Medical science has sought, found, and continues to uncover ways to extend human life — in theory certainly a good idea, but sometimes one taken far beyond the point at which a functioning body seems practical or even desirable for the very ones driven to sustain it. This phenomenon has resulted in an increase in the number of older persons, with a particularly significant increase in the numbers of the oldest old, in our culture. We are now not only supposedly "feeling good" about ourselves within our therapeutic culture, but we are getting older while doing it. Throughout the past century, general life expectancy in Western nations has risen at a dramatic rate, jumping in the United States from about age forty-seven at the beginning of the century to seventy-six for men and eighty for white females. The oldest old is one of the fastest growing groups, with centenarians increasing from a group of about 15,000 in 1980 to 100,000 as we began the twenty-first century.[7] The medical dream of having an average life expectancy of one hundred years is becoming a reality. Of course, with this fact come fresh medical, psychological, ethical, and certainly theological problems — all of which are integrally interconnected. This ongoing sociodemographic shift, with its inherent corporate in-

---

6. Stephen Toulmin, *Cosmopolis: The Hidden Agenda of Modernity* (New York: Free Press, 1990). Toulmin argues that in this final phase of modernity, or, as it could be called, postmodernity, a humanizing effect is and should be taking place in which we are working to "reclaim" the philosophies and discoveries of modernity in an attempt to make them more practical; or, as Toulmin himself puts it, "humanity needs people with a sense of how theory touches practice at points, and in ways, that we feel on our pulses" (p. 180).

7. These figures come from Mildred M. Seltzer, ed., *The Impact of Increased Life Expectancy: Beyond the Gray Horizon,* Springer Series on Life Styles and Issues in Aging (New York: Springer, 1995), p. ix.

crease in physical frailty and cognitive decline, challenges another problematic assumption of therapeutic modernity, the presumption of medical cure and restitution. This presumption often includes a functional denial of the inevitability of suffering and the contingencies of living and dying well.

Aging in Postmodernity: The Historical Framework

Adequate interpretation of the excesses of contemporary therapeutic culture and our response in consideration of older Christians require a brief discussion of the historical framework in which this culture evolved. It is important that we understand the basic cultural forces at work both within and outside of the church that have formed the therapeutic cultural milieu within which we now live. A brief retracing of what some see as modernity's stages is helpful for establishing a better grasp of the context within which we are working.

The observable "scaffolding" of modernity in Western society[8] in the sixteenth century led first to a demand that all thought and conduct be reasonable, and to increasing toleration of diversity in all its cultural forms — intellectual, social, artistic. Then, after Descartes, we attempted to stop asking what distinctives were brought by the varied players to any intellectual or cultural project and the search for a purely rational method was initiated, which it was believed could ultimately lead us all to the correct solution to any problem. This trend of decontextualization had effects upon both philosophy and science all the way until, approximately, World War II. Around 1950 some intellectuals began to notice that we seemed to be, and perhaps even should be, entering a new phase, one in which we seek for ways to "humanize" not only philosophy but certainly science and technology as well.[9] Such a humanizing of modernity — whether seen as part of a third phase in modernity or as postmodernity — can be described as the attempt to hang onto positive achievements in sixteenth-century humanism and seventeenth-century exact science, rather than reject them both altogether.

This humanizing can have positive implications for late modernity in

8. See Alasdair MacIntyre, *Whose Justice, Which Rationality?* (Notre Dame: University of Notre Dame Press, 1988), in which MacIntyre carefully analyzes the development of major European cultural traditions, dividing them into four distinct periods — following upon Aristotle, Augustine, Aquinas, and Hume — each defining "rationality" differently. See also Toulmin, *Cosmopolis,* in which the author uses MacIntyre's findings to corroborate his own, though revising them somewhat in the process. Both MacIntyre and Toulmin argue essentially that there is no such thing as a rationality that is not part of an inherited tradition.

9. Toulmin, *Cosmopolis,* p. 180.

general, and modern medicine in particular, through its rectification of the moral and technical splits that evolved within the scientific advances of the modern era of medicine. A humanizing of science and technology may be seen as the attempt to move on from the received view of modernity in which the exact sciences and humanities were torn asunder. In the context of this humanization Toulmin emphasizes that, "From now on, indeed, the very definition of a 'medical' problem must be given in terms that cover both its technical and its moral features."[10] Postmodern voices are looking for people possessing a sense of how theory is suited to the pragmatic matters of everyday living within the moral, as well as technical, local ecologies of our lives.[11] The therapeutic culture's commitment to self-enhancement and denial of historical contingencies in general — its fundamental tenets — have been driving the entire machine of the sciences (medical science, the social sciences, and so on). The potential for the coming era to engage this situation constructively is dependent upon a commitment to the historicity and the particularity of response to the contingencies of life that is offered by such institutions as the church. This engagement will determine the degree to which this humanizing of postmodernity rectifies the excesses of modernity in both our understanding of aging itself and in the care of those who are old.

Exploring the Problems

Medicine, at least a little like Shelley's modern Prometheus in *Frankenstein*, seems at points in history to seek for and attain betterment in ways that defy its own ability to know what to do next.[12] Doctors, after all, are also characters shaped by the story of our therapeutic culture. And, as we have recounted, human beings functioning in our story are driven by an interest in longevity that reaches far beyond the merely academic, emanating as it does from a desire to avoid suffering and certainly from a fear of death. This is, of course, only possible when those of us who are not medical doctors, includ-

---

10. Toulmin, *Cosmopolis*, p. 181.

11. Toulmin, *Cosmopolis*, p. 180.

12. See Mary Shelley, *Frankenstein; or, The Modern Prometheus* (London: Penguin Books, 1994 [1818]). The classic tale of Frankenstein, far from being merely one of the most interesting horror stories ever penned, remains a very important morality tale. In it, Swiss scientist Victor Frankenstein has one driving aspiration: the creation of intelligent life by his own hands. From the very moment his creature awakens, however, the blindness and destructive power of his folly is revealed. Finally seen for the horror that it is, the monstrous creation is eschewed by all who gaze upon it, including its own maker.

ing those of us in the church who should have plenty to say about such values, desperately *want* these professionals to aid us in such avoidances and fears. But we all have to now ask, just how old do we really want to live to be? And as we age, for how long and in what ways do we care for ourselves?

Research into the project of longevity can be divided into at least five medical categories: the maintenance of perpetual youth, restoring of youth or rejuvenation, postponing of biological aging, prolonging of life, and, finally, the achievement of physical immortality. The medical profession itself recognizes that these five draw strength from our negative attitudes toward suffering and death; although we often express our attitudes instead as something like "the possession of a high value on health and youth," they are no doubt still undergirded by our quest to "feel good" and have self-fulfillment.[13] We not only want to avoid suffering and decline, both physical and mental, but we also expect to retain the strength to accomplish the same things as the young. If we cannot actually turn back the clock, we strive to at least "look" the part by utilizing Retin-A cream, cosmetic surgery, or even the injection of sheeps' placenta into our skin. Since these surface approaches go only so far toward success, we turn to genetics and microbiology in an effort to uncover at the most elemental levels that which causes aging itself. Our hidden hope is that physical immortality can be achieved.

Growing older in the very therapeutic culture that encourages us to desire such perpetual youthfulness and gives us the power to strive for it (to some degree successfully) comes with its share of new psychological challenges, both for those who are older and for those who are living with and caring for them. The aging brain itself undergoes macroscopic, microscopic, regional, and vascular changes, each having great effect upon thought patterns and certainly on any highly prized sense of well-being. With age comes a decrease in the brain's size and weight, inclusive of both gray and white brain matter, with concomitant alterations also in shape — cerebral convolutions narrow, sulci widen, and cerebrospinal fluid collects en masse. At a microscopic level, there is a progressive loss of vital synaptic connections necessary for the processes of rational thinking. Similar changes take place regarding regional brain function, and at a vascular level a disruptive thickening ensues as early as the fourth or fifth decade of life.[14]

These and adjoining factors add up essentially to a decrease in the ability

13. Mildred M. Seltzer, "Racing Against a Pale Horse," in *The Impact of Increased Life Expectancy,* ed. Seltzer, p. 11.

14. See James E. Birren and K. Warner Schaie, eds., *Handbook of the Psychology of Aging,* fourth ed. (New York: Academic Press, 1996), pp. 106-28.

to think as well as we once could, or, worse, to dementia or other "disconnection syndromes," seen as clinical or neuropathological in nature.[15] As we age, these functional difficulties initially generate embarrassment for us and others and eventually even great difficulty in (or the complete impossibility of) carrying out almost all normal activity and behavior. In our therapeutic culture, we tend to hide or deny such behavior in ourselves and have great difficulty coping with it in others — since it reminds us of that which we do not wish to become and is a thorn in the side of an entire society battling to stop such perceivable ravages of the "illness" of aging.[16] The psychological implications of even typical healthy aging, and certainly, then, of the ability to advance in age beyond that which is "normal," create a plethora of aggravated psychological issues surrounding the self, work, family relationships, friendships, and cognitive thinking. Simply put, as we grow old in a therapeutic culture, "the future ain't what it used to be."[17]

Ethically speaking, the complexities proportionate to our growing increasingly old abound. As the average life span rises, life-sustaining medical care must necessarily be divided into two categories: care for elderly patients with decision-making capacity (i.e., the cognitive disruptions associated with aging have not yet impaired basic rationality beyond the ability to make sound decisions), and care for those without such capacity (the same cognitive disruptions *have* impaired sound decision-making). As we grow increasingly older, those around us may be tempted to distrust our ability to make sound decisions even when we are able to do so. Conversely, when we do lose the aptitude to make such choices, others must be trusted with doing so. For this reason we have to ask ourselves such complicated questions as who is qualified to make these choices for both us and others with the appropriate measures of love and justice?

Then, there is a prominent set of prejudices attendant to growing older, particularly in a culture valuing the young and the strong, while at the same time producing so many who are neither. Ageism and even age-rationing are two of the most prominent and consequential to consider. Ageism is the ge-

---

15. Birren and Schaie, eds., *Handbook,* pp. 106-28.

16. One of the better studies on Alzheimer's disease as approached from a Christian perspective can be found in David Keck's *Forgetting Whose We Are: Alzheimer's Disease and the Love of God* (Nashville: Abingdon Press, 1996). In it, Keck reminds us that even when we forget God, particularly if through the ravages of a disease beyond our control, God does not, and cannot, forget us.

17. Attributed to scientist Arthur C. Clarke, author of *2001: A Space Odyssey* and inventor of the communications satellite. See Arthur C. Clarke, *Profiles of the Future: An Inquiry into the Limits of the Possible* (New York: Harper and Row, 1973).

rontological equivalent to racial prejudice or sexism, where in this case "age-ist" or unfair generalizations about any who are old are routinely made. Discrimination in this regard takes place in both subtle and overt ways. "All elderly people are forgetful," "all elderly people are ill-tempered," "all elderly people suffer from depression," "mental impairment is endemic to aging," and "most elderly people have no interest in, and cannot enjoy, sex," are several such sweeping statements.[18] Age-rationing is the systematic denial of potentially life-sustaining health care to the elderly — care not denied the young. The rising cost of health care is often cited as the single vital factor making such rationing necessary,[19] but arguably, prejudices such as those just touched upon tend to play a great part in such decisions. There are moves toward simply identifying a set age where certain forms of life-sustaining medical treatments are routinely denied.[20] These concerns parlay into complex political and public policy issues, where older persons require advocacy in order to sustain their very survival.

On the other hand, the same physicians, nurses, psychologists, social workers, and other cognate professionals who are asked to ration health care, need and often use the elderly in research projects designed to, again, seek new ways to extend life and make growing old more likely.[21] In his confessional book *Constructing the Self, Constructing America*, psychologist Philip Cushman argues that the development of standard psychotherapy is inextricably a product of modernity and its cultural assumptions. Psychotherapy, he writes, has been complicit in creating the very ills it seeks to cure, frequently fostering an "empty self" as it has focused on a consumerist-oriented, interior, privatized understanding of well-being.[22] A system that supports our cultural obsession with feeling good and our longing for cure above all ultimately denies us the ability to "feel good" with integrity in that it leaves us with an empty self grounded in fear, anxiety, and self-deception. We cannot interpret and narrate ourselves as living well without the acknowledgement of death as an integral part of living, thereby distinguishing our practices and expectations as Christians living in the midst of the therapeutic legacy of modernity.

18. Examples of generalizations taken from Mark R. Wicclair, *Ethics and the Elderly* (New York: Oxford University Press, 1993), p. 82.

19. Wicclair, *Ethics and the Elderly*, pp. 80-81.

20. Wicclair, *Ethics and the Elderly*, p. 81. For example, in the British National Health Service long-term dialysis is generally denied to anyone over age sixty-five. Other vital treatment follows a similar pattern of denied access, as consideration of such restrictions is widespread.

21. Wicclair, *Ethics and the Elderly*, p. 160.

22. Philip Cushman, *Constructing the Self, Constructing America: A Cultural History of Psychotherapy* (New York: Addison Wesley, 1995).

Paternalism of the sort that denies even capable elderly people the right to make choices for themselves is also a persistent problem. Such paternalism takes on subtle and at times very cruel forms, wherein older persons are sometimes treated almost like children by their own adult offspring simply because of their age, even when all indicators point to such a practice as being unnecessary. Paternalism in its subtlety is difficult to combat because, as with pornography, one claims to "know it when I see it." In its subjective reality it is much harder than this to identify.[23] Family members are not alone in this paternalism, for medical, nursing, personal, and social service providers that we grow to depend upon as we age also make a practice of such behavior, often unknowingly.

It is clear that we have now become a great deal like the Greek hero Tithonus, who craved an unending life and asked the gods for immortality. They granted his wish — but upon achieving it he realized to his great horror that he had neglected to ask also for eternal youth. He simply grew older and more frail, in a never-ending nightmarish whirlpool of immortality. While attempting to feel good about ourselves by escaping death, we sometimes reach the point in our old age of fearing that it will not come soon enough.[24]

Merely "saying something theological or scriptural" at this juncture should, one would hope, be impossible for the Christian, since as persons belonging to Christ "something theological" should be attendant to every issue of our lives, including the medical, psychological, and ethical themes already outlined.[25] But, since being a faithful Christian is a lot about learning how to ask the right questions, what we must do, certainly, is ask now specifically theological ones regarding these problems.[26] Only then can we reflect upon our cultural narrative and turn with some degree of effectiveness to Jesus and the church for theological engagement.

These theological questions should include such queries as, how are we as

23. Wicclair, *Ethics and the Elderly*, pp. 122-23.

24. Harry R. Moody, *Ethics in an Aging Society* (Baltimore: Johns Hopkins University Press, 1992). Moody relays the story of Florida Scott-Maxwell (p. 19), who composed a journal while a nursing-home resident. She wrote in it, "My only fear about death is that it will not come soon enough. . . . It is waiting for death that wears us down, and the distaste for what we may become."

25. James Gustafson pointed out that theologians frequently receive this or a similar request in "Say Something Theological," *1981 Nora and Edward Ryerson Lecture* (Chicago: University of Chicago Press, 1981), p. 3. Stanley Hauerwas refers to this in his essay "On Keeping Theological Ethics Theological," in *Revisions: Changing Perspectives in Moral Philosophy* (Notre Dame: University of Notre Dame Press, 1983), pp. 16-42.

26. Stanley Hauerwas and William Willimon begin their book *Resident Aliens* (Nashville: Abingdon Press, 1989) with this suggestion.

the church to think and feel about aging in therapeutic modernity, in regard to both ourselves and others? Can our obsessive drive toward a better life and self-fulfillment, amounting to the virtual avoidance of all suffering, be creating even greater problems for all involved? Is not such avoidance antithetical to the story of the Jesus whom we claim to serve? Further, just what should the witness of the church be in all of this? Can we acknowledge our complicity, as the church, in having become participatory authors of such a problematic narrative, even as we attempt to find a new voice within the therapeutic culture in which we live?

Scriptural narratives portray aging as perhaps an initially negative entity, but as positive in the end result.[27] The traditional stories of Genesis teach us that, originally, there was no aging as we know it, nor any death. We were to live out our lives as healthy immortals walking in fellowship with God. We know the rest of the story, too, however, and it is one with an unfortunate ending; with choices came bad ones and then sin, and with sin came both aging and suffering, "until you return to the ground, for out of it you were taken; you are dust, and to dust you shall return" (Gen. 3:19).[28] While yet in Eden we met aging and death and carried them out as our companions.

In other scriptural narratives, at least some humans evidently proved to God that they could with God's grace do better. Growing old became a symbol of blessing, wisdom, and righteousness, an honorable process by which God awarded those who were obedient, for example, in honoring their own parents: "Honor your father and your mother, so that your days may be long in the land that the LORD your God is giving you" (Exod. 20:12). In Proverbs readers are essentially promised a long life if they will "but let your heart keep my commandments; for length of days and years of life and abundant welfare they will give you" (3:1-2). The very display of gray hair itself, a sure sign of growing old throughout the centuries, becomes in Scripture "a crown of glory; it is gained in a righteous life" (Prov. 16:31). The entire New Testament, particularly the Pastoral Epistles, both implies and speaks explicitly of dutifully caring for widows, honoring the elderly, imitating their faith

27. For an excellent inquiry into how Christians should approach the Scriptures, see Stephen E. Fowl and L. Gregory Jones, "Scripture, Exegesis, and Discernment in Christian Ethics," in *Virtues and Practices in the Christian Tradition: Christian Ethics After MacIntyre*, ed. Nancey Murphy, Brad J. Kallenberg, and Mark Thiessen Nation (Harrisburg, Pa.: Trinity Press International, 1997), pp. 111-31. Fowler and Jones make the claim that Scripture provides the primary norm for Christian ethics, but that the ability to read Scripture in this way also requires a life of wisely embodying that which we find therein.

28. All scriptural quotations in this chapter are taken from the New Revised Standard Version of the Bible.

and faithfulness, and in so doing, proving the very faith that we ourselves claim to possess.

How far we have come in our modern culture from growing old as a sign of wisdom, long life as a symbol of God's blessing, gray hair as a crown of glory, and the dutiful care of those who are no longer able to care for themselves. In a church dictated to by a therapeutic culture, we trade these in largely for a premium on youth and surface beauty, rather than acknowledge our aging as a gift from God within the inevitable temporal contingencies of this age. Would anyone reading the scriptural narratives above recognize us as being at all a part of the same tradition?

Transcending the Therapeutic Illusion

We see implicit in the thoughts above the beginnings of a clear answer regarding just how we are to think about growing old and about the elderly in general. It is evident by now also how the values of the therapeutic culture surrounding us have affected our own views, and, therefore, from whence the dread and fear of our own aging and general discomfort with its attendant issues arises. To feel good has become the ultimate desire, and in order to feel good we struggle to avoid whatever we have come to believe will make us feel bad — including signs of aging in ourselves and others and, at a deeper level, sickness and suffering itself. It is therefore to sickness and suffering, particularly with regard to the aging, that we must now turn.

There is an incalculable gulf between that which should be "good" to the church and merely "feeling good" as dictated to us by a societal sickness. That which is "good" for the church cannot be contemplated or written of apart from the account given us in the story of the life, death, and resurrection of Jesus Christ. Through Jesus the idea of "good" takes on radically new meanings, found nowhere else in human history. Good becomes connected to God, God's creation, the gift of Jesus, the Holy Spirit, grace and truth, rebirth, the joyous and at once painful truth, and the news of these things that we take to the world. It is also a name that we earn by the yoke of a long obedience in the same direction,[29] it is what Paul and the rest of us desire to do but have difficulty enacting, it is living for other people at the expense of our own selves, it

---

29. The name of a book that would likely be of interest to anyone wanting a complementary perspective on some aspects of this essay's argument is Eugene H. Peterson's *A Long Obedience in the Same Direction: Discipleship in an Instant Society* (Downers Grove, Ill.: InterVarsity Press, 1980).

is Christ resurrected, and necessarily, then, it is sometimes also preceded by death and suffering, which may include our own participation in both.[30] In the end, we do all die.

A mere sense of well-being or of feeling good cannot be placed into the same category as actual good as narrated through the life, teachings, death, and resurrection of Jesus. Feeling good is manipulable, it is generally fleeting, it can be and often is perverse, and is certainly difficult to concretely define. When Philip Rieff observed that we had "gone too far, beyond the old deception of good and evil, to specialize at last, wittingly, in techniques that are to be called . . . 'therapeutic,' with nothing at stake beyond a manipulatable sense of well-being,"[31] he was, in fact, laying bare a substantive perversion of the very Christian ideas of good that were just touched upon.

In our therapeutic culture, the dominant character type is the "psychological" human being. Therapy as defined within this therapeutic culture of modernity is the attempt to cure illness via the application of science in its broadest sense.[32] In such a scientifically shaped society, the psychological human being takes up the general attitude of a scientist — actually a replacement for the priest or minister who prevailed as a pastoral guide in the former epoch — with herself or himself as the primary object of the science.[33]

It is important to note that faith (the compulsive dynamic of a culture that works to channel obedience to and trust in an authority) has not disappeared in such a system. The faith found in a therapeutic society, however, is not to be confused with Christian faith. It is instead the faith in this new science of self, of forsaking all else and perhaps even all others, simply for the gratification of needs discerned to be central to one's personal sense of well-being. Contrary to Christian worship of the One who made us and gives us

---

30. Cf. Stanley Hauerwas, *Naming the Silences: God, Medicine, and the Problem of Suffering* (Grand Rapids: Eerdmans, 1990), p. 151. Hauerwas argues here that we must not minimize the terrible nature of death, for it is certainly both awful and demonic. While it is not our friend, it also can result from obedience to Christ — a plain fact to which the blood of so many martyrs bears testimony.

31. Rieff, *Triumph of the Therapeutic*, p. 13.

32. Cushman, *Constructing the Self, Constructing America*, p. 67.

33. Rieff, *Triumph of the Therapeutic*, p. 50. The cultural attitude displayed here, of science vs. theology, is one that many long ago discarded and have since been working to revolutionize. Such a division was the product of modernity, and we now seek to rethink such losses in our humanizing. A generally very orthodox, postmodern, or postliberal marriage of the two spheres is alive and growing, evidenced by the thriving existence of a substantial subfield within Christian theology. The work of many theologians — scientists such as Nancey Murphy, J. Wentzel van Huyssteen, Robert John Russell, Arthur Peacocke, John Polkinghorne, and a host of others — is making it increasingly difficult for a science vs. theology view to be viable.

life, it is, rather, the "unreligion" of our era and our entire story.[34] We the church, seeing at least through a glass dimly the differences between these two ideas, must find a different way. Such a narrative as this therapeutic agenda of modernity should not include us, and we have to speak out against this illness lest it consume others. The church is to be true salt and light in such matters. In so being, we are reminded and are to remind others that there is a faithful way of growing old as Christians embodied within the particularity of the story of Jesus and the church.

Why is it, we have to wonder, that such essays as "Growing Old in a Therapeutic Culture" need writing at all? How have we traveled from following a Jesus whose story calls us and "bids us come and die"[35] to becoming placidly silent and without a voice in regard to how we are to grow old faithfully? How have we been led so far down a road of complicity with such a culture that we have to now attempt a retreading of theology and a basic reorientation of our place in the world? Or, regarding growing old and its related issues, how has the salt lost its savor?

Twentieth-century modernity has been one of those times both peculiar and wonderful in Western history when the church has at times been forced to take "one side or the other" for or against a faithful Christianity. The stories of theologians like Karl Barth and Dietrich Bonhoeffer are among the more potent, illustrative, and familiar accounts of the church battling an impending culture. Their histories are particularly helpful for our inquiry at this juncture because their primary battle can aptly be described as one not so much against theological liberalism, or nationalism, or Nazism, or even Adolf Hitler, but as one with a church slowly and unwittingly seduced by foreign cultural phenomena and gradually being silenced by them. While a problem such as our battling with the sick narcissisms of a therapeutic culture certainly does not compare with the seriousness of the issues facing Karl Barth, Dietrich Bonhoeffer, and others in Europe in their time, a strong contention can be made that our problems, at least in respect to the church's identification of Jesus and itself, are no less deadly.

Seeing clearly a general ineptitude for understanding the cultural dangers infecting it, Barth, Bonhoeffer, and others sought to reorient the church toward its own identity and story, not to mention toward a rectified view of Jesus. In so doing, Bonhoeffer wrote to the church of a cross laid upon every Christian. This cross, he wrote, forces us first of all to abandon all worldly

---

34. Rieff, *Triumph of the Therapeutic*, p. 13.

35. Dietrich Bonhoeffer, *The Cost of Discipleship*, revised and unabridged edition containing material not previously translated (New York: Macmillan, 1963 [1937]), p. 99.

concerns and attachments. The "old" person within us dies as a result of encountering the resurrected Christ, and, in fact, we give our very lives over to such a suffering and death. This death is merely a beginning. It commences at the very start of our communing with Jesus. Yes, when Christ calls a person, he enjoins them "come and die."[36]

This line of thinking was powerfully conveyed and translated to include the entire church by Karl Barth, who in drafting the Barmen Declaration — the manifesto for the Confessing Church movement — in 1934 reflected the realization that cultural Christianity had literally become a matter of life and death:

> Jesus Christ, as he is testified to us, is the Holy Scripture, is the one Word of God, whom we are to hear, whom we are to trust and obey in life and in death. We repudiate the false teaching that the church can and must recognize other happenings and powers, images and truths as divine revelation. . . . We repudiate the false teaching that there are areas of our life in which we belong not to Jesus Christ but to another lord. . . . We repudiate the false teaching that the church, in human self-esteem, can put the word and work of the Lord in the service of some wishes, purposes and plans or other, according to desire.[37]

What should be most astounding to us here is how the language used by Barth to decry the dangers of an encroaching culture upon the church in that terrible situation fits so well with our own battle against a therapeutic culture now — particularly since many of us are not even aware that any such struggle exists, or at least are unwilling to give up the prerogatives implied by such a culture. Karl Barth and others were not merely pointing to the fact that the church itself could submit to no other power but Jesus; they were also implying that "other happenings and powers" might have no power at all if the church would see itself as it should in relation to Jesus and then cry out faithfully against such travesties. While we are here merely seeking to rise above the distorted lessons of a therapeutic culture, its cultural philosophy and foreign story are nonetheless robbing us, the church, of our true identity, making it difficult even to grow old faithfully.

---

36. Bonhoeffer, *Cost of Discipleship*. A loose paraphrasing of Bonhoeffer's own powerfully constructed wording.

37. Karl Barth et al., "The Barmen Declaration," in *Creeds of the Churches: A Reader in Christian Doctrine from the Bible to the Present*, ed. John H. Leith (Louisville: John Knox Press, 1963), pp. 517-22.

KEITH G. MEADOR AND SHAUN C. HENSON

Of Leadership, Complicity, and Forgetting Our Story

There are very fine lines between being led into a destructive collusion with the story of a floundering culture, being the one doing the leading, and being a collective society just diseased enough to make it all possible. Who were Barth, Bonhoeffer, and others who were theologically aware of the dangers of their situation supposed to blame for the imbroglio in which they found themselves? The pastors and other church leaders who should have known better? The people who should have known that the pastors should have known better? Theologians like themselves? And who are we to blame that it has become difficult even to grow old well in our world? All of the above, perhaps? That may, in fact, be the best possible answer, for the three are so delicately intertwined in such a plot as ours as to be almost indeterminate as far as culpability is concerned.

If our therapeutic culture is truly the product of a particular time and place, and if pastoral caregivers have been in any sense true leaders, then church leadership should examine its own part in such an unfolding. E. Brooks Holifield offers a trenchant retracing of just such evidence in his exposition on *A History of Pastoral Care in America.* He displays how pastoral care has evolved from a position of concern for the salvation of souls to the embrace and imitation of secular psychological disciplines in an individualized pact of self-realization. Church leadership, he makes clear, has both been influenced by and helped to form our changing social order.

Having inherited traditional ideas of sin and standard methods of both private guidance and public penance dating as far back as the second century, clergy in America began to lose such notions during the nineteenth century, giving way to conversations about the vitality of human nature, the force of the will, and the dynamic powers of the unconscious impulses. Reflecting their times, they displayed a certain fascination with the "natural processes" of human life, indeed, with the entire conception of nature itself, seeing human beings themselves as "powers" within the whole scheme.[38] We could master our ills, formerly known as sins, through the very force of our ability to simply decide. Pastors reveled in stories of coaxing potential parishioners to "decide" for such self-reform, and upon getting them to do so seeing them become faithful church members.[39]

38. Holifield, *History of Pastoral Care*, pp. 17 and 159.

39. Holifield, *History of Pastoral Care*, pp. 181-83. A story is relayed in which a Scottish pastor in Evanston, Illinois, taunts a fellow Scot, an alcoholic, into proving he is a good Scot by displaying his Scottish will through "deciding" to reform himself. The man, it was reported, did so and joined the church.

By the late 1950s there were some who began to wonder publicly whether the pastoral theological tradition had made bad choices. It was only a very brief time later that Philip Rieff made his observations about just how completely the therapeutic had triumphed in Western society. By the late 1960s when his book appeared, our culture was replete with therapeutic options once reserved only for those deeply disturbed. They were now the fodder of the merely discontented or otherwise even facilely unhappy. Pastoral counselors, who readily offered such console, could have proven unique by virtue of their theological training, their sacred role as church authority figures, and their dependence upon traditional theological symbols and practices.[40] But many had apparently forgotten the story of which they were supposed to be teachers. This is a vital point since Christians hope and trust that those to whom they go for help know what they are doing[41] and are rooted in the practices of the historical church. This hope becomes faith, and this faith causes us to look not only to God but to the church for the embodiment of a hope that is much more than the ahistorical optimism of a therapeutic culture. Christopher Lasch, a cultural historian, distinguishes the progressivist optimism of our therapeutic culture from a hope that resonates with the hope of the church embodied in the story of Jesus and a eucharistic hospitality. Hope, he says,

> implies a deep-seated trust in life that appears absurd to those who lack it. It rests on confidence not so much in the future as in the past. If we distinguish hopefulness from the more conventional attitude known today as optimism we can see why it serves us better, in steering troubled waters ahead, than a belief in progress.[42]

Pastors, from the beginning of the church, have inevitably been surrounded by one culture or another. To say with certainty just how much pastors have affected the development of our therapeutic culture or the culture

40. See Howard Clinebell Jr., *Mental Health Through Christian Community* (Nashville: Abingdon Press, 1965), p. 214, and *Basic Types of Pastoral Counseling* (Nashville: Abingdon Press, 1966), pp. 20-22. Cited in Holifield, *History of Pastoral Care*, p. 346.

41. Robert T. Fancher, *Cultures of Healing: Correcting the Image of American Mental Health Care* (New York: W. H. Freeman, 1995), p. 17. Fancher, trained as a psychotherapist as well as a philosopher, entered the therapeutic profession as a second career amid hopes that science, "empirically true, conscientiously arrived at, and demonstrably useful," would offer him the best way to be of help to society. His philosophical training informs his awareness of the limitations of his therapeutic practice.

42. Christopher Lasch, *The True and Only Heaven: Progress and Its Critics* (New York: W. W. Norton, 1991), p. 81.

has affected the pastors is difficult in the context of such interactive social processes. Suffice it to say, however, that both clergy and laity have jointly propagated the development of such a dilemma within the church, since neither could have had the power to promote such a church culture without the consent of the other. This is not to mention the mutual widespread neglect of each in witnessing against such cultural infirmity in society at large.

Our current culture of healing has, like all cultures, itself been shaped by culturally and personally determined meanings of suffering and methods of its alleviation.[43] Suffering in our therapeutic culture has become not just any and all affliction or death, but even the very signs of growing older. Aging is interpreted as a process to endure and suffer through, rather than a temporally contingent gift from God to be approached with gratitude. How did we come to possess such a distorted understanding of suffering, in which we now include the natural processes of growing older? Surely, it is in large part due to the fact that we have, in truth, forgotten — whether willfully or not it doesn't matter — the true story and identity of Jesus and what he has both taught and brought us through his life, suffering, death, and resurrection. And in so forgetting, we lose our own story and even ourselves, as well as the voice for narrating the story for our older brothers and sisters who can no longer tell their stories themselves. Through such forgetfulness, we, as the church, neglect and abuse the hope entrusted by the elders from generation to generation as the inevitabilities of aging and death take away their voices.

Dementias of the Soul and the God Who Remembers

Growing old and forgetting are seen by many as being inextricably related. As was described earlier, certain physical characteristics of aging do lend themselves to the diminution of not only our memories but all higher brain functions. Sooner or later, and to a greater or lesser degree depending upon the individual, we experience a decrease in our brain's size and weight as well as alterations in shape — the narrowing of cerebral convolutions, widening of sulci, cerebrospinal fluid collecting en masse, a disruptive thickening of vascular passages, and a progressive loss of vital synaptic connections necessary for the processes of retaining memory and rational thinking. Dementia in one of its several forms may ensue, the most publicly discussed of these disorders being Alzheimer's — so ruinous as to be termed "deconstruction incarnate."[44]

---

43. Jerome D. Frank, in the foreword to Fancher, *Cultures of Healing*, pp. xiii-xiv.
44. Keck, *Forgetting Whose We Are*, p. 21.

Is there not a sort of dementia of the soul in the life of the church, a forgetfulness of the truth, when we trade in our powerful salvific traditions and give way so readily to such assumptions as those undergirding a therapeutic culture? Are we in such a complete and open rebellion against God that we have, as the prosecutor in Dostoevsky's *The Brothers Karamazov* explained, become so accustomed to "crimes" that "such dark deeds have ceased to horrify us"?[45] Or, more likely, perhaps we have, like God's people seduced by the false dreamers in the book of Jeremiah, forgotten God's name in our dalliance with counterfeit fantasies (Jer. 23:23-27).

In our cultural drive to escape all woundedness and deny its inevitability, we have surely denied ourselves a narrative integrity by pushing from our memories both Jesus and the historical and eschatological hope of the church, and thus our own identity. We have given voice to our enemy, the illusory power of the self-deception of a therapeutic culture. As we engage this therapeutic culture in an aging society, we must recapture our story, accept ownership without self-deception, and remember even as wounded storytellers that which we have been so easily enticed to forget through the lure of "feel good" optimism rather than the hard work of embodied hope.

In a twist of curiosity, the most oppressive of dementias can allow for pockets of memory that often surprise observers. While perhaps not recognizing even the most familiar of friends or family members, the patient may recall quite vividly songs or vast selections of memorized poetry, or remember in explicit detail lengthy narrative episodes from personal experiences of time gone by. Evoking such memories and, in so doing, entering into such stories and memories, can become the most effective way to communicate with a person suffering such losses. Alzheimer's patients and those with similar dementias vividly challenge the naive assumptions of modernity regarding cognition and personhood in this extraordinary ability that some of them have for recalling pockets of hidden narrative from their lives.

In *The Wounded Storyteller*, sociologist Arthur W. Frank argues that we are all wounded, and, further, that the telling of our stories is part of the process of our healing.[46] For Frank, our stories take one of several types that we tell in our suffering, and his hope is that the wounded storyteller acts as a moral witness, "re-enchanting a disenchanted world."[47] While we all have our

---

45. Fyodor Mikhailovich Dostoevsky, *The Brothers Karamazov*, trans. Constance Garnett, in Great Books of the Western World, vol. 52 (Chicago: Encyclopaedia Britannica, 1989 [1880]), p. 369.

46. Arthur Frank, *The Wounded Storyteller: Body, Illness, and Ethics* (Chicago: The University of Chicago Press, 1995).

47. Frank, *Wounded Storyteller*, p. 185.

own stories to tell, we shape and adapt these to the types of narrative forms available, all of which are supplied by the surrounding culture; this signifies the importance of the communities that form us and the stories they tell.[48] Our dependency on the narrative of others increases as we grow older and becomes absolutely vital for our ongoing personhood if we lose our cognitive abilities through dementing processes. The distinctives of a Christian narration within a therapeutic culture embody a hope not subject to the assumptions of a modern therapeutic worldview.

One such assumption of our therapeutic culture is what Frank calls the "restitution narrative," the tale of people getting better. Contemporary society treats both health and youth as the desired states of being, and thus we see these as the conditions to be guarded and restored when lost. Medicine, also, is often blindly concerned with its telos of cure, about which much has already been written in numerous sources.[49] The restitution narrative, then, becomes normative and takes the form, "I was in health yesterday, today I am temporarily sick, but tomorrow I'll be healthy once again." The obvious problem, of course, is that not all who are sick get well, and with age come more and more of these types of illnesses, and eventually death. The restitution narrative, then, which ultimately has the therapeutic triumph of the science of medicine and not the person as its object, is doomed to final failure in this regard.

An alternative plot reveals itself in the "chaos narrative." In this narrative, located at the opposite end of the spectrum from the restitution narrative, stories depict the teller as trapped in a life in which all meaning and truth have vanished, amid situations that will never get better and for which there are no answers. The chaotic storyteller denies that there is any definite order or meaning to be found at all in such events.[50] Chaos narratives take forms such as, "I have a destructive and painful terminal illness and there is no cure, nor will I ever find reason for my suffering," or "I am growing very old in a society valuing youth, and there is no reversing this fact now; all hope is lost and my death approaches." The chaos is so replete in such a telling that the chaos narrative is hardly recognizable as a story at all, if stories are defined conventionally as a sequence of events occurring in order over time.[51] Far

48. Frank, *Wounded Storyteller*, p. 75.

49. Frank, *Wounded Storyteller*, p. 83.

50. See Friedrich Wilhelm Nietzsche, *On the Genealogy of Morals* (New York: Vintage Books, 1967 [1887]). Cf. Alasdair MacIntyre's citations of Nietzsche in his Gifford Lectures entitled *Three Rival Versions of Moral Inquiry: Encyclopaedia, Genealogy, and Tradition* (Notre Dame: University of Notre Dame Press, 1990), which were delivered at the University of Edinburgh in 1988.

51. Frank, *Wounded Storyteller*, p. 98.

from any "triumph of the therapeutic," this form of story can no longer so much as *imagine* life getting better, and represents instead the final ascendancy of all that modernity seeks to transcend, pointing to the emptiness of the overly optimistic therapeutic claims of modernity.

While restitution stories attempt to render infirmity as transitory by an outdistancing of our own mortality, and chaos narratives drown in a pool of hopeless submission to the failures of modernity, the third narrative type, the quest narrative, meets suffering in embodied voices. This story takes ownership of the affliction and uses it. While Nietzsche, who suffered from undiagnosed chronic ailments, called his pain "dog," John Donne transformed his illness, most likely typhus, into a spiritual journey.[52] Such is the practice of the one in a quest narrative, resolutely claiming a narration of the illness, the inevitable aging process, or death that embodies ownership and voice in the story. The quest narrative for the older Christian claims a hope grounded in the life, suffering, death, and resurrection of Jesus and the eschatological vision of a worshiping church.

Such fortitude can be sustained only within the confines of a nurturing tradition. In a reversal of Nietzsche's remark that "truths are illusions which we have forgotten are illusions,"[53] our tradition teaches us that our lives are to be understood as entities that have purpose and meaning, some of which is yet to be discovered. According to such a view, our bodies, which we struggle to keep in such pristine perfection in our therapeutic and narcissistic culture, have only the significance that can come by being part of the whole existence of an accountable agent, one on a quest of discovering that our lives have the unity and continuity of just such a journey.[54] This discovery comes through the telling of our story and the stories of others in such a context.

And, as we have alluded earlier, the church has its own story to tell concerning both Jesus and itself. It responds to the restitution and chaos narratives of modernity with a very particular, historically contingent quest narrative. When people suffering dementia in old age forget all that they know and all who know them, those surrounding them do not forget. We are called to remember for them, reminding the therapeutic culture in which we live that we as a Christian community are one body and are accountable to narrate

---

52. Nietzsche, *The Gay Science*, in *The Complete Works of Friedrich Nietzsche* (Stanford, Calif.: Stanford University Press, 1994), pp. 249-50; and John Donne, *Devotions Upon Emergent Occasions* (Ann Arbor: University of Michigan Press, 1959 [1624]). Cf. these works as cited in Frank, *Wounded Storyteller*, p. 116.

53. Friedrich Nietzsche, *Über Wahrheit und Lüge im Aussermoralischen Sinn I*, in *The Complete Works of Friedrich Nietzsche*. Quoted in MacIntyre, *Three Rival Versions*, p. 35.

54. MacIntyre, *Three Rival Versions*, p. 197.

each other's lives faithfully. We narrate our lives and the story of the communion of the saints grateful that though we may forget God, God in Jesus cannot forget us.

Eucharistic Hope in a Therapeutic Culture

The fear of aging, suffering, and dying so characteristic of our therapeutic culture is indicative of our refusal to die in Christ. We refuse to die in Christ because we have been deceived and have ourselves been our own best deceivers. In a sad psychological indulgence of seeking after self-fulfillment and realization, we forget and forsake our story for one that dares to tell us — with an optimistic wishfulness — that we are our own ultimate hope. We embrace the therapeutic culture's modernist assumption that well-being is achieved through an autonomous psychological self who trusts in the medical restitution narrative. In doing so, we trade in the Christian story of suffering and hope for that of the illusory therapeutic optimist. As a result, we necessarily forget the identity and story that Jesus has already given us, all of which creates a sort of embodied paranoia in which we are not quite certain what to fear most anymore. Through fear and self-deception we have chosen now our enemies to be such things as growing old. But growing old is not an enemy in the story Jesus gave us, and it is that story we must now reclaim. It must be emphasized, however, that this challenge to the therapeutic culture of modernity is not meant to detract from the practices that have existed throughout history of caring for and curing our bodily selves. We are challenging not the practice of medicine per se, but the therapeutic worldview of modernity with its presumptions of medical restitution and its limited psychological vision of personhood. These have had tragic implications for older persons.

The evangelist in Matthew's Gospel records Jesus as having said, "and whoever does not take up the cross and follow me is not worthy of me. Those who find their life will lose it, and those who lose their life for my sake will find it" (Matt. 10:38-39). It is good to remember such words, and if we are to take them as true we must be reminded, and remind others, that to greedily cling to assiduously extended long lives in this world is to lose hold of them, while to give them up for Jesus, the gospel, the church, and others is to retain them forever. Such irony can be learned and believed only as we faithfully witness such truths to one another, and as we each ourselves participate in those practices that serve to remind us of this present reality.

When Jesus at the Last Supper took bread and said, "Take, eat; this is my body," and likewise took the cup and told his disciples, "Drink from it, all of you; for this is my blood of the covenant, which is poured out for many for the forgiveness of sins" (Matt. 26:26, 27-28), this is precisely what he had in mind. The church later witnessed to this fact in handing down the institution first given them, telling us also that Jesus had said to them, "do this" and "drink this" "in remembrance of me" (1 Cor. 11:23-25). Eucharist, the most worshipful, powerful, and intimate of communal activities in the church, not only allows us in its *anamnesis* to recall in truth who Jesus is, but also invites us, as part of our granted identity, to share in the life, death, and resurrection — in the very destiny — of Jesus.[55] This is who we are together, both well and ill, young and old, those called out of the world by the Holy Spirit to live as witnesses to these things toward one another and all others, and perhaps even to suffer and die while doing so as we challenge the therapeutic assumptions of our age. Certainly we are to be faithful in what we know of Jesus and ourselves, as the church present, during a life of discipleship. This life will inevitably include mysteries of illness, suffering, growing old, and dying. But in the end we have a eucharistic hope that surpasses all therapeutic optimism. As Jesus both promised us and exhibited, Christians have a very particular hope in the resurrection and the age to come. We serve a faithful God who cannot forget us. We have Jesus and the Holy Spirit who call us to remember. By remembering Jesus' story and claiming it as our own, we are released from the chaos and restitution narratives of our therapeutic culture. The eucharistic witness found within the quest narrative of the Christian story offers embodied personhood and hope even within the pain of suffering as an alternative to the tragedies a therapeutic culture causes for the older saints of the church.

---

55. See Geoffrey Wainwright, *Doxology: The Praise of God in Worship, Doctrine, and Life* (New York: Oxford University Press, 1980), p. 272. In this section, Wainwright is discussing the book by Catholic author L. Dussault, *L'eucharistie pâques de toute la vie.*

Differences among the Elderly:
Who Is on the Road to Bremen?

PATRICIA BEATTIE JUNG

In 1992, 12 percent of the U.S. population — something over thirty million people — was over sixty-five. By the best estimate, 18 percent of us will be that old by 2020. By 2040 one out of four North Americans will be sixty-five or over. According to the demographic analysis that opens Stephen Sapp's book *Light on a Gray Area: American Public Policy on Aging*, several factors are contributing to the graying of America: declines in both the birth and death rates, the elder boom, even our immigration policies.[1] One of the most important factors behind the growth of the elderly population, however, is the dramatic increase in life expectancy for those living in developed countries during this century.

In the past century our life expectancy has nearly doubled. Of course, such longevity is not without historical, even ancient, precedent for the rare individual; nor is it is completely unknown in nonindustrialized cultures. But a number of factors combined in the last decades of the twentieth century to prolong life for many of us in the United States. Medical sociologist William C. Cockerham argues that because of improved housing, sanitation, nutrition, and medical care, this increase in longevity has become normal for many persons living in industrialized countries.[2]

Though now statistically normal in developed countries, this demographic change has been sudden, and many of us still do not expect to live the life span projected. It strikes us as odd to be among those who go on living when others we know die in their prime or prematurely. It seems mysterious

---

1. Stephen Sapp, *Light on a Gray Area: American Public Policy on Aging* (Nashville: Abingdon, 1992), pp. 1-48.

2. William C. Cockerham, *Medical Sociology*, eighth ed. (Upper Saddle River, N.J.: Prentice Hall, 2001).

somehow that we have been spared, when our encounters with death have been so close. When examined from this angle, the process of aging — regardless of what fears we might have about entering these uncharted waters — seems like "pure gravy." Aging looks quite good, as Woody Allen quips, when you consider the alternative.

This great increase in our average life span has literally added a new developmental stage — what the French have called "the third age" — to our existence. The numbers of people who can be counted among the young old (65-74), old (75-85), and very old (85+) are steadily increasing, with the most growth in the latter category. Indeed, centenarians are the fastest growing segment of the American population! While it is likely that we are brushing up against a sort of biological cap to the human life span, this increase in our life expectancy represents a tremendous change. Elders today are truly pioneers — exploring for us all what it might mean to so age. With them we confront — as individuals, as societies, and as the church — truly unknown territory.

Naturally questions arise. What is the significance of this development for communities? for our species? What does it mean to age? How should we interpret this process? We know little about how we ought to respond to our increased longevity and about what sort of public policies we ought to establish to support such responses. Arthur W. Frank notes that while as Christians we seek a "Christian response" to this reality, "the recurring problem is specifying exactly what we are responding to."[3] It is in our effort to answer this fundamental (even if preliminary) question that we have not always paid attention to the difference age itself makes and the differences among those who do age. In this essay I will detail some of what is at stake in paying attention to these differences and then illustrate how this affects our discourse about aging and the interpersonal and social role(s) we assign to the elderly.

Differences between the Ages

Given the relative newness of this phenomenal increase in human longevity perhaps we should not be surprised by our tendency to measure old age by what it is not: by the scripts which are the privilege and responsibility of either the middle aged or the young to live out. In the light of values such as physical stamina and procreativity, it is not difficult to see elderly people as simply worn out. After all, they have no more such work left in them. They

3. Arthur W. Frank, "The Patient's Vocation: Christian Responses to Bioethics," *The Christian Century* 13 (November 20-27, 1996): 1157.

will exit through retirement social roles they may once have served well and be stripped of other roles by the loss of their children (through maturation), by the loss of their spouse, or by the loss of their edge and endurance (if not health). They appear to be of no use to anyone. They seem, as the cat concedes in the Brothers Grimm fairy tale "The Musicians of Bremen," to no longer be capable of mousing.[4]

Because such an interpretative framework hinges on familiar premises, it is hard to forego. But to age is not merely to be no longer young. Retirement is not the end of life, that is, the end of all public roles and interpersonal responsibilities. Rather, it is a period of transition from the vocations that filled our middle age to the callings of this new third age. Each stage of life has its own tasks. When the cat on the road to Bremen admits that it is old, it asks the others who are traveling: what am I to do? This may indeed be *the* crucial question, but before we can even get to it, we must uncover all the assumptions about aging pilgrims that preclude our consideration of the full scope of possible answers to it. Only then can we imagine what sort of music might be made by those who travel the road to Bremen.

Our clinging to the standards of youth and middle age inevitably distorts the third stage and decimates our ability to see its distinctive vocational significance. This can only make us dread growing old. Our unease with aging finds vivid expression in all those "humorous" fiftieth birthday cards we send to our friends proclaiming them "over the hill." In her book *The Fountain of Age* Betty Friedan tackles the job of deconstructing this "age mystique," which blinds us to the new roles and responsibilities that might spring up for us as musicians on the road to Bremen. Decline is the interpretative key that dominates our cultural understanding of aging, and it does not incline us to search for new opportunities as we age. No wonder, Friedan argues, that so many people experience a midlife crisis. Who would not fear the prospect of simply sliding down that slippery slope, inexorably descending through pitiful states of helplessness into a nursing home and from there into a grave?

The point here is not to pretend that people over sixty-five have only glorious possibilities. Those who sit in easy chairs don't always have it easy. They face a variety of problems: from managing their own or their spouse's chronic illness, to facing the grief caused by the death of loved ones, to the loss of job-related relationships, limitations in mobility, increasing dependence, and

---

4. In the tale, four animals meet on the road to Bremen. They have worked hard and are now old and tired, and their masters, feeling that their usefulness is at an end, plan to kill them. Urging them to flee rather than die, the donkey proposes that they travel to Bremen to become town musicians, and the animals set out on their adventure together.

negative stereotypes about the elderly. Indeed, like everyone else, the elderly must tackle the difficulties that come with the territory they inhabit. But, Friedan argues, these "problems of food, housing, economic support, intimacy, medical care, purpose and respect" cannot be accurately identified and effectively addressed until we as a culture have come to understand that the "problem" is not longevity itself.[5]

Much of what has been assumed mistakenly to be the "plight" of the elderly is in fact the consequence of specific pathologies not properly associated with aging. Alzheimer's, for example, is a disease, not an inexorable or universal characteristic of growing old. In many instances the physical decline linked with people's experience of aging can be prevented or modified "with changes in diet, exercise, lifestyle or environment."[6] The chronic illnesses and degenerative diseases often associated with aging are frequently a result of lifestyle choices: of what we eat, how much we exercise, and how actively we use our minds. Indeed, of all the pithy age-related sayings floating about, the truest appears to be "use it or lose it." Most decline does in fact stem from disuse. Exercise contributes to good health, though it does not work magic.

Clearly, to expose as false those myths that portray the old as inescapably and increasingly physically decrepit, mentally incompetent, desexualized persons best kept isolated in nursing homes is an important first step toward discerning what it means to age. Yet the unambiguously negative account found in the "decline model" that dominates our cultural interpretation of aging is extremely powerful. It persists despite growing amounts of evidence to the contrary. For example, as our very language suggests, senility has been virtually equated with aging in the public mind. While some rote memory loss may correctly be associated with aging, however, recent studies repeatedly indicate that the basic cognitive competence of the elderly does not deteriorate with age. Indeed, there is some evidence of positive growth in certain more complex, integrative mental abilities. In his essay "Biological Theories about Aging," Peter J. Mayer notes that even physical changes like osteoporosis among postmenopausal women and immune system decline which were once presumed to be an inevitable result of growing old are now understood to be the consequence of specific medical conditions or other factors such as malnutrition.[7]

For many, old age is *not* a time of disability or disease; instead it is a time

---

5. Betty Friedan, *The Fountain of Age* (New York: Simon and Schuster, 1993), p. 69.

6. Friedan, *Fountain of Age*, p. 74. See also Peter J. Mayer, "Biological Theories about Aging," in *The Elderly as Modern Pioneers*, ed. Philip Silverman (Bloomington, Ind.: Indiana University Press, 1987), p. 21.

7. Mayer, "Biological Theories about Aging," p. 21.

of remarkably good health. The evidence is clear: deterioration and decay are simply not the rule. Healthy elders are *not* astonishing exceptions to a rule of "decline." Nevertheless, in an essay on aging entitled "A Last Look Around," Edward Hoagland gave poignant voice to a persistent, even if irrational, dread that plagues many of us about to enter the "elder boom." Is it true, he wonders, that "you're only as old as you feel"? Or are those feelings of vigor and vitality just part "of the anesthetic that commonly tranquilizes creatures that are being engulfed by death"?[8]

Why do we persist in stereotyping the elderly as "over the hill"? Partly this is a consequence of not being able to imagine that such aging has any purpose. As the "decline" model rightly suggests, it is clearly not the time to take up the tasks of youth or middle age. To what we might be called in this third age is not clear. Such a blank page can be terrifying to face. Repeatedly the donkey leading the way to Bremen must exhort those who travel that road to have courage. If they are to become musicians, they will have to find their own voice, write their own score.

No wonder we are tempted to jump to the conclusion, as has William Regelson in *The Superhormone Promise*,[9] that aging is not a normal life process but a disease. Why would we not want to slow, even reverse, the aging process? What's so good about growing old? It is clear who profits financially from this medical interpretation of aging: all those involved in the commercial development, production, and prescription of various antidotes to this "disease" — from hormone to hair replacement therapies. But surely there is more than greed behind the $9.5 billion business of disguising, if not denying, what could alternately be seen as the gift of years.[10]

Deconstructing misleading negative stereotypes about aging is important work. It reduces the fear evoked in the young and middle aged about growing old. It frees many elders from distorting their experience of themselves and their peers as a result of the ageist scripts they have internalized. But as Philip Silverman argues, "this should not lead to glossing over that part of aging which does involve loss and inevitable decline in function."[11] Indeed, the tricky element in most distortive stereotypes is that they rest on half-truths or, more precisely, on the blanket application to all of an experience that is indeed true, but only for some.

8. Edward Hoagland, "A Last Look Around," *Civilization* 4, no. 1 (February/March 1997): 35.

9. William Regelson, *The Superhormone Promise: Nature's Antidote to Aging* (New York: Simon and Schuster, 1996).

10. See Larry Reibstein, "Rippling Abs in 30 Days or Your Money Back," *Newsweek* 128, no. 12 (September 16, 1996): 77.

11. Philip Silverman, ed., *The Elderly as Modern Pioneers*, p. 2.

Romantic illusions about life in "the golden years" can be as deceptive and distortive as images of decline. It is true that for many old age is a time of fruition wherein they can enjoy the fruits of their labor — financial security, growing old together, and their children's children. But as Helen Oppenheimer points out, this image, though not false, often covers over part of the truth. In old age some dimensions of our life may begin to decay.[12] If we insist on minimizing or overlooking the problems some face with advancing age, we endanger them and possibly ourselves. The truth about aging — like most of reality — is that it is simply more complex than our predilection for bipolar conceptual frameworks suggests.

To age, as we have noted, is not merely to be no longer young or middle aged. However tempting it is to see this new stage as merely one of loss, we should not interpret this stage of our life through that lens. What such a framework illumines is not what it means to age but the values that underlie our youth-oriented culture. In one sense such a lens proves very revealing, but not of what it means to grow old. Instead, it renders starkly overt the many values upheld in youth and middle age and invites their reevaluation.

To describe this mostly prejudicial pattern of oversimplified generalizations — and the systematic discrimination against elders it evokes — Robert Butler (some years ago now) coined the term "ageism."[13] In her essay "Growing Old with Grace,"[14] Sidney Callahan notes with considerable understatement that ageism has created a general distaste for the elderly in our culture. Many of us have internalized this attitude. In her discussion of the prospects for expanding the social roles of older women, Ruth Harriet Jacobs addresses the affective — gerontophobic — dimension of this perspective.[15] Old people are viewed as socially expendable, if not literally disposable, because they seem through this lens merely to "drain" society. The elderly hate to identify themselves as old and do not want to identify politically with peers on the basis of age. All of this comes from refusing to pay sufficient attention to the differences between the ages.

12. Helen Oppenheimer, "Reflections on the Experience of Aging," in *Aging,* ed. Lisa Sowle Cahill and Deitmar Mieth (Philadelphia, Pa.: Trinity Press International, 1991).

13. Armeda F. Ferrini, with Rebecca L. Ferrini, *Health in Later Years* (Dubuque, Iowa: Wm. C. Brown, 1986), p. 9.

14. Sidney Callahan, "Growing Old with Grace," *Commonweal* 121, no. 10 (May 20, 1994): 11-12.

15. Ruth Harriet Jacobs, "Expanding Social Roles for Older Women," in *Women on the Front Lines: Meeting the Challenge of an Aging America,* ed. Jessie Allen and Alan Pifer (Washington, D.C.: Urban Institute Press, 1993).

Differences among the Old

As many of the essays in this volume have already pointed out, to become an old man is to be on a path different from that traveled by boys or even by young or middle-aged men. And while we must pay careful attention to the difference age itself makes, we must likewise not presume that all those who share the same chronological age are alike. We must pay attention both to the many differences between the young and the old and to the many differences among those who are old. To become (as I am becoming) an old, white, upper-middle-class, heterosexual woman ("week-old wonder bread," as one friend of mine put it) is not the same as becoming a poor, old, black man. To an exploration of some of these important differences this section of this essay will be devoted. Our ignorance of the many differences among the elderly reinforces the temptation to make false generalizations about old people and not to consider aging on its own highly variable terms.

One aim of this volume is to help Christians reevaluate what constitutes "aging gracefully." An element that factors heavily into our current construction of aging is the tendency to think that chronological age alone can create a homogeneous cohort group. But of course many factors other than age influence a person's experience of this stage of life: health but also gender, class, and ethnicity. Many of these differences are filtered out of our current interpretation of the aging process. We assume that these pioneers are basically alike. But in fact this group is tremendously heterogeneous. Indeed, there are more differences among elders than among any other segment of the population.

My working hypothesis is that many previous assessments of and responses to growing old have not adequately accounted for these many differences. What we may now recognize as having significance only for particular subgroups are still blown into universal claims; these false generalizations suppress our recognition of important differences among the elderly. In what follows I will examine some significant differences in morbidity and mortality rates, economic welfare, and sexuality among the elderly. This is not a comprehensive account of all significant differences among the elderly, but instead simply a sampling of three areas of difference that will illustrate the problem that concerns me. As shall become evident, this tendency to homogenize the elderly has proven detrimental not only to predictable subgroups among them but to all concerned, and will undermine our efforts to discern as Christians what practices might befit growing old.

Morbidity and Mortality

Health is perhaps the single most significant factor in an elderly person's quality of life. Yet the truth about the precise relationship between aging and physical health is so complex that even gerontologists are unclear about how to describe it. Cynthia M. Taeuber and Jessie Allen note that expert "analysts disagree strongly about projections of the future health status of the elderly . . . especially regarding the prevalence of disability."[16] It does appear that health may deteriorate with age, but this occurs considerably later for some than others, and its impact varies. Though not a necessary, or even particularly widespread, characteristic of all the elderly, disease and disability are nevertheless more prevalent among the old than among other age groups.

Armeda F. Ferrini explains that while "elders have the highest rate of morbidity of all age groups, in these later years the majority of morbidity is chronic illness: arthritis, hearing and vision disorders, hypertension. . . ."[17] For most old people, however, these chronic conditions do not prove debilitating. Their management requires little alteration in daily routine and most of the young old and old so afflicted adapt well to them, continue to live independently, and evaluate their own health as — for their age — good. Ferrini concludes: "the majority do not have health problems that limit their ability to manage their own households."[18] On the other hand, while about a third of those living beyond eighty-five years could be described as "functionally fit" for independent living, the other two-thirds do become chronically and increasingly disabled survivors. As Colleen L. Johnson and Barbara M. Barer note, "recent longitudinal studies have repeatedly found higher levels of disability with increasing age, a rate that is particularly high among the oldest old." Many — though again not all — are "sinking into weakness" and frequently suffer "pain from head to foot."[19]

In short, it is not only misguided but distortive to try to establish "a rule" for the relationship between aging and physical health. There is more variability among the elderly than among any other segment of the population.[20] It is clearly helpful to distinguish aging per se from diseases — especially those few associated with increased age that do have pathological conse-

16. Cynthia M. Taeuber and Jessie Allen, "Women in Our Aging Society: The Demographic Outlook," in *Women on the Front Lines,* ed. Allen and Pifer, p. 35.

17. Ferrini, *Health in the Later Years,* p. 22.

18. Ferrini, *Health in the Later Years,* p. 13.

19. Colleen L. Johnson and Barbara M. Barer, *Life Beyond 85 Years: The Aura of Survivorship* (New York: Springer, 1997), pp. 57, 65, 66.

20. Ferrini, *Health in the Later Years,* p. 11.

quences (such as cataracts and arteriosclerosis) and that link aging to mortality. But it is also realistic to recognize that for many — especially the oldest of the old — this stage of life may be a period of considerable trial.

Though there is great variability among the elderly, it is not random; certain patterns can be seen among subgroups of the aged. Continued inattention to important differences among the elderly with regard to both life expectancy and chronic illnesses could obscure legitimate health concerns and make less fair the allocation of our public health-care dollar. Reconsider the claims about increases in human longevity with which this very essay was introduced. Before 1850 in pre-industrialized society, the overall life expectancy of men and women was about the same. Any biological advantages associated with females, such as estrogen's capacity to lower cholesterol levels, were counterbalanced by the risks of continual childbearing and inequitable access to food and other resources requisite for survival.[21] But by the end of the twentieth century, a widening gender gap developed in terms of longevity, with females significantly more advantaged today than males. In 1988, for example, there were six and a half million women compared to only two million men over sixty-five.[22] Of all those over one hundred years of age, 79 percent are female. If recent trends continue, this gap may slowly narrow, but the gender gap in longevity is at present large and is likely to remain significant into the foreseeable future, even as more men grow older.[23]

The reasons for the gender gap in mortality rates are several. At birth males are slightly more vulnerable than females, but the gap appears to have social as well as biological roots. Men in our culture die significantly more often of accidents and diseases associated with culturally reinforced, if not constructed, tendencies toward competition, aggressiveness, high-risk activities, and drug abuse. In *The Fountain of Age* Friedan devotes a whole chapter to wrestling with the question of why women age longer and better than men. She wonders whether "the very discontinuity and change that has taken place in women's roles over a lifetime — their continual practice in retirement and disengagement, shift and reengagement — accounts for their greater flexibility and resilience in age."[24]

Mortality differs significantly by race as well. Whites live longer than blacks in the United States, but that may be explained more adequately by

21. Ruth B. Hess, "Gender and Aging: The Demographic Parameters," in *Gender and Aging*, ed. Lou Glasses and John Hendricks (Amityville, N.Y.: Baywood Publishing, 1992), p. 17.

22. Hess, "Gender and Aging," p. 18.

23. Kyriakos S. Markides, "Risk Factors, Gender, and Health," in *Gender and Aging*, ed. Glasses and Hendricks, p. 26.

24. Friedan, *Fountain of Age*, p. 149.

class-related factors. The educated wealthy of all ethnic backgrounds outlive the uneducated poor. Because poverty and lack of education are disproportionately high among African Americans and Hispanics in the United States, it is not surprising that poor black and Hispanic men continue to be at particular risk.

What does all this matter? Clearly, blindness to differences in mortality rates will leave unexamined (and thus inevitably unchanged) all those gender scripts and public policies that contribute to these different rates. This is obviously detrimental to poor men of color, who are particularly at risk. Inattention to gender differences in regard to health has also proved harmful for those women who receive the gift of years, for even though women have indeed been blessed with longer lives, this does not mean they no longer have health concerns. Health is as much a matter of the quality of life as it is a matter of its quantity. The gift of years, while certainly welcomed by women, has not been accompanied by a reduction in the morbidity rate associated with aging. The vast majority of those afflicted by chronic and degenerative diseases like arthritis are old women. Attention to gender differences in longevity must be accompanied by attention to gender differences in regard to morbidity so that the continuing need for research and treatment programs that might prevent disabilities and/or ameliorate the burdens they impose can receive their fair share of the public health-care dollar.[25]

Greedy Geezers and Bag Ladies

The next time you hear the elderly described as affluent — not only as economically better off than the rest of us but as greedy — consider the significance of economic differences among them. In many cases older women are economically disadvantaged in comparison to men, young and old alike.[26] Older people on average are undoubtedly in better shape financially now than they were in 1961, when the first White House Conference on Aging was held. By 1990 the poverty rate for the elderly population as a whole had plummeted to 12 percent, which was below that of the general population. This was a dramatic improvement over the poverty rate of 35 percent overall among the elderly of just thirty years ago. But averages are notorious for

25. Markides, "Risk Factors, Gender, and Health," p. 31; Alan Pifer, "Meeting the Challenge: Implications for Policy and Practice," in *Women on the Front Lines,* ed. Allen and Pifer, p. 244.

26. See James H. Schulz, "Ask Older Women: Are the Elderly Better Off?" *Journal of Aging and Social Policy* 9, no. 1 (1997): 7-12.

disguising wide variables. As Karen Davis, Paula Grant, and Diane Rowland point out, the "elderly population is not homogeneous in composition . . . [and] economic improvements have not been evenly distributed" among them.[27] They report that white men sixty-five to seventy-four years old have the lowest poverty rate in the nation at 9 percent, whereas nonwhite women over eighty-five live below the poverty line at the shameful rate of 59 percent — a rate, I would note, four and a half times higher than the rate in the general population. Some predict that in coming decades poverty for elderly couples and single men may virtually disappear, but it is likely to remain a problem (perhaps almost exclusively so) for old women who live alone.

Today, women constitute nearly three-fourths of the elderly poor.[28] The disproportionate nature of that representation is so stunning that it is worth examining in detail the statistics cited by Cynthia M. Taeuber and Jessie Allen in their study of "Women in Our Aging Society: The Demographic Outlook":

> The elderly poor are disproportionately female, black and Hispanic. Women constituted fifty-eight percent of the elderly population but seventy-four percent of the elderly poor in 1990. Black women make up five percent [of the elderly population, but constitute] sixteen percent of the elderly poor. The poverty rate for all elderly women was fifteen percent, double the rate for elderly men.[29]

To this bleak picture should be added the faces of women near poverty — women who will be quickly rendered poor by either the death of their husband or the onset of a chronic illness. We are not just talking about a few women living near poverty. Julianne Malveaux points out that "one-third of all women (fifty-seven percent of black women and forty-seven percent of Latinos) are within one hundred and fifty percent of the poverty line."[30]

The problem is not that the Social Security system is directly biased against women but that its benefits favor couples over singles and single-income couples over dual-income marriages. In addition, "the basic federal benefits under SSI [Supplemental Security Incomes, for the aged poor, blind,

27. Karen Davis, Paula Grant, and Diane Rowland, "Alone and Poor: The Plight of Elderly Women," in *Gender and Aging*, ed. Glasses and Hendricks, p. 79.

28. Jessie Allen, "The Front Lines," in *Women on the Front Lines*, ed., Allen and Pifer, p. 2.

29. Taeuber and Allen, "Women in Our Aging Society," p. 23.

30. Julianne Malveaux, "Race, Poverty, and Women's Aging," in *Women on the Front Lines*, ed. Allen and Pifer, p. 172.

and disabled] are more generous for couples than singles," according to Marilyn Moon's analysis.[31] The level of Social Security benefit is tied to the employment history of an eligible worker (and if relevant, his or her dependent). Since women have been systematically discriminated against in the marketplace (in terms of hiring, promotions, and so on), and since their work at homemaking (including child rearing and elder care) remains uncredited in the system, it is not altogether unreasonable to conclude that Social Security indirectly "privileges the work and marital experience of older men."[32] In addition, women are disproportionately employed in positions that lack pension benefits altogether. In many cases the economic problems older women face have been socially constructed in the workplace and then reinforced through federal policies. For all these reasons, it is women living alone who are economically most vulnerable at present.

Soon the nation will have to tackle the question of how and to what extent to cut Social Security and Medicare benefits. If not, by 2040 65 percent (up from 30 percent today) of the federal budget will be devoted to sustaining these benefits for the elderly. To declare, as has Robert J. Samuelson,[33] that *the* issue posed by a graying America is simply one of "generational justice" obscures dramatic differences in the economic circumstances of our elders. It is not simply a matter of how much burden should be placed on the young and middle class in support of benefits for the elderly, and of determining what amounts to a fair return for one's contribution to the system (for many elderly today receive far more than alternative investments would have produced). It is *also* a matter of discerning who among the elderly still need to receive such benefits (perhaps even more benefits) in order to live decently. "All of the traits that tend to describe the aged poor — widowed, living alone, very old — are much more characteristic of older women than men," writes Stephen Sapp.[34] Only when such differences among the elderly are ignored can the public policy dilemmas we face be reduced to the issue of justice between generations. Like their younger counterparts, those who are affluent among the elderly have ongoing economic obligations to those — both young and old — in the wider community who live in need.

---

31. Marilyn Moon, "Public Policies: Are They Gender-Neutral?" in *Gender and Aging*, ed. Glasses and Hendricks, p. 116.

32. Allen, "The Front Lines," p. 3.

33. Robert J. Samuelson, "Justice among Generations," *Newsweek* 129, no. 3 (January 20, 1997): 29.

34. Sapp, *Light on a Gray Area*, p. 49.

Oh Wouldn't It Be Loverly?

Despite our cultural tendency to deny it, both old men and old women continue to desire sexual intimacy and to enjoy its delights. Let us conclude this section by considering the differences between people of different ages and among elders in this respect, and the potential impact of these differences on the sexual practices we commend as "fitting" for the old.

Male sexual responsiveness peaks in adolescence, and then ever so gradually declines. In its normal form, the slowing of penile responsiveness may actually prove sexually beneficial at least from a heterosexual woman's point of view, since it affords the man more control over his response.[35] In some men over forty, dense connective tissue develops in the penis and prostate, which may eventually complicate erection, ejaculation, and urination. According to a recent *Newsweek* summary of data, "some fifteen percent of U.S. men are completely impotent by seventy (up from five percent at forty), and a third suffer at least occasional meltdowns."[36] It is important to recognize, however, that such "viropause" (the end of virility) is a consequence of vascular disease, not aging per se. It is not linked to the far more subtle decline in sperm and testosterone production associated with the passing of years, but should be associated with heart disease, hypertension, diabetes, smoking, and alcoholism instead.

Likewise, according to a study on the sexuality of "older adults" by the PCUSA, women after peaking sexually in their mid thirties "tend to maintain this level throughout their lives. . . . The potential for orgasm remains high and in some cases continues to increase well into a woman's later years."[37] In some women certain physiological changes may complicate sexual responsiveness, that is, reduce vaginal lubrications and result in the thinning of vaginal walls and painful uterine contractions during orgasm, but these changes do not reduce sexual responsiveness.

Thus, presuming reasonably good health, the levels or rates of sexual activity for both men and women "tend to remain stable over middle and later life."[38] The main point here is that for both men and women it is precisely "continuity in sexual activity" that is key to maintaining "sexual vitality into

35. Diane E. Rykken, "Sex in the Later Years," in *The Elderly as Modern Pioneers,* ed. Silverman, p. 170.

36. Geoffrey Cowley, "Attention Aging Men," *Newsweek* 128, no. 12 (September 16, 1996): 70.

37. PCUSA (Presbyterian Church in the U.S.A.), "Older Adults," in *Sexuality and the Sacred,* ed. James B. Nelson and Sandra Longfellow (Louisville, Ky.: Westminster/John Knox Press, 1994), p. 300.

38. Ferrini, *Health in the Later Years,* p. 287.

old age."[39] Yet in our culture, sexual activity for both men and women declines (though older women tend to be less sexually active than old men). This is so primarily because they lack a suitable sexual partner with whom to be intimate. Masturbation, same-sex relations, and sexual activity outside of marriage, along with partners who are much younger, are judged unsuitable for a variety of reasons, moral and otherwise. This is especially true for women. As the saying goes, old men get married; old women get lonesome.

Since this is not cross-culturally true, questions arise about what lies behind our construction of sexual activity among the elderly. The PCUSA study suggests (1) that older women have "internalized ageist and sexist assumptions which denigrate their sexuality," and (2) that behind this cultural denial of the sexiness of all older adults (but especially females) is the belief that they no longer *should* enjoy sex.[40]

While sexual pleasure, intimacy, and companionship have been somewhat appreciated within Christianity, until recently they have often been treated as secondary, if not merely instrumental, goods. Childbearing alone was viewed as intrinsically valuable. It tended to eclipse other sexual values, especially in the assessment of female sexuality. This value configuration is directly challenged by the experience of ongoing sexual desire and delight in older post-menopausal females, who now live on average for thirty years beyond their reproductive capacity in many industrialized countries.

At the turn of the century, the average woman's life expectancy was forty-six, whereas now in North Atlantic countries it is nearly eighty. Since the average age for menopause is between fifty and fifty-two, this means that until this century most women never lived past their fertility. Whereas a man's fertility gradually tapers off as he ages, a woman's stops with the completion of menopause. This "change of life" signals a distinct and dramatic change in her reproductive functioning. Today's woman can expect to live a full third of her life after her capacity for procreation has ended. Old women may be the only creatures on earth to whom such a long span of life has been given with no apparent reproductive strings attached, and the human species is most likely unique in the span of life now being devoted to the post-reproductive maturation of its female members, as it is unique in its prolonged infancy and youth.

Increasingly there is an effort to downplay the differences between the experiences of aging men and women in regard to sex hormones and fertility, but there are few points of analogy between menopause and andropause. It is

39. PCUSA, "Older Adults," p. 302.
40. PCUSA, "Older Adults," p. 301.

true that around forty men begin to experience a noticeable change in the production of both testosterone and sperm (even though both have been on a more subtle decline since late adolescence). The level of testosterone in the blood drops more rapidly after forty — by about 1 percent a year. Thus by age seventy the average male has experienced a 30 percent decline in the level of testosterone he produces. On top of that, growing amounts of the testosterone that remain in circulation are effectively neutralized by increases in the blood of a protein called SHBG. Labels like "male menopause," however, which minimize the tremendous gap between women and men in this regard, obscure an important difference in their experiences of aging and of their sexuality. While their sperm count definitely lowers as they age, men have been known to biologically father children well into their nineties. In contrast, when ovulation stops (on average around age fifty), women can no longer be biological or gestational mothers without the intervention of new reproductive technologies. In addition, there is little that is gradual in the cessation of female fertility. During menopause there is a dramatic crash in a woman's estrogen level with correspondingly tremendous effects on everything from a reduction of her risk in certain types of breast cancer to the loss of her estrogen-based protection against heart disease. In contrast, the decline in the production of testosterone is far more gradual. Though the decline of testosterone may have a measurable impact on bone density, muscle strength, size, endurance, and some secondary sexual characteristics, the hormone profiles of most seventy-year-old men stay within the range considered normal for young men.

How these facts might be interpreted can vary tremendously. When the male experience is treated as normative for all, it is hard not to interpret the onset of menopause (as many have done in North America) as pathological in character. Now many question this androcentric framework and the "medicalization" of our response to menopause. Constructions of the goodness of sexuality that make procreative potential essential, if not central, are profoundly challenged by this development in human evolution. The more women enjoy such longevity and good sex within it, the more difficult it will be to dismiss the sexuality they embodied as withered or as biologically serendipitous.

If we fail to reflect inductively and dialogically on the concrete particularities of an inclusive range of experiences of aging, we will make false generalizations both about what we may share in common and about what differentiates us as old folks. Generalizations that mask important differences inevitably result in the unexamined hegemony of certain attitudes toward and practices regarding aging. It is important to recognize just how danger-

ous some of these ideas can be. They undergird not only our dread of growing old but our rejection of the gift of years. (Some, when they consider the
alternative to aging, opt out. At present the suicide rate is quite high among
the elderly.) What is crucial is that we seek not to rise above the diversity of
our experiences but to both appreciate that variety and discern within it those
things that we share.

Conclusion

To what are we called in this third age? What might Christians make of this
dramatic increase in human longevity? Attention to the variety — biologically based as well as socially constructed — in the experience of aging suggests that what might count as "aging gracefully" or as Christian responses to
aging necessarily varies. Some will retire from active lives (both professional
and recreational) and slow down enough to smell the roses, rest, and tell
wondrous "elder tales," if not become outright contemplative. Others will become increasingly productive in new ventures they are now ready and able to
risk. Both lifestyles contribute to the commonweal. Some will experience the
transition into old age as serene; others will find themselves wrenched out of
middle age. Some may pare down to essentials and find that they are able to
detach themselves from things they once pursued but that ironically came to
possess and burden them. Some will learn to delight in the treasure that is
their good health, while others will wrestle perhaps for the first time with
chronic and degenerative diseases. Loss and grief will be accompanied by the
growth of new kinds of friendships. From the perspective of this stage, much
of what once preoccupied us with urgency may seem less important. As Jenny
Joseph warns, some "shall wear purple."[41]

The exact timbre and harmonies in the music we compose on the road to
Bremen hinge a lot on the instrument we bring to the journey, that is, on who
we are at that turning point, and on the character of those with whom we
choose to band. But key to the process is our willingness to embark on the pilgrimage itself. Instead of denial, aging and the aged should be received with
gratitude.

If we continue to construct this stage of life on the "decline" model, it
cannot be seen as the gift it is. Given the grim outlook on aging that domi-

---

41. See Joseph's charming poem "Warning," which begins "When I am an old woman I
shall wear purple/with a red hat which doesn't go, and doesn't suit me. . . ." "Warning" can be
found in Joseph's *Rose in the Afternoon, and Other Poems* (London: Dent, 1974).

nates in our culture, most of us want to deny our age, trying to "pass" as younger, as "ageless." Frieda Kerner Furman in her book *Facing the Mirror: Older Women and Beauty Shop Culture*[42] tells the sad story of a woman well into her seventies who adamantly insisted during her interview that she was not old. By attending to the differences between the ages and among the elderly — and breaking the hold of many stereotypes on the moral imagination — we may be able to face more fully the ambiguity of our own experience of becoming old.

Henri Nouwen and Walter Gaffney argue that our need to segregate the elderly — in some instances to deny their very existence — is rooted in our denial of the old man or woman awakening within. "No guest will ever feel welcome when his host is not at home in his own house."[43] Perhaps honesty is a key to hospitality — to becoming people capable of caring for the elderly and of celebrating the gift of the years wherein we shall be aged.

42. Frieda Kerner Furman, *Facing the Mirror: Older Women and Beauty Shop Culture* (New York: Routledge, 1997).

43. Henri J. M. Nouwen and Walter J. Gaffney, *Aging* (New York: Doubleday, 1974), p. 96.

The Language of Death:
Theology and Economics in Conflict

D. STEPHEN LONG

How shall we assist our elders in dying well? When we answer this question we will also know how to live well because living a good life includes learning to die well. Such an art has become a neglected and forgotten theme in Christian theology. This was not always the case. Works such as Jeremy Taylor's *Holy Dying* recall a time when theologians put forth obligations to prepare the faithful for death. The "art" of "dying well," suggested the Anglican divine, required daily practices of general preparation. For Taylor, this general preparation was based on three precepts: First, the person who would die well "must always look for death every day knocking at the gates of the grave; and then the gates of the grave shall never prevail upon him to do him mischief." Second, "he that would die well must all the days of his life, lay up against the day of his death." The necessary provisions, stated Taylor, were "faith and patience." Third, to die well required a life that eschewed "softness, delicacy and voluptuousness" in favor of "a life severe, holy and under the discipline of the cross." Taylor then suggested daily activities that would assist us in this general preparation for death such as examination of conscience and the exercise of charity.[1]

Jeremy Taylor put forward these duties in the mid seventeenth century,[2] and they provide a context within which we think about not only our own deaths but also the deaths of our elders. To honor one's elders would be to help them complete life with a holy death. But more than two centuries later, Taylor's general precepts seem alien, if not morbid, to us. We focus our atten-

---

1. Jeremy Taylor, *Holy Living and Dying; With Prayers Containing the Complete Duty of a Christian* (New York: D. Appleton, 1859), pp. 42-57.

2. Taylor himself was no stranger to death and suffering, having faced imprisonment, poverty, and the burial of two sons.

tion not on death itself, but on that period prior to death known as "retire-ment" or the "third age."[3] We speak of "aging" rather than of "dying." We still possess preparatory duties for death, but these duties take as their primary purpose a comfortable retirement before death so that we will be the least burdensome on our relatives, friends, and enemies. Such duties can easily conflict with previously practiced theological duties to prepare daily for death at all ages through a severe and holy discipline. The language of dying is no longer cloaked in garments such as fasting, prayer, and preparation for suffer-ing. Instead, it is dressed up with retirement, pensions, and security.

This change in dress has some distinct advantages and reflects positive social changes since Taylor's time: we bury our children less, our parents and grandparents live longer and healthier lives, we physically suffer less from dis-eases and poor health.[4] These changes have resulted in a new language. We now speak of a "third age," or a third stage in life where we must learn to ad-just to the process of aging — adjustments our forebears had little opportu-nity or necessity to make. Only a masochist could find in these new develop-ments something to bemoan, for no one should seek suffering and an early death for their own sake. Yet the difficulty with acknowledging the positive gains of these changes is the social and political narrative that is often given credit for them. That narrative suggests that these gains were realized primar-ily by the creation of the free market as a neutral technical instrument that al-locates scarce resources in the most efficient way possible, diminishing pain and suffering and furthering life and prosperity.

This narrative creates two problems. First, by viewing the market as a neutral technical instrument, it abstracts it from any analysis or consider-ation of the social, political, and theological conditions that make such a market possible and that such a market produces.[5] Second, once this narra-

3. See Peter Laslett's *A Fresh Map of Life: The Emergence of the Third Age* (London: Widen-feld and Nicolson, 1989).

4. Who constitutes the "we" in these sentences is intended in a limited sense. It applies to those who might read this essay — educated, middle- or upper-class people. These changes are not uniform throughout all places and among all people. It is still the case that one's socioeco-nomic status while working basically determines one's socioeconomic status in retirement.

5. Another problem with this interpretation is that it seems to be false. Sociological inter-pretations of statistics do not show direct correlations between increased life expectancy and modernization and industrialization. Laslett notes, "The developing countries today have al-ready been described as beginning to age in the sense of the lengthening of life, well before in-dustrialization has been achieved. If present trends and politics continue, it could be that aging in the further sense of having large proportions of old will also supervene in those countries, es-pecially China, before industrialization and 'modernization' have made much progress" (*Fresh Map of Life*, p. 83).

tive is conceded as the source of this best of all possible worlds we now live in, then the dominant language available to think and speak about aging and death is the language of the economists. That language will always find preparatory duties such as Taylor's alien. It will also produce false contexts within which people of faith can easily be misled in their good intentions to fulfill religious obligations such as honoring one's elders.

Perhaps the reason we find terms such as "fasting, severe discipline and preparation for suffering" strange and yet are comfortable with the language of "retirement, pensions, and security" is precisely that our dying is defined more by considerations of "economics" than by moral, political, and theological considerations. Our language of aging and dying has implicitly and explicitly become defined by the "burden of dependency," which is given definition by economists:

> From an economic point of view, a person who has retired from the labor market is a "burden" on society in the specific sense that his current consumption expenditure outweighs his current contribution to the total marketable output.[6]

This technical definition of retired persons is not intended to imply a value judgment; it supposedly reflects nothing but a necessary presupposition for the economic analysis of intergenerational resource distribution. Nevertheless, such language does produce different moral considerations for the process of aging and dying than did language such as Taylor's or obligations to honor one's elders. It prompts us to secure our future aging so that we will be the least burdensome on others. Our preparatory duties for death include securing our future not only against want but also against any dependence on the charity of others. But these preparatory duties are not the result of some natural desire for autonomy; they arise from the demands of a particular sociopolitical order, one that was given shape by the marginalist revolution.

---

6. See Richard Disney, *Can We Afford to Grow Older?* (Cambridge, Mass.: MIT Press, 1996), p. 17. Such "conventional approaches to the 'economics of aging'" then give rise to discussions of aging in a "burden of dependency" model, which uses "static . . . measures of the burden, calculated with varying degrees of sophistication" (p. 12). It should be noted that Disney's work develops a different model than this burden of dependency model, although he does assume the retired are a "burden" in this putatively neutral technical sense.

Speaking of Death as the Optimal Allocation of Scarce Resources: The Language of Economics

Economists describe the relationship between the elderly and the young in terms of the marginalist rationality (also known as neo-classical liberalism) that revolutionized economics in the latter part of the nineteenth century.[7] This rationality assumes that the starting point for economic analysis is individuals who must make choices concerning exchanges in conditions of scarcity.[8] The market is a neutral, value-free technical instrument to effect these exchanges in the most efficient and rational way possible. Such reasoning abstracts both from the social conditions within which these individuals are situated and from conditions of accumulation by assuming that "the initial allocation of goods is taken as given historically and so is no matter for the economist to investigate."[9] The task of the economist is to optimize efficiency with the social and political conditions assumed as given.

Marginalist Rationality: Natural or a Political Abstraction?

Marginalist rationality does not describe something which is natural, i.e., just the way things are; rather, it assumes the normativity of a social order — capitalist society — which it seldom acknowledges, because economics presents itself as something of a natural science. This is important for intergenerational economic analyses because marginalist rationality also assumes a "natural" conflict of interest between the generations. In fact, some economists believe we will face an economic crisis because of our aging population. We shall examine this possible crisis below; however, whether such a crisis exists or not, intergenerational economic analyses assume conflict. As one economics textbook puts it,

7. For a good analysis of the marginalist revolution see Simon Clarke's *Marx, Marginalism and Modern Sociology: From Adam Smith to Max Weber* (London: MacMillan, 1982), particularly pp. 145-85.

8. This language is not only prevalent in economics; it is also the language within which sociologists work. For example, Ronald and Jacqueline Angel begin their sociological analysis of care for the elderly by stating, "In the United States today, programs for the old and for the young compete for the same limited resources. If real economic growth remains relatively low, increased outlays for the elderly can only come at the expense of other social goods, including programs for children" (Ronald L. Angel and Jacqueline L. Angel, *Who Will Care for Us? Aging and Long-Term Care in Multicultural America* [New York: New York University Press, 1997], p. xxi).

9. Clarke, *Marx, Marginalism, and Modern Sociology,* p. 153.

Is a $20,000 hip replacement for a ninety-year-old with a life expectancy of a few years the most valuable use of society's resources? These are difficult and unpleasant questions but as long as society as a whole bears the brunt of these costs, through its Medicare and Medicaid programs, there is no way of avoiding them.[10]

The economist's question seems "natural" enough. We have a straightforward and stark choice and we are told there is no way to avoid it. Either we expend "society's resources" on a ninety-year-old individual's hip replacement or we expend these resources on something else more valuable. The mathematics is simple. We have X amount of resources. Y equals the value of a ninety-year-old individual's hip replacement. Z equals other "more valuable uses of society's resources." The result is an obvious equation: $X = Y + Z$. If we increase expenditures on Y then we decrease possible expenditures for Z. But a little reflection and this apparently natural choice disappears, and we see how misleading and abstract it is because it hides its politics behind a putatively "natural" choice.

The first abstraction we encounter is in the terms of the comparison itself. We find "ninety-year-old individual's hip replacements" compared with "more valuable uses of resources." But the comparison assumes that all ninety-year-old people in need of hip replacements share a similar socioeconomic status. This is simply false. Some ninety-year-olds will have access to resources other than federal expenditures for health care. All such people should be exempted from the comparison. Then we realize that the comparison works only between those who depend on federal expenditures for their health care and other "more valuable uses of resources"; the comparison is between the poor and "more valuable uses of resources." Yet what are these "more valuable uses of resources"? What does "Z" represent? Nuclear armaments? Tobacco subsidies? Bicycle trails? Enterprise zones for inner cities? Expenditures for special prosecutors? Until we know what we are comparing, we simply are incapable of exercising any practical judgment.

This brings us to the second abstraction with which we meet. Who is the "we" that is assumed to make these practical determinations about the allocation of "society's resources"? We are asked which use of "society's resources" is more advantageous as if "we" had some direct political mechanism to make this determination. But of course "we" do not, and marginalism works on the assumption that we should not. No political mechanism should exist other

10. Joseph E. Stiglitz, *Economics*, 2nd ed. (New York: W. W. Norton, 1997), p. 920. Stiglitz has served as President Clinton's chairman of the council of economic advisers as well as chief economist at the World Bank.

than the choices of individual consumers. Choice is exercised by individuals, each of whom determines for herself what she wants, and the market merely acts as a neutral instrument to index those preferences by matching wants with products and services. Thus if either the elderly or those concerned about them find it useful to employ their resources for hip replacements, then the market will provide. The market will provide such services until the marginal utility of such an employment of resources is no longer viable; that is to say, until individual consumers determine that the employment of their limited resources for other services or products is of more use to them than hip replacements for ninety-year-olds.

These collected and indexed preferences are all that the marginalist economists can mean by "society's resources." Politically, the logic of their position entails that institutions refrain from social constraints on the market; otherwise, the "rationality" of marginal utility would be adversely affected. If the government, or some other institution, subsidizes hip replacements, then I as a consumer might be able to employ my resources for both my grandmother's hip replacement and my son's college education, not recognizing that this is an "irrational" employment of resources because the costs are hidden in such a way that I am not forced to allocate my own resources in the most efficient way possible. So to use the expression "society as a whole bears" is within a marginalist analysis both an abstraction and misleading. Few, if any, "social resources" exist, and "we" have no political mechanism to make judgments about the control of such resources other than as individual consumers.[11]

Of course, in the equation above X (the amount of resources available at a given time) is not indefinitely fixed. It may be fixed momentarily at the point where I must choose between utilizing my resources on hip replacements or on a child's education, but it is not fixed over time. The only possible alternative to difficult decisions between competing values is to increase X as much as possible. So the best possible answer to our social problems will always be increased economic growth. But here we see a contradiction, because the very same economists who argue that in the long term we must increase growth and that the advantage of capitalist society is that it is the most efficient form of wealth production also tell us that the means to achieve this most efficient form of production is by recognizing that we must choose in the present between our elders' hip replacements and our children's education or other "more valuable uses of resources."

---

11. The one exception would be through taxation, but what impacts us directly is the amount we will be taxed. We have little recourse as to how those taxes will be utilized, for all the political options present accept the basis of marginalist rationality.

So we are confronted with the economist's abstract logic: "These are difficult and unpleasant questions but as long as society as a whole bears the brunt of these costs . . . there is no way of avoiding them." But of course what we have discovered is that we do not have a society that bears the brunt of these costs and that economics works to prevent us from any concrete discernment about uses of resources other than as individual consumers. It permits us the privilege of avoiding social and political questions about the allocation of scarce resources. The purpose of the economist's question is not to exercise practical judgment about the expenditures of social resources; the question functions merely as a way to legitimate the economist's social and political starting point — we are all individuals who must make choices about scarce resources and the most efficient way to do this is to leave it to the "neutral" working of the market.

The market decides, and we must realize that the market is the most rational form of life available to us. We have no politics available to us that would allow us to live otherwise, for such a politics would require that questions such as "What is a good use of our resources?" could be answered. We would need some common conception of a good life for which people should aim. But this is precisely what our democratic process protects against.[12] Thus, the market is our only politics.

Once the market has become our politics, then we should not be surprised that we begin to speak of the elderly, aging, and death in terms intelligible within the market. To honor our elders is to submit them to the logic of the economist's rationality. We must now think of our elders as economic burdens whose care should be subject to the conditions of marginal utility. This is not because health care is "by nature" a scarce resource whereby choices must inevitably be made between hip replacements and children's education. This is a feature of our particular social order.

The Impending Social Security Crisis

Even those programs which could potentially be "social resources," such as Social Security, Medicare, and Medicaid, do not function within social and political arrangements whereby people can exercise practical judgments

---

12. For a fuller explanation of this point, see Michael Sandel's *Democracy's Discontent: America in Search of a Public Philosophy* (Cambridge, Mass.: Belknap Press of Harvard University Press, 1996), particularly his first chapter, "The Public Philosophy of Contemporary Liberalism," pp. 3-24.

about what constitutes a good expenditure of society's resources. The debates around all social security programs occur within the logic of marginalism. Economists tell us that federal expenditures for the elderly are currently $16,000 while they are only $1,200 for children under the age of eighteen.[13] Such figures raise questions about the optimal use of resources by an aging population. Of course, these figures are also abstractions that overlook the social and political context within which the elderly and children live. These federal expenditures to the elderly are the entitlements granted by Social Security and Medicare. The extent to which the economy can continue to provide these kinds of entitlements to the elderly is a question beguiling economic prognosticators.

We are told that the Social Security system in the United States faces an impending crisis. A number of factors account for this. First is the increase in life expectancy. In 1935 the expectation for those who had lived to sixty-five was that they would live another twelve years. In 1995 that expectation had increased to seventeen years and it is estimated that by 2040 it might climb as high as nineteen to twenty-one more years.[14] Such increased life expectancy places an added burden on Social Security, which has been a mixture between a "pay-as-you-go" model and a trust fund. The pay-as-you-go model works on the basis of economic transfers between current working generations and those who are retired. Increased life expectancy places burdens on the revenues that will need to be redistributed from the current working generation to those in retirement as well as on the funds available for the elderly.

Second, the numbers within, and the age of, the working generation have been decreasing at the same time that the numbers of the retired generation have been increasing. The past century's declining fertility rates have led to fewer persons available to support the elderly and thus restrict the potential for the pay-as-you-go system, creating more of a demand for a trust system.[15] That declining fertility rates pose serious intergenerational economic problems contains a curious irony, since both the classical liberal economists and the marginalists told us that population control (especially among the poor) was essential for a healthy economy. Fertility rates in the United States reflect the very measures economists urged on society. Now we are told that the success of this population control could place the ability to care for the elderly in jeopardy.

13. Stiglitz, *Economics*, p. 918.

14. Stiglitz, *Economics*, p. 916.

15. See P. A. Samuelson's "The Optimum Growth Rate for Population," in *International Economic Review* 16 (October 1975): 531-38.

A third reason for the possible impending crisis is that the trust system has been primarily placed in government bonds, which are used to finance the debt; thus the rate of return is not as high as it could be.

A fourth reason for the crisis is public opposition to increased taxation. To fix the system, some economists suggest, would require a 3 percent increase in taxes. But the suggestion of a tax increase in the current cultural climate is simply not possible.

A fifth reason for the crisis stems from changes in family and community structures and in the nature of work. As Angel and Angel state, "For most of human history, as is still the case for a large fraction of the world today, people worked until they could no longer participate in paid or domestic labor, and then they survived on the charity of family and community until they died."[16] This social practice, however, has now been replaced by a relatively new one known as "retirement" in which we hope to age free from charity doled out by family or community.[17]

The current practice of retirement has developed within the last fifty years and was brought on by changes in the family structure that resulted from capitalism. From 1947 to 1976 the "labor-force participation rate of men over 65 fell from 47.8% to 20.0%."[18] This declining participation ratio is not only for workers sixty-five and older; it is also found among workers between the ages of forty-five and sixty-five. As a social practice, retirement has been both forced and voluntary. Insofar as it has occurred through layoffs, plant closings, and shifts in labor employment resulting in changes from industrial production to a service economy, such retirements were forced. Insofar as it has occurred from choices made available because of private pension funds and Social Security, it is viewed as voluntary. Even if retirement is a function of choice, suggest the economists, it may still not be "utility maximizing," for many of these retirees are still capable of "produc-

16. Angel and Angel, *Who Will Care for Us?* p. 2.

17. One of the reasons for this loss of family structure is mobility, which works against the perseverance of family and community structures and is central to the logic of capitalism. Within capitalist society, people, like commodities, must be mobile. Without mobility strains are placed on the most efficient allocation of scarce resources, including labor. We all must go where the jobs are. While some of the technological achievements of the past few decades make it easier to maintain contact with family, these achievements have not allowed us to sustain a bodily presence to our elders. Current efforts underway to provide "elder care" long-distance are certainly one way the market allows some of us to address this issue, but such care remains a contractual arrangement between producers and consumers.

18. Disney, *Can We Afford to Grow Older?* p. 193. Most of my reflections on retirement are indebted to Disney's chapter, "Retirement: The Labor Supply of Older Workers in an Aging Society."

tive" services. Thus, incentives may be needed to entice the elderly to remain in the workforce.[19]

Social Security and private pension funds have made those who cease working less dependent on family and community structures. Sociologist Peter Laslett, however, views the decline of the family structure not as a loss but as a gain for the elderly. He suggests that the diminishment of the extended, residential family structure was necessary for the development of retirement because "the co-residential family group is very difficult to adapt to all the eventualities of the individual life course, and providing for old age seems to be beyond its capacities."[20] Co-residential families, he argues, produce dependency and intergenerational hostility. For the elderly to be free from such dependence they must first have sufficient means to sustain themselves separate from familial means. Intimacy at a distance, he suggests, is more conducive to healthy third-age living. Thus his "theory of the third age" suggests that retirement reflects a natural desire of the elderly to be independent from familial constraints, a state now made possible by capitalist society.[21]

Should those in the "third age" expect a comfortable, independent existence free from the burdens of family, work, and the needs of community life? What moral resources could we draw upon to answer such a question? Would provisions for such a life fulfill the religious obligation to honor one's elders? If this is a morally valid expectation, can the economy continue to support an elderly generation marked by increased longevity, higher medical bills, early retirement age, and fewer family and communal networks, by a declining

19. "An alternative view [to that of involuntary early retirement] is that the secular decline in labor-force participation rates, especially among elderly men, is an outcome of choice. For these individuals, the prospect of higher retirement income, stemming from (e.g.) the growth of private pensions and the ability to liquidate other assets such as housing equity, exceeds the utility derived from continued employment at an age when they might expect to live for another 25 years. Then the decision to retire is optimal for the individual. . . . In a 'forward-looking' (lifetime) model, the individual will evaluate the expected streams of earnings and nonwork income and the marginal utility of leisure per remaining period. This could lead still productive individuals to choose to forgo paid work. In such circumstances, it is hard to think of a social regime under which it would be desirable to force such individuals to work beyond their chosen retirement age. What is then needed, if the decline in the participation rates of the elderly is to be curtailed, is a structure of economic incentives that persuades the potential worker to continue working" (Disney, *Can We Afford to Grow Older?* p. 199).

20. Laslett, *Fresh Map of Life*, p. 125. For a historical analysis of retirement see his chapter, "Retirement and Its Social History," pp. 122-39.

21. Laslett writes, "In disposing of the myth that the English elderly in the past always lived and died surrounded by bevies of their relatives, we need not accept the belief that it would always and necessarily have been better for them if these had been the circumstances" (*Fresh Map of Life*, p. 126).

number of workers? Economists suggest that it can, that we face no economic crisis of aging;[22] but the economy will not be able to provide for the practice of retirement through the current re-distributive practices of Social Security. Only through increased private pensions will the economy continue to work for the elderly. But this of course raises the possibility of increased relative disparities between the poor and the rich. We face no economic crisis of aging, but we continue to suffer deep divisions between rich and poor, and these categories cannot be equated with working and retired.

Increased utilization of private pension plans is many economists' remedy for the problems brought to the economy by an aging population. Another possible remedy is to increase the power of the state. This seems to be a remedy more favorable to sociologists. "All of these changes mean that in the future the elderly will have little alternative but to turn to the state when they become dependent," write Angel and Angel.[23] But of course, turning to the state will also entail turning away from family and other community structures. Either the state or the market will give us the language to speak about preparing our elders to die. In the face of such a reality, preserving a theological language for aging is itself politically significant, for if it gives us nothing else, it can give us the moral resources by which our expectations of aging and dying should be formed.

Dying as a Participation in Charity: The Language of Theology

How can we relate theology to this socioeconomic analysis? The question is improperly stated. It assumes that economics is a technical science like auto mechanics, gall bladder surgery, or housing construction. Because these are neutral, technical disciplines we need not relate theology to them; nor should they encroach upon theological language. While this may be the case with carburetor adjustments, economics constantly surpasses its proper limits and imposes its logic on all aspects of human life; and theology must refuse to concede any intellectual space free from its own intrinsic logic. This is a necessary feature of Christian theology because it is a "meta discourse" that positions all other discourses within its own narrative order of creation and redemption. Any Christian theology which refuses to do this will cease

22. See Angel and Angel, *Who Will Care for Us?* pp. 150-53.

23. Angel and Angel, *Who Will Care for Us?* pp. 17-19. In fact, without federal intervention such as Social Security, "retirement" is not possible for many persons who were gainfully employed throughout their life. In 1990, 41 percent of retirees had nothing but Social Security to live on.

to express adequately its own internal logic and become dependent upon other discourses for its intelligibility.[24] Theologians on both the political left and right have denied this claim by making space for economics or social analysis as an autonomous sphere. But such concessions inevitably reduce theology to the status of the irrational, cultural, or valuational over against the factual.

All Things Fulfilled in Christ and Subject to His Authority

Christian theology cannot concede space to other intellectual disciplines because the logic of theology arises from a universal meta-claim (always mediated historically) that Christ is Lord and that such lordship cannot be superseded. The strength of a theological analysis of aging is that it explicitly gives us what economics conceals — a common conception of a good life for which people should aim and to which judgments about good uses of resources can and should be subordinate. This is because no higher authority exists than Christ's. Thus no intellectual discourse can position theology within some authoritative structure other than the logic of Christ's sacrifice. As Karl Barth put it,

> His sacrifice meant the closing of the time of the divine holding back, the time of the mere passing over of human sins endlessly repeating themselves, the time of the alternation of divine grace and divine judgment, in which human priests had their function and the offerings made by men had a meaning. His sacrifice means that the time of being has dawned in place of that of signifying — of the being of man as a faithful partner in covenant with God, and therefore of his being at peace with God and therefore of the being of the man reconciled with Him and converted to Him. We are told in Jn. 19:28 concerning the crucified Jesus that He knew "that now all things were finished (tetêlestai)." And His last word when He died was "it is finished (tetê-

24. I recognize that many theologians would find this claim objectionable, but I find John Milbank's argument in *Theology and Social Theory: Beyond Secular Reason* (Cambridge, Mass.: Basil Blackwell, 1991) convincing on this point. Milbank writes, "The pathos of modern theology is its false humility. For theology, this must be a fatal disease, because once theology surrenders its claim to be a meta-discourse, it cannot any longer articulate the word of the creator God, but is bound to turn into the oracular voice of some finite idol. . . . If theology no longer seeks to position, qualify or criticize other discourses, then it is inevitable that these discourses will position theology: for the necessity of an ultimate organizing logic cannot be wished away" (p. 1).

lestai)" (John 19:30). Jesus knew what God knew in the taking place of His sacrifice. And Jesus said what God said: that what took place was not something provisional, but that which suffices to fulfill the divine will, that which is entire and perfect, that which cannot and need not be continued or repeated or added to or superseded, the new thing which was the end of the old but which will itself never become old, which can only be there and continue and shine out and have force and power as that which is new and eternal.[25]

In the all-sufficient, unsurpassable sacrifice of Christ, Christian theology suggests, *all things* are completed. Nothing escapes the force of the "all things" here, all things have received their proper end. Christ's sacrifice is the "perfect redemption."[26] The logic of this perfect redemption is such that all other intellectual discourses must be positioned in terms of its truth and never vice versa.

While theological engagement with other intellectual discourses must position all other discourses within its own internal logic, it must also reflect the nature of its own logic, which is Christ's sacrifice, and not become a form of tyranny. As Milbank reminds us, "There is a continuity between Jesus' refusal of any seizure of power and the early church's refusal to overthrow existing structures, in favor of the attempt to create alternative ones, as local areas of relative peace, charity and justice."[27] This continuity should exist not only between Jesus and the early church; it must be a permanent feature of the church's life, for it is intrinsic to the logic of the gospel. The task of relating theology to economics is not then to overthrow the existing structures in some cataclysmic revolutionary act. We are not waiting for the proletariat to rise up and control the means of production through a violent seizure of power any more than we are waiting for the free market to work its miracle and provide its always-not-yet-achieved wealth of nations. Neither are we waiting for the imposition of some "righteous" theocracy. Instead, the theological task is to create space for faithful Christian practice wherever that space can be found and whatever the consequences entailed in the production of such a space. For this reason, a theology of aging need not begin by re-

---

25. Karl Barth, *Church Dogmatics* IV.I.

26. The language comes from the Anglican and the United Methodist Articles of Religion. The expression is ecumenical. I do not intend to eclipse the "not-yet" character of this eschatological claim into a fully realized eschatology. The very effort to subordinate an economic analysis of aging to theological considerations is a sign of the "not-yet" character present in these claims.

27. Milbank, *Theology and Social Theory*, p. 116.

sponding to the economists' and sociologists' analysis. They should seek to be relevant to theology and never vice versa.

Christian theological reflection does not begin with the allocation of scarce resources among individuals; it begins with the appropriate distribution of the fullness of life Christ offers in his cross and resurrection. This claim must be something more than pious sentiment if theology is to matter substantively. By beginning with the fullness of life Christ offers I am not denying the possibility of tragic conflicts; we still might need to tell ninety-year-olds that hip replacements are not the appropriate use of our resources. Such judgments, however, will be based on an understanding of an ecclesial mission subject to Christ's authority and not simply on the abstract calculations of marginal utility, which always hide politics behind "usefulness."

Jesus' fullness of life breaks the boundaries of race, class, family, and nation to produce a new form of social reproduction which we call "church." The church is the visible inauguration of God's reign, which is both founded by Jesus in his teachings, death, and resurrection and endowed with certain sacramental structures by which all people are called to Jesus' ongoing mission through participation in his life. Jesus' actions reveal to us the role our elders have within the new community he has established. They provide the context within which we can faithfully honor our elders. Jesus provides this by fulfilling the law revealed to Moses on Mount Sinai.

When Jesus tells us that the entirety of the law is fulfilled in the commandment to love God and our neighbor, he is directing us to the realization of the Torah revealed at Sinai to Moses and now fulfilled in him.[28] This does not constitute a decisive break with Israel, but retells the story from the perspective of Christ as the one who decisively brings and enacts God's reign.[29]

---

28. See Thomas Aquinas, *Summa Theologiae* I-II.108.

29. Oliver O'Donovan has persuasively narrated the political implications of Christ's victory in his *The Desire of the Nations: Rediscovering the Roots of Political Theology* (Cambridge: Cambridge University Press, 1997). He notes that "The kingly rule of Christ is God's own rule exercised over the whole world. It is visible in the life of the church, but not only there. St. Paul declared that God has 'disarmed the principalities and powers and made a public show of them in Christ's triumphal procession' (Col. 2:15). That must be the primary eschatological assertion about the authorities, political and demonic, which govern the world: they have been made subject to God's sovereignty in the Exaltation of Christ. The second qualifying assertion is that this awaits a final universal presence of Christ to become fully apparent. Within the framework of these two assertions there opens up an account of secular authority which presumes neither that the Christ-event occurred nor that the sovereignty of Christ is now transparent and uncontested" (p. 146). O'Donovan then narrates how secular authority both submits to and contests Christ's rule. Something like O'Donovan's argument must also be made with respect to the family. As Christ subjects, and will subject, all nations to his authority, so

All social, political, and economic institutions are now subjected to the authority of Christ. We can begin to see how this works for the family, and the care of the elderly, by observing the odd way Christ fulfills the fourth commandment — honor your father and mother.

Honoring Our Elders

Law is never an end in itself; if it were, obedience would be arbitrary, it would mean merely observing commandments. Law directs human actions to virtuous ends; it assumes a virtuous life as the context for its intelligibility. Law without virtue is capricious; virtue without law lacks direction. Jesus presents to Christians the social and political life that directs our actions toward virtuous ends. When we examine the fourth commandment, however, the social life Jesus presents to us seems to contradict rather than complete the commandment. His treatment of his elders appears dishonorable.

Luke tells the story of Jesus' disappearance from his parents' care for three days to spend time in the temple. When Mary finds him and says, "Son, why have you treated us so? Behold your father and I have been looking for you anxiously," Jesus' response is, "How is it that you sought me? Did you not know that I must be in my Father's house?" (Luke 2:48-49). Jesus dismisses his parents' anxiety as unwarranted, and this is not the only occasion on which Jesus seems dismissive of his family. Mark records Jesus' response to the announcement that his mother and brothers are waiting for him as "Who are my mother and my brothers? . . . Here are my mother and my brothers! Whoever does the will of God is my brother, and sister, and mother" (Mark 3:31-35). In their narration both Matthew and Luke seem to soften this encounter by retaining Jesus' words but not juxtaposing them to his mother's search quite so severely (Matt. 12:46-50; Luke 8:19-21); yet both Matthew and Luke record a statement of Jesus against the family that Mark does not have. Luke puts it in its starkest form: "If anyone comes to me and does not hate his own father and mother and wife and children and brothers and sisters, yes, and even his own life, he cannot be my disciple" (Luke 14:26; see also Matt. 10:37-39).

Both Matthew and Luke record one of Jesus' harshest sayings against the family, when he turns to a disciple who wants to bury his father and says, "Follow me, and leave the dead to bury their own dead" (Matt. 8:22; Luke

---

also does he, and will he, subject the family. To understand how he subjects the family to his authority we must be attentive to the scriptural narratives that characterize the subordination of the family to Christ's mission.

9:60). Such statements do not seem to hold forth much promise for any attempt to develop a theology of aging and dying. John's Gospel likewise recounts a shocking statement of Jesus to his mother when she tells him that the wine has run out at a marriage at Cana in Galilee: Jesus says, "O woman, what have you to do with me? My hour has not yet come" (John 2:4). So we find in Scripture multiple attestations from diverse sources that Jesus acted almost dishonorably toward his own elders. The urgency of his mission seems to leave little room for a theology focused on the needs and concerns of the elderly, including the needs of his own parents.

Jesus' harsh actions toward his elders, however, need to be supplemented with the poignant scene in John's Gospel when Jesus, suffering on the cross, saw his mother and John "standing near" and said to Mary, "Woman, behold, your son!" and to John, "Behold your mother!" (John 19:26-27). This agonizing scene does not contradict the harsh ones mentioned earlier. Rather, it sets them in an appropriate order. In fact, this scene occurs right before Jesus remarks, "It is finished" (tetêlestai). The bequeathment of his mother to the disciple is part of Jesus' completion of all things. From this we learn that the family has been restructured and brought into submission to the authority of Christ. Beneath the suffering of the cross, John receives Jesus' mother and provides a space for her in his own home.

This scene can serve us well in our efforts to think about an appropriate theology of aging and death. Raniero Cantalamessa explains its significance well: "Beneath the cross, Mary therefore appears as the daughter of Zion, who after the death and loss of her sons received a new and more numerous family from God, but by the Spirit and not the flesh."[30] The fourth commandment is fulfilled not by dishonoring the family, but by restructuring it. Just as there is no longer male nor female, Jew nor Gentile, slave nor free in the community of faith, so there is also neither parent nor child. As Jesus commanded, all the faithful are to be brothers, sisters, and mothers to one another. This commandment assumes the virtues of charity and hope. Charity is present because we must take others into our homes, and provide for them out of our resources, as John did for Mary. Hope is present because death will not leave the widowed and orphaned abandoned. Within the church, they are to find new homes. Our use of resources must bear witness to this new reality that is made present beneath the cross.

That we are to be brothers and sisters to one another is easily explained, but that we are to be mothers is certainly surprising. This surprised St. Augus-

---

30. Raniero Cantalamessa, Mary: Mirror of the Church, trans. Frances Lonergan Villa (Collegeville, Minn.: Liturgical Press, 1992), p. 121.

tine such that he wrote, "I understand that we are Christ's brethren and that the holy and faithful women are Christ's sisters. But how can we be mothers of Christ?" Augustine did not let his puzzlement prevent him from using the expression and he explained it ecclesiologically.

> Who gave you birth? I hear the voice of your hearts answering "Mother Church!" This holy and honored mother, like Mary, gave birth and is virgin. . . . The members of Christ give birth, therefore, in the Spirit, just as the Virgin Mary gave birth to Christ in her womb: in this way you will be mothers of Christ. This is not something that is out of your reach; it is not beyond you, it is not incompatible with you; you have become children, be mothers as well.[31]

St. Augustine also finds in Jesus' bequeathment of John and Mary to each other evidence of his humanity and divinity. The harsh sayings of Jesus toward his elders represent for Augustine Jesus' divinity; they reveal that Jesus is not bound by biological ties to the family. Jesus' bequeathment, on the other hand, evidences his humanity. "Then it was, as a man on the cross, that He acknowledged His human mother and commended her in a most human fashion to the Apostle he loved most."[32] The love for his mother was natural and more; it was also supernatural. And thus it was grounded in grace, in his freedom to love through and beyond the biological ties of family. It was not necessary; it was gift.

The bequeathment of Mary and John to one another occurs prior to Jesus' proclamation, "It is finished." The all-sufficient sacrifice on the cross includes Christ's restructuring of the family so that our duties toward the elderly are no longer merely obligations to biological family. Instead, the family is expanded. To honor one's parents is for John to take Mary into his home now that she has lost her son. To honor one's parents is also to honor those who are parents to us in the faith. Our obligations to our parents include not only that we be children to them but parents as well. Vice versa, parents' obligation to their children includes not only the role of parenting but also a readiness to allow our children to be mothers to us, to birth in us faith. This does not imply any disrespect for our own parents, for as Jesus made preparations for his mother on

---

31. St. Augustine, *Sermons* 72A; quoted in Cantalamessa, *Mary: Mirror*, p. 69.

32. Augustine, *Faith and the Creed*, p. 325. St. Augustine also finds in the relationship between Jesus and his mother evidence for God's love and redemption of both sexes. "We must likewise repudiate those who deny that the Lord Jesus Christ had Mary for His mother on earth, since His temporal plan ennobled each sex, both male and female. By possessing a male nature and being born of woman He further showed by this plan that God has concern not only for the sex He represented but also for the one through which He took upon Himself our nature."

the cross, so he teaches us that disciples are to prepare such a place for their own parents within the community of faith.[33] Nor does this imply that "Mary" stands as some symbol for the "elderly" per se. Mary is,

> as St. Ambrose taught, . . . a type of the church in the order of faith, charity, and perfect union with Christ. For in the mystery of the Church, which is itself rightly called mother and virgin, the Blessed Virgin stands out in eminent and singular fashion as exemplar both of virgin and mother. Through her faith and obedience she gave birth on earth to the very Son of the Father, not through the knowledge of man but by the overshadowing of the Holy Spirit, in the manner of a new Eve who placed her faith, not in the serpent of old but in God's messenger without wavering in doubt. The Son whom she brought forth is he whom God placed as the first born among many brethren (Rom. 8:29), that is, the faithful, in whose generation and formation she cooperates with a mother's love.
>
> The Church indeed contemplating her hidden sanctity, imitating her charity, and faithfully fulfilling the Father's will, by receiving the word of God in faith becomes herself a mother.[34]

By her faithfulness, Mary is mother to us all. She is the symbol of the church and a symbol of the restructuring of family bonds.

The way we think, speak, and act concerning our aging, and the aging of our elders as well, should reflect that the family has now been restructured and subordinated to the authority of Christ as have "all things." The well-known description of Mary as the "daughter of her son" reflects the completed ordering of the family. This restructuring of the family should become our politics and provide us with the language we use in speaking of preparing our elders, and ourselves, to die.

Languages in Conflict

Once we begin not with the abstract calculations of marginalism but with a theological politics where all things are, and shall be, subordinated to the au-

---

33. That the disciple took Jesus' bequeathment seriously can be seen in the Acts of the Apostles where Luke tells us that Mary was with the disciples when they returned to Jerusalem after the Ascension (Acts 1:12-14).

34. *Lumen Gentium,* in *Vatican Council II: The Conciliar and Post Conciliar Documents,* ed. Austin Flannery (Collegeville, Minn.: Liturgical Press, 1981), para. 63-64.

thority of Christ, we do not then have ready-made answers to perceived economic problems of aging. Instead, what we have is a different context within which arguments and concrete determinations could take place.

1. An alternative space must be created.

The first theological task in preparing our elders to die is to create some alternative space where the elderly can be cared for within the context of the ecclesial community. Only such a space allows for theology to circumscribe the language of aging and dying with its own logic. Such a space will include subordinating all our needs to the authority of Christ and the ecclesial mission. It involves duties and habits of preparation which recognize our sufferings and those of our parents as purposive; they fulfill what is lacking in the all-sufficient sacrifice of Christ (Col. 1:24).

Theology must not accommodate the analysis of aging to either the economists or the sociologists. Instead, it should show the abstract nature of their arguments as well as their hidden political and social valuations. Aging cannot be adequately assessed solely on the basis of marginal utility, for usefulness per se does not give us sufficient resources to exercise concrete determinations necessary for the sake of our ecclesial mission. As St. Thomas stated, an action is useful because it is directed to an end.[35] Until we know that end we cannot properly speak of the useful. To speak of the useful without knowledge of any end is foundational to marginalism. This is why it always reduces politics to market considerations. Christians should not countenance such a political reductionism. Our politics must bear witness to the end of all creation present in Christ. This entails that economic considerations find their purpose in the ecclesial mission, which is to be a sign and foretaste of the subordination of all things to Christ. Such a mission does not give us a priori principles about whether we as the elderly, or the elderly entrusted to our care in hospitals, nursing homes, and families, should be given hip replacements. But it could provide a political context within which such a debate could take shape. We can begin to ask questions such as, "Must we practice medicine in such a way that it is viewed as a scarce natural resource?"

The "we" here takes on some definitiveness in its reference to people of faith bound together into a catholic unity serving a common mission. We can now ask in a concrete way, "What 'other valuable resources' could serve our mission better?" Free medical clinics in the inner city? Perhaps we could ask our suburban elderly to forego such operations for the sake of some greater mission, thus extending the life of charity.

35. Aquinas, *Summa Theologiae* I-II.7.2 ad 1.

2. The healing power of the resurrection is essential.

At the same time that subjection to the authority of Christ recognizes a place for suffering, and recognizes that suffering does not diminish the life of charity, it also must bear witness to the healing power brought by the resurrection. Suffering is not the only enemy we know, but it remains an enemy. As Mary always had a place among the disciples, should we not expect that our parents will also receive a place where sons and daughters will tend to them? Such "tending" will seek to diminish the pain associated with aging and dying as much as possible. Death and its entourage is no friend; it remains an enemy, and one that was vanquished in the cross and resurrection even if it is not yet fully vanquished. For this reason we must not sacrifice our elderly to the idols of a false security. When a ninety-year-old foregoes a hip replacement and endures suffering for her last few years, and the Pentagon is granted more money than it requested, then we can be sure we have denied the healing power of the resurrection.

3. No solution can be found in the biological family (or the state or the market).

The church should never rest content with a care for the elderly situated in the biological family, the market, or the state. There may be some truth to Laslett's contention that co-residential families create intergenerational hostility rather than structures for virtuous living; yet Christians need not fear such revelations about the family since it has been restructured, and we need not hold romantic illusions about it. Nevertheless, Laslett's replacement of charity by earned assets and autonomy is problematic, for the community of faith has as part of its task the charitable redistribution of its resources to care for those who no longer have them. A system of care such as Social Security, insofar as it redistributes wealth across biological family lines, reflects more an appropriate subjection to Christ's authority over the family than does either leaving such care to the family alone or leaving such care to individual earnings. Nevertheless, not even the state is entrusted with the charisma to restructure the family along the lines of God's reign. That is the task of the church alone, a task it accomplishes through the sacrament of baptism. The church must assist in the practice of redistribution so that needs are met rather than wants satiated. This has been an ancient teaching of the church,[36]

---

36. See Acts 2-5. A similar sentiment is found in Catholic teaching on the church: "in accordance with the venerable example of former times, bishops should gladly extend their fraternal assistance, in the fellowship of an all-pervading charity, to other Churches, especially to neighboring ones and to those most in need of help" (*Lumen Gentium*, para. 23).

and it implies that families within the church should recognize Christ's authority over their resources. By providing for those who cannot provide for themselves, the church fulfills the pentecostal mission.

4. The threat to God's rule is not the division between the elderly and the young but between the rich and the poor.
The serious threat to God's rule is not the disparity that exists between young and old in our churches but that between poor and rich. Only insofar as the elderly are found among the broader category known as the poor should they be entitled to charitable provisions. While our Social Security system may be facing a crisis, this does not necessarily translate into any "crisis of aging" per se.[37] The crisis is between the increasing relative distance between rich and poor, both culturally and economically. The church cannot begin to address the problems of the elderly poor only during their "third age"; such problems must be addressed from birth. The crisis for the church is that this economic disparity is insufficiently challenged; instead, it is reflected in the church's increasing divisions based on class interests.

5. The elderly are not individuals in a calculation of burden.
The elderly must not be treated as individuals in a calculation of burden of dependency — even in a technical sense. They are persons who by virtue of their baptism were granted gifts for the upbuilding of the church. Baptism, like ordination, brings with it lifelong tasks. The goal of the Christian life is not leisure, forced or voluntary, at the end of life, but faithful service. This must be demanded from the faithful even when we rejoice with them in their cessation of work as daily toil.

6. We must think again about the creation of an alternative practice.
But all of this requires the creation of an alternative space where Christians would practice medicine and care for the elderly in ways that we do not yet

37. See Disney, "Some Salient Conclusions" (chap. 11 in *Can We Afford to Grow Older?*), where he argues, "There is not a crisis of aging." He suggests, "It is common to blame 'aging' for the budget deficits and payroll-tax increases associated with social security programs in the 1980's. But the sources of these (correctly perceived) crises have little to do with aging per se. In pay-as-you-go social insurance, financing crises have far more to do with the chain-letter or Ponzi-scheme nature of such programs as practiced by governments and voters, which precommit future generations to excessive forced transfers" (pp. 307-8). While he reassures us that aging itself is not the problem we face, his prediction that increased private pension plans will increasingly replace Social Security is not so reassuring, for this will only exacerbate the class divisions between the poor and others.

see prevalent in contemporary church life. Such alternative arrangements are present both within the church's ministries and outside of them. The church could learn from community-based health care such as the On Lok program in San Francisco's Chinatown, where medical and social services are provided to the elderly so that they can remain in their own homes and community.[38] Insofar as the church has a financial interest in the proliferation of nursing homes for the well-to-do elderly it will be hampered in its ability to subject even our family relationships to the authority of Christ. This poses a serious problem for any theological analysis of the economics of aging, for the conflict between theology and economics occurs not at some abstract level of linguistic differences; it must be a conflict of languages made necessary by ecclesial practice. If such concrete practice is not forthcoming, we will have no alternative but to use the dominant language of the market; our dying will be described in terms of the burden of dependency.

38. See Angel and Angel, *Who Will Care for Us?* pp. 150-53.

The Last Gift: The Elderly, the Church, and the Gift of a Good Death

JOEL JAMES SHUMAN

Any definition of health that is not silly must include death. The world of love includes death, suffers it, and triumphs over it. The world of efficiency is defeated by death; at death, all its instruments and its procedures stop. The world of love continues, and of this grief is the proof.

WENDELL BERRY

One short sleep past, we wake eternally,
And death shall be no more; death, thou shalt die.

JOHN DONNE

The distorted and altogether circular logic of the relationship between aging and death in our culture is this: Because we know that it is old people who most often die, we fear becoming old or being long in the presence of those who are old, for we fear death. But one of the reasons we fear death is that we have no sense or experience of what it might mean for us or someone else to have a good death. And we have no sense or experience of what it might mean to have a good death in part because we have separated ourselves from those who are in the process of dying — usually the elderly — by allowing them to be placed in institutions and cared for by professionals, often long before death comes. Their deaths are frequently unnecessarily protracted, lonely, and miserable; we know (or at least we suspect) this, and so we stay away from them, because we fear seeing ourselves and our own deaths reflected back to us in their eyes. Thus at the very time our participation in their lives and theirs in ours could make the most difference for us and for them, we abandon them, and with them the possibility that things might be different. The cycle of fear and alienation with respect to death is perpetuated, seemingly without end or hope for an end, and we continue to believe that death is absolutely the worst thing that can happen to us, something alien to life, something to be avoided or at the very least controlled.[1]

This logic constitutes a powerful force that penetrates nearly every aspect of modern life. It is a force that the Christian church must strive to oppose. Because Christ has triumphed over death, rising on Easter morning as the first fruits of the new creation, those baptized into his body, the church, live with the hope that they too may be raised from death to life. Because death no longer must be experienced as terror and judgment, we need no longer flee in fear from the prospect of death, especially as it presents itself to us in the lives of the sick and the elderly.[2] We are free to imagine ways to help those within and beyond our community to die well, and to do so in our presence. In so doing we are formed as members of a people who bear witness in our common life to the fact that death is defeated, and that, in the words of John Donne, we look with hope to the time when death itself shall die.

Such imaginings must begin, however, with the admission that in spite of the grace that has been made available to us, we scarcely know how to begin. For how can we speak in concrete terms of a good death, having never experienced such a thing? I am past forty years old and have written about these things on more than one occasion; I have experienced the death of more than one person for whom I have cared deeply. But none of these deaths could by any stretch of the imagination be called "good."[3]

---

1. Sherwin Nuland, *How We Die: Reflections on Life's Final Chapter* (New York: Alfred A. Knopf, 1994), pp. 254-55. Nuland explains that 80 percent of all deaths in America occur in hospitals, a fact he attributes partly (following Philippe Aries) to the general inability of our modern culture to stomach the harsh realities associated with the process of dying. See also Robert C. Atchley, *Social Forces and Aging*, seventh ed. (Belmont, Calif.: Wadsworth, 1994), pp. 349-57. To this general removal of ourselves from death as a daily reality, we can juxtapose our immersion in the surreality of death as depicted by popular media. Ray Anderson remarks that "we are a society that views more simulated deaths on television in a few days than most of our ancestors confronted real deaths in a life-time!" He goes on to say that the average child in 1971 had seen by age fourteen about eighteen thousand television deaths (think how this number must have grown since), yet could not be expected to experience the death of someone close to him for the next forty years (*Theology, Death, and Dying* [New York: Basil Blackwell, 1986], p. 21).

2. Anderson, *Theology, Death, and Dying*, pp. 3-13; 56-59.

3. I am not suggesting by my use of the term "good death" that death itself should be regarded as a good. I have no interest in arguing one side or the other of this very complex philosophical and theological question. Rather, I mean to suggest that there are better and worse

This is not to say that the distorted way we think about aging and dying has gone unnoticed. Daniel Callahan has considered these matters as thoughtfully as anyone, and he is persuaded that where the care of the dying elderly is concerned, contemporary American culture has arrived at a point of crisis.[4] The problem, as he sees it, is that we have lost our sense of what constitutes a "natural" life span; consequently, we tend uncritically to pursue the extension of biological life without regard to its quality.[5] We need, he argues, to develop an account of the medical care of the elderly in which "the proper goal of medicine for those who have already lived out a natural life span ought to be the relief of suffering rather than the extension of life."[6]

On one level, Callahan's arguments are extremely powerful and deserve serious consideration. From a theological perspective, however, they are problematic, in the sense that it is not altogether clear that we can ever agree about precisely what a "natural life span" is. We can say, on the one hand, that when a person is no longer able truly to live she should be permitted to die; but such a claim requires that we understand clearly what it means "truly to live." But this is an understanding that is not simply a matter of intuition or individual desire but of moral agreement. Apart from a substantive, commonly held account of the proper goods and the good of human life, we simply cannot say whether or not a person is finished living.

Nevertheless, Callahan does have a point when he suggests we need to learn to think differently about these matters. Perhaps the best place to begin thinking differently is to consider why we think the way we do *now* about death and aging, to think about why the notion of a good death seems to so many of us so nonsensical.[7] In what follows, I want to suggest that the modern logic of aging and death is shaped by a constellation of (at least) three forces, each of which is mutually interdependent with the other two. First, we can describe in late modernity a steadily increasing trend toward what has been called the biomedicalization of death. This trend treats aging and dying as akin to diseases, as phenomena fundamentally alien to life and therefore to

---

ways of dying and of caring for the dying, ways that are more or less consistent with our most basic convictions about how we are to live.

4. Daniel Callahan, *Setting Limits: Medical Goals in an Aging Society* (New York: Simon and Schuster, 1987).

5. Callahan, *Setting Limits*, pp. 160-64.

6. Callahan, *Setting Limits*, p. 160.

7. By putting the matter in this precise way I do not mean to suggest that the theological problem of the fallen human experience of death as terror and judgment is not in some sense transcultural; I simply want to attend especially to the ways that problem tends to be instantiated in our own culture.

be controlled or, if possible, defeated by medical technology. Second, we can identify a progressively growing hegemony exercised by our capitalist political economy. This force shapes us to think of ourselves and others as "normal" or not primarily in terms of the capacity to participate in cycles of production and consumption, a tendency with devastating consequences for our relationships to those who are aging and dying. Finally, we can show the gradual erosion of the practices and the moral significance of those tradition-bearing communities which, until very recently, were the carriers of alternative practices of dying and caring for the elderly and dying. It is this erosion, finally, that leads us to think in such a severely attenuated way about the so-called "ethics" attending the ways we care for those facing the end of their lives.

The Medicalization of Aging and Death

In laying certain of our culture's distorted ways of thinking and acting about aging and death at the feet of modern medicine, it is important that we do so in a way that does not divorce medicine from the whole cultural fabric of late modernity. We cannot, in other words, simply "blame it on the doctors"; to a very significant extent medicine *is* a cultural phenomenon. Medicine's understandings of the body and what happens to the body as it ages, and especially of how we should respond to those changes, are formed *by* the culture it serves nearly as much as those understandings *form* the culture. Hannah Arendt made a point very much like this one when she said in her reflections on the scientific and technological explosion characterizing the second half of the twentieth century that there is a sense in which science has but "realized and affirmed what men anticipated in dreams that were neither wild nor idle."[8]

This assertion notwithstanding, it is certainly possible to say that medicine has been one of the more significant carriers of modernity's largely uncritical positivist turn. This is especially true of medicine's assumption of one form or another of the body-as-machine metaphor, which is at least partly responsible for the ways we have come in this culture to think about aging and death.[9]

8. Hannah Arendt, *The Human Condition*, second ed. (Chicago: University of Chicago Press, 1998), p. 2.

9. Sharon Kaufman speaks of the "biomedicalization of aging," explaining that this trend "is thought to result from the dominance of scientific models for understanding the life course

The modern habit of thinking of the body as being like a machine probably has its origins in Descartes' assertion that the mind, which he believed was
free, active, and immaterial, is the true locus of human being and agency,
while the body, which he saw as material and altogether passive, is something
other than the agent herself. Because the body is material and passive, Descartes believed the body was explicable solely in terms of certain irreducible
mechanical laws.[10] So understood, the body could easily be seen as what is,
according to Alasdair MacIntyre, "an object for or an exemplification of the
results of scientific research."[11]

With the rise of scientific medicine, the assumption of the body-as-
machine metaphor led to the understanding that illness is best described as a
contamination or failure of one of the machine's constitutive parts. This notion, which Dubos called the "doctrine of specific etiology," has provided the
basis for many of modern medicine's greatest achievements.[12] It also, however, has led to the uncritical assumption that the body and those forces that
afflict it — including aging and death — are finally understandable primarily
in terms of simple, efficient causality.[13] Because death, like disease, is primarily understood to be the result of particular efficient causes, and because
medicine is directed toward ferreting out and eliminating such causes, there
arises in the culture a generalized, vague sense that medicine should have as
one of its primary goals the cure of death itself, and that in the interim, medicine should do all it can to extend life and to better understand precisely why
we grow old and die. Thus, says Sherwin Nuland, "modern biomedicine has
. . . contributed to the misguided fancy by which each of us denies the certain
advent of our own individual mortality."[14]

In order to illustrate this tendency, Nuland refers to the peculiar concern
of modern medicine to identify in every case the "cause of death," a concern

---

and the use of proliferating biomedical technologies for solving the problems of disease associated with old age" ("Intensive Care, Old Age, and the Problem of Death in America," *The Geron-
tologist* 38, no. 6 [1998]: 721). For an account of the ways positivism became — and continues to
be — a foundational part of the thought world of modern medicine, see James P. Browder,
"Elected Suffering: Toward a Theology for Medicine" (Ph.D. diss., Duke University, 1991).

10. Owen Flanagan, *The Science of the Mind*, second ed. (Cambridge, Mass.: MIT Press,
1991), pp. 1-11. Cf. Browder, "Elected Suffering," pp. 66-68; 87.

11. Alasdair MacIntyre, "Medicine Aimed at the Care of Persons Rather Than What?" in
Philosophical Medical Ethics: Its Nature and Significance, ed. H. T. Engelhardt and S. F. Spicker
(Dordrecht, Holland: D. Reidel, 1977), p. 90.

12. Peter E. S. Freund and Meredith B. McGuire, *Health, Illness and the Social Body: A Critical Sociology* (Englewood Cliffs, N.J.: Prentice Hall, 1991), p. 227.

13. Nuland, *How We Die*, pp. 70, 72.

14. Nuland, *How We Die*, p. 10.

that is shaped by and reflected in the federal government's annual "Advance Report of Final Mortality Statistics." In that report, he says, one cannot locate

> a listing for those among us who just fade away. In its obsessive tidiness, the Report assigns the specific clinical category of some fatal pathology for every octo- and nonogenarian in its neat columns. . . . Everybody is required to die of a named entity, by order not only of the Department of Health and Human Services, but also of the global fiat of the World Health Organization. In thirty-five years as a licensed physician, I have never had the temerity to write "Old Age" on a death certificate, knowing that the form would be returned to me with a terse note from some official record-keeper informing me that I had broken the law. Everywhere in the world, it is illegal to die of old age.[15]

This is not to say that acknowledging old age as a "legitimate" cause of death would solve this particular problem. So long as we presume that death is alien to life, making aging a cause of death does little more than make aging itself a pathology to be investigated and cured.[16] The emphasis remains on the control and cure of death rather than with guiding its performance; medical science remains more enamored with discovering the molecular-chemical or genetic bases for aging and age-related physiological changes than with developing ways to assist the human passage into aging and death. Thus by virtue of its strong desire to improve the quality of human life, medicine is in the case of those who are aging ironically contributing to what amounts (from the perspective of Christianity, at least) to a heretical hope that we are moving by force of technological progress toward a day when — to refer once again to the words of John Donne — "death shall be no more."

Market Hegemony

A second great force shaping our contemporary attitudes toward aging and death is the free-market capitalist political economy that is so much a part of our lives. Increasingly, we live in a world shaped by the ideology of the market, an ideology that trains us to be acquisitive people who are constituted primarily by our desires for commodities and who understand ourselves to be connected to others only in very narrowly specified ways. In an essay dis-

---

15. Nuland, *How We Die*, p. 43.

16. Atchley (*Social Forces and Aging*, pp. 69-71) suggests this is a central development in modernity.

cussing barriers to genuine practices of caring in contemporary American culture, Charles Taylor observes that there is an inextricable link between market economies and a type of procedural liberalism that "does not concern itself with substantive goals in people's lives, but rather acts as a traffic director coordinating resources that enable people to work toward their own life goals."[17] This political philosophy, he explains, produces a cult of the individual "that understands social relations and larger social entities as put together by the choices and actions of individuals. This deeply entrenched philosophical vision holds individual freedom — negative freedom — as the highest value."[18]

Yet, as Taylor goes on to suggest, negative freedom is just that — negative. "Freedom from" is not freedom in any absolute sense, but freedom *for* something else. The rather illusory self-identification of people first of all as autonomous agents who are essentially unencumbered by substantive commitments to others is an integral part of the success of capitalist political economies. Indeed, our contemporary culture shapes us to believe this about ourselves, that we are more than anything else "getters and spenders" who are identified by ourselves and others "only as a unit of consumption or of labor."[19] Being effective producer-consumers requires of us an infinite flexibility, for producer-consumers

> must not be tied to place, but prepared to move to follow employment. They must not be tied by time, but prepared to work all hours and days of the week, especially Sundays. It follows that they must not be tied to any particular group of people or community: that they have families, even, is of no social significance since it is of no significance in the market, except as distracting from their flexibility. . . . They are in short to be dismembered, reduced to a series of functions that they exercise in accordance with no principles of continuity of their own choosing but only with the demands of the market. For only in this way can they meet the increasing and changing variety of the desires of the consumers. But who are the consumers? None other than the workers themselves. The assumption behind the demand for flexibility

17. Charles Taylor, "Philosophical Reflections on Caring Practices," in *The Crisis of Care: Affirming and Restoring Caring Practices in the Helping Professions,* ed. Susan Phillips and Patricia Benners (Washington, D.C.: Georgetown University Press, 1994), p. 176.

18. Taylor, "Philosophical Reflections on Caring Practices," p. 177.

19. Nicholas Boyle, *Who Are We Now?: Christian Humanism and the Global Market from Hegel to Heaney* (Notre Dame, Ind.: University of Notre Dame Press, 1998), pp. 38, 27. I am grateful to Alex Sider for directing me to Boyle's book.

in the workers — which denies them the continuity of a fixed identity — is that as consumers too they will have no fixed or limited desires, not give themselves an identity by voluntarily renouncing any of those desires for some more general — and therefore non-marketable — good.[20]

Our participation in this infinite cycle of production and consumption therefore shapes us increasingly to believe that we live in a world characterized by a struggle of all against all, a world in which, as a particularly crass (albeit popular) bumper sticker says, "he who dies with the most toys wins."[21] This attitude corrodes community and tradition, for it is totally incompatible with the notion that our lives are at any serious level constituted by our relations to one another.[22] John Milbank puts this as well as anyone when he says quite simply that capitalism

> in its most innate tendency precludes community. This is because . . . it makes the prime purpose of society as a whole and also of individuals to be one of accumulation of abstract wealth, or of power-to-do things in general, and rigorously subordinates any desire to do anything concrete in particular, including the formation of social relationships.[23]

What this has to do with the modern logic of aging and death I posited above is fairly obvious. The requirement of capitalism that we remain flexible — unencumbered by excessive attachments to particular people or places — alienates us from one another. Our obligations to one another are minimized but do not disappear altogether; we understand that those to whom we are bound and who are unable to care for themselves need to be cared for by somebody. Yet we are unable or unwilling to provide that care ourselves, for to do so would distract us from what we understand to be our primary task, which is participating responsibly in the political economy. We are consequently persuaded that the care of those unable to care for themselves must be professionalized, not simply for their own good, but for the good of the economy as well.

It is precisely at this point that the ways our attitudes toward the elderly are shaped by the medicalization of death and aging come into direct contact

20. Boyle, *Who Are We Now?* p. 28.

21. See Boyle, *Who Are We Now?* pp. 314-16.

22. Christopher Lasch, *The True and Only Heaven: Progress and Its Critics* (New York: W. W. Norton, 1991), pp. 38-39, 51, 58-59.

23. John Milbank, "Socialism of the Gift, Socialism by Grace," *New Blackfriars* 77, no. 910 (December 1996): 535.

with the ways those attitudes are shaped by our participation in the market. The market confronts us with the notion that just to the extent they can no longer participate in the cycle of production and consumption, the elderly are no longer "normal" members of society. And because we have come to view the changes associated with aging and death through a medical lens, we believe that the best place for such persons is a medical institution, such as a hospital or a skilled nursing facility, where the things that make them less than normal may be treated or controlled.

In terms of the political economy, this model of care may be perceived as a relative good in at least two ways. First of all, a generalized belief in the efficacy of professional care, along with its wide availability, frees families and members of local communities to participate more fully in the market. And second, the elderly themselves once again become participants in the economy, and this in an entirely new way. An entire industry of care for the sick and dying elderly now exists, and their considerable wealth, otherwise relatively inactive, is again being circulated in the economy.[24]

The Erosion of Tradition

Our growing tendencies to view life through medical and market lenses are both parts of a much more comprehensive way of thinking about ourselves and others that has its origins in modernity's hostility toward tradition.[25] The same shift in thinking that gave rise to the scientific positivism that is part and parcel of modern medicine and to those market economies that shape us to think of ourselves as producers and consumers has also *directly* undercut the ways of life of those tradition-bearing communities with substantive commitments to particular accounts of the human good and to the peculiar practices that sustained those accounts, accounts and practices that have traditionally been sustained to a significant extent by the older members of these communities.

Kant's "What is Enlightenment?" is an exemplary text in this regard; in pronouncing the advent of a new era in which humanity would be released from its "self-incurred tutelage,"[26] Kant was in effect announcing the creation of a new, ostensibly public space that was to be a democratic realm ruled by

24. I engage these matters in more detail in my book *The Body of Compassion: Ethics, Medicine and the Church* (Boulder, Colo.: Westview Press, 1999), pp. 41-44.

25. See Kaufman, "Intensive Care, Old Age," p. 721.

26. Immanuel Kant, *Foundations of the Metaphysics of Morals*, trans. Lewis White Beck (New York: Macmillan, 1959), p. 85.

facticity and universal rationality where traditional authoritative claims about how all humans ought to live would be disallowed.[27] In that space, says Alasdair MacIntyre, the "self had been liberated from all those outmoded forms of social organization which had imprisoned it simultaneously within a belief in a theistic and teleological world order and within those hierarchical structures which attempted to legitimate themselves as part of such a world order."[28] Autonomous human rationality *as such,* and not the wisdom of a tradition accumulated through time, was what really mattered.

The appearance of this sort of public space of course did not lead to the immediate and absolute dissolution of what MacIntyre refers to as "outmoded forms." Rather, that appearance contributed to the production of the commonly held modern understanding that we live simultaneously in two worlds, each governed by its own particular rules. There is first of all a public realm, governed by a morality structured by universal reason, in which our commitments to one another are freely chosen and contractual; this is the realm of science and of the market, the world where we make our livings and in which we interact with strangers. The second world is the private realm, the realm of family and of belief, governed by sentiment and affection, where relationships are based not in the expectation of mutual benefit, but in affective sympathy.[29]

But the assumption of the public-private distinction is highly problematic, especially for those who would seek to establish or reestablish alternatives to the status quo. The very idea that the public world is the world of fact suggests that it is somehow more real than the private world of value and mere belief. Such matters (as value and belief), moreover, are thought to have little or nothing to do with medicine and money; at best they might provide some raw material from which a few abstract moral principles may be extracted. Consequently, those communities that might otherwise provide concrete counterexamples of ways to care for the dying elderly find themselves unable to do so, because they have succumbed to the temptation to translate their convictions and practices into a more universal idiom in the name of achieving incremental improvements in the dominant system.[30]

The elderly consequently find themselves assaulted culturally on several fronts at once, all of which make it difficult, if not impossible, for them to age

27. Alasdair MacIntyre, *After Virtue* (Notre Dame, Ind.: University of Notre Dame Press, 1981), pp. 43-46, 52-59.

28. MacIntyre, *After Virtue,* p. 60.

29. Alasdair MacIntyre, *Dependent Rational Animals* (Chicago: Open Court, 1999), pp. 113-15.

30. MacIntyre, *After Virtue,* p. 252.

and die well and to teach us to do likewise. Many of the changes in their bodies associated with aging are viewed culturally and medically more as diseases than as things proper to their existence as embodied creatures; we thus suspect that they are inherently diseased and consequently in need of highly specialized care. The emphasis on efficiency characteristic of market economies and their cycles of production and consumption tempts us further toward alienating them; their inability to participate in the economy makes them a burden, particularly in terms of the time demanded by their care. Who can afford to take time away from work or career to care for an aging relative? And when professionalized institutional care is so widely available, who needs to take such time?

This attitude is magnified by our culture's general disregard for traditional authority. The aged are finally segregated because we believe they are superfluous. MacIntyre writes,

> In a society where the role of tradition is recognized, the old have a corresponding role; take away the tradition and the old become functionless and redundant people. Where tradition is recognized, the telling of stories by the old to the young about their own youth and about the inherited past is an indispensable part of the transmission of the culture. When tradition goes unrecognized, the stories of the old become boring anecdotes.[31]

Thus the wisdom of the elderly is absent from our lives largely because we no longer believe it exists. And nowhere is this more evident than in our attitudes toward death, which we prefer, when it becomes inevitable, to ignore.

> As with aging, so with death. The concept of a tradition is the concept of a relationship extending through generations in which each generation finds the significance of its activity a part of a history which transcends it. No generation can usurp the place of another, and therefore for each there is a time to die. Death is not to be fended off, it is at a certain point to be welcomed and embraced.[32]

The way of life suggested by MacIntyre is one very different from our usual experience. It suggests that there is a proper and even, if we dare use the word, a "natural" rhythm to our lives together through which we discover

---

31. Alasdair MacIntyre, "Patients as Agents," in *Philosophical Medical Ethics*, ed. Engelhardt and Spicker, p. 203.

32. MacIntyre, "Patients as Agents," p. 203.

that we are always and everywhere bound to one another in nearly innumerable ways. The question we must confront is how to go about getting from where we are now to where we would like to be.

Can Christians Offer an Alternative?

If Christians are to offer an alternative account to the modern logic of aging and dying, we must begin where the quotation from MacIntyre leaves off, with the assertion that there is for each of us indeed a time to die, and that an important part of dying well is not simply this acknowledgment but also the community's proper discernment in individual cases of the proximity of that time. Christians are not vitalists, in that we do not hold biological life to be an absolute good to be grasped at all costs.[33] Ray Anderson explains that whereas death as the cessation of personal existence is the consequence of humanity's alienation from God — an alienation overcome by Jesus' life, death, and resurrection — the same thing cannot be said for death as the end of our biological lives as embodied creatures, which is a phenomenon proper to our creatureliness:

> A theology of death for human personhood must also then include the realistic aspect of death as that which belongs to one's natural life. This biological continuum of life and death, which includes a finite and mortal creaturely nature, is a limit which God established upon the human person's earthly existence. Yet this limit does not become fatal because God also promises to uphold the human person through that natural limit through a personal and spiritual relation with Himself.[34]

But the articulation of an adequate theology of embodiment, death, and resurrection is not in and of itself a sufficient basis for a Christian alternative. Such an alternative also requires, in addition to a well-developed theology of aging and dying, a thoroughgoing description of the forms and practices of communal life that make it possible for each death to be a faithful one. This is where we begin to see how Christianity is genuinely countercultural. Wendell Berry remarks of the community that accounts within its vision and its practices the continuity of death with life:

33. John Breck, *The Sacred Gift of Life: Orthodox Christianity and Bioethics* (Crestwood, N.Y.: St. Vladimir's Seminary Press, 1998), pp. 203-42.

34. Anderson, *Theology, Death, and Dying*, p. 51.

Learning the correct and complete disciplines — the disciplines that take account of death as well as life, decay as well as growth, return as well as production — is an indispensable form of cultural generosity. It is the one effective way a person has of acknowledging and acting upon the fact of mortality: he will die, others will live after him.[35]

Broadly speaking, the "correct and complete disciplines" that enable Christians to age and die faithfully are the same disciplines that enable us to live faithfully. We discover very quickly that the notion that there might be something called a good death makes sense only in light of the firm conviction that we can name and describe a good life, and that a good death is finally nothing more or less than a death approached and performed in a manner consistent with a good (that is, a well-lived) life.[36] A well-lived life, moreover, is a life lived in faithful communion: with God, with other persons, and with the rest of creation and its characteristic rhythms of birth, growth, life, aging, and dying. The liturgical practices of baptism and Eucharist are perhaps the lenses through which the fundamentally communal nature of the Christian life is best seen; Christian baptism is not simply being initiated into a particular relationship with God, but also into membership in that people called the communion of saints, a people who include, as the eucharistic liturgy reminds us, God's "people on earth and all the company of heaven."

And aging and dying *look* very different from within the communion of saints. It is not simply that the practices of the church subvert our fear of death by training us to approach the end of life with confidence and even with joy, though that certainly is true;[37] it is also that the communion of saints is a community constituted by God's grace by its extension backward and forward through time *and* by the persistent, immediate presence and participation of all its members, including those who have died. In this sense the communion of saints is a tradition-bearing community sine qua non. The fact that the church names and looks to the example of its saints is but another reminder that it is a community that treasures and in fact cannot do without the accumulated embodied wisdom of those who have lived faithful lives. Indeed, this is the means by which the church is preserved as a community of memory. The

35. Wendell Berry, "Discipline and Hope," in his *A Continuous Harmony: Essays Cultural and Agricultural* (New York: Harcourt Brace, 1970), p. 147.

36. Stanley Hauerwas, "Happiness, the Life of Virtue and Friendship: Theological Reflections on Aristotelian Themes," *Asbury Theological Journal* 45, no. 1 (Spring 1990): 7-16.

37. Karen Westerfield Tucker, "Christian Rituals Surrounding Death," in *Life Cycles in Jewish and Christian Worship*, ed. Paul Bradshaw and Lawrence Hoffman (Notre Dame, Ind.: University of Notre Dame Press, 1997), pp. 196-213.

church thus aspires always to be a flourishing community in which "the young and the old must take care of one another. The young must learn from the old, not necessarily and not always in school. There must be no institutionalized 'child care' and 'homes for the aged.' The community knows and remembers itself by the association of old and young."[38]

And here we see another way in which death is properly part of the normal rhythms of life in the Christian community. For if we understand that dying well is a morally significant act insofar as it bears evangelical witness to our most profound theological convictions, we also will come to see that there is no more important lesson that the old can teach the young than the lesson of how to receive the gift of such a death. In this way the church bears witness to the world of a basic truth:

> concepts of renewal are always accompanied by concepts of loss or death; in order for renewal to take place, the old must not be forgotten but relinquished; in order to become what we may be, we must cease to be as we are; in order to have life we must lose it. Our language bears abundant testimony to these deaths: the year's death that precedes spring; the burial of the seed before germination; sexual death, as in the Elizabethan metaphor; death as the definitive term of marriage; the spiritual death that must precede rebirth; the death of the body that must precede resurrection.[39]

This lesson is not one that the elderly can teach us well unless we create a space of honor and respectful care in our very midst in which they might live out their days. But the creation of such a space requires our presence, and that presence is an impossibility unless we are willing to call into question our typical economic practices. The presence of the elderly to the community and the community to the elderly takes time and money and the development of certain skills, and these requirements are not feasible for most of us given our present ways of life, dominated as they are by the pursuit of careers that demand an almost idolatrous allegiance to our employers and by a political economy that underwrites that allegiance in the name of "economic growth." If we are to be faithful, then we must be willing to repent, that is, to embrace a different way of life more commensurate with our convictions about what really matters.

In the long run this means we must give serious consideration to adopt-

---

38. Wendell Berry, "Conserving Communities," in *Another Turn of the Crank* (Washington, D.C.: Counterpoint, 1995), p. 20.

39. Berry, "Discipline and Hope," pp. 160-61.

ing radically different ways of life. While we cannot and should not all expect to "go back" to the simpler era of the village doctor and the extended agrarian family[40] (although some of us probably should), we can imagine alternatives based in the Christian community's unique status as a social, political, and economic counterculture. The church is a baptismally reconstituted, extended family whose members affirm a fundamental obligation to care for one another in a way that can certainly be described as familial. Moreover, the church testifies to the existence of a political economy that is characterized not by competition, efficiency, and the endless cycle of production and consumption but by the notion that all of the good things in our lives, and indeed, life itself, are gifts from a gracious God.

Because we understand that our lives and our resources are gifts, we are free to engage in creative redistributions of wealth and other resources in order to enable different ways of life among our sisters and brothers. Freed from the drive to accumulate wealth and status, those of us with an abundance of time and money who are unencumbered at a given time by the particular demands of child rearing or caring for significantly dependent parents or grandparents can make ourselves and our resources available as gifts to those in our community who need to take the time and acquire the skills requisite to offering the gift of caring presence to those who are dependent upon them.

This turn toward non-professional care in non-institutional settings is not a rejection but a proper subordination of scientific medicine to the goods — and the Good — of the communion of saints. Medicine can help us discern the relative proximity of the time to die by advising us of the probable consequences of pursuing one treatment option as opposed to another, and it can help us manage the pain and suffering often associated with the end of life. This is only possible, however, when both patient and practitioner understand that the overarching concern of all parties is neither the prolongation of life nor the control of death itself, but faithfulness. This is an understanding that may require a very different medicine from the one we currently possess. Sherwin Nuland at least gestures in this direction when he claims that

> Each one of us needs a guide who knows *us* as well as he knows the pathways by which we can approach death. There are so many ways to

40. In *Theology, Death, and Dying,* Anderson says: "It is clear that the human environment of dying was itself a casualty of the modernization of medicine and health care. We cannot go back, ever again, to that earlier state of the art where the limits of preservation were reached without breaking out of the boundaries of family love and care. The humanization of dying must not be viewed as an attempt to sentimentalize dying, nor should our concern for the recovery of the human environment of dying be motivated by nostalgia" (p. 149).

travel through the same thickets of disease, so many choices to make, so many stations at which we may choose to rest, continue, or end the journey completely — until the last steps of that journey we need the company of those we love, and we need the wisdom to choose the way that is ours alone. The clinical objectivity that should enter into our decisions must come from a doctor familiar with our values and the lives we have led, and not just from the stranger whose super-specialized biomedical skills we have called upon. At such times, it is not the kindness of strangers we need, but the understanding of a longtime medical friend. In whatever way our system of healthcare is reorganized, good judgment demands that this simple truth be appreciated.[41]

For Christians, skilled, discerning friends like the ones Nuland describes are those who share with us the story of baptism. Like all of the good things in our lives, they are gifts to be graciously received and carefully cultivated. In this sense, dying is part of an entire way of life revolving around the notion of life as gift: During their lives the elderly bless us with the gift of their wisdom by telling us the stories that have made them the women and men they are. The power of these stories forms us morally to be, among other things, the kind of people who love and respect the elderly and understand the significance of their lives for our own.

As this understanding grows, we discover (one hopes) within ourselves the capacity and the desire to respond to them in gratitude; we notice and embrace their increasing dependence and offer them the gifts of our time and our resources. And when the time of their death approaches, we offer them the gift of our presence. We gift them with the hard and often unpleasant work of caring for them, feeding and bathing them, and holding them in the night. We share in some small way in their suffering and their fear as the hour of their death approaches. And when that hour arrives, in the midst of our very real grief at their passing, we discover that we have received as much or more than we have given. For they, in accepting our care with grace, have given us the example of how to die well, an example we may one day be privileged to pass along.

41. Nuland, *How We Die*, p. 266.

PART III

THE CHRISTIAN PRACTICE
OF GROWING OLD

Captured in Time: Friendship and Aging

STANLEY HAUERWAS *and* LAURA YORDY

Growing Old in America

In our society the single most striking portrayal of old people is their loneliness. Friendship with the elderly is almost unimaginable, as our very conception of what it means to be old is one of isolation. This isolation compounds with frailty, lack of usefulness to the world, dislocation from home and possessions, forced dependency, and nostalgia to construct a pitiable picture of a person who is unloved and, in many ways, unlovable.

We think, therefore, an exploration of the relation of friendship and aging long overdue. Obviously, any account of the relationship between aging and friendship involves questions of how one conceives of aging itself. Though we all grow old, how we grow old and its significance obviously varies from one historical context and community to another. We cannot pretend to speak for all communities concerning the relation between friendship and aging. Rather, we intend to draw on Christian resources to illumine how Christians should understand how friendship is possible not only between the elderly but across generations.

We need to be as candid as we can, however, about our own perspective. Our account is shaped by our own experiences in middle-class, white, Protestant America and consciously directed toward mainstream, middle-class churches (which are too often "white"). African-American, Asian-American, and Hispanic experiences of aging and friendship seem substantially different from those of whites. Nonetheless, we hope that the stories and practices we share in the Christian tradition can illustrate both the issues and resources for addressing those issues. We want to understand how friendship is not only possible but necessary for that community through time we call the church.

Of course, there are and have been many ways of being old even within the Christian community, just as there are many ways of being young. We are not suggesting that all elderly people will be the same, but rather that the very diversity of gifts present in the young and the old is a resource for the building up of a community in time that has time enough for friendship.

Our account is at once descriptive and normative, but it will not be easy to distinguish clearly one from the other. We begin descriptively by providing an account of aging and loneliness particularly as it occurs in American society. We do not pretend, however, that our account is free of normative presumptions; we make generalizations about the relation of growing old and death which we assume should not be avoided. The middle section of the essay is more explicitly normative. We draw, perhaps somewhat surprisingly, on monastic accounts of friendship in order to develop an account of Christian friendship. We think this account is important for teaching us the nature of friendship in a community determined not to let time alienate us from one another. In conclusion, we make some suggestions about what churches might do to make friendship within and between generations a reality.

Although we write from an explicitly theological perspective, we hope that our willingness to speak from our own tradition will illumine other perspectives. We need to make clear, however, that assumed in the "method" of this essay is what some would characterize as a "postmodern" theological point of view. That is, we assume that no universal perspective on aging (or anything else) is possible. Accordingly, we can do nothing else but speak from the traditions in which we live. We make no apology for the tack we take in this essay, but rather hope it will encourage others to write from other traditions.

To grow old is to lose our acquaintances and lifelong friends to distance, illness, and death. As our friends move away or die we lose the confirmation of our own life stories and identities. We are not even sure, as we grow old, that we are still the same people we were. We are unable to recognize in our flesh and bones the image of who we thought we were. The face and body that stares back at us from the mirror just does not seem to be "our body." So we are alienated not only from others but from ourselves.

Of course, the old have memories, but memory itself may fail, thus contributing to our alienation from our own lives. Alternatively memory may remind us, in excruciating detail, of the person we used to be but are no longer. The stories that make up our lives, that constitute who we are, are in many ways too rich to be told. So our telling them can increase our loneliness because the telling is always less than the life lived or shared. In short, growing old cannot help but be a continuing alienation from who we once were.

In his wonderful book *Old Friends,* which describes life in a retirement home, Tracy Kidder reports that one elderly man had since his wife died "suffered from memories." That describes our situation perfectly — we suffer from our memories just to the extent we cannot live without our memories. For example, Kidder notes that the same elderly gentleman recalled the time early in his marriage when his wife dropped a frying pan and he yelled at her. "If she could come back to life now, she could drop a hundred of them and I wouldn't give a darn," he says.[1] Kidder observes that such a remembrance is an indication that we do not control our memories so much as they control us. This man remembered his marriage as a happy one overall, yet the stories he now recalled and most wanted to tell were about a dropped frying pan and his sixty-year-long disagreement with his wife about demonstrativeness.

> His wife would say she wished he'd tell her that he loved her, and he would protest that he preferred to do the sorts of things that proved it. She would say she understood, but that any woman wants to hear the words, and Art would answer, "It doesn't run in my family to be like that." He started telling his wife he loved her several times each day, in their room in Sunrise, during the weeks before she died. But she never said a word. Not "Yes, dear, I forgive you." I would've liked that. It seemed it hurt her all her life.[2]

Later in his book Kidder notes that a basic principle of neurology holds that failures in memory tend to proceed inversely with time. "As memory fades, the past comes nearer."[3] This process, Kidder observes, no doubt has a biological origin, but the psychological result has a logic of its own. In old age many people seem to remember best what has mattered most to them. Such memory cannot help but create a kind of sadness just to the extent it is a reminder that what we so cared about is no longer "us."

Another way to put the matter is that as we grow old, our attempts to live in the past, which should be one of the benefits of growing old, can also be alienating to the extent that nostalgia distorts the story of our lives. This is particularly the case given the artificial life created by retirement and nursing homes. There the elderly discover they are not only strangers to one another but to themselves. They try to create commonalities through the telling of stories as a way to discover friendships, but too often such tellings make the story foreign for both the narrator and the listener. What seems lacking is any

1. Tracy Kidder, *Old Friends* (New York: Houghton Mifflin, 1993), p. 83.
2. Kidder, *Old Friends,* pp. 83-84.
3. Kidder, *Old Friends,* p. 235.

shared tradition through which such tellings contribute to the building of a wider community.

The obituaries commonly seen at retirement homes are poignant indications of the loneliness that seems unavoidable in such circumstances. Kidder describes the obituaries often posted on the ubiquitous obituary board. The activities director or her aid usually writes the brief encomiums, which consist in a standard line or two — "'a loving woman,' 'will be missed by family, friends, and staff.'" Some attempt is usually made to say something of the person's individuality but not much can be said — "'a lover of plants,' 'an avid bingo player,' 'enjoyed children.'"[4] Anonymous deaths testifying to the sad fact that if you live too long in this society you will, by necessity, die alone.

Such anonymity is not just the fate of the elderly but rather the intensification of our society's emphasis on autonomy. We believe that our first task is to create our own stories, to make our lives ours, without the help of others. We can never accomplish that task without the help of others, of course, but our very attempt to be autonomous prevents the acknowledgment that we are dependent. And, unfortunately, we bring these habits with us to our aging.

For example, one of the ways we try to fend off the anonymity that is the inextricable byproduct of the quest for autonomy is to try to become "successful." This effort is closely tied to our cultural habits of consumption. Many expensive "luxury" products are advertised as marks of the buyer's "arrival" at a status of wealth, financial security, or worldly achievement. You, the buyer, have worked hard, made a contribution to society, hoarded your money ("invested wisely"), and now in retirement "deserve" to drive an expensive car. You are someone; you have arrived. You stand on the peak of success.

Contrast this advertisement image with the far more common reality: a person (usually male in this scenario, but more and more often female) works hard for many years, may acquire a house and possessions over time, and reaches the age of voluntary or forced retirement. He no longer makes a tangible contribution. He receives a smaller income and gradually has to give up the possessions he worked so hard to acquire: the house is too hard to maintain, the driver's license relinquished, the furniture given away. You are nobody; you have arrived. Instead of standing on the peak of success, however, you have tumbled into the abyss of old age in working-class or middle-class America. Because achievement is so often defined as "having it all," having less *means* failure. And who wants to be friends with a failure?

To grow old, therefore, means to learn to live without friends. This unfortunately means in our society that we are put completely at the mercy of the

---

4. Kidder, *Old Friends*, p. 214.

family. Many old people, especially widows and widowers, are directly cared for by the family — most often spouses, daughters, daughters-in-law, or nieces. The old person depends on family for anything ranging from financial advice to transportation to daily feeding, toileting, and bathing. This dependency violates our sense of autonomy; we cannot manage by ourselves. But it also violates the autonomy of the family caregivers. Contrary to the common cultural image of adults as people who make choices about their lives, we do not choose our aging family members and we may not feel we chose to care for them — even as we engage in that care for long time periods. Moreover, because we often view friendship as a chosen relationship between equals, this dependency seems to erode or even prohibit any friendship between adults and aging parents.

Of course, as we have already indicated, retired people can escape the family by moving away from their homes and their communities into retirement homes. Such "homes" can be and often are quite wonderful and may provide the additional care needed. Or the move may be prompted by social mandates to seek a more comfortable climate or a city with cultural resources and activities directed toward the elderly. Such moves may be quite appropriate, but they have the effect of making the elderly displaced people — without clear membership in community and its attendant responsibilities, without close neighbors, without friends to remind us who (and whose) we are.

In fact, one of the ways the elderly are isolated in our society is through the assumption that to be old is to be free. The elderly are assumed no longer to bear "normal" responsibilities. They can return to "childhood," seeking nothing but their own immediate gratification. Too often such "freedom," however, turns out to be a form of abandonment by family and community. Such an abandonment is what we should expect in a society that assumes it can survive without memory; on the other hand, surely the most important obligation the elderly have toward the young is not to just remember but to be our memory.

That the elderly are freed from such obligations in our society correlates with the view that human development ends in early adulthood, or at least in middle age. Many dominant images in American culture portray old people as set in their ways, that is, as not capable of learning anything significant, much less growing in virtue. The elderly are thus thought capable of engaging in superficial friendships with other old people through time-filling "activities" rather than in profound friendships of character. Old people are portrayed as simpler creatures than younger adults; an old person typically is either "sweet" or "irascible," neither of which images indicates the interesting and complicated character of close friends. It is as though there is little reason to get to know old people because they are not very compelling as persons. Yet what could be more important than friendship between the old and the not so old, for otherwise how will the young ever know how to grow old and die? It is not, for example, unimportant that this essay is being written by an older person (Hauerwas) and a younger person (Yordy). Youth still has energy and enthusiasm (or so say the old). The older one of us says that while he has known death is always a theoretical possibility, it is only recently that he has begun to think it might happen to him. Though the possibility of death still remains largely an abstraction, he cannot help but begin to think that it changes one's perspective on one's life. It is the kind of perspective that aging inextricably brings.

To become old means, for example, that we are forced to be reintroduced to the fact that whatever else we are, or think we may be, we are our bodies. To be old, to be subject to the small and not so small pains and illnesses, makes us aware that we do not just have bodies, but we are bodies. We can become obsessed by our bodies as every little ache and pain frightens us, intimating our deaths. Indeed, it is interesting how often the elderly forge common judgments, if not friendships, through the ongoing comparison of illnesses and what can and cannot be done for and, far too often, *to* them in the name of "cure."

We believe the awareness of death which growing old brings is a gift, but it can often appear as just another impediment to friendship. Why even begin the difficult struggle toward intimacy when one of us is going to die soon? Surely this is one of the most poignant aspects of life in a nursing home. For as desperately as those in such homes desire to overcome loneliness through friendship, such friendships seem so fruitless because they are threatened by a not-too-distant death. Most of us can rightly stand only so much death. Grief is hard and friendship requires mourning. The isolation of the elderly from the young is surely one of the cruelest aspects of our need to house the elderly in "one place." Young people often lack the experience to be good friends with the old, for they do not really believe they will ever die. The only way to overcome the superficiality of cross-generational friendships, however, is through more opportunities for these friendships to arise and develop over time.

Christian Friendship

We think these obstacles to friendship for old people are real, but we also think that Christianity has rich resources to make possible friendship between the elderly and, perhaps most important, becoming and remaining friends with ourselves as we age. Actually, friendship across generations as well as friendship among the elderly becomes crucial if we are to be the kinds of communities in which aging can be seen as an opportunity for a rich life of service. We need, however, to be clear: we do not regard the church as another social service agency simply to provide the benefits of "support structures" as do other associations. Instead, the Christian story as embodied in the practices of the church offers a different understanding of both aging and friendship than we have just described.

We can only gesture toward the complex relation between Christian ways of growing old and how Christians have understood the nature and importance of friendship. To this end we will draw on the work of Aelred of Rievaulx (1109-1167) because he left us rich accounts of friendships we believe embody Christian wisdom. It may seem odd to enlist a medieval monk to illumine Christian friendship among people in the twenty-first century. Not only does his account of friendship among brothers in a religious community provide a prismatic account of Christian friendship, however; we think it also highlights by contrast the problematic status and concept of friendship in our culture.[5]

Of course, we are not claiming that Christians have some corner on friendship. Plato, Aristotle, and Cicero wrote profoundly about friendship and what they wrote certainly influenced Christian practice and thought. Aristotle, for example, distinguished between three kinds of friendships — friendship of use, pleasure, and character. He thought the first two forms of friendship deficient because the friend is loved not because he is a friend but because he is useful or pleasant. The problem with such friendships is that they are easily dissolved when the partners "do not remain unchanged: the affection ceases as soon as one partner is no longer pleasant or useful to the other."[6]

---

5. Some readers may object to our drawing on the writings of a twelfth-century monk because his world seems so distant from our own. And in many ways this is true. It was not, however, a more idyllic world; human envies, hates, and disputes were not only present in a monastic setting but intensified, partly because "autonomy" was simply not an option. The brothers and sisters had to learn how to negotiate such antagonisms in the light of a common telos that transcended the individual. That learning is what we hope to implement here.

6. Aristotle, *Nichomachean Ethics,* trans. Martin Ostwald (New York: Bobbs-Merrill, 1962), 1156a20-24. Future references to *Nicomachean Ethics* will be given parenthetically in the text. For an extended discussion of Aristotle's account of the interrelation of happiness, virtue, and friendship, see Stanley Hauerwas and Charles Pinches, *Christians Among the Virtues: Conversations with Ancient and Modern Ethics* (Notre Dame, Ind.: University of Notre Dame Press, 1997), pp. 3-51.

In contrast, Aristotle describes the perfect form of friendship, that is, character friendship, as that between good people who are alike in excellence or virtue. "For these friends wish alike for one another's good because they are good men, and they are good *per se,* (that is, their goodness is something intrinsic, not incidental)" (1156b5-10). Such friendships are lasting because such people are constituted by virtues that are perduring. On the other hand, according to Aristotle such friendships are rare because such people are few. Moreover, time and familiarity are required for such friendships to develop. Aristotle notes that nothing characterizes friends as much as the pleasure they derive from living in each other's company (1157b17-20).

Christian accounts of friendship agree with Aristotle that any intelligible account of friendship must consider the pleasure intrinsic to friendship. Nonetheless, the Christian account of friendship assumes a quite different context, one that reshapes Aristotle's understanding of friendship. Christians do not begin by trying to develop an account of friendship in the abstract, for friendship among Christians is only intelligible in the context of corporate, timeful discipleship which they call the body of Christ.[7] Aelred put it this way: "Friendship excels everything . . . for friendship is a path that leads very close to the perfection which consists of the enjoyment and knowledge of God, such that [one] who is a friend of man is made into a friend of God, according to what the Savior said in the Gospel: 'Now I will not call you servants, but my friends' [John 15:15]."[8]

Christian friendship, therefore, seems to have three closely related aspects: (1) to enable and assist each friend in the acquisition and practice of

---

7. We do not mean to imply that Aristotle had an "abstract" account of friendship. He was acutely aware that friendship required for its specification a wider politics. Yet he thought he lived at a time when such a politics was absent. Accordingly, character friendship became for him an end in itself. In the last book of the *Nichomachean Ethics* Aristotle writes sorrowfully that "with a few exceptions, Sparta is the only state in which the lawgiver seems to have paid attention to upbringing and pursuits. In most states such matters are utterly neglected, and each man lives as he pleases, 'dealing out law to his children and his wife' as the Cyclopes do. Now, the best thing would be to make the correct care of these matters a common concern. But if the community neglects them, it would seem to be incumbent upon every man to help his children and friends attain virtue. This he will be capable of doing, or at least intend to do" (1180a25-32). This passage surely explains why Aristotle devoted two books of his ethics to friendship. Friendship became, in the absence of any good politics, the only place that a school for virtue might exist. One cannot help but feel he is not just describing his time but ours. For Christians, however, no account of friendship can be justified that is not shaped by the more fundamental community we call the church.

8. Aelred of Rievaulx, *Spiritual Friendship,* trans. Mark F. Williams (Scranton: University of Scranton Press, 1994), 2:14. Future references to *Spiritual Friendship* will be given parenthetically in the text.

Christian virtues; (2) to build up the Christian community as the body of Christ; (3) to make possible, under God's gracious favor through the Holy Spirit, friendship with God. The fact that Christian friendship has functions does not, of course, mean that its value is "merely" instrumental rather than intrinsic, for the nature of these functions should make clear that Christian friendship is itself a goal worth seeking and a gift from God. We should note, however, that these functions have little to do with spending time together in diverting activities. Christian friendship as described here is much tougher than a diversion *from* the preoccupations of aging; rather, it is a redirection *to* the gift of aging in a Christian community.

The first purpose of friendship is to encourage the good character of the friends. As Aelred explains, "friendship bears fruit in this life as well as in the life to come. Friendship establishes all the virtues by means of its own charm, and it strikes down vices by its own excellence . . ." (2:9). This assumes that friends, regardless of age, can be moved to the good by God's grace acting through the influence of their friends.

> [T]he Lord says in the gospel of John, "I have chosen you, so that you may go and bear fruit," that is, so that you might love one another. For in this true friendship one makes progress by bettering oneself, and one bears fruit by experiencing the enjoyment of this increasing degree of perfection. And so spiritual friendship is born among good people through the similarity of their characters, goals, and habits in life. (1:46)

Old people, therefore, are not necessarily "set in their ways," incapable of conversion, transformation, or even minute, imperceptible steps in virtue. Think, for instance, of the many biblical examples of God calling quite elderly people to greater faithfulness, to surprising acts of discipleship: Abraham and Sarah, Jesse, David, Zechariah and Elizabeth, Anna. These stories tell us that our common cultural images are not truthful depictions of Christian life: old people are still called to discipleship in the community, and that discipleship may involve radical change in their way of life.

How do friends enable this sort of vigorous, difficult discipleship? They do so first by understanding that friendship itself is a gift of God. Like all such gifts, it is inherently christological. Friendship, Aelred writes, "is both formed in Christ and preserved according to Christ, and . . . friendship's goal and usefulness are ultimately referred to Christ" (1:10). To say that friendship is christological means that the fundamental shared good between friends is the love of Christ, that friendship occurs in Christ and is sustained in Christ, and that friendship will ultimately be perfected only in Christ's kingdom. This christological basis of friendship calls friends to be Christ-like to one another in particular ways: to give and receive service to each other, to offer correction when appropriate, to be patient, and so forth. Friends help us live into our own stories through enacting the story of a Christian life.

Aelred's assumption that we must live into our own stories stands in stark contrast with the modern desire for autonomy. He says, "these are not so much humans as beasts who say that one ought to live so as to be a consolation to no one, to be a burden or a grief to no one; who derive no enjoyment from another person's good, who would cause through their own misfortune no bitterness at all to another person" (2:52). Christians understand that our lives are gifts, not achievements. By that we mean that we are completely vulnerable, dependent creatures of a gracious God who has "storied" us prior to any choices we might make. We call rebellion against our giftedness "sin." Sin is part of the story we must tell about our lives if we are to be truthful. Therefore, we need friends in order to learn to tell the truth about our lives; otherwise, we are tempted toward delusional stories about our righteousness.

Consequently, friendship for Christians is both a necessary activity for the discovery that we are less than we were meant to be, and the resource to start us on the journey through which we become what we were created to be. So "practicing" friendship, both in the sense of rehearsal and of habit, makes us disciples. As Aelred observes, "friends are concerned for each other, pray for each other, one blushes for the other, another rejoices for the other, one mourns the fall of the other as his own. A friend uses whatever means he can to encourage the timid, strengthen the weak, console the sad, and check the enraged" (3:101). Cross-generational friendships manifest this mutual upbuilding in particularly important ways. The older person can teach, by example, how to age and die well; the young learn to honor the elderly as those with such an obligation. The young, too, can remind the old that aging is not an excuse to slip into irresponsibility, indifference, or despair. Most people never think of how we must live when we're younger in order to be able to live well when we're older; it is through friendship with an older person that a young person can both appreciate the lifelong value of friendship and acquire friendship's virtues.

It is important, in the context of a discussion of aging, to note that the limit of friendship is not death, but sin. Aelred says,

We can see the certain and true goal of spiritual friendship: that is, nothing should be denied to a friend, and anything should be undertaken for a friend, even to the point at which we must lay down our life for our friend — a sacrifice ordained by divine authority. Therefore, since the life of the soul is far more important than the life of the body, I believe that only this one thing should be denied to a friend: that which causes the death of the soul, which is nothing other than sin — that which separates God from the soul and the soul from life. (2:68)

Aelred's observation about what should be denied to a friend startles those of us who have been trained to believe that death, not sin, is our deepest enemy. Yet we believe that Aelred is right to remind us that when our lives are constituted by the fear or the denial of death, our friendships cannot help but be fragile. Friendship cannot be a hedge against death, because there is no hedge against death. Instead, friendship must be constituted as part of a narrative that makes our lives good. Put dramatically, what makes Christian friendship possible is the Christian presumption that we are bound together in a story that gives us something worth dying for.

This brings us to the second aspect of the Christian understanding of friendship, that is, that friendship among Christians is understood to build up the community of faith, the body of Christ. For Christians, friendship between individuals is not and cannot be opposed to the community, but rather serves the community good. Such a good is called common because we do not understand it as a good comprising the sum of our individual interests but rather as a good unknowable without the discovery through friendships that, as Aelred writes, "friendship has its source in God; the happiness of individuals is the happiness of all" (3:79). Moreover, for us such friendship is not only with those now present but with those who have gone before, those we call the communion of saints.

That is why Christian communities live by memory. Our central feast is a feast of memory by which we are made part of God's very life in memory for the world. It therefore becomes crucial for Christianity to be about the formation of communities in which memory is not only a possibility but a necessity. Christianity can be Christianity only if we remember those who have gone before and made our faith possible. The very language of faith implies faithfulness to those who have gone before. They live on through our memories and we live on in the memories of those who follow. The church, therefore, cannot be the church without the elderly. They are the embodied memories of the church's story. Of course, we do not expect that all the elderly of the church should express the "wisdom of their years." But there can be no substitute for some old people in the church being wise. Someone must know how to tell the stories well.

Because the church's story is our story, the church offers an alternative to family just to the extent that through our baptisms we understand that we have been made part of one another in a more determinative way than biology could ever do. By being so made, we also discover the possibility of friendships we had not otherwise imagined. So old people are not stranded in their families; instead, they are members of Christ's body along with all the children and other adults of all backgrounds, talents, sexualities, races, and classes. We become who we are, we become truly ourselves, only through Christ. Christian worship enables our lives to be enmeshed in practices and narratives through which we can discover ourselves in our growing old as well as others in their growing old. This requires, of course, that old people not merely be "Sunday acquaintances," but that they be entangled and succored in close friendships.

Moreover, the fact that old people are often stripped of worldly power becomes a resource for the church. For through such "stripping" we are left with what matters — presence to one another. We are reminded that Christian life is less about doing than about being, and that being happens only by way of our bodies. Bodies that cannot "do" very much anymore — bear children, drive cars, read small print, climb steps — can still "be," can offer through their very presence the knowledge of God's Spirit present with us.

The third aspect of friendship is actually its culmination, its telos: friendship with God. Perhaps no image, we believe, is more powerful than Aquinas's suggestion that beatitude — blessedness — is ultimately friendship with God. Aelred, anticipating Aquinas, notes that Christ has made such friendship possible in a manner that defeats the loneliness of aging and death.

> Is it not a certain share of blessedness so to love and be loved, so to help and be helped, and thus to fly higher, from the sweetness of brotherly charity to that more sublime splendor of divine love, and now to ascend the ladder of charity to the embrace of Christ himself, and then to descend by the same ladder to the love of one's neighbor, where one may sweetly rest? (3:127)

For Aelred, then, friendship with God happens through human friendships, and only for those who are friends with themselves and others.

The possibility of friendship with God does not mean we are, or may become, God's equals.[9] On the contrary, friendship with God requires first of all a profound acknowledgment of our inequality. Acknowledgment of difference is important in any friendship, lest we merely project our self-image

---

9. Paul Waddell, *Friendship and the Moral Life* (Notre Dame, Ind.: University of Notre Dame Press, 1984), p. 139.

onto the other in such a way that friendship disintegrates into narcissism. Christians believe that difference need not impede friendship just to the extent we share the same body in Christ. In our relationship with God, of course, the difference is infinite. God is creator, eternal Lord of all, and we are God's flawed, finite creatures. Here is another reason why friendships among and with old people, and participation of elderly people at worship, become crucial. To be elderly means to be vulnerable. The elderly, like the sick, need help. But their very need of help creates the conditions for them to help community members come to enjoyment of one another as *fellow creatures* of God. We are all vulnerable; we all need help. For a few years as young adults we may pretend (egged on by social and cultural forces) that we can live forever as autonomous, self-reliant, self-fulfilling beings. The pretense, however, collapses soon enough. So the presence of the visibly vulnerable elderly is a reminder that we are not our own creators. Consequently, Christians must ask the elderly to be among us so we will not take our lives for granted.

The acknowledgment of our creatureliness, that we will die, is a necessary condition for our ability to be our own best friend. Aristotle maintained that in order to be friends with others we must be our own best friends. As he observes, we count as friends those who (1) wish for and do what is good for their friend's sake, (2) wish for the existence and life of their friend for their friend's sake, (3) spend their time in our company, (4) desire the same things we do, (5) share our sorrows and joys. A good person has, Aristotle maintains, all these feelings in relation to himself and therefore must be his own best friend. In particular, a good person wishes to spend "time with himself, for he does so with pleasure. The memory of his achievements gives him delight, and his hopes for the future are good; and such memories and hopes are pleasant" (1166a23-27). All this is true if we remember that Christians should not be anxious, for we believe we can "rest easy" in the face of death.

We are creatures "caught in time"; the span from birth to death is short and inexorable. Christians believe, though, that our being made part of God's life transforms time from threat to gift. We have the time, in time, to be friends with one another, destined as we are for death. We were created for and are destined to friendship with God; this creation and destiny makes us friends with ourselves and, thus, with one another. Christians mourn no less our own deaths or the deaths of our friends, but such mourning does not make us doubt that we should be lesser friends to one another. Rather, we discover in and through friendship that we have been made part of a common memory; and that common memory makes growing old a pleasure, a discipleship, and a blessing.

The Church and the Elderly

We are acutely aware that this account of friendship and aging may seem un-realistic given the reality of the contemporary church. Churches are more likely to be shaped by the American way of growing old than by the kind of responsibilities we think are incumbent on the elderly in the Christian com-munity. We do not believe, however, that the church is without resources for response. Indeed, we hope Christians might see themselves enough in our ac-count of aging and friendship to begin to act differently. We have no ready-made "solutions." We do, however, offer some suggestions about small — but we believe significant — practices that may help Christians recover the art of friendship between generations.

First and foremost, we believe the church must be the kind of community that insists that those who have grown in years are not relieved of moral re-sponsibilities. They cannot move to Florida and leave the church to survive on its own. For Christians, there is no "Florida" even if they happen to live in Florida. That is, we must continue to be present to those who have made us what we are so that we can make future generations what they are called to be. Aging among Christians is not and cannot be a lost opportunity, but rather must be a transformation of what the world understands to be a loss of power into service for the good of the Christian community.

The problem, however, is that when we are old, it is too late to learn how to grow old. We must be taught how to live well when we are young if we are to know how to live well when we are old. (In fact, one of the great problems of our time is the assumption that we can and should live as if we will never grow old.) This will, of course, require the church to find ways to avoid isolat-ing the young, the not so young, and the elderly from one another. If, as we maintained above, the church is a community of memory, such isolation cer-tainly makes the church's work impossible. What it means for the church to be a community of memory is the gospel; it is not some truth that can be known without memory. The gospel is a story with myriad subplots, intrica-cies, colors, and textures. Stories live through memory, through being told over and over again, and in the telling new aspects of the story are discovered. That is why the church is so dependent on those who can help us remember the complexity of the story that constitutes who we are.

So the church names a community that depends on those who have gone before to remember the skills necessary for the telling and retelling of the story. We do not mean to suggest that the full responsibility of this task falls particularly on the elderly, but we do think they have work to do if the church is to survive as church. In short, we rightly expect Christians to grow old wisely, for the church is a community constituted by wisdom. And wisdom is acquired not through means-end principles but through corporate experience, by living the church's stories. We do not presume that all Christians as they grow old should be wise, but we do expect the church to live as a community that requires the wise, particularly the elderly among us, to exist.

In this respect it is quite interesting to contrast the church as a community of wisdom with the generalized acceptance of the "expert" as the assumed legitimate authority in modernity.[10] The expert is not expected to be wise, but rather to know the best ways to achieve results through the use of technical rationality. The whole point of a society constituted by the authority of the expert is to be a community that can live without stories. The elderly, similarly, simply are not required. Obviously we do not think the church is this type of community, living as it does through memory. As a community dependent on the wisdom of the elders, therefore, the church inevitably stands in tension with the culture of modernity.

Of course, to say that the church is a community that lives by wisdom means that it must also be a community in which friendship is possible between generations; for wisdom is not learned easily but requires the ongoing transformation provided by friendships over time. As Aelred says on the relation between friendship and wisdom, "friendship cannot even exist without grace. Therefore, since eternity thrives in friendship, and truth shines forth in it, and grace likewise becomes pleasant through friendship, you be the judge whether you should separate the name of wisdom from these three" (1:63). So the church must find ways to have children and those we currently call "the youth" sit at the feet of their elders where they learn the wisdom of the past. This "sitting" requires that the church not be a people in a hurry, but rather a people who have learned to wait. That is, Christians should be oriented toward witnessing God's work in God's time rather than achieving our goals in our own time.[11]

Perhaps the hardest thing the church must ask of the elderly is to teach us how to die. Such teaching requires a vulnerability none find easy, particularly in a society based on autonomy. Yet none of us knows how to die "by nature"; we must be taught how to die through friendship. Contrary to the oft-made claim, we do not need to die alone, but rather we can die knowing that we will not be abandoned by our friends simply because we are dying. If the church

10. Alasdair MacIntyre, *After Virtue* (Notre Dame, Ind.: University of Notre Dame Press, 1984), pp. 79-84.

11. "Waiting" and "witnessing" do not mean "preserving the status quo." They mean testifying to the truth of Christ's kingdom in the midst of the world, without expecting that we humans can enact that kingdom ahead of its appointed time.

could be such a community, then we might discover that we are again able to attract young and old alike if only because they see that these people are happy. We conclude with Aelred's idyllic description of this happiness, which he wrote as a relatively old man:

> When I was walking around the monastery cloister three days ago, as the beloved crowd of brothers was sitting together . . . I marveled as though walking among the pleasures of paradise, enjoying the leaves, flowers, and fruits of each single tree. I found not one brother in that whole multitude whom I did not love, and by whom I did not think I was loved in turn; and so I was filled with joy so great that it surpassed all the delights of this world. Indeed, I felt as though my spirit had been poured into all of them, and their affection had been transplanted into me, so that I could say with the Prophet, "Behold, how good and pleasant it is, when brothers dwell together in unity [Psalm 133:1]." (3:82)

Rather than dismissing this passage as an unrealistic portrait, we believe that Christians should read it as a prescription for friendship with and among the elderly. In such friendships do we become church; in church are such friendships possible.

Worship, the Eucharist, Baptism, and Aging

SUSAN PENDLETON JONES *and* L. GREGORY JONES

Two of the most powerful intellectual and social forces of the twentieth century have been the hard sciences and capitalist economics. They have conspired to produce increasingly dominant images of personhood that undermine theological conceptions of the purpose and destiny of human life. For example, a "scientific" conception of human nature presumes that rationality is the defining characteristic of personhood. In a widely influential book on medical ethics that draws on this scientific conception, H. Tristram Engelhardt describes a person as one who is "self-conscious, rational, free to choose, and in possession of a sense of moral concern."[1] On these grounds, Engelhardt suggests that not all humans are persons. He notes, "persons, not humans, are special."[2]

Similarly, capitalist economics defines persons not only as rational choosers but as those capable of contributing productively to the economy. Personhood is defined not by who one is but rather by what one is capable of doing. Hence, individuals are valued as persons so long as they are useful workers. If they are no longer useful, then they become replaceable parts in a large economic system.[3] On an economic understanding, productive individuals, not human beings as such, are special and counted as persons.

1. H. Tristram Engelhardt, *The Foundations of Bioethics* (New York: Oxford University Press, 1986), p. 105.

2. Engelhardt, *Foundations of Bioethics*, p. 104. It should be noted that, since the publication of this book, Engelhardt has changed his views, renounced his secular approach, and become a Christian. We use his description both because of the influence of this book and because it aptly and concisely articulates a widespread view. Indeed, this view of rationality and personhood is enshrined in the most influential book in political theory of the last half-century, John Rawls's *A Theory of Justice* (Cambridge, Mass.: Harvard University Press, 1971).

3. Barry Schwartz has criticized this view of human nature and personhood in two books:

Such descriptions of the hard sciences and capitalist economics are by no means identical. Their overlapping assumptions, however, have converged in impoverishing our conceptions of the purpose and destiny of human life. They have been shaped by the presumptions of modern atheism. These descriptions exclude any conviction that human beings are valuable not because of their rationality or their productivity but because they are created in the image and likeness of God and destined for communion with God.

These descriptions, along with the social and economic forces that accompany them, have made it difficult for many Westerners, and especially Americans, to know what to do with people who are not rational and productive. We can marginally tolerate those who are rational but not productive, as well as those who are productive but not rational. But we do not know what to do with those who never will be fully rational or productive — for example, the severely mentally and physically handicapped. Nor are we sure what status we ought to give to those who are not yet rational and productive, the unborn and the newborn, and those who are no longer rational and productive, the elderly, the chronically suffering, and the dying.

Indeed, Engelhardt acknowledges that his definition of personhood excludes a variety of human beings. Examples of excluded groups include fetuses, infants, the severely senile or the mentally handicapped, the severely brain damaged. Engelhardt acknowledges that we may give reasons for wanting to extend treatment and care to such groups, but they are not, strictly speaking, to be considered "persons." Hence, he concludes that abortion is not really a serious moral issue, and that the moral fabric does not depend on condemning infanticide. He states that "it is difficult to mount a plausible, nonculturally biased, strong argument against infanticide. The best that can be produced is a speculative, circumstantial argument."[4] Opposition to euthanasia would fall in the same category.

These assumptions become particularly dangerous when linked to our technological imperative that everything should be fixable or curable as well as to Western culture's aversion to — and denial of — death and dying. Thankfully, we have not reached the point of actively practicing infanticide or euthanasia. Even so, unless we begin to change our thinking and challenge the social and economic forces around us, the conceptual and practical forces are not far away.

Christian worship ought to be one of the sites for challenging our think-

---

The Battle for Human Nature (New York: W. W. Norton, 1986), and The Costs of Living (New York: W. W. Norton, 1994).

4. Engelhardt, Foundations of Bioethics, p. 229.

ing as well as the social and economic forces that threaten to shape us. Yet, too often, Christians — and here we mean especially Protestant Christians — have allowed our worship to be shaped by the very presumptions of rationality and productivity that are regnant in the wider culture. Many Protestant services are so dominated by words that those who are mentally incapacitated are unable to participate. Further, the physical and social spaces of worship often powerfully communicate to persons that only the mentally and physically able ought to attend.

In this essay we want to suggest how Christian worship can play a central role in resisting corrupt notions of human personhood and in reshaping our habits of life and of thought. In particular, we will suggest that Christian worship provides a site for reclaiming the sense that all of us — from the youngest of children to the oldest of the elderly — are creatures made in the image and likeness of God, destined for communion with God, and worthy of participation in the praise of God.

To be sure, we do not assume that all elderly persons lack either rational capacities or productive abilities, or both. Many elderly continue to be both rational and productive. Because the loss of such faculties is one of people's deepest fears as they grow older, however, and because part of those fears is the conviction that they will be lost to God and of "no use" to others, we want to show how Christian worship ought to challenge the root of those fears. Further, we are convinced that the contemporary marginalization of the elderly from our families, our communities, and our imaginations is significantly shaped by our broader understanding that personhood is fundamentally rooted in narrow conceptions of rationality and productivity. Challenging those presumptions, and focusing our understanding of personhood on the communal praise of God centered in the Eucharist, will equip us to appreciate more profoundly those elderly in our midst who do not maintain strong cognitive and productive capacities.

We begin with two stories of the Eucharist, one about a mentally handicapped person and one about a severely brain-damaged person, to explore the ways in which we too often limit who counts as persons or what they can "understand." We then turn to a brief constructive description of why worship ought to be central for us as we age, and for the ways in which we honor the elderly in our midst. We conclude with a vision of what it means to honor the wisdom of the elderly through practices in the church. Overall, we will suggest that worship is central to shaping our vision of the purpose and destiny of human life throughout the life span, regardless of whether a person is born with limited cognitive abilities, loses the capacity for memory through illness or tragic accident, suffers from severe dementia or Alzheimer's, or is able to function vitally with their reason, emotions, and soul intact until their dying days.

I

Too often, healthy middle-aged adults presume that others who are different from us must lack the capacities for understanding that we have. We impose on them our understanding of what they must be capable of grasping. Yet often the practices of Christian living, and centrally the Eucharist, shape an understanding of God and of community that exceeds our limited imagination.

One such instance is told by Sue Mosteller, who in 1975 became the international coordinator for the L'Arche communities for the mentally handicapped. There are more than one hundred L'Arche communities in over twenty-six countries, and they are premised on the conviction that the mentally handicapped and other persons are capable of living together in Christian community. Such communities regularly eat, work, and live together, even as they also worship and celebrate the Eucharist together. Such practices have a powerful impact in shaping the lives of the participants.

Mosteller displays this impact through the story of Michael, a mentally handicapped resident of L'Arche whose grandmother died.[5] After his grandmother's death, Mosteller writes, "Michael's mother felt physically and emotionally unable to cope either with her own grief and loss, or with Mike's anticipated reaction, so she decided not to tell him about the death until after the funeral." L'Arche communities ordinarily advise against this, because it is important that those who are handicapped learn to "live" through sorrowful as well as joyful times. They wanted, however, to respect the mother's position during her time of grief, and so they agreed.

Michael went home the weekend following the funeral. On Saturday morning, his father announced the news to him. In response, Michael found his mother "resting on her bed and sat beside her, holding her hand, not speaking, but only offering the comfort of his presence." He did this for almost forty-five minutes, and his mother later remarked that it was precisely the thing that she needed at that moment.

But that was not all. "Spotting a silver vase of flowers, [Mike] haltingly asked his father to fill the vase with coca cola. An exchange of views ensued and Mike, who stutters and sometimes finds it hard to speak his mind, finally

---

5. Sue Mosteller, "Living Wish," in *The Challenge of L'Arche,* ed. Jean Vanier (London: Darton, Longman & Todd, 1982), pp. 11-23 (quotations are from p. 17).

succeeded in convincing his dad that he knew that the vase was for flowers and not for coke, but he still needed his father to fill the vase with coke." In the meantime, Michael had gotten a table and put three chairs around it.

When his father returned, Michael put his parents on one side of the table and himself on the other, and placed the coke and a piece of bread on the table. "'Now,' he announced, 'we will pray for Grandma.' Breaking the bread, he handed a piece to his mother and asked her to pray. He repeated the action with his dad and then he himself took the bread and prayed aloud for his grandmother. He followed through with the 'vase' and each in turn prayed for the deceased. Then he finished by announcing to his parents that God would surely look after Grandma from now on, but that they must begin to think of Grandpa, who was now alone and would need their support."

How do we begin to make sense of Michael's profoundly Christian vision? Even his parents underestimated his capacity to understand or cope with the death of his grandmother. But Michael had developed habits of being present to one another and of eating together, paradigmatically through the celebration of the Eucharist in L'Arche communities. Drawing on those habits, he was able to bear witness to God and to the power of Christian community by ministering to his mother and father. Though he may be cognitively impaired, Michael had a more profound "knowing" schooled by the habits of his participation in a worshiping community than many people whose cognitive abilities are seemingly stronger.

This knowledge that challenges modern conceptions of rationality is displayed even more explicitly, and dramatically, in the story neurologist Oliver Sacks tells of Jimmie G.[6] Jimmie was a charming, intelligent, and handsome forty-nine-year-old man. Unfortunately, he also was memoryless. Sacks was puzzled by the phenomenon of an otherwise healthy man whose intelligence was intact but who had lost his capacity for memory. Hence, he was prompted to ask: "What sort of a life (if any), what sort of a world, what sort of a self, can be preserved in a man who has lost the greater part of his memory and, with this, his past, and his moorings in time?" (p. 23).

Jimmie's life had, for all intents and purposes, stopped in 1945 when he was nineteen, some thirty years before the time in 1975 when Sacks began to see him. He could remember anything that happened prior to 1945, but nothing since then. He could describe his early life in great detail, vividly and with affection. But as he moved to describing his days in the Navy, he began to

---

6. The story is told as "The Lost Mariner," chap. 2 of Oliver Sacks, *The Man Who Mistook His Wife for a Hat and Other Clinical Tales* (New York: Harper and Row, 1987), pp. 23-43. Further references to this story will be given parenthetically in the text.

speak in the present tense. Indeed, Sacks discovered that Jimmie believed he was still nineteen.

Curiously, on intelligence tests Jimmie scored very well. As Sacks describes it, Jimmie "was quick-witted, observant, and logical, and had no difficulty solving complex problems and puzzles — no difficulty, that is, if they could be done quickly. If much time was required, he forgot what he was doing" (p. 26). He knew the periodic table quite well, but included only those elements that had been discovered prior to 1945.

Jimmie had virtually no capacity for remembering recent events. He could not remember events or people from day to day. Indeed, he was apt to forget anything said or shown to him within a few seconds' time. He sometimes retained faint memories of recent events, but could not put things together into a coherent recollection. As Sacks notes, "It was not, apparently, that [Jimmie] failed to register in memory, but that the memory traces were fugitive in the extreme, and were apt to be effaced within a minute, often less, especially if there were distracting or competing stimuli, while his intellectual and perceptual powers were preserved, and highly superior" (p. 27).

Sacks found himself wrung with emotion, heartbroken and deeply perplexed by the case of a highly intelligent man whose life seemed "lost in limbo, dissolving" (p. 29). Neurologically, Sacks diagnosed Jimmie as having Korsakov's Syndrome. But Sacks struggled with the deeper questions — he wrote in his notes that Jimmie was a "man without a past (or future), stuck in a changing, meaningless moment." Sacks found himself recurrently wondering about "'a lost soul,' and how one must establish some continuity, some roots, for he was a man without roots, or rooted only in the remote past" (p. 29).

Sacks and others had begun their work hoping to be able to help Jimmie; he was so personable, so likable, so intelligent, that Sacks found it difficult to imagine or believe that "he might be beyond help." But, he added, "none of us had ever encountered, even imagined, such a power of amnesia, the possibility of a pit into which everything, every experience, every event, would fathomlessly drop, a bottomless memory-hole that would engulf the entire world" (p. 35). Sacks found himself bewildered, wondering whether there was anything he could do. He thought of Jimmie as being a lost self, a lost soul, unaware of his condition because it engulfed him and the world into the vortex of a meaningless present. Or so Sacks thought.

Perhaps Sacks's bewilderment was as much a factor of modernity's restricted conception of personhood as anything else. Note that Sacks concluded that, since medical science was unaware of a way to help Jimmie, he might be "beyond help" from any source. He couldn't be cured, so how do we go on?

It is to Sacks's credit both as a doctor and as a humanistic scholar that he continued to ask the questions rather than conclude definitively that Jimmie *was* beyond help. He even asked the Roman Catholic nuns who ran the Home for the Aged, where Jimmie was being treated, what they thought of his condition. Sacks reports their conversations as follows: "One tended to speak of [Jimmie], instinctively, as a spiritual casualty — a 'lost soul': was it possible that he had really been 'desouled' by a disease? 'Do you think he *has* a soul?' I once asked the Sisters. They were outraged by my question, but could see why I asked it. 'Watch Jimmie in chapel,' they said, 'and judge for yourself'" (p. 37).

Jimmie was a regular participant in worship at the Home. So Sacks went to observe Jimmie in worship. Sacks's observation is remarkable:

> I was moved, profoundly moved and impressed, because I saw here an intensity and steadiness of attention and concentration that I had never seen before in him or conceived him capable of. I watched him kneel and take the Sacrament on his tongue, and could not doubt the fullness and totality of Communion, the perfect alignment of his spirit with the spirit of the Mass. Fully, intensely, quietly, in the quietude of absolute concentration and attention, he entered and partook of the Holy Communion. He was wholly held, absorbed, by a feeling. There was no forgetting, no Korsakov's then, nor did it seem possible or imaginable that there should be; for he was no longer at the mercy of a faulty and fallible mechanism — that of meaningless sequences and memory traces — but was absorbed in an act, an act of his whole being, which carried feeling and meaning in an organic continuity and unity, a continuity and unity so seamless it could not permit any break. (pp. 37-38)

Sacks recognized that here, in worship, Jimmie discovered his soul. He recognized that personhood could not be circumscribed by memory, mental activity, or the mind in isolation from other faculties.

Indeed, Sacks discovered in chapel that Jimmie's soul was discovered in moral attention, in aesthetic and dramatic activity in the praise of God. Again Sacks's observation is compelling:

> Seeing Jim in the chapel opened my eyes to other realms where the soul is called on, and held, and stilled, in attention and communion. The same depth of absorption and attention was to be seen in relation to music and art: he had no difficulty, I noticed, "following" music or simple dramas, for every moment in music and art refers to, contains,

other moments. . . . If Jimmie was briefly "held" by a task or puzzle or game or calculation, held in the purely mental challenge of these, he would fall apart as soon as they were done, into the abyss of his nothingness, his amnesia. But if he was held in emotional and spiritual attention — in the contemplation of nature or art, in listening to music, in taking part in the Mass in chapel — the attention, its "mood," its quietude, would persist for a while, and there would be in him a pensiveness and peace we rarely, if ever, saw during the rest of his life at the Home. (pp. 38-39)

Undoubtedly, Jimmie's participation in worship reflected a similar "knowing" to that which Michael displayed in the service in memory of his grandmother. For both of them, the Eucharist signifies a participation that involves the body and the soul in the praise of God beyond the limits of ordinary cognitive ability.

Jimmie's story, moreover, signifies an additional way of understanding personhood and participation in a community. His life and soul are continually shaped in worship by dimensions that transcend merely speaking and reading and hearing words — music, drama, and the dramatic activity of bending the body to receive the Eucharist. Jimmie "came alive" in worship. Perhaps, in Jimmie's life, only the Sisters fully understood what it means to care for persons who do not seem to fit the empirical sciences' narrow description, and perhaps only they embodied a commitment to care for those who cannot be productive and are actually, from an economic perspective, a "drain" on scarce financial resources.

Sacks's concluding reflections illustrate the powerful lesson he learned from watching Jimmie in chapel.

> I had wondered, when I first met him, if he was not condemned to a sort of 'Humean' [froth], a meaningless fluttering on the surface of life, and whether there was any way of transcending the incoherence of his Humean disease. Empirical science told me there was not — but empirical science, empiricism, takes no account of the soul, no account of what constitutes and determines personal being. Perhaps there is a philosophical as well as a clinical lesson here: that in Korsakov's, or dementia, or other such catastrophes, however great the organic damage and Humean dissolution, there remains the undiminished possibility of reintegration by art, by communion, by touching the human spirit: and this can be preserved in what seems at first a hopeless state of neurological devastation. (p. 39)

There is a philosophical as well as a clinical lesson in Jimmie's case, and Sacks describes both well. Yet there are also theological lessons that Sacks hints at but does not fully articulate.

Thus we turn in our next section to describe those theological lessons and what they reveal about the centrality of Christian worship both for us as we age and for the ways in which we honor the elderly.

II

Stories such as Michael's and Jimmie's are moving in the ways they display the limitations and inadequacies of modern conceptions of personhood. But it is worship, centered in the Eucharist, that reveals that all of us — including Michael, Jimmie, the elderly, Alzheimer's patients, as well as neonates and young children — are fundamentally creatures created for the praise of God. Art, music, and communion offer, as Sacks notes, opportunities for "reintegration" of the soul and the recreation of identity. They do so not so much because of the importance of aesthetics per se, but rather because who we are as persons is fundamentally dependent on whose we are — creatures made in the image and likeness of God.

It is thus not surprising that the Eucharist is often of central importance to the elderly in nursing homes. The sacrament, including the gestures and the ritual, offers a powerful opportunity for integration. Indeed, when Susan has taken the Eucharist to elderly parishioners in nursing homes, she has discovered that even those persons suffering from significant cognitive impairment would sometimes join in participating in parts of the liturgy. Even more, one elderly woman who rarely could communicate in ordinary conversation, and earlier during the day had not been able to recall her own name, recited parts of the Great Thanksgiving along with Susan, and then joined in saying the Lord's Prayer. The habits of a lifetime had shaped her life of communion.

Similarly, we should not be surprised that music would be able to touch Jimmie's soul so profoundly. Music touches us at levels far deeper than cognitive understanding. For example, the Letter to the Ephesians emphasizes the power of music, explicitly contrasting singing to drunkenness (5:18-20) as alternative forms of life. David Ford offers illuminating comments on this passage:

Singing psalms, hymns and spiritual songs, by contrast [to drunkenness], enables a "sober intoxication" which attunes the whole self —

body, heart and mind — to a life attentive to others and to God. It is a practice of the self as physical as drinking — and as habit-forming. One of the main habits formed is that of alertness. There is also the habit of obedience, a word closely connected in many languages with hearing. Singing is a model of free obedience, of following with others along a way that rings true. In this often the body leads the self, and we find ourselves absorbed in a meaning which only gradually unfolds and pervades other spheres.[7]

Often the body leads the self. . . . One of the reasons that music is so powerful in sustaining people amid suffering or cognitive impairment, in causing us to overflow in praise, is that music touches the entirety of our being: body, soul, and passion as well as mind. Beautiful music calls us out of the immediacy of our current situation into a world far greater than we could otherwise imagine, into the praise of God. St. Augustine, in a sermon on Psalm 32, testifies to this extraordinary power of music.

Wherever [people] must labor hard, they begin with songs whose words express their joy. But when the joy brims over and words are not enough, they abandon even this coherence and give themselves up to the sheer sound of singing. What is this jubilation, this exultant song? It is the melody that means our hearts are bursting with feelings words cannot express. And to whom does this jubilation most belong? Surely to God, who is unutterable. . . . If words will not come and you may not remain silent, what else can you do but let the melody soar?[8]

We begin to discover that the unutterable God is most aptly praised in music and jubilation that lets the melody soar.

Further, we discover that our personhood, our identities as creatures created for the praise of God, is fundamentally social. We bear the image and likeness of the Triune God in the overflowing abundance of communal praise in worship. Again music provides a central image. As Ford describes it,

Sounds do not have exclusive boundaries — they can blend, harmonise, resonate with each other in endless ways. In singing there can be a filling of space with sound in ways that draw more and more voices to take part, yet with no sense of crowding. It is a performance of abundance, as new voices join in with their own distinctive tones. There is

7. David F. Ford, *Self and Salvation: Being Transformed* (Cambridge: Cambridge University Press, 1999), p. 125.

8. Quoted in Fergus Kerr, *Theology After Wittgenstein* (Oxford: Blackwell, 1986), pp. 166-67.

an 'edgeless expansion' (Begbie), an overflow of music, in which participants have their boundaries transformed. The music is both outside and within them, and it creates a new vocal, social space of community in song. The *en pneumati* (with/in the Spirit) resonates with the repeated use of the same phrase in Ephesians 2:18 and 22. There the Jews and Gentiles are seen, after the demolition of the dividing wall between them, having access through Christ in the Spirit to the Father. The community is pictured being joined together ('harmonised together' — *sunarmologoumene*) into 'a holy temple,' the space which above all is filled with psalms and hymns, 'a dwelling place of God in the Spirit.'[9]

Music provides a way of incorporating the diverse range of differences among participants within a complex unity of praise.

Hence, worship includes those who sing as well as those incapable of using words, for whom the melody soars in their souls. But it is not just any music that makes the crucial difference — it is music fit for the soul, for the praise of God. Fundamentally, Christians proclaim that worship appropriate to the praise of God bears the face of the crucified and risen Christ. Our praise should be shaped by cruciform joy, music capable of embracing our deepest fears and our highest hopes, our most intense griefs as well as our most focused triumphs.[10]

Such praise of God should shape communities that refuse to abandon those who are suffering, including those who are not yet, no longer, or never were able to function cognitively. This praise testifies to the vision at the conclusion of Romans 8, a chapter that acknowledges the painful realities of suffering and the groaning of creation for fulfillment: "For I am convinced that neither death, nor life, nor angels, nor rulers, nor things present, nor things to come, nor powers, nor height, nor depth, nor anything else in all creation, will be able to separate us from the love of God in Christ Jesus our Lord."

Theologically, we learn through worship, through prayer and praise of God, that our identity as persons and our hope for the future are shaped by God's memory and hope manifested in Jesus Christ. The stories of our lives, broken and fragmented as they are by sin, by oppression, by tragedy, by the realities of aging and dying, find their full meaning and intelligibility by being located in the story of the Triune God. Life as we know it is filled with a vari-

---

9. Ford, *Self and Salvation*, p. 121.

10. Those who are deaf are also capable of "making music" that touches their souls, whether it be through the use of bass drums that create vibrations the deaf can feel or through the use of signing the music and moving their bodies as they do so.

ety of perils, threats, and disorders; the reality of death cannot be avoided. Even so, nothing can separate us from the love of God in Christ Jesus our Lord because the story does not begin and end with us; it begins and ends with God.

David Keck develops this theological conviction with great clarity and power in his study of Alzheimer's disease and the love of God, *Forgetting Whose We Are*.[11] Since Alzheimer's is a disease that tests the limits of our personhood, it provides a crucial test case for the theological claims about God's story and God's memory and hope as the carriers of our personal identity. After all, the Alzheimer's patient suffers a disintegration of virtually any form of personal identity. Keck writes, "An Alzheimer's hermeneutic learns through the humiliation of disease, dissolution, and death that we approach the Bible's narratives as creatures in need, creatures whose own selfhood is dependent on the support of the family, the church, and God. It is a disposition which acknowledges that, above all, we must interpolate our narratives into the narrative of Christ's suffering, death, and resurrection."[12]

Theologically, nothing can separate us from the love of God in Christ Jesus our Lord; yet too many communities, even worshiping communities, have allowed themselves to be defined by sinful conceptions of personhood in ways that marginalize and isolate people in need. Ecclesially, there are far too many things that separate people from experiencing the love of God in Christ Jesus that ought to be expressed by the caregiving of others but often is not.

The church as a worshiping community gathers for the praise of God and so is called to locate people's personal and diverse, complex, and even disintegrating narratives in the narrative of Christ's suffering, death, and resurrection. That requires that we learn to practice the church, and especially the church's worship, as a site for sustaining human dignity across the generations, regardless of cognitive ability.

We do so especially through the celebration of baptism and the Eucharist. Baptism identifies and claims us as creatures of a gracious God, identifying us as people with dignity regardless of the world's definitions of personhood.[13] We are baptized into Christ's death and resurrection, dying and rising to new life in Christ. Further, in baptism, members of the community welcome the newly baptized and commit themselves to caring for those baptized throughout their lives.

---

11. David Keck, *Forgetting Whose We Are* (Nashville, Tenn.: Abingdon, 1996).

12. Keck, *Forgetting Whose We Are*, p. 228.

13. See chap. 6 of L. Gregory Jones, *Embodying Forgiveness* (Grand Rapids: Eerdmans, 1995), for a description of how important this claim about baptism has been in sustaining a sense of identity for African Americans amidst conditions of slavery.

Similarly, the Eucharist sustains us on our journey by locating our lives, and our community, within the drama of Christ's suffering, death, and resurrection. It is not accidental that the narrative of the Great Thanksgiving spoken or sung, the real presence of Christ in the bread and wine, the bodily gestures of those receiving the Eucharist, and the music of the liturgy all coalesce to shape and sustain communities that praise God. Further, frequent celebrations of the Eucharist develop habits that cultivate the kind of knowing made manifest in the stories of Michael and Jimmie. Most particularly, the Eucharist is a sacrament of hope that is crucial for all of us, and especially the elderly, as a reminder that our lives are not bounded by death but by the resurrected and resurrecting Christ.

This suggests that, ecclesially, we discover authentically Christian community precisely as we practice worship in ways that develop habits of life, thought, and interaction that school us to discover one another's identities as creatures of a gracious and holy God who promises to recreate our lives in God's eternal kingdom. We do so in worship, and in giving and receiving care and friendship across the generations; those who are infirm or cognitively impaired are as important in the ways they receive care and friendship as are those who offer it. We can learn much from hospice physician Ira Byock's words to a generous and giving man who, in his dying, was despairing because he was no longer in control of his own life:

> You know, the social responsibility that you have so well exemplified is not limited to doing things for others. Interactions just like this, caring and being cared for, are the way in which community is created. I believe that community, like the word *family*, is really more of a verb than a noun. Community comes about in the process of caring for those in need among us. It's unfortunate now that you're getting to see that side of it, but in allowing yourself to be cared for, and being a willing recipient of care, you're contributing in a remarkably valuable way to the community. In a real sense, we need to care for you. Not just those of us in hospice, but the community we represent, the community that funds and supports us.[14]

Community is a verb. We would add to Byock's description that community comes about most faithfully and authentically in the process of praising God in worship, shaping the habits and dispositions that enable us to care for and be cared for by one another across the generations.

Thus far, we have been focusing on the ways in which we need to rethink

14. Ira Byock, *Dying Well* (New York: Riverhead, 1997), pp. 96-97.

our theological and ecclesial assumptions about personhood. We believe that we need those habits of life and thought shaped by worship, and especially by the Eucharist, in order to sustain patterns of care and commitment across the generations regardless of cognitive ability. Even so, our descriptions have focused more on the elderly as recipients of care, and as persons worthy of continuing dignity even as cognitive functioning may diminish or be lost over time; yet many elderly have crucial roles to play in caring for others, and in offering wisdom, care, and commitment to the younger generations. If we understand our lives and our identities in relation to the praise of God, sustained by communities of giving and receiving care, then we will be better able to appreciate and honor the elderly in our midst.

III

People are called to honor the elderly as well as young children, not because of their rational capacities or their productivity but as creatures created in the image and likeness of God for the praise of God. Hence, there are no replaceable people, nor is there anyone that we are permitted to abandon, marginalize, or ignore. We will be measured by the care we offer to the least among us.

Even so, we ought also to honor the elderly because they are a source of wisdom and guidance for the future. The elderly have lifetimes of experience to draw on, and many elderly have crucial wisdom to offer the young. To be sure, not all elderly are wise or virtuous. Even so, those who have cultivated good habits and served God faithfully over the years have much to offer to others. Worship is a central activity that brings the generations together and provides opportunities for the elderly to establish and sustain crucial relationships across the generations. Regular participation by the elderly in worship and involvement with children often increase physical and spiritual health among the elderly.

Drawing on our experience as pastors of United Methodist congregations, we want to suggest some key ways in which the elderly can offer care to others across the generations. First, people schooled by the Eucharist ought to develop habits of eating together in other contexts as well. In one congregation, we intentionally planned meals for the elderly to share with the children and youth of the church. Sometimes the elderly prepared the meal, but on other occasions the children and youth prepared it. The intention was to cultivate relationships and to give the elderly an opportunity to share their time, their wisdom, and their faith with those just beginning their journeys in life and in faith. The results were extraordinary. The elderly appreciated the time with younger folks, and the children and youth appreciated the attention they got from adults who clearly had time for them. Indeed, in some cases relationships were forged that extended into regular visits and phone conversations across the generations. Some elderly became "surrogate grandparents" for kids who valued having additional support nearby.

Similarly, baptism and confirmation offer opportunities to formalize important intergenerational relationships between the elderly and younger generations. For example, godparenting is a central practice for Christians to emphasize that raising Christian children cannot be left to parents alone.[15] Rituals for infant baptism ask the rest of the congregation if they will help raise the child; godparenting formalizes that process for specific persons. While people often ask friends of their own age to serve as godparents, we have also witnessed examples where elderly persons have served faithfully and powerfully as godparents to young children. After all, the elderly have both the time and the wisdom to offer.

This relationship may continue through the confirmation process. But it may also be that confirmation offers a separate occasion for asking the elderly to participate in concrete ways in the care of others. We asked several elderly members in a congregation to serve formally as mentors for youth as they went through confirmation. We wanted each confirmand to be mentored by a member of the congregation to learn to think and live as a Christian, and we discovered that several of our elderly members had the Christian wisdom we were looking for. We did not anticipate, however, how much time the elderly would devote to their mentoring relationships with the sixth and seventh graders. Though we should not have been surprised, we were delighted to discover that this task of mentoring in which we asked the elderly to give care to others also became an occasion where the elderly described that they felt they received more from the relationships than they offered.

In this same congregation, the elderly became key volunteers for an after-school program at the church. The elderly would come to the church to help the elementary and middle school children with their homework, to play with them, and to talk with them about problems they faced. These elderly offered a significant alternative to the latchkey syndrome in a community where many children were being raised by a single parent or by two blue-collar parents who both had to work in order to make ends meet.

---

15. See Ellen Charry, "Raising Christian Children in a Pagan Culture," *Christian Century,* Feb. 16, 1994, pp. 166-68.

In all of these circumstances, the activities of Christian worship and their underlying theological presumptions provided ways to honor the elderly and to draw them into life-giving relationships of caring for others. To be sure, there are countless other ways to develop practices of honoring the elderly in Christian community. But the celebration of the Eucharist and eating together, prayer to and praise of God, singing and other music, godparenting and mentoring confirmands, are all examples of the ways in which community is a verb in which we are sustained through caring and being cared for. We honor the elderly through such practices, we school ourselves and them to recognize that wisdom is expected of us as we age, and we shape our own habits of resisting the world's definitions of personhood and embodying holy care for those whom the world would abandon, ignore, or marginalize.

IV

We conclude this essay by briefly recounting an unusual service that illumines the central ways in which Christian worship reflects and shapes our assumptions about aging, wisdom, habits, and Christian holiness. The service was the baptism of our first child, held in the care center of the retirement home where Greg's grandfather lived.

Greg's grandfather Arthur was a retired United Methodist minister. He had performed our wedding at the age of eighty-six, and at that time promised to return to baptize our first child (if we should eventually have one). By the time our son was born, his great-grandfather was no longer well enough to travel. Grandpa Arthur was a saintly man of great wisdom, and we wanted both to honor his life and to fulfill his promise to us. So we decided to take the child to him in Iowa to be baptized, to the sunroom of the care center of the retirement home.

Grandpa Arthur prepared himself very carefully for the day. He ordered a new stole for the occasion so he could present it to us, and he crafted special prayers to be spoken as part of the baptismal ritual. We gathered others from our family, our church family, and our extended Christian community for the baptism. As we gathered on that Sunday, the atmosphere at the care center was electric. The elderly were thrilled to have a sign of new life in their midst, and all eyes seemed focused on the baby and the impending baptism.

The congregation that gathered for the baptism was, by the standards of the world, a rather motley crew. The celebrant, Greg's grandfather, was an eighty-nine-year-old man who would die five months later, shortly after his ninetieth birthday. He was so frail that he could not stand; he would have to sit in a wheelchair for the baptism, the Eucharist, the prayers, and the homily.

Gathered for the service were members of our family, including Greg's great-aunt, a retired minister's spouse suffering from Alzheimer's disease. Friends of ours from seminary days were there, as were a number of the residents of the care center and the retirement home. Throughout the service, Greg's great-aunt kept blurting out questions and comments that revealed her confusion. Although she could talk to Greg about times they had spent together twenty years earlier, she could not figure out who the baby was and had very little sense of the present. Aunt Ruth also became quite focused on the action of the liturgy, however, especially the music. The words were meaningless to her, yet she responded in loud and unrestrained ways to the gestures and the music.

The highlight of the service for us was the care we received from Grandpa Arthur's homily and prayer. It embodied so much wisdom and insight, so much hope for the future of our world and for our child's life, and so much confidence in the goodness of God that our eyes filled with tears of gratitude. He had summoned up the strength to offer a powerful gift to us. By most standards, Grandpa Arthur's life was beyond much usefulness — his mind was failing, his energy was low, and he needed far more than he could give. By the rationalist assumptions of Engelhardt and his fellow travelers, or the productivity standards of capitalism, only a few of the people gathered could actually be identified as persons. Yet we will never forget Grandpa Arthur's leadership of worship that day, or those persons who joined together with us.

We knew, and know, that this service was a gathering of persons in community for the praise of God. Community was a verb that day. That congregation, including persons ranging from a three-month-old baby to people a few months away from death, only some of whom possessed very strong cognitive capacities or much productive usefulness, provides an extraordinary example of life shaped by worship and of worship transforming life.

As we learn from Grandpa Arthur, Aunt Ruth, Michael, Jimmie, and countless others, Christian worship can play a central role in resisting corrupt notions of human personhood and in reshaping our habits of life and of thought. Christian worship provides a crucial site and set of practices for reclaiming the sense that all of us — from the youngest of children to the oldest of the elderly — are creatures made in the image and likeness of God, destined for communion with God, and worthy of participation in the praise of God.

The Virtues of Aging

CHARLES PINCHES

Aged to Perfection?

What could it mean to speak of the virtues of aging? There are some things —
wines, for instance, and certain kinds of cheese — that grow markedly better
with age. Aged to perfection, we say. Of course, to certain other things age
brings little but decay or rottenness, processes quite frightening in their final-
ity. No use in waiting on the blackened banana in the fruit bowl to reacquire
its firmness or beauty nor in encouraging the sagging jack-o-lantern to
brighten up for next Halloween. Aging has taken from these things their principal function; they are of use now only as they join with other has-beens in
the mulch pile, losing altogether their particular identity and form.

If we are discussing human beings rather than bananas, one might suppose the question about whether age is a virtue must change focus. It might
be noted, for instance, that questions of virtue for human beings must not be
about age itself; after all, a person either is or isn't aged, this has nothing to do
with anyone's choice, and so can have little relation to whether she has human
or moral virtue. To speak of her virtue we don't need so much to focus on
whether she is young or old as on whether she possesses certain qualities of
character such as courage or temperance.

Moving too quickly to character and virtue, however, as if they come only
in one-size-fits-all, may hide from us certain crucial aspects of what it means
to age well as a human creature before God, as well as subtleties about what
having human virtue involves. Consider in this regard the simple fact that we
understand those who are "aged" as having a special standing among us. Old
bananas do not occupy any similar sort of space. They are not so much aged
as *overripe*. We define them in terms of what they have passed by, what they

202

once had but now lack. By contrast, older human beings are not rightly understood to be people who lack youthful vigor. This may be true of them, but that is not who they are. This very point, that aged human beings have a special status that is not due merely to some lack but rather to something they have acquired or represent that is peculiar to the aged, actually suggests that there may indeed be virtue in aging, and that there are virtues those who are aged have, or can have, that the rest of us might not.

This point may not sit well within our standard pattern of moral presumption. In modernity, we do not typically like it if someone imagines that some distinction between one and the other human being counts morally, which is why we have spent a great deal of energy establishing "rights" for the elderly who, we assert, are just exactly like the rest of us. To quote Dr. Seuss's Horton (who heard the *Who*), "a person's a person, no matter how small" — or elderly. Horton is in one sense correct. By no means do I mean to say that the elderly are not "persons" in every sense of that widely used term. But Horton's tiny *Whos* actually provide us an interesting contrast: they are people who happen to be small. Elderly people, on the other hand, are not just people who happen to be old, they are the elderly — just as young people are not just people who happen to be young, they are, in fact, children.

The point is this: when it comes to being human, as opposed to hair color or size or even race, age is special. There are many reasons why this is so. To begin with we humans are mortal, and so it is not so odd for us to orient ourselves in relation to the relative temporal proximity of our death or birth. Moreover, the human life, as the narrative theologians remind us, is a kind of journey or story; like all stories it has a beginning, a middle, and an end.

I am not yet old, so I cannot say for sure. But I should think that this point might provide relief for the elderly, particularly in a society such as contemporary America where we are bombarded with messages about how important it is to avoid the signs of aging. As William May has perceptively noted,

> Americans tend to identify themselves and others with their doing rather than their being. When retirement strips them of their work, people often forfeit their identity. They lose their self-respect and therefore their hold on the respect of others. The aged thus slip to the margins of consciousness for the ruling generation. America ranks as one of the most secular countries — not in the meaning of secular as irreligious but in its original characterization of a culture that orients to the current generation, the generation that holds power and exercises authority. A consumerist society is secular in the sense that it ori-

ents with a vengeance to the current generation. It squanders the resources of generations to come and it distances itself from the heritage
of generations past all for the sake of the generation now in charge.[1]

As May sees, what results from this hegemony of the ruling generation is that
when it turns its attention in either direction, to children or to the elderly, it
either forces conformity or patronizes. Children are directed to enjoy the sort
of thing the ruling generation imagines they would want were they still children, and the elderly are directed to pretend that one can grow old without
becoming elderly. To illustrate this last point: I drive daily by a billboard advertising a local hospital's new "geriatric center." It shows a grinning older
man . . . snowboarding. The caption beneath shouts out saucily: "ACT YOUR
AGE!" I suspect that those at the "geriatric center" have more wisdom than
their billboard. But as a bit of public discourse it shows us something of the
depth of our deception. We establish a "center" for the elderly — then force
them with our rhetoric about it to imagine a form of life that is decidedly not
theirs.

Here our discussion of the aged banana may yet bear fruit. We took the
phrase "the virtues of aging" to mean that age itself is a virtue, as it is for
many wines. Points made in the interim have opened the possibility that age
for humans neither rots nor perfects them, although it does change them.
The change makes them different from many of us in a significant way: they
have become elderly. Life for the elderly is, then, importantly different from
the life led by those of us who are not elderly. As such, it very well may require
(as well as make available) a distinct set of virtues. These virtues will not be
entirely separate from ones acquired earlier in life, for it is, after all, the same
life. But becoming elderly may require a significant retooling of the virtues
one has prior to the change.

One final point before moving on. If it is true that being elderly is not
rightly thought of, like size, as simply something an older person happens to
be, but, like being a child, part of what he or she is, then we can ask our first
question, now in a bit less muddled way. We are quite sure aged wine is good
to have on hand; an aged banana . . . well, perhaps not. What, though, of aged
human persons? Is it a virtue of human life, a good, that we have the elderly
among us? Or, more respectfully put, is it good that some of us come to bear
the distinction of being elderly? For Christians there is no hesitation. It is
good, very good. We are convinced that God has made us different for our

---

1. William F. May, *The Patient's Ordeal* (Indianapolis: Indiana University Press, 1991),
p. 122.

mutual joy and benefit, which is also to say for our instruction. As Jesus did with the children, the elderly person can be placed in our midst, not merely as a demonstration of our diversity but also as a sign of truths we are at other ages tempted to ignore. In this way, the continuity between all ages, young, old, and in between, must be consistently recalled. The elderly person is different from those of us of other ages, but precisely for this reason she is able to see and represent to us, particularly if she is virtuous, what human life is really all about.

The Virtues and the Notion of "Retirement"

Supposing that there is something to find, we turn now to look within the life of the older person to see what about it might give rise to distinct virtues. Since the life of any human being is continuous, however, we cannot imagine that an entirely new set of virtues arises with age. While age calls from us a particular kind of vision and strength, if we wait until we are old to develop the roots of these, we will be stymied. As with sickness, we need particular virtues to be sick well, but it is foolishness to suppose these can be developed in an instant, just as we become sick.[2]

One of the great strengths of the classical tradition of the virtues is that it assembles the life of virtue around specifically human tendencies or appetites. Some of our appetites are particularly strong; if unchecked they will carry us away like a river. These appetites need to be tempered. On the other hand, in other situations, faced with adversity of a certain sort, we tend to retreat, and so we need to be strengthened to bear these situations well. Temperance and fortitude, the first two of the four cardinal virtues, address these essential human appetites or tendencies. They keep our lives from being distorted by them.

As Aquinas held, while the virtues are not entirely different things in different people, it is nonetheless the case that our specific natures will make for a certain variance, particularly in these two cardinal virtues that have to do with the appetites (or, for Aquinas, the passions). For instance, our sexual appetite is for Aquinas a concupiscible one, and so will need tempering. Yet clearly sexual appetite varies from person to person, and so the precise shape of temperance as it deals with the sexual appetite in one or the other person will vary.

---

2. See my and Stanley Hauerwas's discussion of developing patience in sickness in *Christians Among the Virtues* (Notre Dame, Ind.: University of Notre Dame Press, 1997), pp. 171-78.

This is one place to start when thinking of the virtues of the elderly. Appetites not only vary from person to person, they vary over the space of a person's life. Sexual desire is an obvious example here, so temperance with regard to sexual desire may be a different thing for an old man than it was for him thirty years earlier. But there are other relevant changes besides this one. There is a change, for instance, in what frightens. The bustle, for example, of a busy airport or a city street may excite us when we are young but in later years become a source of great anxiety, so much so that considerable courage is needed for an old man to fly to Los Angeles to see his son.

Yet this sort of analysis, while important, will not take us to the heart of our concern. To be sure, we are speaking here of changes that have their roots in the life of the human body — to which, in a way, everything about aging is tied. The hearing fades and the mind slows, so one can never be sure in a busy airport that one is getting everything straight. But the changes that come with aging, while related to these bodily changes, have more to do with the place of the aging person in the community she inhabits, and with its form of life.

My father-in-law, who is retired, is fond of saying that there is no retirement from the Christian life. Of course he is right. The point might be pressed: one might imagine that when Christians get old they ought not to retire from their jobs or professions. After all, if a Christian was seriously engaged at fifty-five in doing what she thought she ought to be doing in the workplace — caring for the sick, let us imagine, or teaching the uneducated — why should she stop doing this when she turns sixty-five? Indeed, if she does, doesn't this demonstrate that she did what she did less for its own sake, as a service to God and community, and more for the external reward of her salary?

Mother Teresa notwithstanding, and with due respect and admiration to those Christians like her who work tirelessly at one calling till their death at an extreme old age, there does seem to be something important carried by the notion of retirement — not from the Christian life, but from one's lifelong job in society. To begin, it is a bit snobbish of those who work in the professions to assume that someone's job is necessarily also his calling, i.e., that we fulfill our obligations to God and to our community through the work we perform for our daily bread. Suppose one's job, the only one he could find, was to mine for coal.

But more importantly, in some societies "retirement" functions as a passage of a life from one calling to another. In traditional Hinduism, the passage from one stage or *asrama* of life to the next is quite distinct and pronounced. In his middle years a man is understood to inhabit the householder *asrama*, when he cares principally for his family and his job. When his skin is wrinkled and his hair white, he can, and in some sense should (although many do not), move to the stage of forest dweller. This stage merges with the final ascetic stage of his life, what he does until death, and it is the most highly honored of all stages.

In Western society, retirement typically releases one from the daily responsibilities and cares of the world of work, so one is able to pursue other things. Of course, for many this is crushing, since increasingly the world of work is the only source of meaning and purpose in our lives, as well as the patterned routine around which we build our daily schedules. Those with money often set off on a frenzied search for the "fun" they were cheated out of in those earlier days when they were busily building cash reserves. Theirs is a double emptiness, for not only is the fun they seek an illusion, but their determined pursuit of it reveals that the work of their earlier days was itself a kind of lucrative pastime, what they needed to do then in order to be able now to set about to fill their empty hopes.

Whatever a person makes of it, retirement nonetheless functions as the swing point, the gateway to old age. My hunch is that some form of the concept is necessary if we are to make full good sense of the notion that there are virtues of aging. As opposed to the aging of the body or the diminution of the sexual appetite, what retirement introduces is a change of description about what one does. So the retired person will say of himself, "I used to do that, but I don't any longer. Now I do this."

One unfortunate feature of our societal concept of retirement is that we typically apply it to paying jobs. This is particularly pernicious if it is accompanied by the presumption that the time one spends employed in a job serving the gods of capitalism is truly the core of human life. So youth becomes a time when we prepare for getting a job, and old age the time when, since we can no longer produce, we can be sent to pasture. When retirement is so closely tied to work in the capitalist system, the term can be used only ambiguously of spouses who didn't work in that system, my mother and mother-in-law to name two, who now nonetheless adopt the term when they say of themselves together with their husbands that "we're retired." Their *joint* adoption of the term is for our purposes quite helpful. My mother no less than my father can say, "I used to do that, but I don't any longer. Now I do this." In her case, she raised five children, one or the other of whom occupied her house for the space of thirty-six years. But we are all gone now, and she no longer does that. She has retired.

Armed with this modified sense of retirement, I believe we can make our way back round to the virtues of aging — that is, after one more caveat. If we think of retirement as expressed in the phrase "I used to do that, and I don't any longer; now I do this" — with the "that" taken not to mean any *thing* at all but rather a life-defining pursuit — we must finally add that the "this" is what we anticipate doing until we die. Retirement, taken now as a stage in life, is importantly the last stage. This marks it as, in some cases, quite a long stage indeed, one that will, not unlike the middle stage of production or caregiving, itself include very many changes and adjustments. After thirty-six years raising and caring for children in her house, my mother retired with my father in 1977. So, for twenty-five years, she has been retired. Now eighty-two, she is all the more aware of the imminent possibility of her own death, although I suspect she has spent time in all of those twenty-five years preparing in one way or another for it. But it may not come soon — indeed, given her current health it is not likely to. There have been a great many changes in her life in these twenty-five years, almost as many as in the thirty-six years previously. But in those twenty-five years (and this is the point about retirement) she has had to come to see herself, her life, and her work in a different way than she saw it in the phase or stage before. Importantly, she has understood it throughout as in one way or another the final stage of her life. This is one central factor that marks it as distinctive and, as such, provides one key ground for thinking about distinctive virtues of aging.

The Virtues of Aging: As It Is Now

It has not been my purpose in the foregoing analysis to argue that "to be elderly" is always the same thing as "to be retired," as if, no matter how old, one is not elderly until one has retired from a job, or, in the reverse, as if all those who "retire" at any age are, ipso facto, elderly. Rather, my concern with retirement relates to what I take to be quite true, namely that "to become elderly" involves more than merely a set of bodily changes that come with age. What it involves in addition is the entrance into a stage of life that is different from the middle, active phase of worker/homemaker. To employ the phrase used by May, the elderly person is one who is no longer a member of the "ruling generation." As I have further suggested, this phase is not merely to be understood negatively, in other words, that to be elderly involves the loss of a certain kind of power, but also in terms of its place within the story of a human life. It is the final phase, the conclusion, where all that has gone before can be summed up and brought to an end.

As we have seen, the notion of retirement in present society is subject to a great deal of corruption. Nonetheless, I am proposing that it be redeemed; indeed, it is an important task for Christians in America and similar societies to do this work of redemption. A key part of this work, both for the elderly and for the rest of us, is to see that and how there are virtues of aging.

Let me begin reflecting on the specific virtues of aging with a story. A few years ago while on a long cross-country trip our family stopped to spend a day or two with my wife's aunt and uncle. Uncle Day, who was then eighty-four, greeted us with great glee, for at that time we were partly comprised of four children under the age of twelve. As Uncle Day knew, no one likes better to play games than children under the age of twelve — unless it is Day himself. Soon after our arrival the games came out, interesting and somewhat obscure games such as "Othello," a game related to checkers where the pieces are colored differently on either side and are inverted by various moves. The person who successfully turns the most pieces on the board to his color wins. Uncle Day, we found out, had actually made this particular Othello set in his wood shop in the garage. A "tour" of the shop was forthwith arranged and we all learned how pieces could be cut on the band saw and shaped on the lathe. Uncle Day, I could tell, had developed an affection for these machines for what they could do, but his chief love there in the shop was the raw woodpile. Day and Blanche spent their working years as Presbyterian missionaries. Their life there is another story, one you can guess is not unrelated to this one. But we are speaking of them now in retirement. And the specific relevance here is that in retirement Day and Blanche, while hardly poor, must adhere closely to a budget. It is one reason why Uncle Day's woodpile is entirely composed of pieces that have been scrounged: This is a piece of oak that came from an old pallet — you know, they make some of those pallets out of oak since they need to be strong. And here's a piece of black walnut that Billy (son Billy) brought me. I forget where he picked it up. But black walnut! Look at the color. I think there's enough to make croquet mallets out of it for my grandkids. Imagine, black walnut croquet mallets!

The tour over, back at the game table the action switched to card games. If you have ever played cards with young children you know that there is one nagging problem even with the simplest game of "Go Fish." Most card games require that a hand be splayed and held unseen by opponents around the table, but this is a quite difficult task for children. It is usually tried once and thereafter abandoned by the youngest children, their cards laid face up on the table for older brothers and sisters to plainly see. For the next age up it is a source of endless frustration, for they understand the significance of not showing your cards but their hands are yet small and young enough that holding the cards splayed in one hand while picking from them with the other more often than not results in several cards falling to the floor.

Othello and croquet and "Go Fish" continued throughout our weekend at Day and Blanche's, the time came to say goodbye, and we were off for home. That was in late summer. Shortly before Christmas a package arrived from Day and Blanche with gifts marked for the children. Inside each child found an oblong block of wood, yellow pine, sanded smooth, each with his or her name wood-burned into its shellacked facing surface. The bottom of the block is flat and sits firmly on any table. The top is slanted, and into it are cut deep, narrow groves, arranged down the slanted surface like stadium steps. Each is a personalized, handmade stand in which to display your cards to yourself, and no one else.

In detailing virtues of the elderly William May makes the following comments about a virtue he calls *simplicity:*

> Simplicity should mark the elderly, and not merely because memory lapses into the familiar, repetitive grooves, but because the pilgrim has at long last learned to travel light. He has learned to live by simple truths and simple gifts. The prophet Micah describes such a soul as it winnows down . . . "He has showed you, O man, what is good; and what does the Lord require of you but to do justice, and to love kindness, and to walk humbly with your god?" (Micah 6:8).[3]

May is right to use the term *simplicity* to describe a principal virtue of those elderly who, like Uncle Day, can teach the rest of us the virtues we will need near the end of our journey, and which all of us, of any age, very much need displayed in our lives together. Short of dying young, there is no clearer way someone is cheated of her old age than if she must live it in turmoil and complication. Our lives are complicated, particularly in the middle, and that this may later ease does not change things much for those in the midst of the complications. This is one reason why having the elderly living among us is so important. For they become an emblem to the rest of us that, despite their reality and power, crisis and turmoil do not rule the day. *Dona nobis pacem.* And God will grant us peace at the end of the day, in the quiet of twilight, when we have the eye to notice a child's struggle with her cards, the mind to imagine a solution, and the time to craft it for her with care and love.

If we begin with May's suggestion that simplicity is a central virtue for living well as an elderly person, we are able to see our way clear to identify a related virtue. For the story of Uncle Day to have the ending it did, he needed to see what he saw, namely the minor but genuine frustration of young children struggling with their cards. To do this, Day had to live very much in the

---

3. May, *The Patient's Ordeal*, p. 134.

present; he had to be attuned to the world as it was right then, as he sat on the floor playing cards with his grandnieces and grandnephews.

This very present sense of things I shall call the virtue of *delight*. It is a special gift both to and of the elderly that comes, as May notes, partly because they have learned to travel light, and so are weighed down by fewer cares. It is partly due as well to the fact that they are nearing the end of their journey and so are released from having to notice and care about only the "significant things." For instance, while my wife and I might have in passing noted our children's frustration with their cards, it was the least of our worries, concerned as we are about how they are doing in school, whether they'll need new coats this fall, and so on.

The virtue of delight was on display in Uncle Day not only when he noticed the trouble with cards but as he admired the black walnut. My father, recently deceased, showed it in his last years as he tended his roses. When we visited, I always admired my father's roses. But I did not see them as he did; he took in them a delight I suspect I can at this stage in my life only know in glimpses. My father with his roses, as Day with his wood, was in his final years particularly adept at admiring, at breathing in deeply, what is the simplest and best in God's world.

The virtue of delight in Day led, as virtues should, to an action. His virtues of simplicity and delight made the time he spent playing cards with our children different from the time I spent doing the same — it was more present, which made him able to see their struggle with their cards in a way different from how I saw it. But what needs further to be added is that this vision in Day carried along with it a readiness to engage simply with the world he saw. This is not to say that what Day did was simple in the sense that it was easy. To the contrary, making the card stands, even hatching the plan to mail them for Christmas, involved time, care, and skill. Rather, it was simple in the sense that it engaged directly and specifically one item in the world. It saw a child's struggle and then set about with focus and single-mindedness (and delight) to address that struggle.

Simplicity and delight are related in a surprising way to the physical aspects of aging as well. I am speaking of a concern that the elderly have of necessity, namely a concern about their own physical health. This is a simple although often very great trial. The elderly must live every day with the awareness that their bodily powers are diminishing, which forces them to live with a constant sense of their own limitation. This may not sound much like a virtue, and for our culture it decidedly is not. Indeed, as the billboard of the snowboarding senior attests, there is nothing that horrifies our culture more than the thought that we might have to live within the limits of what we are truly able to do rather than what we imagine we want to do. Christians, however, see how *limitedness* can appear not only as a gift but also as a call. If lived well, it can be called a virtue.

Concern about one's own health, along, perhaps, with concern about the health of a spouse or close friend who is also elderly, can become an obsession. But if it does not, and is properly placed, it enhances the virtues of simplicity and delight we have been speaking of. For those who are seriously impaired, the body may seem a prison from which to escape. But for many of the elderly whose bodies yet serve them, there comes a heightened sense of the goodness of the body and a thankfulness for all that it can yet do. An older woman might say, "I may not be able to snowboard (as if I ever wanted to!), but I can walk out on a bright, sunny afternoon to get the mail. Ah, and what a pleasure it is!"

One step further, this intimacy with the body leads in those who are virtuous to a quite focused *empathy* for others. Young or old, we all share the needs and gifts of the body. The virtuous elderly who are especially aware of these needs and gifts in their own bodies will be also aware of them in others. I do not doubt that one of the reasons Uncle Day saw so well the struggle in our children's fingers properly to grip the cards is that his fingers do not work as they once did and he has come to understand and live within their limitations. Concern about the body in those who lack virtue remains (and often increases) as principally a concern about *me*, about *my* body and its ailments. By contrast, in the virtuous elderly it expands without effort to a concern for another. After a restless night of their own they will ask without a hint of envy, "How did you sleep last night?" Or, "I feel a chill in the air this morning; are you warm enough?"

It has become a joke within our family that if you visit grandparents in Florida you had better be ready to talk about the weather. It is discussed numerous times in the day; routinely everyone at church, which is comprised mainly of the elderly, knows at least one forecast (pooled, of course, they often cancel one another out) for the coming day. Whatever the forecast, the hope of sun and warmth for our visit is expressed by each one. Some may suppose this is a sign that these elderly people have little else to think about. Perhaps. But bodily creatures are right to be concerned with the weather. Moreover, as opposed to so many of us who live for what might happen next year or next decade when our ship comes, for those who are concerned with what happens today or maybe tomorrow, what is more important than whether the sun is soon to shine? Concern about the daily weather may indeed signal a kind of simplemindedness, but not, as we suppose, a vice, but a virtue, a gift that the virtuous elderly give to the rest of us. They can teach us in this to live, and delight in, what is now present, a thoroughly sufficient time, the gift of a gracious God whose promise it is to remain always present with us.

The Virtues of Aging: As It Was

By definition old age requires accumulated time, by which we mean human time, time carried by memory. Carrying memory is not the work of this or that person only; rather, it is done by a people whose life extends beyond a generation. The elderly have a special role with respect to this accumulated memory. More than any others among the living, it is they who represent the past for us.

Virtues attributable to the elderly in this sense, however, cannot be described formally. No doubt, there is a certain function that all elderly perform irrespective of what sort of people they serve, for the passage of memory cannot be accomplished in any other way than by elders communicating in one way or another with their juniors. This means that some skills or gifts related to the passage of memory in a community will be identifiable apart from what in particular is remembered. Some old women, for instance, are wonderful storytellers, and they are rightly held in esteem by their people for this skill. Yet there is more to virtue than skill. The storyteller does more than pass memories without careful selection and judgment; she does more than tell them for our simple entertainment. Rather, she tells her stories to shape us. In stories the past is put to work in the present, not only in what old men or old women tells us, but in them as they tell us. They embody the past, but they bring it to us for a present purpose. Perhaps they remind us of something that was lost and needs to be regained, of some gift given that needs yet to be received with gratitude, or of some deed once done that outstrips our present achievements whose glory might even yet be reclaimed. The elderly person who carries and communicates these memories remembers with design. She wants us to be instructed in our lives now.

This means that old storytellers may compete with one another in the different memories their stories recall. To discover not only skill but also virtue in the storyteller, we must ask not only how they tell their story but what story they tell. To explore this, and to note how different old men serve their people differently, I should like to consider a remarkable old story, Homer's *Iliad*.

In the *Iliad* the warlike and adventurous Akhaians are fixed upon the utter destruction of the more cultured and domesticated Trojans, hunkered down behind the walls of their great city. These two peoples, and the war that rages between them, are the focus of this great epic poem throughout. As one might suppose, the story dwells upon the clash between the two mighty champions of the opposing peoples, Akhilleus and Hektor, members each of the ruling generation. Less noticed, however, are the two old men who serve the peoples: Lord Nestor of the Akhaians and King Priam of the Trojans. Both Nestor and Priam are, in our earlier sense, retired. The main work of the two cultures — attacking and defending, warring in full strength and glory — has passed on to the next generation. The two old men are hardly disengaged, however. Instead, they have the distinct and important function of placing the present action of each people into a context that is sustained by its past. This relation to the past is vital if those now at work in the ruling generation are to muster the strength and courage to rise to the task before them.

Nestor's role in this is particularly apparent. Besides providing sage counsel, he continually inspires the Akhaian warriors with wild tales of past heroics in battle. Sometimes, in fact, he even taunts them with this past, suggesting that if they fail to match its glory (which, as they contemplate retreat, they are plainly doing) they are unworthy of their forefathers. As such, Nestor has a great deal to do with whether or not the war between the Akhaians and Trojans continues. Indeed, early in the *Iliad*, Homer gives the impression that warring parties might avoid war. In one case, for instance, Hektor has challenged the Akhaians to send forth a champion to meet him in single combat. With Akhilleus sulking in his tent, the lesser champions of the Akhaians are reticent to step forward, for Hektor is formidable. In this moment of uncertainty Nestor publicly remembers a time when a similar challenge was issued by the champion Ereuthalion, and he, then a young man, rose to the call.

> . . . he challenged all our best,
> but all were shaken, full of dread; no one
> would take the field against him. Well, my pride
> drove me to take him on with a high heart,
> though I was still youngest of us all.
> I fought him, and Athena gave me the glory.
> Tallest and toughest of enemies, I killed him,
> that huge man, and far and wide he sprawled.
> Would god I had my youth again, my strength
> intact: Lord Hektor would soon be engaged!
> But you that are the best of men of Akhaia
> will not go forward cheerfully to meet him![4]

4. Homer, *The Iliad* 7.175-86, trans. Robert Fitzgerald (New York: Anchor Books, 1974). Hereafter, references to the *Iliad* (and to *The Odyssey*, also translated by Fitzgerald [New York:

As the oldest warrior, Nestor speaks with authority. He has the special role of mediating the glories of a past generation to this one, the one that has for the moment become unsure, gripped by fear in the face of Hektor's might. His story is effective. The creeping cowardice is arrested and champions arise. "So chided by the old man, volunteers arose then, nine in all . . ." (7.177-88). From the nine Aias (Ajax) is appointed and the war resumes its course.

In this brief episode Homer displays how war is a practice that is carried from generation to generation. This is perhaps all the plainer at the end of his other epic, the *Odyssey,* when the youthful Telemakhos finally comes of age as he joins with his father Odysseus and grandfather Laertes in readying himself for battle. Pride swelling in his heart, Odysseus hails his young son:

> "Telemakhos,
> you are going into battle against pikemen
> where hearts of men are tried. I count on you
> to bring no shame upon your forefathers.
> In fighting power we have excelled this lot
> in every generation."
> Said his son:
> "If you are curious, Father, watch and see
> the stuff that's in me. No more talk of shame."
> And old Laertes cried aloud:
> "Ah, what a day for me, dear gods!
> to see my son and grandson vie in courage!" (24:561-72)

The mantle has been passed, and it is armored. Old men like Nestor or Laertes find joy only as they are assured that the next generation has learned to offer war its soul. Nestor is a courageous man, to be sure. But in old age the courage required of him is less valor in battle, more the courage to represent to his successors what past valor demands in the present. Nestor fearlessly employs all the authority that rests in his age and person to ensure that the code by which he lived will guide the lives of his children and his children's children.

This is in many ways a captivating picture, but it must be drawn out fully; for we speak here of a past of carnage that is once again activated in the present. Indeed, it is the thirst for war, the courage of battle passed from Nestor to Ajax, or from Laertes to Odysseus to Telemakhos, that leads to the destruc-

---

Vintage Classics, 1990]) will be included in the text. Fitzgerald's translation uses a phonetic rather than traditional spelling of the names of many of the characters in the epic. (Hector is Hektor, Achilles is Akhilleus, and so on.) I will follow Fitzgerald in most cases, noting the more traditional spelling in parentheses when necessary.

tion of Troy and the slaughter of its citizens, and to the obliteration of Ithaca's civilized life.[5] Thus one might make the suggestion (is it Homer's?) that old men like Nestor, while no doubt admirable in their steel-heartedness and in their concern to challenge and teach the next generation the same, can be blinded by the stories they so faithfully pass along. In this light, the story of the latter deeds of Priam, the old Trojan king and grandfather, provides a striking contrast.

Priam's key scene in the *Iliad* comes after the battle his contemporary Nestor so fervently inspired. It has borne its awful fruit. Hektor, Priam's son, is dead, and his body is being dragged daily behind Akhilleus' chariot, a plaything now, and a sign of Akhilleus' prowess. Priam goes by night to visit Akhilleus to plead for his son's body, in order to take it back to Troy for respectful burial. The journey behind enemy lines is difficult, one Priam makes against the advice of many in Troy. Sorrowfully dragging himself from the security of his city toward the enemy's tents, he feels the disorientation of an old man in a stranger's world. He is met, however, by Hermes the Wayfinder, disguised as one of Akhilleus' men. The man treats Priam with respect, partly because Priam reminds the man of his father "whom he holds dear" (24.449).

This memory of a long-lost father foreshadows the exchange between Priam and Akhilleus that occurs once Priam, with the young man's assistance, arrives at Akhilleus' tent. His first act is to kneel and kiss "the hands of wrath that killed his son" (24.572). Then he speaks as follows:

> "Remember your own father,
> Akhilleus, in your godlike youth: his years
> like mine are many, and he stands upon
> the fearful doorstep of old age. He, too,
> is hard pressed, it may be, by those around him,
> there being no one able to defend him
> from the bane of war and ruin. Ah, but he
> may nonetheless hear news of you alive,
> and so with glad heart hope through all his days
> for sight of his dear son, come back from Troy,
> while I have deadly fortune. . . .

---

5. In the *Odyssey* the three generations mentioned stand poised to do battle with virtually all the other established families on Ithaca. The only thing that saves Ithaca is Athena's intervention; she steps in and halts the war. This intervention differs in character from all other cases of her intervention in the epic. We are left with the impression that without this uncharacteristic supernatural strike, the world of men, coached as it has been by the gods of war, will utterly self-destruct.

Akhilleus,
be reverent toward the great gods! And take
pity on me, remember your own father.
Think me more pitiful by far, since I
have brought myself to do what no man else
has done before — to lift to my lips the hand
of one who killed my son." (24.582-608)

Like Nestor's, the words of the old man have effect on this fiercest representative of the ruling generation. Yet the effect does not this time issue in a battle cry. The memory awakened is not that of mighty deeds of war; Priam does not chide Akhilleus to rival his forefathers in blood thirst. Instead, in his words and bearing, his very person, and the fact that he is enemy, father of the vanquished, Priam reminds the mighty Akhilleus of the limited span of human life we share.

The reckless passion of two young lovers or the lusty, swaggering love of men at the height of their powers wading together into some great and terrible test of strength — these loves by nature deny time; they are purposefully forgetful precisely so that they might imagine themselves eternal and invincible. Akhilleus, whose behavior throughout the *Iliad* is best summarized as rage of various sorts, has been locked firmly in this passionate forgetfulness. The power, an unexpected and alien power of Priam's words and presence, breaks this spell. Akhilleus is suddenly touched by a cross-generational love that by nature places each human life in its time. He remembers his father and so remembers, in a way, himself. In an instant, the war that has brought him so far from home, his victory over Hektor, the death of his friend Patroklos, are placed within the context of life, his and his father's, Priam's and his son's. So the deep sadness of their unhappy intersection is suddenly seen for what it is. Here, these two men for whom hatred and enmity could have no better ground, share grief.

Now in Akhilleus
the evocation of his father stirred
new longing, and an ache of grief. He lifted
the old man's hand and gently put him by.
Then both were overborne as they remembered:
the old king huddled at Akhilleus' feet
wept, and wept for Hektor, killer of men,
while great Akhilleus wept for his own father
as for Patroklos once again; and sobbing
filled the room. (24.610-17)

This moment of shared grief comes upon the two men without plan. Nevertheless, it was Priam's courage that made it possible. What sort of courage is it, and how does it compare to the fervor of Nestor, who by virtue of his old age carried the force and authority to shame younger men into battle? The difference lies in the different relation each has to the world of war, which is, of course, the world in which the ruling generation rules. Nestor is a witness from wars of the past, a testimony to the glory they can bring and the courage they require. But wars, at least in the *Iliad*, are not important for what they accomplished in time, in other words, for the fact that they brought a period of peace; to the contrary, they provide men with a way to transcend time, in a moment to achieve eternal glory. Nestor does not remind the younger men of what they eventually will become — old men who have journeyed through time. To the contrary, he incites them with the picture of the glory he once achieved, and so shames them for supposing in weakness and fear that the temporal context this glory transcends might rival it in significance.

Priam's courage lies in his readiness to challenge the hegemony of war as the lord of all that matters. In so doing, he challenges the presumption that our lives shine the brightest only as we stand at the pinnacle of our powers. His old age calls Akhilleus out of the passion of the present time, or, perhaps better put, the old man who comes to beg for the body of his beloved son from his wrathful killer testifies to the truth that the so-called glories of war will live in true memory not for what they were in a moment's proud flash, but rather for what they reap in time, namely grief. And this, Akhilleus suddenly sees, is true not only for Priam but for Akhilleus' own father, for himself, and for all men and women as shaped by those loves that tie us together in our temporality. This why Priam and Akhilleus, who have been the cause of each other's grief, can nonetheless unite in it and in the remembrance of the timeful loves that lie at grief's root.

The virtue, then, of Priam as an old man is the *courage of truthful remembrance*. Its truthfulness resides in its readiness to bear sadness and grief. Its courage lies in its readiness to be old. Nestor displays a semblance of courage when he chides his juniors into battle. But he does so by representing to them what he once was, not what he now is. His memories, then, do little more than aggrandize the present. He supports rather than challenges the ruling generation's pursuit of power and glory. By contrast, Priam elicits from Akhilleus and the young man who leads him to his tent an awareness of how the present time fits within the past and the future. They are reminded of their fathers, not as they once were, brilliant in the valor of war, veiled in its trance of transcendent glory, but as they are now, old men who miss the sons they have always loved. So Akhilleus sees in a flash who he is — and what is the true meaning in time of what he has done to Hektor. He is not just the one who in a glorious moment vanquished a noble foe; he is, rather, a man who must bear his deeds and the deeds of others through time. Importantly, what he must bear, as does this old man Priam before him and as does his father on a distant shore, is the sadness of loss. In this moment of truthful remembrance, the question of who is to be blamed for the loss recedes; what matters is that these two mortal men both bear it.

Priam's courage as an old man, then, lies in its challenge to the rule of power by which the Akhaians lived. While admitting Akhilleus' mastery and might, Priam's truthful courage nevertheless refuses to give it the status of ultimate truth. Indeed, Priam stands as a witness to the falsity of Nestor's story of war since that story fails to place war in time; it ignores the sadness that must be borne by those who suffer its results. In this way, Priam's courage is no private virtue.[6] He does not simply come to this conclusion about war privately, in his own mind. He does not stay safely behind the walls of his city and share his grief for Hektor only with those who also loved him. Rather, he leaves this security — an act made all the more difficult by his age — and walks with trembling resolve across the very battlefield on which his son was killed to face the ferocious destroyer of what he had for so long loved. In this he allows his age to be displayed, and so offers witness to the truth of another story than the one that has so far been told in the *Iliad*.[7] Homer's great epic poem is, no doubt, a story of the strong and mighty clashing in glorious battle. But, as Priam shows, behind it lies another perhaps more truthful story, one wives, children, and old men must bear in memory. A story of the loss of loves, of sadness and of grief.

The Virtues of Aging: And As It Will Be Forever, Amen

The point just made about which story, Nestor's or Priam's, bears the truth, is actually a theological one that cannot be attributed to the storyteller Homer without qualification. For in Homer's world we must ask what good Priam's

---

6. As Stanley Hauerwas and I argue elsewhere, there is no such thing as private courage. See *Christians Among the Virtues*, chap. 6.

7. This is not unlike the Buddha who, it is told, sees an old man and so is opened to a world that his father has tried to hide from him by immersing him so thoroughly in the rich life of the warrior caste. Next, as the story goes, he sees a sick man, and then a dead man. Upon asking, he is told by his chariot driver that these were common to the lot of humanity. The next step, of course, is Buddha's great renunciation of the world.

witness to the truth serves. As the battle has been passed from Nestor to Aias and others, so it will be passed from Aias or Akhilleus to the next generation, Laertes to Odysseus to Telemakhos. This is a truth as well, one that is made no less true by the suffering this cycle brings to the like of old men like Priam. Akhilleus says as much.

> But when Akhilleus' heart
> had known the luxury of tears, and pain
> within his breast and bones had passed away,
> he stood then, raised the old king up, in pity
> for his grey head and greybeard cheek, and spoke
> in a warm rush of words:
> "Ah, sad and old!
> Trouble and pain you've borne, aplenty.
> Only a great will could have brought you here
> among the Akhaian ships, and here alone
> before the eyes of one who stripped your sons,
> your many sons, in battle. Iron must be
> the heart within you. Come, then, and sit down.
> We'll probe our wounds no more but let them rest,
> though grief lies heavy on us. Tears heal nothing,
> drying stiff and cold. This is the way
> the gods ordained the destiny of men,
> to bear such burdens in our lives, while they
> feel no affliction. . . .
> gods out of the sky sent you this bitterness:
> the years of siege, the battles and the losses.
> Endure it, then. And do not mourn forever
> for your dead son. There is no remedy.
> You will not make him stand again. Rather
> await some new misfortune to be suffered." (24.623-61)

Akhilleus' regard for Priam has grown after this display of courage and love for son Hektor. But the anger that earlier seethed in Akhilleus' breast has been replaced, at least toward Priam, with *pity* for one so gray and old and sorrowful. In his pity, Akhilleus has quickly found a place to store grief, both his own and Priam's. It comes to us by fate, and so it is to be endured. Time, which brought grief, can again carry it away. For now, Priam must endure his sad heart; bearing this sadness in the full knowledge that it will not change what is may help the sadness pass. There is, after all, no remedy, something an old man should know better than most of us.[8] Old age, and the perspective it brings to those who have the courage of their years, does indeed remind us of the futility of the pursuits of the powerful. It points us, however, to nothing beyond. There is, after all, no remedy.

Yet for Christians this is not the final word, for they live (and die) in hope. And the Christian virtue of *hope* transforms the virtues of aging we have been discussing. It is why elderly Christians can bear the sadness of memory without being overcome by it, and why they can insist on the truth of a story that challenges the ultimate rule of the momentary transcendence of the glories of war. Indeed, it is also why old men like Uncle Day can take such delight in the simple yet profound work of crafting a card stand for young hands.

The hope that elderly Christians may have is best displayed by hearing from another old man named Simeon who makes a cameo appearance at the beginning of Luke's Gospel. The remarkable thing about Simeon is that he dies at the beginning of the story. Generally we think it is an awful thing to die at the beginning of a story. This is why the deaths of children affect us so deeply.[9] Their story had only just begun. Simeon's death, however, comes not at the beginning of his own story, but at the beginning of the Gospel story. As to his story, we know very little. And that, in fact, seems part of the point. Simeon's story serves to point to the greater story of God's redemption of God's people. This fact does not obliterate Simeon's own story, one he yet

8. Homer's view, of course, is difficult to settle upon in so great a work of art. For myself, I suspect that this greatest of all stories of war is also meant as a critique of war. Akhilleus' comment here provides this critique with a home in which room can also be made for war's continuance, as one of those afflictions that must be endured. If we read, as I have, Priam in these last moments as a figure who embodies a different sort of courage altogether than that displayed by the heroes throughout the poem, there is yet a way to suppose that Akhilleus' apparent acceptance and admiration of Priam has been too quick in these last comments to return to its own way. What authority, after all, does Akhilleus have to write the horrors that have come of his own deeds off to the account of the gods? Indeed, Priam bristles at Akhilleus' philosophizing and pious invocation of the fates. He refuses Akhilleus' offer of a seat and with firmness asks plainly for Hektor's body. In his turn, Akhilleus' temper flares, and we are reminded that, despite this remarkable display of affection, he is yet the man of the murdering hands. Priam — and Priam's challenge, if I am right in understanding it as such — has but the little room that pity provides in this ferocious heart.

9. It is not clear, however, that the children always see it this way. (See, for instance, Myra Bluebon-Langner's *The Private Worlds of Dying Children* [Princeton, N.J.: Princeton University Press, 1978].) Children's deaths rightly remain excruciatingly sad. It is a form of atheism, however, to suppose there is nothing worse. We are tempted into this view precisely as we suppose that there is nothing beyond each of our individual stories; that each of our stories is itself the source of its meaning.

lives even after the infant has settled into his arms. He is, after all, an old Jew, appearing in a story being told primarily for Gentiles. But in this lies his hope, which transforms his story. He is not released from his story, but its weight is shifted. He can go to his death in hope, for he has glimpsed God's salvation for the whole world. This means that he goes in the knowledge that what is yet to come is far greater than what has been.

Simeon's relationship to this, the what-is-yet-to-come, is one of hope, not of knowledge. The infant he holds in his arms conveys to him more than blind optimism about the future, for he sees in it pain and death, even as he grips the squirming new life. Yet his cannot be a full view. It is not his to see the full unfolding of the story that will later wrap itself around the infant in his arms. This affects Simeon's relation not just to the story but to his own death. Indeed, Simeon dies outside the story — we know little of his death except that it will shortly occur. Neither Simeon nor his death is what the story focuses upon. T. S. Eliot, who imaginatively pauses on Simeon longer than does Luke, suggests this. "Not for me the martyrdom, the ecstasy of thought and prayer, / Not for me the ultimate vision." Moreover, in his hope Simeon does not become a giddy old man, brimming with the excitement of having gotten to hold precious baby Jesus. At the close of Eliot's poem Simeon speaks of being tired of his life, echoing the biblical words, "Now let thy servant depart in peace."[10]

It is not uncommon for an aging member of the ruling generation to find himself suddenly awash in the (to him) terrifying thought that the best is behind him. To such a one, death appears as the greatest threat, and so begins his race against the clock to find something new and more meaningful to pin his life upon. But this is not how Simeon hopes in the Messiah, nor how he thinks of his death. Rather, Simeon's hope in the Messiah carries him to his death in the knowledge that the good life he has lived (says Luke, Simeon was "righteous and devout") is not futile precisely because it need not save itself. Put another way, it does not need to bring itself to its own completion. Its full completion lies yet ahead, in the fullness of the story that is only now beginning. The virtue of hope, in other words, makes possible the end of a life without the end of a story. In this sense Simeon has lived toward the coming of the one who will bear his story up into a new life, the form of which Simeon has, in hope, caught only a glimpse. In this knowledge he can go peacefully to his own death.[11]

10. T. S. Eliot, "A Song for Simeon," in *The Complete Poems and Plays of T. S. Eliot* (London: Faber and Faber, 1969), pp. 105-6.

11. It is important to distinguish between dying in hope and hoping for death. The confu-

Classical Christian sources locate the theological virtue of hope between those of faith and love. This middle position may puzzle us. We understand that faith is a virtue of the intellect; for Aquinas it is that by means of which we grasp onto God with our minds. So it is that faith seems the right place to begin. And, in an apparent next step, it is easily seen that faith cannot be the end, for if by it we see God, then in love we are united to him. We cannot be united with something we disbelieve in, so plainly love requires faith — and faith leads to love. But what, then, of hope? What does it do other than occupy the gap between faith and love?

In response to something like this question, Aquinas drew the following distinction between love and hope, bringing the latter into full view.

> [L]ove and hope differ in this, that love denotes union between lover and beloved, while hope denotes a movement or a stretching forth of the appetite towards an arduous good. Now union is of things that are distinct, wherefore love can directly regard the other whom a man unites to himself by love, looking upon him as another self: whereas movement is always towards the term which is proportionate to the subject moved. Therefore hope regards directly one's own good, and not that which pertains to another.[12]

Hope, then, is a virtue for someone who is yet on her way. Importantly, it is her way and not another's. This is not to say we cannot share with others in hope. But we do so differently than sharing in love, for love shared is between us, whereas hope shared is each of us striving together toward what yet lies ahead. To use the first person possessive with hope — "my hope" — is to draw a primary association as opposed to the secondary association in the phrase "my love." Unlike "my hope," "my love" is derivative of and secondary to the full meaning of love carried in the phrase "our love."

This is why hope relates particularly to the journey each of us is on in our life, which is nothing if it is not "my journey." So too it relates to our deaths, which are arguably even more our own than our lives. As we sometimes refer to it: "my time." It is important in this respect that Simeon, upon receiving

---

sion in some cases is absolutely pernicious. Hoping for one's own death can sometimes be a sign of despair, according to Aquinas (*Summa Theologiae,* II-II.20), precisely the opposite of Christian hope. Or only slightly better, such a "hope" can be rooted in a stoic resolution, which, if not the opposite of Christian hope, is particularly resistant to it. We need not decide that it is always wrong to hope (or, better put, to wish) for one's death — an old man suffering in constant and great pain surely is justified in doing so — to be clear that it bears no particular connection to the Christian virtue of hope.

12. Aquinas, *Summa Theologiae,* II-II.17.4.

the infant, turns from him and from his parents to address God directly: "Lord, now lettest thou thy servant. . . ." Simeon prays this prayer in hope for himself, which is not to say hope in himself. Rather, he hopes in God to whom he addresses his prayer. As Aquinas suggests, Simeon stretches toward his own good, which is arduous, not the least because it includes his dying, having caught just a brief glimpse of what is to come — which he sees will also be arduous, since, as Simeon must tell Mary, "a sword will pierce through your own soul" (Luke 2:35).

Dying, and preparing for one's own death, is arduous work. This is true for anyone, even those who die in hope, although it is a different sort of work for those who die without hope. Preparing for death is one of the great tasks given to the virtuous elderly. We can recall that "retirement," as we have been speaking of it, represents not just the time when what we do in life changes; it is also the phase of the final work of our lives. For the Christian, however, "preparing for death" does not involve merely loping toward the inevitable moment of expiration. Nor is it a matter simply of settling one's affairs. And the reason it is not merely this lies in Christian hope. Like Simeon, what the Christian looks for when death comes is a vision not of the completeness of his own life but of the story by which his life has been borne up. And this he can know only in hope. Guided by hope, the Christian can point beyond himself to the full completion of God's story, to the redemption of the whole world. In this the hopeful Christian is freed of the fear of diminishing, of fading away, even of dying alone. Rather, his hope in his death is that it, like Simeon's, might point toward the new life that has come into the world in Christ.

This is not to suggest that death must become an obsession for the hopeful elderly Christian, something that occupies his thoughts daily. If anything, the reverse is the case. For hope, as we have said, frees us from the anxiety of having to see our story reach any particular conclusion, the conclusion that we or others might want it to reach for it to be complete. What the hopeful elderly Christian knows, however — and this is how she differs from those of us of other ages — is that she will die soon, maybe next week, maybe next year, or maybe in ten years, but, nonetheless, in some sense, soon. It is by this that she resolves to engage now in the work of pointing her life beyond itself. It is this work that we see in Uncle Day as he takes simple delight in the texture and color of black walnut or as he takes the time to craft card stands for children who, most likely, he will never see use them. It is the work as well of Priam as he makes his way across the battlefield, risking his life for the body of his son and preparing en route to challenge the formidable Akhilleus, Hektor's bane, with truthful memory. In their lives, words, and actions these elderly persons draw our attention beyond themselves, beyond even the lives and troubles of the current ruling generation, to the truth that anchors all our lives. They point beyond what is now to what is yet to be, in hope.

As he cradles the child in his arms Simeon symbolizes this perfectly. In the midst of the temple and for the benefit of Mary and Joseph (who, he knows, are in for some unpleasant surprises), Simeon holds aloft God enfleshed. Despite the moral weightiness of his own life, despite the authority he wields as one who was throughout his life "righteous and devout," our gaze is not rightly fixed on Simeon but on the child in his arms. Those of us who are young and easily impressed are tempted to watch old man Simeon with awe. But like others of his kind, the virtuous elderly, it is his own gaze that teaches us, for his eyes are fixed in hope on the one newly born, in whose life, death, and resurrection the world will know peace. "Now lettest thou thy servant depart in peace, according to thy word: for mine eyes have seen thy salvation."

Generational Conflict: Continuity and Change

DAVID MATZKO McCARTHY

Introduction

"The most critical task among the very old is to retain a sense of identity when confronting physical decline and the loss of loved ones . . . to maintain a sense of sameness when confronted with all the losses associated with advancing age."[1] This essay will consider issues of identity and aging in relation to both social pressures that come between generations in the modern world, and, in contrast, possibilities of continuity within the intergenerational life of the church.

First, we will look to images of continuity and change within Scripture and to the church as an ongoing yet changing tradition. Then we will consider intergenerational dynamics and concerns of the aging in American culture. By way of comparison, we will look again to biblical and theological resources and conclude with suggestions for enhancing intergenerational life. Intergenerational issues are not one set of discrete concerns among others (or simply a subtopic of church programming) but are at the heart of what it means to be a community gathered by God. The church is the continuing historical presence of God's self-giving in Christ, and, as such, the church is deeply concerned with its continuity through the ages and with unity among the diversity of its members, young and old.

Though I have chosen to title this essay "Generational Conflict," it would be a mistake to assume that a generational divide is the primary issue under

---

1. Sheldon S. Tobin, James W. Ellor, and Susan M. Anderson-Ray, *Enabling the Elderly: Religious Institutions within the Community Service System* (Albany: State University of New York Press, 1986), p. 4.

consideration. Rather, while the essay points to questions about intergenerational dynamics, about continuity and conflict across the generations, I invite the reader to think about the issues of aging treated here as the backdrop for a deeper theological question, the question of who we, as Christians, are called to be as a people of God.

Consider, as an example, the aging of the body. The diminishing vitality of the body is a significant pressure on the elderly, that is, on our continuity of self as our declining physical abilities do not allow us to be the kind of people we once were. We are embodied agents, and the stories of our bodies are the stories of who we are. As we age, our bodies present us with a challenge of holding together our identities amid change. We face changes whether we are an eighty-year-old woman who no longer has the facility to drive her car or a forty-year-old man who cannot run the basketball court the way he once did. The stories of our own lives, seen through our bodies, reveal a complexity of continuity and change. Undoubtedly, a conflict of generations can be told from within each of our lives, as we find that in significant matters we are not what we once were. The same can be said on a corporate level as we ponder who we have come to be as God's people.

On a theological level, we ought not overlook the fact that we are, first of all, embodied in a social life, as the body of Christ. This language of the body is not simply a convenient transition from issues of aging to comments about the church. The body metaphor shows an essential connection. The social body is the context where our personal bodies become intelligible, where they communicate, where they speak about who we are to others and to ourselves. The interpersonal communication that constitutes our bodies gives to us our own sense of identity. While our physical bodies may not be the whole of who we are, the social body, as the body of Christ, does provide the landscape for the many facets of our personalities and extends our identities beyond the confines of our individual lives.

Trans-generational continuity is essential to the church, which by definition includes the unity of all generations and all times and places in communion with God. The fulfillment of the Christian life is communion with God in a great company of all who have been drawn into God's self-giving. This community always makes us much more than we would have been otherwise, and this "more," this coming out and going beyond ourselves, is the pattern of grace. Insofar as God's grace is in the world, its presence establishes a social body — the concrete, historical presence of a people. Because the church is bound in time, however, change is inevitable and necessary. Issues of continuity and change are, for Christians, issues about the life of the church and its identity as a people of God.

DAVID MATZKO MCCARTHY

Continuity and Change

The modern world celebrates discontinuity with the past, and the bonds of the past are usually considered obstacles to future progress. Think about the classic tales of rags to riches. The stories of admirable figures are told so that their notable positions of wealth or political prominence are attained as a victory over some other more likely fate. Abraham Lincoln was born in a humble log cabin. Albert Einstein was considered a dull-witted child. Andrew Carnegie began life in poverty. The end of these stories is radically different than the beginning: from the log cabin to the president's mansion, dimwit to genius, pauper to robber baron. Brilliance pulls up roots.

The stories could be told differently, in terms of continuity. But they are not. For instance, the popular imagination overlooks the fact that Einstein showed genius at an extraordinarily young age. The sorts of obstacles he typically encountered were not due to a lack of intelligence but to the arrogance and impatience of his genius. Whatever the case with Einstein, Lincoln, or Carnegie, the important point for us is that discontinuity with the past is embedded in our modern stories of self-making, hard work, cunning, and resolute action. Discontinuity is a powerful source of identity. Sociologist Robert Bellah has shown that detachment from family, church, and received "values" is the customary (and expected) means of becoming a mature adult in America.[2] Breaking with tradition is the tradition of our culture.[3]

The modern world itself, as a historical era, is also identified in terms of discontinuity, in terms of its break from the age that preceded it. The medieval age is considered a time of continuity and oppressive cultural unity, while the modern world is seen as an age of change and diversity. The contrast becomes that simple. Modern people are able to understand change because they see that ideas, attitudes, and practices are relative to history, to time as well as to culture and social location. At its core, modern self-understanding is characterized by a conflict of generations, which is assumed to be part of the very constitution of personal and social identity. We make ourselves by distinguishing ourselves from the past. We see immaturity in depending upon others for our understanding of self and the world, and to this degree, independence from the past is a mark of maturation and freedom.

Discontinuity is not, of course, the whole of the story. Nations, cultures,

---

2. Robert N. Bellah et al., *Habits of the Heart* (Berkeley: University of California Press, 1985), pp. 55-84.

3. Alasdair MacIntyre, *Whose Justice? Which Rationality?* (Notre Dame, Ind.: University of Notre Dame, 1988), pp. 326-48.

ethnic groups, communities, neighborhoods, and families draw lines of continuity in order to make their very existence intelligible. Continuity is essential to questions about who we are and why we live the way we do. Change is steady and transitions are often not smooth, but for the church, the goal of change is the continuity of one faith. The church is called to unity and catholicity, to common worship and corporate faithfulness. The church is Christ's bond with humanity and his continuing presence to the world. The church, in its widest scope, is a community that is assembled throughout the ages and in all places of the globe. The church is called not to break away but to be gathered.

The biblical story is forged with the tensions between continuity and change. One of the most pronounced struggles is the very emergence of the Christian assembly as distinct from the synagogue. How do the early Christians proclaim the new events of God in Christ while sustaining continuity with God's enduring relationship with Israel? The Gospel of Matthew explains the transition by showing that Jesus is the fulfillment of God's covenant promises and Israel's prophetic witness. Matthew highlights the theme of fulfillment in Jesus' birth and infancy, his Sermon on the Mount, his gathering and sending out of disciples, and virtually all aspects of his ministry and way to the cross. Continuity, though, is also established through conflict. Jesus' Sermon on the Mount (Matt. 5–7), for example, carries on a disputation about Mosaic Law, on the basis of the law's original intent. Jesus' conflict with his contemporaries is understood in relation to his appeal to Israel's covenant tradition and the unity of his ministry with God's fundamental purposes for Israel.

The Apostle Paul made similar claims in his letters to the Galatians and Romans. In Galatians 3 and Romans 4, he shows that the covenant of faith, given through Christ, restores God's covenant with Abraham. Torah law, in Paul's view, proves to be only an interim stage of God's enduring faithfulness. In Romans 9–11, he indicates that God's offer of a covenant to the Gentiles sustains and is, in fact, the route to the fulfillment of God's promises to the Jews. We ought not overlook the radical nature of Paul's claims here. He argues that Christ represents the utter consistency of God's plan of salvation, even though Paul's Jewish contemporaries would have seen a fundamental departure. Gentile Christians broke from circumcision and the Torah law (Acts 15), and Christian eucharistic practices appeared strange and blasphemous to faithful Jews (John 6). What from the rabbinical side looks like a radical break is continuity for Paul and Gentile Christians. God's covenant with Israel, according to Paul, is sustained through the (temporary) division between Jewish faithfulness and Gentile Christianity.

This short discussion of the biblical narrative comes down to a single theme: from the beginning, adjustments and judgments pertaining to continuity-through-change are basic to the church's identity. To cite another example, the correspondence between Paul and the Christians of Corinth reveals the struggles of a community undergoing profound changes brought by the Spirit in their lives. Paul is concerned with various divisions among the community, with rival appeals to authority, with sexual immorality, with the habit of settling disputes in the courts, with segregated eucharistic practice, and with divisions created by contending claims about the gifts of the Spirit. He calls the Corinthian Christians to unity. "For just as the body is one and has many members, and all the members of the body, though many, are one body, so it is with Christ. For in the one Spirit we were all baptized into one body — Jews or Greeks, slaves or free — and we were all made to drink of one Spirit" (1 Cor. 12:12-13). Differences are not denied but put in service to the unity of all under God.

Generational Dynamics: A Representative Example

Before we consider generational divisions and isolation, we will begin with an example of good intergenerational relations in the church. Our example comes from a study of support systems for the elderly as they are found in twenty black churches in Philadelphia.[4] In the study, John Morrison discovers that support systems are at work within small groups, such as choirs, Bible studies, and fellowships for men and women. The groups involve the active elderly, as well as others, in the care for infirm elderly and others in need. Morrison is impressed that the churches do not concern themselves with questions of age. He sets out to find conflict, but he reports a lack of age-segregation in the churches, along with what seems to be a shared intergenerational mindset.

> The lack of age designation allows participation by older people on a non-stigmatizing basis. Activities begun at an earlier stage in life can continue into later years without interruption, providing an important sense of continuity as one gets older. Church informants often had difficulty in telling whether a member was under or over 65 and they frequently used such phrases as "I know Mrs. Smith is in her 70s

4. John D. Morrison, "The Black Church as a Support System for Black Elderly," *Journal of Gerontological Social Work* 17, nos. 1/2 (1991): 105-20.

but she seems more like 50." Clearly a functional rather than chronological criteria was used to define membership in groups. In fact, some
churches had made provisions to assure that younger people had opportunity to participate in key governing groups, because these groups
tended to be dominated by older members. Development of specific
senior citizen groups within churches may not be wise. In fact, a number of pastors felt that age designations or age segregated programs
were inherently problematic and should be avoided. . . . One parish
minister reported success with efforts to match parochial school children with older people needing chore services. Respondents often referred to the church as a "family," and made statements that the church
should reflect the range of differences that might be found in a family.[5]

Morrison points out that an "important sense of continuity" is sustained by the integration of roles and functions in the church — activities
that hinge on abilities and common purposes rather than age. He notes that
functional rather than chronological criteria determine membership in particular groups. On the positive side, the church provides continuity throughout the life span and across generations through its constancy of worship,
mutual care, and service to the surrounding community. Again, distinctions
are made not between age groups but within them, according to roles within
the church. The young and old alike will sing, pray, worship, and reach out to
the sick and those in need. It is the church's identity and mission that bring
all together.

On the downside, it appears that the churches on which Morrison is re-
porting, and from which his findings spring, are aging congregations. Most
of the members of these congregations are beyond middle age, and the
churches are pressed to integrate younger adults. If this is the case, one
wonders whether the continuity enjoyed by the members is a result of a
subtle isolation of the elderly. Is there a lack of generational concerns because a single generation, the older generation, is dominant? The small
group structure Morrison identifies may not resolve these questions of isolation and generational change as much as it avoids them. In addition, this
small group system produces a distinction between functioning and nonfunctioning members. Morrison sees this as a problem in relation to how
the churches are able to involve the homebound and infirm. The "nonfunc-
tional" are not integrated because they have not made themselves "useful."
Obviously, this divide between functioning and nonfunctioning is not a fit-

---

5. Morrison, "The Black Church," p. 115.

ting way to describe the unity of Christ's body, which is always sustained through grace.

Are Morrison's positive examples unraveling? Not necessarily, but we will do well to recognize that both unifying and isolating forces are working upon these congregations. The basic unifying practices have been mentioned and will be developed later (for example, the church's liturgy and its mission). In the meantime, we will consider modern tendencies toward intergenerational conflict and segregation. These tendencies impinge on the church's ongoing journey as the body of Christ.

Generational Dynamics: Autonomy and Isolation

Recent philosophical and sociological works have provided convincing accounts of problems that come with a modern sense of discontinuity and detachment.[6] These problems are not universal, and an isolation of the elderly does not characterize all families or communities in contemporary culture. While detachment and loneliness may or may not dominate in one place or another, however, they are distinctive problems of modern life. Our culture is marked by both impulses toward isolation and desires for interconnection. Most of us live amid the crossfire.

Inasmuch as the modern self is forged by the ideal of autonomy, a quest for the "true" or "inner" self forms a pattern of disengagement. The self is freed to pursue its own destiny, released from burdensome social constraints — from roles and duties within common practices and traditional ways of life. We make our own way, our own values, and our own meaning in life, but in the process a fragmentation of social life is produced. We assume that common life will be made anew for each generation. When a couple is married, for instance, we talk about beginning a new family (rather than a new branch of old ones). The implications of this fragmented social world reach from the so-called culture wars to a popular disillusionment with politics and decreased involvement in social life.[7]

In concrete terms, the modern course of life, in pursuit of personal identity and career, is likely to require a series of relocations or dislocations. A successful person leaves his or her hometown and constructs a network of relationships and a future from scratch. Aside from work, the goals of modern

---

6. See, for example, Charles Taylor, *Sources of the Self: The Making of Modern Identity* (Cambridge, Mass.: Harvard University Press, 1989).

7. Bellah et al., *Habits of the Heart*, pp. 167-95.

life typically include setting up a separate residence in a neighborhood unified only by social and economic status.[8] A person may seek community, but he or she finds a "community" bound by leisure activities and economic consumption.[9] On the one hand, neighbors share only shallow commitments — garbage pick-up and a concern for lawn care. On the other hand, real friends are found at work. Work is where we are able to pursue a common life and common goals with others, but in large part, our careers make few links with other aspects of our lives. Our jobs may simply dominate (rather than integrate) all other concerns.

With the pattern of dislocation comes a compartmentalization of our lives into distinct spheres of home, work, play, and perhaps something we distinguish as our religion. After we have isolated ourselves from our families and traditional communities, we lose the connections that once held the various aspects of our lives together. The disconnection might have occurred generations before we were born, so that a fragmentation of social life may be our cultural inheritance. Whatever the case, we should know we are in trouble when the Worldwide Web and interactive television are extolled as great hopes for modern community. Common life remains part of our moral language, but it has become a distant aim rather than the context from which we encounter the world.

If detachment is basic to change, our sense of usefulness will be confined to what we can produce now, that is, to what we can see that we have done and the meaning we have made. The modern imperative is to be the interpreters of our own lives. Here, the danger of autonomy and detachment is not selfishness or egoism — the autonomous agent may want to do things for others and have notably selfless intentions. The real danger is discontinuity and a sense of meaninglessness. Discontinuity leads to a limited conception of how our lives fit within the scheme of things. It cuts me off from the hopes of generations past and my dependence on those who carry on in the future. It leads to impa-

---

8. Peter N. Stearns, "Historical Trends in Intergenerational Contacts," in *Intergenerational Programs: Imperatives, Strategies, Impacts, Trends*, ed. Sally Newman and Steven W. Brummel (Binghamton, N.Y.: Haworth, 1989), pp. 21-31. Stearns gives a historical outline of intergenerational contacts, noting their decline in recent years. He explains that "there are less regular and structured interactions between old and young in the later 20th century than ever before. Not only families but also other institutions in modern society have reduced the chance for old and young to share activities in meaningful ways" (p. 30). He does not point to an ideal time in the past, although some eras (early nineteenth century) have been more promising than others. The middle decades of the twentieth century, according to Stearns, witnessed "a real, society-wide revolution in family structure and a growing separation of older people from the most direct, immediate relationships with younger family members" (p. 28).

9. Bellah et al., *Habits of the Heart*, pp. 71-75.

tience about making our lives worth something. Making our lives meaningful for ourselves is a lonely prospect. In this sense, the isolation of the elderly, when it does occur, may be partly self-imposed. Insofar as our independence is our aim, we are already isolated.[10] The elderly in North American culture are thus isolated not just in nursing homes but alone in their own homes.[11] And they have played a large part in sectioning themselves off.

Our quest for self-making fits with our obsession with youth. A common goal among many aged is to stay young.[12] Youth represents vitality, and the declining health that often accompanies aging has an obvious effect on our perception of being old. Physical disabilities and a lack of mobility are considered typical marks of old age rather than wisdom, virtue, or a substantial accumulation of experiences. Our negative conception of aging should give us pause. Poor health is now seen as an intrusion, and so is old age. Aging intrudes when we experience a disjunction between our declining abilities and what we know to be our proper (independent and autonomous) social roles and relationships.[13] Insofar as an elderly person is able to sustain his or her identity through the relationships and social practices that have been continuous in life, he or she is likely to be considered "young."

Youthfulness represents vitality, but it is also interesting that the prolonged span of adolescence in American culture represents a time of freedom and the opportunity for life-determining choices. Youth represents a state of life when we are not yet bound by our own past. Being young provides opportunity for defining one's own identity and goals for one's future. The energy

10. A surprising study on depression links the likelihood of depression among the elderly with the frequency of visits by their children. Charlotte Dunham, "A Link Between Generations," *Journal of Family Issues* 16, no. 4 (July 1995): 450-65. "Receiving support may lead to fear of increased dependency with aging and therefore increase the risk of depression" (p. 462).

11. Tobin et al., *Enabling the Elderly*, pp. 6-14.

12. Winnifred Peacock and William M. Talley, "Intergenerational Contact: A Way to Counteract Ageism," *Educational Gerontology* 10, nos. 1/2 (1984): 13-24. Stearns, in "Historical Trends in Intergenerational Contacts," places a shift toward valuing youth in the early nineteenth century. "Images of the elderly serving as repositories of collective memory are less common in pre-industrial Western history than in some other agricultural societies. . . . [But] there is evidence that young people looked forward to reaching a relatively advanced age as a badge of wisdom and dignity . . . and many people were prone to claim to be older than they actually were. . . . By the 1820s people, when they lied about their age, lied toward youth, in the pattern that remains today. By the later 19th century, old age was increasingly linked with medical infirmity as doctors, in well-publicized reports, probed the inevitable degeneration of the human mind and body" (pp. 22-23).

13. Susan Eisenhandler, "More Than Counting Years: Social Aspects of Time and the Identity of Elders," in *Research on Adulthood and Aging: The Human Science Approach*, ed. L. Eugene Thomas (Albany: State University of New York Press, 1989), pp. 163-82.

of the young is often directed toward segregating themselves and identifying the character of their own lifestyles. A person's social relations and activities, ones that he or she will continue until old age, are thought to be dependent upon the independence of youth.

There is a great irony here. Autonomy and self-making are primary goals; yet, social engagement gives life its purposefulness. The elderly hope to remain independent and young, but it is a network of interdependence that sustains their youth. Many gerontologists work hard to dispel popular assumptions that the elderly are passive and wasting away in retirement homes. They cite statistical evidence that the vast majority of seniors maintain their own residences and provide for their own needs. They emphasize that most people over sixty-five live an active and independent lifestyle characterized by good health and mobility.[14] But does not this continuing pursuit of independence contribute to isolation rather than solve it? When a person does reach an age when he or she is not mobile and independent, what then? All we have done is pushed the problem back further from the youthful aged to the elderly who act old (i.e., to the "non-active" and dependent).

Intergenerational Conflict: An Interest Group Approach

Classifications such as "senior citizens," "baby boomers," and generations "X" and "Y" are common parlance among pundits and sociologists. The baby boomers (b. 1945-1962) seem to get the most press. Experts study and debate this generation's effect on everything from Hollywood fixations to the housing market to the fate of Social Security. As the baby boomers age, the American population, as a whole, is aging. Whereas in the 1980s slightly less than 12 percent of the population was sixty-five or over, by 2020 the elderly may comprise close to 20 percent.[15] What do these numbers imply? Many predict a drain on the resources for the young. Much anxiety is being created by the prospect that baby boomers move out of the workforce and into retirement

---

14. Grace Craig, *Human Development* (Englewood Cliffs, N.J.: Prentice Hall, 1989), pp. 540-41.

15. Tobin et al., *Enabling the Elderly*, p. 5. See also Eric R. Kingson, "The Social Policy Implications of Intergenerational Exchange," in *Intergenerational Programs*, ed. Newman and Brummel, pp. 91-100. "The population of persons age 65 and over is expected to increase rather dramatically, from approximately 29 million persons today to 65 million by 2030. The very old population, those persons 86 and over, are projected to increase the most rapidly among our older population, from approximately 3 million in 1988 to 4.9 million in the year 2000, to 8.6 million in 2030 and to 16 million in the year 2050 (U.S. Bureau of the Census 1984)" (p. 93).

like locusts devouring the harvest. The elderly, from the start, are assumed to be a burden, and the well-being of one age group is believed to detract from another.

In the language of public policy, generations are understood as interest groups, and senior citizens are thought to be a "special interest" that seeks to protect Social Security benefits, Medicare, and other age-based entitlements.[16] An apparent source of intergenerational conflict is the fear that the American economy will not be able to bear the burden of the entitlements that elderly baby boomers will demand. The real source of conflict, however, might be deeper than this battle over resources.

The root of the problem might be the very polity of competing interests. Contending interests have become key to political relationships because American society has little other means of determining what people deserve. We assume that we can demand economic benefits that we have earned on our own (which is an important justification for the Social Security retirement benefits). Apart from this economic merit, we seem to lack a common language for judging what people deserve. When the elderly or handicapped do not contribute to the economy, how do we determine their due? The polity of competing interests shifts the question from what people deserve to an individual's responsibility to protect his or her well-being. We protect ourselves by making demands and applying political pressure. Contending social interests, of course, parallel the capitalist system of economic competition. Conflict is believed to be the best and most disinterested way of balancing one interest against a host of others.

A theological conception of justice, on the other hand, is set within the memory of God's grace and steadfast faithfulness.[17] Justice, in its ancient formulation, seeks a balance or a harmony of distribution according to what people need and what they merit. If one "interest" overcomes another, justice restores. Justice requires agreement about common goods and a (relatively) clear network of social roles that would allow judgments balancing what one person deserves in relation to another. Such social networks and common goods are hardly (or thinly) operational in a modern interest group polity, so

16. Mark Schlesinger and Karl Kronebusch, "Intergenerational Tensions and Conflict," pp. 152-84, and "The Sources of Intergenerational Burdens and Tensions," pp. 185-209, in *Intergenerational Linkages*, ed. Vern L. Bengtson and Robert A. Harootyan (Washington, D.C.: Springer, 1994). The authors argue that seniors do not constitute an interest group with a unified set of interests. They claim that intragenerational conflicts among the elderly are more prevalent than an intergenerational clash of interests.

17. Karen Lebacqz, "Justice," in *Christian Ethics*, ed. Bernard Hoose (Collegeville, Minn.: Liturgical Press, 1998), pp. 163-72.

that a language of market competition and interests also dominates the American political discussion of intergenerational relations.

A conflict of generations, as it is expressed in standard social and political terms, is only part of a larger conflict-based system. Merit and what people deserve is difficult to determine, except by an economic criterion: what people earn, they deserve. What we deserve, therefore, is most difficult to determine for those outside the market, for the poor, infirm, and those who provide care for others apart from an economic relationship; the polity of the so-called public sphere has little means to judge, for example, the merit of parenting or caring for one's elderly parents. It is not coincidental that the current debate on welfare has emphasized "welfare to work," with the argument frequently being made that it would be better for welfare mothers to get a job than to stay home with their children — as though in caring for their children mothers are somehow cheating active, contributing members of society. Granted, there are nuances involved that we cannot examine here, but it is interesting to note how raising children is seen as an economic drain and a social liability. The political battle cry is to get those welfare mothers into the workforce and cut them off if they have any more children. One generation is set against the interests of another.

Generational Conflict in the Church

The first part of this essay considered questions of continuity and change by drawing a contrast between a modern means of shaping identity and the challenge of sustaining continuity through change. On the one hand, we might be inclined to idealize a radical break with the past; on the other, we could be committed to an ongoing conversation within a tradition that is extended through many generations. In the contemporary world, the first scenario tends to be more natural insofar as it fits with a common configuration of the modern identity (i.e., autonomy and our conflict-based polity). The second option, therefore, cannot be defended on the grounds that we will be more psychologically satisfied or have an easier route to understanding our own identities if we follow it. It is easier to live alone and define who we are for ourselves, even at the risk of loneliness. When the elderly maintain their own homes, separate from their children and siblings, one important reason seems to be that living with others, even those in our own families, causes intolerable stress. Living together and sharing a common life are difficult.

The unity of common life is basic to the call to be the church, so that for Christians a desire for intergenerational continuity makes sense as a journey of a people called to faithfulness. While autonomy has been written into the goals of modern identity, Christians are called to the unity and mutual dependence of Christ's body. Christians confess that human life is discovered in the story of God's creative and redemptive activity. We receive life as a gift, and our lives come to us as part of an ongoing history far more expansive than our own self-making. God, from the beginning, is not the One in isolation, but is the One interpersonally expressed in the love that binds Father and Son in Spirit.[18] Likewise, the image of God in men and women marks them, fundamentally, as community. The pilgrimage of the Christian life is an ongoing response to God's self-giving through Christ and to the return of love in Christ's Spirit. The church is a sacrament of God's invitation to common life, gathered as the body of Christ.

The biblical story of God's covenant includes both retrospective and prospective accounts of generational change. Generation after generation is held up to the standard of Abraham's faith. The story of the patriarchs is the renewal and progression of God's promise from generation to generation, which ends with the dubious prospects of Jacob's blessings to his twelve sons (Genesis 49). The sons of Jacob receive mixed judgments about their faithfulness and future. God's promises, nevertheless, are set in motion once again with the liberation of the Hebrews from slavery in Egypt. Unfaithfulness, however, is the cause for this liberated generation to pass away, after wandering in the wilderness, before the next enters into the promised land. Likewise, the prophetic books connect past, present, and future through a look toward a renewed generation, enlivened by God's Spirit (Ezekiel 37), with the imprint of God's way upon them (Jeremiah 31), as a witness and light to all the nations of the world (Isaiah 40–43).

The prophet Micah, when speaking God's word against Israel's corruption, denounces animosity between parent and child. "[F]or the son treats the father with contempt, the daughter rises up against her mother" (7:6). This divisiveness is an image of Israel's dishonesty, injustice, and greed. Like Micah, the prophet Malachi calls for justice. When he looks with hope toward God's gathering of a faithful people, he uses the relationship of parent and child as his metaphor. "Lo, I will send you the prophet Elijah before the great and terrible day of the LORD comes. He will turn the hearts of parents to their children and the hearts of children to their parents, so that I will not come and strike the land with a curse" (4:5-6).

The New Testament, as well, provides some significant references to relations between the young and old. The Gospel of Luke, for instance, cites the

---

18. Augustine, *The Trinity*, trans. Edmund Hill (New York: New City Press, 1991).

passage from Malachi when Gabriel announces the coming of John the Baptist. "[He comes] to turn the hearts of parents to their children, and the disobedient to the wisdom of the righteous, to make ready a people prepared for the Lord" (1:17). Through the birth of John to Elizabeth and Zechariah, Luke also sustains Old Testament themes of God's promise of a new generation born to those assumed to be too old and barren. Likewise in Luke, Jesus is presented in the temple with the prophetic words of Simeon and Anna. Both are elderly and waiting for God's redemption of Israel. Their old age represents a persistent yearning, a continuity and unity of Israel in its hope for God's promises fulfilled.

Elsewhere in the New Testament, a prophetic hope of restoration parallels the call of life in the church. Relations between young and old are of a piece with the unity and mutual care of Christ's body.[19] In 1 Timothy 5, for example, the young are encouraged to treat all older men and women as their fathers and mothers — an indication of the community's self-understanding as family. First Timothy sets young and old in a reciprocal relationship. The letter gives special concern to care for widows, and widows, for their part, have a special role in the prayer of the community and guidance of the young.[20] Leaders of the church are referred to as elders *(presbyteroi)*, providing an interesting connection between age and function. This connection is not always literal, but we can say that insofar as young and old are divided by particular needs and gifts, their differences are directed toward mutual benefit and the unity of the body.

Although the foundation of the church is unity, we will not be free from dealing with divisions and disagreements, and certainly not free from generational conflict and misunderstanding. Younger people may see the elderly as rigid, and the seniors may think that the young show a lack of regard for the community. The elders may seem to care too much about order in the kitchen cabinets and silence in the sanctuary. Young adults may appear to want change without understanding the logic and coherence of existing practices. They may seem set on altering the structure of church programs and introducing new elements in the liturgy without being formed by existing ones. The seniors may want to sustain practices, while the younger generations expect to reshape them.

In these few examples, we can identify modern goals of self-making and corresponding intergenerational pressures. If, in modern terms, we are sup-

---

19. See Warren Carter, "A Survey of Recent Scholarship on the New Testament and Aging and Suggestions for Future Research," *Journal of Religious Gerontology* 9, no. 2 (1995): 35-50.

20. See also the role of widows in Titus 2:3.

posed to make ourselves and determine our own futures, then, in fact, we are fundamentally alone. Modern culture lacks a means to make judgments about intergenerational conflicts inasmuch as we want for a common future, a common understanding of human goods, and a network of social practices in pursuit of those goods. A common good, in contrast, is fundamental to the church, as it is a sacrament of God's unity and of humanity's common end. The church's social life, its goods, its conflicts, and its reciprocity of generations are made intelligible by its faithfulness to the way of God in Christ. The church is a community bound by the resolution of differences, Jew and Gentile, slave and free, male and female (Gal. 3:28). Generational conflict certainly exists in the church, but these conflicts can be put to a good purpose through God's forgiveness and reconciliation.

The Church Is a Social Body

Salvation is social. God's promises to Abraham hinge on the creation of a people as God's people, and God's covenant with Israel outlines a way of life as community with God and neighbor. Jesus calls for a new set of social relationships, and the giving of the Spirit at Pentecost is the seal of a community gathered as a witness to the coming kingdom. The notion of the kingdom of God is unavoidably social, but it is not social or political in terms of social reform movements, interest groups, or political parties. The kingdom that Jesus calls for transforms what it means to be social or political. Social relations in the church are established according to life in Christ, according to God's self-giving, according to the death of the way of envy, vengeance, and violence.

If secular social life were patterned according to God's way, the dominant political order (as it is sustained by violence) would fall apart. For this reason, many have supposed that the church and the coming kingdom are not social and not relevant to political questions. They claim that the way of discipleship is not fit to support a social order but is merely a matter of private attitudes and beliefs. In making this assertion, they confuse the prevailing social order, which defines current politics, with social life as such. The inability of Jesus' way to sustain the current political order points precisely to the social character of discipleship. The salvation that Christ brings is a call for repentance and transformation. If Jesus' social program is not relevant to national politics, this is so because God's kingdom lays bare the world's order of domination and violence.

The church will always have an ambiguous social character (in secular terms) because it is a social body patterned on the future of God's redemption. St. Paul understands the church as a community of God's new age amid the old. Jesus claims that his kingdom is not of this world; it is a kingdom of heaven, not because salvation is merely spiritual, but because it is radically social. It is radical in its unity, a unity that becomes demonic if it is wagered on human self-making. It is a unity of forgiveness and gift. Through God's self-giving in Christ, people are brought together in a common life, which reveals that all other so-called social orders are really orders of competition and antagonism.

Up to this point, this essay has drawn a contrast between two types of intergenerational conflict. The first is characterized by autonomy and individual self-making, and the second by a common journey with a common end and a common set of social practices. On the one hand, a conflict of generations fits within a story of distancing oneself from others in order to enhance personal identity, while on the other, intergenerational tensions can be put to a unifying purpose in terms of a move toward greater faithfulness, toward repentance and reconciliation. In the first case, we must determine the meaning of our own lives. In the second, personal identity is found when a person discovers his or her place in the lives of others, on the landscape of a continuing story. The story of generations is marked by conflict and change, but when that story is set within God's enduring presence to the world, constancy is its underlying theme.

Some contemporary accounts of the church's life have been marked by the first version of personal identity rather than the second. These accounts assume that salvation is fundamentally an individual matter. Such individualist conceptions of the church are embedded in current strategies for church growth, as they are based on a market view of the church and, therefore, cannot avoid a fractional system of social relationships. The typical strategy is to increase the size of a congregation by forming several small groups, in order to give members and potential members an intimate network of family-like relationships. The strategy appears benign enough; the structure of small groups meets the need for a sense of community, and it allows a good bit of adaptability to the market.[21] But, at bottom, the small group strategy is fragmented.

The popular "church growth movement" conceives of the local church as a confederation or collection of groups. According to the logic of this movement, small groups and the church as a whole are more effective when they

---

21. George Barna, *Marketing the Church* (Colorado Springs: NavPress, 1988), pp. 111ff.; Kennon L. Callahan, *Twelve Keys to an Effective Church* (New York: Harper and Row, 1983), pp. 35-40.

are homogenous. Homogeneity is effective because the attractiveness of a group depends on immediate interpersonal relationships. The groups, then, will build on and reflect the type of relationships already existing in a neighborhood, city, or town. You might meet someone at a PTA meeting and invite her to your Bible study. Why would she be inclined to accept your invitation? She sees how much the two of you are alike and that she is likely to feel comfortable in the type of group that you are in. Person to person contact is the key to this church growth strategy.[22] This method appears to expand community, but because small groups are the primary context of one's connection to the church, there is a splintering effect. According to the wisdom of the growth experts, a growing church must always form new small groups in order to accommodate new interests and relationships. Here, we see the splintering of common bonds. Existing small groups, which have endured for several years, have established a pattern of relationships; therefore, new members will not be integrated with much success.[23] Not one but a multiplicity of communities (and relational systems) is created, under a single management structure.

Amid the fragmentation, the strategy leads to isolation of the elderly for several reasons. First, the small group system seems to baptize whatever social networks exist in a neighborhood or town, so that, if the elderly are isolated in the civic community, then isolation will continue in the church. If the church is formed as a coalition of tightly knit groups and if these groups are internally homogenous, any differences among groups will again exacerbate isolation. Second, the church growth strategy reflects an interest group polity. Members of a church are bound together by common interests in the Christian faith, but their common life will be patterned along the lines of typical civic organizations. The groups may work hard to serve those in need, but their strategies for growth will reach out to those who are active or potentially active in fulfilling the particular mission of a particular church. The growing church will assess the market and tap the predominant constituency in an area. If young families are the growth population, then programming should be focused on their needs. If a church is set in an aging community, social programs for the elderly will be appropriate. In either case, generational divisions are built into this model of church.

The market model fails insofar as it diminishes the social character of the church. We confess our faith as one and are called to live as the concrete presence of God's new possibilities for human community. Church growth strate-

---

22. Barna, *Marketing the Church*, pp. 109-10.
23. Callahan, *Twelve Keys*, p. 37.

gies, on the other hand, are likely to understand worship as an opportunity for common prayer or an occasion for all the groups in the church to express their faith together. The liturgy, in this framework, expresses a task of building community, which has already been worked out by the small groups. Small groups in themselves, however, are not the sources of the problem. The failing of the market model is to make the small group and its interpersonal relationships the primary source of communal identity. What such church growth strategies lack is an understanding of worship as a social practice which is the social bond of the church. The Lord's Supper, for instance, is the articulation of God's self-giving in Christ that makes the gathered community into Christ's body.[24] God's reconciliation and the passing of Christ's peace are our intimate bonds, and the basis upon which we are able to call each other friends.

Rather than a market strategy, the church is God's jubilee. The church is an invitation to the ineffective and the infirm, a banquet for the sinner and outcast, who are enlivened by new possibilities for life together with God. The church is a context where our presence in the company of others is a work of grace, so that the isolation of generations cannot be the last word. The church does not serve the poor, infirm, or isolated elderly as much as it is called to a common life with them. Breaking bread, breaking the bonds of isolation, feeding the hungry, clothing the naked, and visiting the imprisoned are aspects of the church's call to be God's people.

Intergenerational Programs

A strong movement toward intergenerational programming in the church is growing, and its aim is to match the gifts of aging with the needs of younger generations, and vice versa.[25] Seniors can be mentors for confirmation candidates or staff the church's after-school programs and daycare. Younger generations can bring the Eucharist to the homebound or provide help with domestic tasks. Young and old participate together in continuing religious education and retreats.[26] These programs take advantage of the differences

24. Kathleen Fischer, *Winter Grace* (New York: Paulist, 1985), pp. 15-16. The author uses the Eucharist as the context from which to understand the graces of growing old.

25. Shari Reville, in "Young Adulthood to Old Age," in *Intergenerational Programs*, ed. Newman and Brummel, pp. 45-54, uses Erik Erikson's stages to show that the needs and gifts of different generations can be understood in a complementary manner.

26. James W. White, *Intergenerational Religious Education* (Birmingham, Ala.: Religious Education Press, 1988).

between generations and stages in the life cycle. If the elderly are becoming more dependent, they will complement the needs of those in middle adulthood who are seeking to expand their networks of community and care. If young adults are beginning to cultivate their identities, the elderly can offer a wealth of experience and the patience that comes through having been there before.

An interesting element of these programs is that the main purpose of each is something other than the formation of intergenerational bonds. Intergenerational contact is certainly a conscious goal, but only a secondary or indirect outcome. The primary foci are shaped by the enduring practices of the church, the spiritual and corporeal works of mercy such as visiting the sick and instructing the ignorant.[27] These practices form a long tradition of discipleship. If visiting the sick and the imprisoned are intimately related to faith, intergenerational contact is already in place in terms of what is assumed to be the widest generational gap (i.e., contact between the elderly shut-ins and younger members of the church). Intergenerational programming, then, depends on existing social tasks of the church. Efforts to enhance intergenerational bonds do not require a new set of social practices but rather a renewed understanding of the old ways of faithfulness. Intergenerational efforts are not a discrete set of concerns but part of the identity and mission of the church.

Amid the age segregation of modern life, however, intergenerational connections will often be an intentional part of the church's life. People of different ages will have different orientations to the life of the church, and distinct groups organized according to stages of life or generations are likely to flourish. Intergenerational programs will attempt to mitigate isolation and divisions, but some differences between young and old may in fact be celebrated — as they contribute to the life of all. The elderly have concerns, expectations, and gifts to offer. Certainly the aging bring continuity to the living traditions of a community by contributing to common memory. Our elders bring the past to those who follow. This rooted quality of community might lead to inertia, but the task of both young and old is to remember and sustain the enlivening ways of the faith, so that our aging is not a time of regress but a source of important judgments about changes and continuing life.

We ought to avoid considering old age itself as a particular gift. Such

---

27. The traditional lists: the corporeal works — feed the hungry, give drink to the thirsty, clothe the naked, shelter the homeless, visit the sick, ransom the captive, and bury the dead; the spiritual works — instruct the ignorant, counsel the doubtful, admonish sinners, bear wrongs patiently, forgive offenses, comfort the afflicted, and pray for the living and the dead.

would only deepen the segregation of generations. Nevertheless, it might be appropriate to claim that our elders, as aging Christians, contribute to the life of the church through their longevity, through their embodiment of memory. Our imagination, hope, and patience are enlivened through the storytelling of our communities, so that many of us have vivid recollections of events we did not experience or experienced before we were old enough to interpret the events. When we look to understand who we are, we rely on the stories that our parents, grandparents, and others in our communities have told us again and again. We are told who we are from the beginning of our lives, for good or for ill, and some of us spend years attempting to reinterpret or edit or undermine these stories. The power of this "reception" is that it shapes who we are and who we believe ourselves to be. It is virtually impossible to sort out what has been given and what we have made for ourselves. In the modern world, it is assumed that the "givenness" of identity makes us less free, but in theological terms, dependence (our being created and being gathered in community) is the source of freedom. An attempt to escape the bonds of memory is part of the modern quest for autonomy and the dubious achievement of personal independence.

Inasmuch as received memory has marginal importance for modern identity, intergenerational memory will not be considered vital to practical wisdom. We think that our elders ought to be wise, but more often than not we find that age does not bring sagacity. We are likely to be bored with the insights of seniors, and we may be inclined to lack trust in their judgments about our lives. The wisdom of the elderly is their memory, and if a community does not recognize memory's place in an ongoing pilgrimage, then the remembering of older persons will not be seen as a source of common life. When received memory is considered only the trivia of history, the continuity that the elderly bring will have a diminished role. Practices of the present will be understood in terms of their contrast with the past (fitting with the typical modern divide between the past and our present self-making).

Social displacements and discontinuity with the past have obvious effects on the process of aging, especially as we come near to death. In the face of divided community, we are likely to believe that our lives have lost value and that our contributions to our communities have been betrayed.[28] If we know that the wisdom of our experiences is received as useless, we are likely to become defensive or nostalgic about our generation and our era, believing in a golden age of our social contributions. Our deaths will mean the death of the

28. Daniel J. Levinson et al., *The Seasons of a Man's Life* (New York: Alfred A. Knopf, 1978), p. 38.

meaning of our lives. The full meaning of one life for young and old, in fact, depends on the living remembering of others. Shared memory gives meaning to past and present and a direction for the future. Discovering the meaning of our lives is necessarily an intergenerational conversation.

According to common stereotypes, the young are hungry for change, and the old are sated and protective of the past. These caricatures are often accompanied by a view of "tradition" as old and stagnant. Tradition, it is assumed, comes to a person in a solid lump, as a completed whole. If traditions are understood to be living, on the other hand, the church will assume that change and conversion are continuing processes. If ongoing conversation is recognized as an articulation of a historic faith, those with longevity will be recognized as best situated for wisdom about sustaining continuity through change. Note my use of the phrase "best situated." It is not the same as saying that longevity itself produces wisdom. The point here is that memory, continuity, and change fit together. Continuity and change are not opposites. Indeed, if older generations bring memory and continuity to common life, they will provide a vital resource for understanding change.

The Pressures to Die: Reconceiving the Shape of Christian Life in the Face of Physician-Assisted Suicide

DAVID CLOUTIER

The elderly in our society are often faced with two rather overwhelming fears: the fear of becoming a burden and the fear of a lingering, painful death. That is, they fear dependence and suffering, both of which ostensibly diminish the ability to live what is defined as a fulfilling life in our society. My own grandmother, a German immigrant, who was a widow for forty years and worked when few women did, faced a great deal of suffering in her own life, and so did not seem to fear suffering as she aged into her nineties. But her increasing dependence, first on my parents, then on the health-care system, was something she did not and could not handle well. Her final years, when the slow but steady loss of both physical and mental capacities deprived her first of the ability to get around the neighborhood, then of the ability to live alone, and finally even of the ability to live without more constant supervision and assistance than my parents alone could provide, tore her apart. Her fierce independence, such an asset for most of her life, made her final years apparently very difficult, a constant and losing struggle against her own weakness and against those who would try to care for her. My grandmother never would have considered euthanasia. But certainly in her last years she wished for her own death. Could a different view of the meaning and practice of dependence have allowed her to live more fully? Could others benefit from a similarly reworked idea of suffering? And could recovering the Christian meaning of suffering and mutual dependence in our common baptism in Christ defend the Christian people against the powerful impetus toward euthanasia that haunts the elderly in our world today?

At the intersection of many of the issues discussed elsewhere in this collection is the pressing question of physician-assisted suicide, or euthanasia.[1]

---

1. For the purposes of this essay, I will assume the "standard case" where physician-assisted

This question includes consideration of, and is at least partially a consequence of, the complex technological nature of modern medicine, the economic burdens imposed by such medicine, the isolation of the old and sick in our society, and the valorization of youth and activity as models of the good life. Physician-assisted suicide is the flashpoint where these issues all come together and demand decision in the most concrete terms: ought the suffering and terminally ill person end his life? Ought she not to be liberated from the twin fears of a lingering death and debilitating dependence?

The answer to that question given here will involve considerations of the Christian view of life and its goodness and shape which are normally given short shrift in discussions of the issue. Too often decisions about physician-assisted suicide are worked out in isolation from larger questions; this has led to a shrill debate that embodies the incommensurability of moral discourse in this culture, about which philosopher Alasdair MacIntyre has written at length.[2] Such incommensurability leads not to rational moral discernment but to reciprocal shouting. By considering the unique place of suffering and dependency in the Christian picture of the good life, I hope to provide a more persuasive case for the inadmissability of physician-assisted suicide in the lives of those who follow Christ.

Christians and Suicide

Physician-assisted suicide, as the phrase suggests, can be seen as a possible special case within Christian teaching on suicide. Nearly all Christians still seem to agree that suicide is wrong, even though the basis for such a rejection, especially in the larger society, is no longer very clear. Given the increasing emphasis on individual autonomy and self-determination that pervades our society, arguments against suicide no longer seem as self-evident. Ancient Stoicism saw suicide as a potentially noble course of action, and the classic

---

suicide becomes a moral question. As Gilbert Meilaender states it, it is the case where a person who is suffering great pain from a terminal illness is killed with his or her own consent, with only mercy as a motive. Questions about miraculous recoveries, ambiguous motives on the part of those involved, and what constitutes adequate "consent" are all set to the side, under the assumption that these issues certainly complicate real life but are not at the heart of determining whether, and why, physician-assisted suicide is right or wrong. See Gilbert Meilaender, "Euthanasia and Christian Vision," in *On Moral Medicine,* ed. Stephen E. Lammers and Allen Verhey (Grand Rapids: Eerdmans, 1987), pp. 454-60.

2. See Alasdair MacIntyre, *After Virtue,* second ed. (Notre Dame, Ind.: University of Notre Dame Press, 1984), pp. 6-35.

modern argument by philosopher David Hume certainly gains power in our present environment.

Hume argues that "if suicide be criminal, it must be a transgression of our duty either to God, our neighbor, or ourselves."[3] Regarding ourselves, Hume makes the common-sense argument that "I believe that no man ever threw away life, while it was worth keeping."[4] Regarding the neighbor and the wider society, Hume says, "Suppose I am a burthen to [society]; suppose that my life hinders some person from being much more useful to society. In such cases my resignation of life must not only be innocent but laudable."[5] Finally, in terms of our duty to God, Hume states that "were the disposal of human life so much reserved as the peculiar province of the Almighty that it were an encroachment on his right, for men to dispose of their own lives; it would be equally criminal to act for the preservation of life as for its destruction."[6] Hume's line here is a profound response to Christians who would argue that only God can determine when it is that we are to die.

Christians ought not, however, be taken in by these arguments. The Christian prohibition on suicide ought not rest on considerations of utility or on an overly simplistic reservation to God of matters of life and death. The common argument, "You have so much to live for," ought also to be subordinated, especially since such language can make appeals to physician-assisted suicide more intelligible than they deserve to be.

The Christian is able to understand the prohibition against suicide — and indeed, able to understand what the term itself indicates — only from within the practices and narratives that constitute the Christian story. The Christian life is shaped by its participation in the Triune life of God through the liturgy, sacraments, stories, and habits of speech of the community of the church. Thus, the Christian prohibition against suicide receives its intelligibility most centrally from the practice of baptism, which turns our bodies themselves into gifts at the service of God, the community, and the world.

The sacrament of baptism, Paul tells us, initiates us into a community called the body of Christ. The bodiliness should particularly be noted here, since the implication of the sacrament of baptism is that our bodies are no longer our own — our relation to our own bodies is not one of ownership. Instead, our bodies are given as gift into the hands of the community, and ultimately into the very person of Christ ("It is no longer I who live, but Christ

---

3. David Hume, "On the Naturalness of Suicide," in *Life and Death*, ed. Louis Pojman (Boston: Jones and Bartlett, 1993), p. 196.

4. Hume, "On the Naturalness of Suicide," p. 201.

5. Hume, "On the Naturalness of Suicide," pp. 200-201.

6. Hume, "On the Naturalness of Suicide," p. 198.

who lives in me," Gal. 2:20). Therefore, we are no longer able to determine on our own what happens to us; the community does that. The body could, in theory, tell us that we have to die, but in fact the nature of the community as the body *of Christ* does not allow such a command. That our new lives in baptism are a gift from God to be used exclusively in God's service to the mission of Christ in the world is why Christians cannot imagine a situation where suicide would be the appropriate course of action for such sanctified flesh. As Stanley Hauerwas notes, "our living is an obligation," and no longer simply a natural desire or instinct.[7] Hence, a community in which suicide happens is a judgment on that community, for it usually represents a failure on the part of the community to make every member essential to its survival and flourishing, as Paul says it ought to be.

Let us note carefully what has and has not been said. I have not appealed to any principle such as "the sacredness of all life," since, as many commentators on both sides of the physician-assisted suicide debate have pointed out, "life" does not name the ultimate good for Christians. As our friend Hume notes, "If my life be not my own, it were criminal for me to put it in danger, as well as to dispose of it. . . ."[8] The universal Christian obligation to martyrdom, or, if you prefer, to the cross, means that the preservation of life is not something Christians do at all costs. But I have appealed to a particular description of life and its goals without which the whole argument doesn't work. The reason Christians oppose suicide is that life is meant for faithful service to God and God's community, and suicide cannot fit under that description, given the sort of act that it is.

Is It Merciful to Kill?

Nevertheless, many Christians who would certainly oppose, let's say, the suicide of a teenager or a thirty-something find in physician-assisted suicide a totally different issue. Over against those who hold the argument about the sacredness of all life, these Christians argue that the ethical value or principle of life is not an absolute but must be weighed against other goods and values in order to determine the best course of action.

Lisa Sowle Cahill's analysis of the ethics of physician-assisted suicide is a classic example of this sort of reasoning. Life is indeed a good, but physician-

---

7. Stanley Hauerwas, "Rational Suicide and Reasons for Living," in *Suffering Presence* (Notre Dame, Ind.: University of Notre Dame Press, 1986), p. 106.

8. Hume, "On the Naturalness of Suicide," p. 199.

assisted suicide may be allowable so long as it "would involve only terminal or comatose patients for whom it is impossible to continue to pursue those human values for which the Creator intended life to serve as a condition." In these cases, "life may cease, in some sense, to be a 'good,'" for it is only a conditional or instrumental good — that is, a good so long as it serves some other ends.[9] Now note that this position is not that different in some ways from the position I outlined above; Cahill and other commentators like her draw on the fact that for Christians death is not the ultimate enemy.[10] Laurel Arthur Burton tells the story of a Mrs. Carlson who seems to fit all the usual criteria for physician-assisted suicide, and who says to the chaplain, "God doesn't ask people to live under insufferable conditions. He shows the way over. I'm no more afraid of dying than the Hebrews were of crossing the Red Sea."[11] Burton seems to typify the standard "feeling" that it is not right to be an absolutist on this issue: "I believe that life must be valued, but we must be careful not to embrace mere vitalism."[12] Life, in these standard cases, no longer seems to be worth living.

But there are two difficulties with these sorts of arguments. First, nearly all the Christian arguments in favor of physician-assisted suicide rely on a sort of weighing or comparing of goods or values, generally known as proportionalism or utilitarianism. Proportionalist moral arguments simply do not work for a variety of reasons,[13] yet beyond appeals to Aquinas's teleology and the principle of totality, Cahill's argument ends up simply comparing goods, or, in her words, "responsibly" mediating "between conflicting values and the rights and duties which are devolved from them."[14] Are such cost-benefit analyses at all helpful in actually determining what one *ought* to do?

9. Lisa Sowle Cahill, "A 'Natural Law' Reconsideration of Euthanasia," in *On Moral Medicine,* ed. Lammers and Verhey, p. 451.

10. Cahill, "A 'Natural Law' Reconsideration," p. 447.

11. Laurel Arthur Burton, "Negotiating the Faith: A United Methodist Chaplain's Perspective on Euthanasia and Doctor-Assisted Suicide," *Quarterly Review* 16 (1996): 169-88. When Burton suggests that others might interpret the Exodus story differently, Mrs. Carlson replies, "Other people can believe what they want. It's what I believe that's finally important. The Hebrews responded to God, all right; and I am, too. I know what's best for me, and I know about my relationship with God." Such a response vividly displays the difficulties with religious individualism and underlines the urgency of the communal response I outline below.

12. Burton, "Negotiating the Faith," pp. 185-86.

13. For example, they weigh values which simply cannot be compared on any basis and they give little or no specificity to the agents in a given situation. For a nicely detailed critique, see Germain Grisez and Russell Shaw, *Fulfillment in Christ* (Notre Dame, Ind.: University of Notre Dame Press, 1991), pp. 64-71.

14. Cahill, "A 'Natural Law' Reconsideration," pp. 446-47.

But beyond this technical argument lies a much more important one for the case at hand: the way in which most of these commentators define (explicitly or implicitly) the good life. Cahill is fairly explicit: she speaks of the good of life as the development of the highest, or spiritual, goods of life ("conditions of meaningful personal existence"). An example of a terminal cancer patient she gives indicates what is meant:

> He is undergoing extreme personal suffering, involving both physical and "spiritual" aspects. Bodily pain is intimately related to mental stress, to one's total outlook on life and to one's ability to make the most of biological existence as the condition for fully human meaning, centered on personal relationships. . . . The integrity and maturity of personality which he has acquired as the goal of his lifetime thus far is slipping rapidly away as he endures the demoralizing experience of physical and mental deterioration. He acknowledges that life which was once a good to him is now approaching its conclusion.[15]

The description suggests that the good life cannot include suffering, which is supposed to impair personal relationships. It also suggests that "maturity of personality" is irretrievably impaired in this situation because of "physical and mental deterioration." In another place, Cahill refers to "the continuation and development of a personal life history" as a high value, high enough to consider the loss of it cause to end one's life.[16] This sort of description of personhood is troubling for many reasons: those who are physically or mentally disabled appear to be unable to achieve life's good, the notion of "making the most" out of life strikes a terribly hubristic and titanistic note for the Christian, and there is little if any reference to the goods of prayer and praise. Cahill's case is nuanced: she does not simply endorse the typically American view of the good of autonomy, for she speaks of relationality as the heart of "fully human meaning"; yet her notion of relationality itself seems to rest on an idea of autonomy that, when endangered, makes relating no longer genuine and fulfilling.[17] It hovers too close to what John Paul II has identified as the "culture of death," which identifies the goods of life with efficiency and

---

15. Cahill, "A 'Natural Law' Reconsideration," p. 448.

16. Cahill, "A 'Natural Law' Reconsideration," p. 451.

17. Timothy Quill, a physician who is one of the most morally serious advocates of physician-assisted suicide, offers a powerful though unwitting demonstration of some of these problems. See "Death and Dignity: A Case of Individualized Decision-Making," *New England Journal of Medicine* 324, no. 10, pp. 691-94. In a longer, more general treatment of physician-assisted suicide, the case of Diane would merit a very close reading for what it tells us about why people seek to die, their notion of self, and their practice of dying.

productivity.[18] Simply put, her anthropology does not take as its norm christology; the Christian self is given in baptism, and it is nothing other than a sharing in the redeemed and redeeming life of Christ. Thus, any account of death and dying in the tradition cannot be grounded in basic premises but only "in Christ's humble acceptance of crucifixion."[19]

Patricia Beattie Jung, by contrast to Cahill, notes that the terminally ill may be drawn more deeply into the goods of the Christian life. In a culture that values autonomy, "their dependence and need reveal our notion of individual strength to be an illusion. They disclose everyone's interdependence."[20] Moreover, "as is the case throughout life, in suffering Christians are called to embody God's passion for communion with all of creation,"[21] contra Cahill's suggestion that suffering must inhibit relationship. Most descriptions of the good life like Cahill's buy into two nonchristological components of the good, typical of wider society: the avoidance of all "unnecessary suffering" and the value of personal autonomy and independence. Cahill is right, however, to ask us to look at what the "conditions of meaningful personal existence" are; the rest of this essay is an attempt to draw the terminally ill (and others persons who suffer and/or are dependent) back into such meaning.

Suffering in Christ's Body

One cannot help but be filled with shock and even perhaps a bit of scandal when hearing Paul proclaim that "even now I find my joy in the suffering I endure for you. In my own flesh I fill up what is lacking in the sufferings of Christ for the sake of his Body, the Church" (Col. 1:24). Finding joy in suffering? Is this just more evidence that Paul ought to be read selectively, if at all?

Despite such a reaction, we can find it in ourselves to admit that suffering can be good sometimes, though we don't like it. Even if we'd love it if there were a simple pill we could pop to lose the weight we wanted to, we ruefully admit that the saying "No pain, no gain" has something to it. Few myths are as powerful in our culture as the one in which a person must overcome many obstacles, often with great personal sacrifice, to achieve an honorable goal.

18. See *Evangelium Vitae* in *Origins* 24 (1995): 689-727; here, para. 12.

19. H. Tristram Engelhardt Jr., "Physician-Assisted Death: Doctrinal Development vs. Christian Tradition," *Christian Bioethics* 4 (1998): 115-21; here, 120.

20. Patricia Beattie Jung, "Dying Well Isn't Easy: Thoughts of a Roman Catholic Theologian on Assisted Death," in *Must We Suffer Our Way to Death?* ed. Ronald P. Hamel and Edwin R. Dubose (Dallas: Southern Methodist University Press, 1996), p. 183.

21. Jung, "Dying Well," p. 188.

Even if most of us secretly are lazy and would prefer to win the lottery or do as little work as necessary, we nevertheless cannot hide our admiration for these stories. So perhaps we can make sense of suffering by saying that we can come out on "the other side" stronger, more resilient, wiser. Perhaps Paul, the spiritual athlete who keeps his eye on the prize and runs the race (2 Tim. 4:7-8), isn't really so far off after all. Suffering is a sort of education.

Theologian Hans Urs von Balthasar, however, quickly dismisses "this kind of domestication of suffering . . . as a shortsighted, petit-bourgeois rationalism."[22] Such a view of suffering as educative utterly fails to address the gross excess of suffering in the world, the innocent suffering. In the book of Revelation, in fact, the "wrathful justice" that makes the unjust suffer "only hardens the guilty, and makes them turn away even more decisively."[23] The excess of suffering forces humanity into a darkness, for "suffering cries out much too loudly: [humanity] cannot fail to hear it, nor can [they] integrate it into an all-embracing system of world harmony — for example, as the 'necessary shadow' that must be there for the sake of the beauty of the whole picture."[24] The suffering of the terminally ill provides a very appropriate example of this sort of "excess," and of the despair it can produce in humanity's response, for where is the "gain" at the end of the pain? In the end, "no answer is to be found in words."[25]

Still, Balthasar reminds us, there must be an answer, for if there is not, who would not join Ivan Karamazov in his refusal of a God who permits this? And yet in the name of what can one rebel except in the name of this very "good" God? Humanity "can only wait for God's own answer. And God gives no answer but the folly of the Cross, for the Cross is the only thing to rise above the 'folly' of the world's suffering."[26]

All this may be true, yet how does it do us any good? How is the cross an answer? Here we look at the even more scandalous claim from Paul that his

22. Hans Urs von Balthasar, *Theo-Drama*, vol. 4: *The Action*, trans. Graham Harrison (San Francisco: Ignatius, 1994), p. 192.

23. Balthasar, *Theo-Drama*, p. 193.

24. Balthasar, *Theo-Drama*, p. 194.

25. Balthasar, *Theo-Drama*, p. 194.

26. Balthasar, *Theo-Drama*, pp. 194-95. Balthasar's narration of the cross as the most important "act" in the divine drama that is God's life wholly excludes any interpretation of Jesus' death as a sort of heroic suicide, as a giving of life for others which might justify physician-assisted suicide. David Thomasma's argument ("Assisted Death and Martyrdom," *Christian Bioethics* 4 (1998): 122-42) along these lines fails to recognize our lives as gifts we give to the community rather than as possessions of which we can dispose, even if such an act seems noble. Jesus' death is not a noble, other-regarding act, but rather is fundamentally obedience to the will of the Father.

own sufferings fill up what lacks in Christ's suffering, a claim that hearkens back to the importance of baptism I noted earlier. The "joy" of suffering can be seen only if there is a genuine relation between Christ and the Christian, a sharing, a mutual obligation. Balthasar, while not denying the uniqueness of Jesus' suffering, suggests the eucharistic bond that can explain Paul's strange metaphysics: "To receive into me the One who was sacrificed for me means to grant him space in, and power of disposition over, my whole existence, both spiritual and physical, and thereby to follow him."[27] And participation in the Eucharist presupposes the gift of our bodies that God receives in baptism. About this baptism, Paul admonishes the Romans, "You cannot have forgotten that all of us, when we were baptized into Christ Jesus, were baptized into his death" (Rom. 6:3). Therefore, Jesus is the true owner of all churchly suffering.[28]

Joel Shuman makes a similar point, but is perhaps more careful than Balthasar to address questions of the possible valorization of suffering engendered by this. He states that "Jesus' gathering disciples is morally significant because it is the means by which he *bodily* reproduces himself and his ministry in and to the world."[29] This "reproduction" of Jesus' body and embodied ministry cannot and should not avoid the implication that Jesus' body is a suffering, broken body at the central point in his ministry. Still, Shuman notes,

> None of this means that there is a precise correlation between Christ's suffering and Christian suffering. The cross does not in any clear sense *explain* suffering; indeed, I am persuaded that most suffering will remain absolutely inexplicable. Yet Jesus' performance of suffering service seen most clearly in the cross offers Christians the opportunity to make some of their suffering and their service to the suffering among them an expression of discipleship.[30]

Like Balthasar, Shuman affirms that the cross is not a "theodicy" in the classical sense; it is not an explanation. It is, rather, an offer, an offer to participate in God's life. This should not be surprising to us: Jesus came not as a philoso-

---

27. Hans Urs von Balthasar, *Mysterium Paschale,* trans. Aidan Nichols (Grand Rapids: Eerdmans, 1990), p. 99.

28. Balthasar, *Mysterium Paschale,* p. 135.

29. Joel Shuman, "Beyond Bioethics: Caring for Christ's Body" (Ph.D. diss., Duke University, 1998), p. 130. This dissertation appears in book form as *The Body of Compassion: Ethics, Medicine, and the Church* (Boulder, Colo.: Westview, 1999).

30. Shuman, "Beyond Bioethics," p. 135.

pher offering explanations but as the suffering servant offering himself. Similarly, suffering gives us the opportunity to "fill up what is lacking" in Christ's suffering "for the sake of the body," by offering ourselves, whether in suffering or in caring for the suffering (and there is both suffering and service on *both* ends), in the mutual giving of discipleship.

This understanding of suffering shared with Christ has radical implications for the way we think about the place of suffering in the good life. Rather than exclude it, the temptation now is to require it. So Shuman is right to remind us that "suffering, no matter what the cause, is not a gift to the suffering or to anyone else and should not be sought. What *can* be understood as a gift, however, is the *way* we suffer — and with whom — where suffering is for whatever reason unavoidable. . . ."[31] And so Paul suggests to the Colossians that the suffering is not merely a test or an exercise but is endured "for you," that is, for the sake of the Christian community. While persecution, missionary work, and the like are perhaps more common exemplifications of this, there is no reason to think that any sort of suffering within the body of Christ should be excluded from the notion of suffering "for you." Suffering should not, for the Christian, be an isolating experience, nor a shameful or unnormative one. Rather, suffering offers a peculiarly powerful place for the practice of discipleship, for it gives the community the time to show its "willingness to be present to and for one another in various ways during less than happy and even horrific circumstances."[32] The suffering servanthood of both the ill and the caregiver is made possible and life-giving by their common participation in the broken body of Christ, which seeks to reconcile the world in itself.

To "fill up what is lacking in Christ's sufferings" is to continue the reconciling work of the cross. The cross does not explain suffering; rather, it shows us how the practice of suffering can be offered as a gift that can and does reconcile others, despite surface appearances to the contrary. Thus, even the suffering of the terminally ill, which can rarely be seen in an educative light, can be swept up in God's redemption, which is, right now, making all things new. Balthasar reminds us in closing his reflections on suffering that the slain Lamb on heaven's throne proclaims, "Behold, I make all things new." "Not: Behold, I make a totally new set of things, but: Behold, I refashion and renew all that is."[33] So long as we "are," we are being refashioned. Suffering is an in-

---

31. Shuman, "Beyond Bioethics," pp. 136-37.

32. Shuman, "Beyond Bioethics," p. 137.

33. Balthasar, *Theo-Drama*, p. 200. A similar, but much more sweeping and impressive, account of suffering and redemption that intertwine in Christ, with a very suggestive politics of apocalypse attached to it, is given by David Toole, *Waiting for Godot in Sarajevo* (Boulder, Colo.: Westview, 1998).

tegral part of that refashioning, for all concerned. Why? Christians can offer no explanation; they can only try not to abandon each other, just as Christ, though abandoned and suffering, did not abandon the world that the Father loved.

Mutual Dependence in Christ's Body

So much for "meaningless" suffering; it is apparent that suffering is indeed a part of the renewal of life in Christ, or, at least, that it can be. Shuman reminds us that our presence to each other in these times of suffering is "genuinely possible . . . only when we understand ourselves as bound to one another on the level of being-in-relation that membership in the Body of Christ makes possible."[34] Perhaps even more distressing to the terminally ill than their own suffering is the specter that haunts them of being a burden to others. Independence and autonomy are so much a part of "personhood" in contemporary America that persons who cannot get along without help must be greatly pitied. Hence, the goal of the Americans With Disabilities Act: to make sure that anyone in a wheelchair has no more need of asking for help than others do. This is the way we respect the "personhood" of the handicapped, by making them as independent as the average American. What then of the terminally ill, who, beyond the financial burden often present, are profoundly troubled to find that they can no longer get along without assistance, which, unfortunately, can often only be delivered impersonally?

Shuman reminds us that in the church, the inverse relationship of personhood and autonomy is true. Mutual dependence is perhaps the most important hallmark of what it should mean to be the one body of Christ as the church. In this way, the care given to and received by the terminally ill ought not to be seen as an embarrassment or a burden but as a rare chance to see what church really means in modern America. There is a danger here of valorizing the terminally ill as merely objects of charity, but my emphasis on mutual dependence should avoid falling into that trap. Needless to say, such a patronizing motivation for charity does not deserve the name "charity" in the first place.

Recovering the importance, and even the daily mutual practice, of dependence is vital to rethinking our attitude toward the terminally ill and their attitude toward themselves. "It may be that the demand for euthanasia comes because we lack the skills humanely to know how to be with and care for the

34. Shuman, "Beyond Bioethics," p. 137.

dying, especially when we are the ones doing the dying," write Stanley Hauerwas and Richard Bondi.[35] Many ethicists tend to normalize autonomy when attempting to describe the good life; not only must the terminally ill learn a life that is less focused on autonomy, but caregivers will also find their own autonomy "limited." If a limiting of autonomy is incompatible with the good life, then dependency is refused from both sides. On the other hand, many Christian ethicists have sought to recover the relational character of the good life, over against Enlightenment-inspired pictures of the lone ethical hero or the isolated pursuer of virtue or success.[36] This emphasis on a relational anthropology goes a long way toward weaving our lives together with others'.

Still, there is a significant difference between relationality, as the term is usually used, and mutual dependence of the sort suggested here. Relationality often has that petit-bourgeois ring to it, conjuring up images of freely chosen, free-floating relations. This falls short of helping us understand the dependence required of the terminally ill and their caregivers. My use of the word "dependence" is deliberately provocative. Jung rightly notes that, while Christians must challenge the notion of autonomy present in our society, "radical dependence" is also a "diminishment" of our lives. Yet her term, "interdependence," still gestures toward a sort of contractual reciprocity that is too narrow to describe the relations of love, marriage, genuine friendship, and, most especially, relations with God. "Mutual dependence" expresses the utter self-gift required in those sorts of relations — a genuine binding of the self — while avoiding the connotation that what one depends on is self-sufficient and all-powerful, which I would take to be the case with "radical dependence." In the case of the terminally ill, it is of the highest importance that the larger Christian community see and experience the extent to which the community depends on its members in difficult circumstances.[37] The mutual dependence of the Christian community ought to be exemplified by the church's utter dependence (modeled on Christ's own dependence) on the gracious gifting of God. Jesus challenges us in the Sermon on the Mount: "That is why I am telling you not to worry about your life and what you are to eat, nor about your body and what you are to wear. . . . Your heavenly Father knows you need them all. . . . So do not worry about tomorrow: tomorrow

---

35. Stanley Hauerwas with Richard Bondi, "Memory, Community, and the Reasons for Living: Reflections on Suicide and Euthanasia," in *Truthfulness and Tragedy* (Notre Dame, Ind.: University of Notre Dame Press, 1977), p. 112.

36. See, for example, Anne Patrick, *Liberating Conscience* (New York: Continuum, 1996), and John Mahoney, *The Making of Moral Theology* (Oxford: Clarendon, 1987).

37. Jung, "Dying Well," pp. 183-84.

will take care of itself" (Matt. 6:25, 32-34). Our dependence on God is not simply a relation but rather, as Jesus suggests, goes to the core of our being and must be exemplified in all we are and do, especially materially.

The Christian community is the most obvious locus for the activity of dependence. Paul, speaking of the many parts of the one body, further specifies this dependence: "it is precisely the parts of the body that seem to be the weakest which are the indispensable ones" (1 Cor. 12:22). The unity of body itself comes only in the Holy Spirit, and thus through baptism: "We were baptized into one body in a single Spirit" (1 Cor. 12:13). Just as with suffering, recognizing the place of dependence in the Christian life requires a baptismal anthropology. Gerhard Lohfink brilliantly illustrates the mutual dependence assumed by the earliest Christian communities in their sharing of daily work, of goods, and of care. "Care was extended above all to widows, orphans, the elderly and sick, those incapable of working and the unemployed, prisoners and exiles, Christians on a journey and all other members of the church who had fallen into special need."[38] This care stems directly from the Christian injunction to love, which "was not a noble feeling, but very concrete assistance — especially for fellow believers."[39] These stories may seem almost sentimental, but it should alarm us how far most Christian communities have drifted from these practices.

The mutual dependence required by the terminally ill person and his or her community — a dependence which is most definitely material — ought to seem continuous with the normal, daily life of Christian brothers and sisters, rather than a sudden, disturbing, and dignity-diminishing onset of a fall from the ideal state of autonomy. Teaching us how to live in such a way that our final years do not need to be experienced as a decline is particularly valuable and imperative in a society where the vast majority of us will live long lives and will be forced to deal with bodily decay.

It is true that the "dependence" feared by many who might consider physician-assisted suicide is not a personal one but rather a dependence on the impersonal and often incomprehensible forces within the modern medical establishment. Certainly the desire "not to be a burden" on friends and family is often voiced, but the desire to avoid dependence on medical technology is even more powerful in our thoughts. Worse still, as Wendell Berry notes, modern medicine itself fosters a sense that medical care is best performed in isolation. As he puts it, "the modern medical industry faithfully

---

38. Gerhard Lohfink, *Jesus and Community,* trans. John Galvin (Philadelphia: Fortress, 1984), p. 155.

39. Lohfink, *Jesus and Community,* p. 156.

imitates disease in the way that it isolates us and parcels us out."[40] Not only are parts of our body ruthlessly isolated, but treatments (especially specialized ones) require patients to be wrenched away from their own communities, often far away, to regional centers like Duke Hospital, where the plethora of nearby hotels testifies to the distance many patients and their closest friends and relations have traveled. Berry equates health with "wholeness" or "membership," and that wholeness includes "the sense of belonging to others and to our place."[41] I will return to consider the difficulties of practicing mutual dependence amidst medicine as we now see it near the end of this essay.

Recovering the Daily Practices of Vulnerability to Suffering and Dependence

I have displayed now how suffering and dependence, as the two main factors that lead persons to consider physician-assisted suicide, cannot be seen as pure negatives within the Christian story. In fact, it is not incorrect to say that suffering and dependence are constitutive of the Christian life, a christological anthropology grounded in the practice of baptism. Yet "words" are certainly not enough, especially for elderly patients themselves; the above words are best read and pondered by those who are not suffering now. What is required for the patient is action.

Thinking about the actions necessary to make the above description "live" in the common life of Christians raises some hard questions. First and foremost, it is obvious that Christians must pastorally practice and experience the above story *before* the critical situation of terminal illness arises. We cannot live lives that pursue autonomy as a praiseworthy goal and then suddenly discover the goods of mutual dependence when we can no longer achieve autonomy; instead, we must always live as if we have obligations to all our brothers and sisters. We must learn anew to rely on our neighbors, as most people in most places have done naturally from time immemorial. Too often, it takes tragic and destructive circumstances for us to actually practice this communal life. For example, in North Carolina a few years ago, Hurricane Fran swept through Durham, knocking out power to nearly all households. The transformation of life was astonishing to everyone: people shared food and shelter and tools in ways normally unseen. Deprived of the gentle,

---

40. Wendell Berry, "Health Is Membership," in *Another Turn of the Crank* (Washington: Counterpoint, 1995), p. 88.

41. Berry, "Health Is Membership," p. 87.

alluring hum of electricity, households in effect lost their walls. All were in a common boat, and no one seemed embarrassed to ask for "favors." Despite the destruction, people discovered many of the joys of communal dependence of which our civilization had deprived them. If our lives, especially as church, embodied this sort of visible and expected sharing on a regular basis, not only would the terminally ill lose the trappings of independence and feel less as though their dignity and personhood were being robbed, but the community would be conditioned in such a way that the burden of care would not fall on isolated families but could be shared among an entire congregation. This is not a network that can be formed and implemented at a moment's notice; it can come only from a daily life of "membership" (in Berry's sense) in which mutual dependence is the usual way of life.

In a similar way, suffering — or perhaps it would be better to say openness to suffering, or *vulnerability* — also should become more "common" in the community. Normally, we almost instinctively turn our eyes away from suffering, even as we worship a suffering God at the center of our sanctuaries. Moreover, we act in a way that often seeks to minimize our own suffering and vulnerability, regardless of other considerations. The movement of the nation into isolated suburbs and gated communities, the segregation of exploited farm workers and garment workers from our shiny supermarkets and discount stores, and, of particular importance to the issue at hand, the institutionalization of physically and mentally ill all suggest the extent to which we shape our world by our desire to be as invulnerable as possible. While suffering is certainly to be avoided, it is certainly *not* to be avoided at all costs. The God with whom we are one is a God who is "a man of suffering, accustomed to infirmity" (Isa. 53:3). To enter into the servanthood of Christ is to live in a communal way of life in which we constantly find ourselves participating in and with suffering, and thus suffering ourselves, in such a way that our final illness need not seem a sudden outset of pain which we cannot bear. When the evasion of vulnerability becomes the marker of so many of our everyday practices, it is no wonder that physician-assisted suicide is seen as "merciful." But as John Paul II notes, "True 'compassion' leads to sharing another's pain; it does not kill the person whose suffering we cannot bear."[42] None of this is to minimize the excruciating anguish endured by some ill persons in approaching their deaths; certainly that is not something I can claim to know anything about. Yet I am sure I would know more about it, and therefore more about what it would take to die well myself, if I practiced a sharing of suffering through service with others as an integral part of the Christian life.

---

42. *Evangelium Vitae*, para. 66.

All of this is to say that the church's most important "response" to the growing problem of physician-assisted suicide is to rethink and re-form the day-to-day life of individual Christians and the community in which we live. In an important (though not complete) sense, it is already "too late" when a person is dying in pain. To die well in accord with the death of Christ can happen best when it is done within a community that *lives* the cruciform life of Christ well, and within a personal narrative that is formed and nurtured by the same life throughout. As Stanley Hauerwas puts it, to die well is to die being able to remember the manner and good of one's life, and for others to remember it in the same way.[43] One dies the way one lives; to die via physician-assisted suicide is a judgment on the community, for it is a death formed more by the culture of instant gratification and disposability than by the gospel preached among Christians.

Today we do not generally die (physically, at least) within these Jesus-storied communities but "within the confines of health care institutions,"[44] institutions that have their own stories attached to them. As Nicholas Christakis notes, "the change in attitudes regarding euthanasia has largely been forced upon the medical establishment by exogenous forces, prominently by patient dissatisfaction with current ways of dying."[45] He goes on to say that "people are dissatisfied with the technicalization, medicalization, professionalization, institutionalization, and sanitization of death."[46] Physician-assisted suicide appears almost as a liberator from these byzantine "-izations." Dissatisfaction is perhaps too weak a word; people are scared of dying within the current medical establishment, and perhaps rightly so.

Thus, any perspective on physician-assisted suicide, especially concerning the elderly, must focus its attention on this problem. How can suffering be made communal when the suffering are so isolated? How can dependence be seen in continuity with the previously described daily life of Christian dependence if all of a sudden it becomes dependence on a bureaucratic and impersonal monster?[47] How can a system that promises to "cure" act to "care" in a case where "cure" is not really an option? And, perhaps most importantly,

---

43. Hauerwas, "Rational Suicide," p. 106.

44. Nicholas A. Christakis, "Managing Death: The Growing Acceptance of Euthanasia in Contemporary American Society," in *Must We Suffer Our Way to Death?* ed. Hamel and Dubose, p. 15.

45. Christakis, "Managing Death," p. 16.

46. Christakis, "Managing Death," p. 17.

47. Of course, I do not mean to condemn here all medical professionals, many of whom do their best to mediate between the bureaucratic system and the patient, thus being the sort of caregivers advocated in this essay.

how can the presence of overwhelming (and, I might add, overwhelmingly profitable) medical technology not end up unnecessarily prolonging and even intensifying suffering?

Here we encounter the most difficult problem related to physician-assisted suicide, the distinction between euthanasia and "letting die." Ethicists have attempted various solutions to this problem: some have attempted to make a distinction between extraordinary and ordinary means,[48] others have tried to distinguish acts of commission and omission, still others have sought to constrain medical technology by means of a criterion of just distribution of scarce resources.[49] As helpful as some of these distinctions are, none are really able to clear away what seems to be an inherent fuzziness on this question. Medical science is unable to provide ironclad pronouncements of terminality; treatments often produce different responses in different patients, so the temptation is to try everything. Nearly all religious positions accept the proposition that there *is* a distinction to be made here, and that there is a proper limit to treatment, beyond which it is acceptable and even obligatory to allow a person to die. The trouble of course is defining that limit.[50]

All ethical theories which attempt to do so in a detailed way cannot help but suggest that there is no need for, as Aristotle called it, *phronesis,* or practical moral reasoning. There comes a limit in any concrete ethical situation where the agent is required to make a judgment that cannot be previously given in theory or simply determined by the application of existing rules and parameters. This is, in effect, what our highest courts do in ruling on difficult cases of the law. Doctors, too, are used to making a phronetic distinction between customary and unusual procedures. Yet, as with the courts, this should not inspire a sudden situational ethic, for two reasons. First, the agent, like the judge, is meant to be formed in a particular practice or set of practices. The quality of the agent's judgment rests substantially on the quality of his prior formation, of his initiation into the life of the virtues, as Aristotle and Aquinas would have it. Second, phronesis functions most appropriately in a communal fashion, again in parallel to the communal nature of our supreme

48. See, for example, the Sacred Congregation for the Doctrine of the Faith, "Euthanasia," in *On Moral Medicine,* ed. Lammers and Verhey, pp. 443-44. Interestingly, the argument used against euthanasia in *Evangelium Vitae,* while retaining the standard natural law account, overshadows it, in favor of a more christological approach. See Philip LeMasters, "John Paul II on Euthanasia: An Analysis of *Evangelium Vitae,*" *Encounter* 58 (1997): 193-206.

49. Jung seems to take this approach; see pp. 189-90 of "Dying Well."

50. Paul Ramsey's discussion of the details of various approaches and their problems remains strikingly relevant and helpful. See "On (Only) Caring for the Dying," in *The Patient as Person* (New Haven: Yale University Press, 1970).

courts. Thus, the practical moral reasoning that allows a distinction to be made between physician-assisted suicide and "letting die" can best be done by a community deeply formed in the story of suffering, dependence, and death performed paradigmatically by Jesus. As Paul Ramsey notes, "there may be meaningful specifications of moral rules without certainty in the applications of them."[51] Needless to say, the modern medical institution (or the modern legislature, which is likely to be the place where the "acceptable" limits of euthanasia are worked out) is not such a place. With the support of the various ideas delineated above, *healthy* Christian communities can and should be trusted with determining the exact distinction. Ramsey adds that the Christian tradition already has developed "flexibly wise categories of traditional medical ethics" to handle these sorts of problems, and that these categories (themselves dependent on Christian claims about God, creation, and so on) should be further developed and nuanced rather than dumped because they cannot provide complete prescriptions for every particular case.[52]

I cannot help but add that the very presence of this problem is a result of the confusing maze of modern medical technology, which is correspondingly a result of the vast wealth we as a society have accumulated. The fact that we worry about these sorts of problems so intensely in specialized research hospitals while so much of our own population, not to mention the world's population, goes without basic medical care, immunizations, and potable water is incredible. Incredible, that is, until you realize that most medical research and development is "directed" by the invisible hand of capital which, far from distributing resources fairly, distributes them according to profit, according to the place where the most money is to be made. Further, the United States seems particularly averse to making significant changes in the ends the medical establishment seeks. This is not simply a "justice" issue, as many commentators put it, but must be seen as part of the judgment Jesus continually and consistently levies about the perils of wealth.

As Sondra Ely Wheeler has noted in her study of the New Testament on this issue, wealth is problematic not only because it tends to be distributed unequally but because its very presence encourages idolatry (in the case of modern medicine, a fear of death greater than a fear of God) and "repeatedly thwarts the response to Jesus' preaching. . . ."[53] Put another way, our freedom to see Christ and follow the gospel is severely jeopardized by the presence of

---

51. Ramsey, "On (Only) Caring," p. 120.

52. Ramsey, "On (Only) Caring," pp. 148, 156-57.

53. Sondra Ely Wheeler, *Wealth as Peril and Obligation: The New Testament on Possessions* (Grand Rapids: Eerdmans, 1995), p. 129.

wealth.[54] In the case of the technologization of dying, wealth has impeded the fundamental Christian practice of visiting the sick and comforting the dying, as well as encouraged us to place more faith (and resources) in technological prowess than in genuinely basic care. Perhaps this is not a very helpful analysis, and it certainly risks ignoring and demeaning the real benefits ("miracles," a telling term indeed!) produced by modern medicine — after all, I would hardly wish to undo immunization. But a far more limited supply of wealth might tend to produce the basic, inexpensive, widely needed treatments. Ramsey reminds us that "the advancement of medical science and practice is not alone sufficient to transform elective into morally imperative treatments."[55] If this analysis of the "letting die" distinction in terms of wealth is unhelpful and frustrating for actual, present-day decisions, at least it should help us understand how and why we're stuck in the first place. As Stanley Hauerwas and Richard Bondi remind us, "Most of what is important to our moral existence is not what causes us problems, but what is behind those problems and never raised as a question."[56]

Conclusion

The technical difficulties of negotiating the prohibition against physician-assisted suicide notwithstanding, my analysis of the problem should at least make this ultimate fact clear: as long as Christians insist on isolating terminally ill individuals and their families, both personally and economically, they will find themselves facing the compelling temptation of physician-assisted suicide; thus, like the description of suicide in general that I initially provided, the presence of physician-assisted suicide among us is a judgment on our communal failure to live as persons baptized into Christ and his church. The elderly in our communities are particularly haunted in their loneliness and inadequacy, made to feel as out-of-date and worthless as a ten-year-old computer in our disposable society. Ramsey's claim that "the chief problem of the dying is how not to die alone" is even more true today.[57] It will require more than a simple prohibition to root out the problems engendered by our present situation. A "consistent ethic of life" or a cost-benefit analysis is not likely to help those who really need aid. Rather, a christological reconception

---

54. Wheeler, *Wealth as Peril and Obligation*, p. 130.

55. Ramsey, "On (Only) Caring," p. 145.

56. Hauerwas and Bondi, "Memory, Community, and the Reasons for Living," p. 104.

57. Ramsey, "On (Only) Caring," p. 134.

of Christian life together which includes suffering and dependence, and the presence of that community with the terminally ill (as well as the potentially even more valuable presence of the terminally ill to that community), will help Christians, even those suffering terminally, to die well, sharing in the death of him with whom they shared their life. His was not a peaceful death. But it was a good one.

Memory, Funerals, and the Communion of Saints: Growing Old and Practices of Remembering

M. THERESE LYSAUGHT

Lord, for your faithful people, life is changed, not ended.[1]

Introduction

When I was ten, I first glimpsed that death and growing old were connected. That June, I spent the first of many three-week summertime visits, *sans* siblings, *sans* parents, with my then eighty-five-year-old great-grandmother, Nonny Dodie, also known as Mary Waldo (hence "Dodie") Nall Thume Foltz. Twice widowed, Nonny was a farm wife who, upon the death of her second husband Alfred a few years earlier, had sold the farm and moved into a small house in "town." A wide-eyed girl from a middle-class Chicago suburb, I learned much during those summers in the small, rural community of Sweetser, Indiana (population 967). Life was hard-earned. Things wore out before they were thrown out. Nonny taught me how to make egg noodles and oatmeal cookies, applesauce, fried chicken, and wilted lettuce; that the makings of a good meal came mostly out of the cellar or were dropped off by friends; and that bacon grease was a necessary ingredient for making most dishes. She likewise taught me about aches and pains, support hose, and that teeth could be taken out at night.

These summers also afforded me my first foray amongst Protestants. I not only attended Nonny's Methodist church but, more formatively, spent a good

---

1. The Catholic Church, "Preface of Christian Death I," in *The Sacramentary,* English translation prepared by the International Commission on English in the Liturgy (New York: Collins World, 1974), p. 493.

bit of time with the initially forbidding ladies of the church's sewing guild (to whom my mother sternly warned me *not* to broadcast the fact that I was Catholic, for fear of negative repercussions or bringing scandal on my great-grandmother, I don't know which). We sewed bandages for the Red Cross.

It was in this setting that I first learned about obituaries. Each morning, as we sat at the breakfast table with the heavy and already-too-hot summer breeze blowing the smell of musty wood through adjustable screens, my great-grandmother would pick up the newspaper and, before reading anything else, turn to the obituaries. This was how she started her day. More often than not, she would slowly raise her hand to her mouth, clasping her chin, shaking her head, and say, "Well, Lord have mercy. So-and-so's dead." Then would follow the eulogy — her story of who the dead person was, what kind of work he was in, who he was related to, how long she'd known the family, the troubles and triumphs in their life, some personal anecdote. She would wonder aloud how the family was bearing up, read to me the funeral information, and invariably close with the refrain: "I guess I'm gettin' old. Every week it seems I lose someone else. God'll be taking me one of these days. I wonder who'll be left to go to my funeral."

At first I thought it was rather morbid to start one's day by seeing who had died. Over time, however, I began to realize that this morning routine and the funerals that Nonny subsequently attended were of a piece with the textures and rhythms of life in Sweetser. It was a rare day that Gladys (her "young," sixty-ish friend) did not come by to pick her up to drive her somewhere: to visit relations, to visit acquaintances, to visit especially those widowed and those whose children had moved away, and to visit Alfred's grave. I, of course, accompanied her. It seemed that most of my time in Sweetser was spent making visits.

What is more, Nonny was far from the only one in Sweetser attending funerals and making visits. How did I know? My great-grandmother also happened to write the "social" column for two local newspapers. Her phone and doorbell rang many times daily with folks calling in or stopping by to report "the news," to report who had gotten married or been born or died, who had come to town, who had come to visit, who they themselves had gone to see, what they'd discovered thereupon, as well as who-wore-what and what sort of food was served. It soon became clear to me that in Sweetser, Indiana, not only was it nice to be visited; it was newsworthy.

Now, while my Nonny's habits of newspaper reading and visiting were no doubt in part artifacts of life in a farming community as well as semi-covert means of gathering information for her column, I am convinced that these interconnected activities signaled something more profound. They bespoke a set of underlying practices that were subtle yet deeply formative and that witnessed to convictions about what mattered most. Indeed, if our beliefs are the way we live — or, rather, if what we believe is known best through the actions and practices that concretely structure our lives — then the citizens of Sweetser, Indiana, in the 1970s believed it to be crucially important to remember others and to be, in turn, remembered.

I tell this story because I think the lives of my Nonny and her community display an alternative to the contemporary professional discourse on aging. Circumscribed as they were by the medical-therapeutic-social work paradigm that dominates analyses of aging, they simply carried on a way of life that witnessed to fundamentally different convictions about growing old. Although my Nonny passed on a dozen years ago and I unfortunately cannot query her directly, I am going to take the liberty of trying to reconstruct the sort of convictions required to sustain the practices in which she participated. I will argue that these convictions challenge both the contemporary demonization of aging and the trend that seeks to counter that demonization by rehabilitating the notion of "memory." Increasingly in the therapeutic and pastoral literature, memory becomes both the primary service the elderly render to the community and the process through which growing old finds meaning. This rehabilitation of memory vis à vis aging arises from good intentions. Given that it subscribes to the same anthropological presuppositions as its opponents, however, it fails in the end to provide an adequate bulwark against those forces which would render the reality of growing old and care for the elderly among us unintelligible.

My Nonny's advanced age, her rural piety, and her practice of obituary reading suggest that while memory is certainly not unimportant for understanding what it means to grow old, memory needs to be construed differently. In fact, I believe her life points toward a theological re-reading of memory, encountered concretely through the Christian practice of the funeral liturgy and its affirmation of the communion of saints. Such a re-reading, I will argue, suggests that for Christians, growing old is read best not through "memory" but rather through practices of remembering. Such practices provide Christian communities and those who grow old among them a more adequate response to contemporary realities of aging as well as theologically formed habits of discipleship.

To outline this argument will require a number of steps. I begin with a brief display of the phenomenon of aging and the role of memory as it is presented in contemporary discourse. This leads to a discussion of the notion of memory, both in its philosophically normative mode and theologically re-read. This theological re-reading is displayed through the practice of funerals and the doctrine of the communion of saints through which Christians learn to remember the dead. These practices, in conjunction with remembering theologically construed, lead finally to an allied set of practices that circumscribes the realities of growing old within the discipleship of the body of Christ.

The Ambiguity of Aging

Aging is ambiguous. As Helen Oppenheimer notes, old age can be characterized as both fruition and decay, a time of both fulfillment and loss.[2] Bernard Nash describes aging as a paradox: "Does it strike you as strange that we all want to live longer but none of us wants to grow old?"[3] Both sides of this ambiguous paradox deserve brief exploration.[4]

What fruits and fulfillment does growing older bring? Why might people rightly desire to live longer? Apart from hopes for a secular sort of immortality, a certain degree of advanced age is simply required in order to experience particular joys and pleasures. These joys come as serendipitous gifts as well as fruit intrinsic to lifelong work in the service of valued practices: seeing one's grandchildren, having "old" friends, celebrating decades of marriage, earning the honor that attends a lifelong career. Growing older provides the opportunity to truly master certain skills, to practice them effortlessly, and to share them with new generations of apprentices. The prospect of retirement, attractive to those whose financial security is assured, promises the leisure to shift one's energies to new pursuits and areas of interest, unfettered by the responsibilities of raising children. And as Oppenheimer notes, "just to have learnt more, to have seen more and to have more experience to draw upon are benefits bestowed by time which even the brightest youngster will have to wait a while to attain."[5]

As should come as no surprise, many elderly people do not feel "old" but rather maintain "that they still feel the same: perhaps still in their twenties."[6] The poet May Sarton, in her journal *At Seventy,* concurs and further remarks that she *loves* being "old":

2. Helen Oppenheimer, "Reflections on the Experience of Aging," in *Aging,* ed. Lisa Sowle Cahill and Dietmar Mieth (Philadelphia, Pa.: Trinity Press International, 1996), pp. 41-44.

3. Bernard Nash, "Reworking the Image," *The Witness* 76 (January/February 1993): 11.

4. Given that the social construction of aging has already been well described by previous essays in this volume, I shall here note only the most general contours.

5. Oppenheimer, "Reflections on the Experience of Aging," p. 41.

6. Oppenheimer, "Reflections on the Experience of Aging," p. 41.

What is it like to be seventy? If someone else had lived so long and could remember things sixty years ago with great clarity, she would seem very old to me. But I do not feel old at all, not as much a survivor as a person still on her way. . . . In the course of [a poetry reading] I said, "This is the best time of life. I love being old." At that point a voice from the audience asked loudly, "Why is it good to be old?" I answered spontaneously and a little on the defensive, for I sensed incredulity in the questioner, "Because I am more myself than I have ever been. There is less conflict. I am happier, more balanced, and" (I heard my- self say rather aggressively) "more powerful." I felt it was rather an odd word, "powerful," but I think it is true. It might have been more accu- rate to say "I am better able to use my powers." I am surer of what my life is all about, have less self-doubt to conquer. . . ."[7]

Further on in her journal, Sarton extends these reflections in the context of inverting one of the biggest bogeys of aging (especially for women): wrinkled faces.

Why do we worry about lines in our faces as we grow old? A face with- out lines that shows no mark of what has been lived through in a long life suggests something unlived, empty, behind it. . . . Still, one mourns one's young face sometimes. It has to be admitted. I now use a night cream for the first time in my life. At the same time, as I went over photographs yesterday for a children's book of biographies in which I am included, I felt that my face is better now, and I like it better. That is because I am a far more complete and richer person than I was at twenty-five, when ambition and personal conflicts were paramount and there was a surface of sophistication that was not true of the per- son inside. Now I wear the inside person outside and am more com- fortable with myself. In some ways, I am younger because I can admit vulnerability and more innocent because I do not have to pretend.[8]

The joys that attend aging, however, vary from person to person, espe- cially as actual realities of growing old are shaped by personal context, class, gender, and culture. Even within the span of an individual life, one who finds seventy a time of fruition may find eighty-two more ambiguous or adverse. Indeed, cultural stereotypes generally construe growing old only in terms of its myriad possibilities for physical, mental, economic, and social diminish-

---

7. May Sarton, *At Seventy: A Journal* (New York: W. W. Norton, 1984), p. 10.
8. Sarton, *At Seventy,* pp. 60-61.

ment. Not only is aging accompanied for many by real financial impoverishment, the disappointments of dreams unattained, betrayal by children or
spouses, and the burdens of caring for physically and mentally diminished
parents, spouses, and friends, but it also carries with it the threat of "dementia, deafness, blindness, arthritis, helplessness, even repulsiveness; and worst
of all the loneliness of outliving one's contemporaries."[9] We see in the elderly
around us that

> aging restricts mobility, diminishes senses, and impairs speech and
> thinking. It leads to a withdrawal from active public life, and forces us
> in time to rely on the help of others to carry out the most basic daily
> activities; . . . the loss, suffering, and diminishment of old age [entail]
> disengagement, isolation, and dependence.[10]

Those who grow old inevitably find their lives becoming undone on a number
of levels — their bodies and their minds begin shockingly to fail; capacities diminish; former proficiencies fade; youthful appearance disappears. Identity
transmutes, as the former centers of their lives — either career or home — are
literally taken away. Their communities unravel in a particularly poignant way,
as they find themselves facing again and again the deaths of those with whom
they have lived for decades, with whom their entire lives have been intertwined: parents, siblings, spouses, children, mentors, friends. It seems — with
all of this taken together — that as one grows old, one's very self dissolves.

This latter dynamic lies at the root of contemporary constructions of aging. Just as Sarton describes the bounty of growing old in terms of the full
bloom of her true "self," it is the dissolution of the self that is aging's bane.
Given the modern positioning of the self as the source and end of all meaning, anything that threatens it will be feared. Indeed, even the most cursory
survey of contemporary literature on aging reveals fear to be a dominant motif. The nature of this fear, however, is culturally determined. As Lucien Richard notes: "the fear of becoming old in our society is determined by the fear
of losing those elements which constitute life's goal, and are perceived as the
foundation of self-worth and personhood."[11] Thus behind the "problems"
that aging poses within late-capitalistic, technologically hyperdriven, liberal
Western culture lies a set of anthropological assumptions, convictions about
what it means to be a "person."

9. Oppenheimer, "Reflections on the Experience of Aging," p. 43.
10. Drew Christiansen, "A Catholic Perspective," in *Aging, Spirituality and Religion: A Handbook,* ed. Melvin A. Kimble et al. (Minneapolis: Fortress, 1995), p. 404.
11. Lucien Richard, "Toward a Theology of Aging," *Science et Esprit* 34, no. 3 (1982): 274.

The clearest and most compelling display of this anthropology can be found in H. Tristram Engelhardt's unvarnished articulation of the logic of liberal capitalist culture, *The Foundations of Bioethics*. Here Engelhardt identifies those elements required for personhood, namely that an entity be "self-conscious, rational, free to choose, and in possession of a sense of moral concern."[12] While others might name these characteristics slightly differently (as autonomy, freedom, self-sufficiency, etc.), a review of the traumas of aging listed above suggests that aging ultimately attacks and impairs personhood: rationality and self-consciousness are effaced via dementia and the impairment of speech and thinking, economic impoverishment, physical afflictions such as the restriction of mobility, blindness, deafness, arthritis, and the need to rely on others ravage freedom-to-choose and self-sufficiency.[13]

That aging can so dismantle the constituents of personhood has led Drew Christiansen to identify "the twin fears" of aging as the fear of dependence and the fear of abandonment and neglect.[14] While these may seem to point in different directions, they are integrally related. The prospect of dependence — whether it be physical, financial, or decisional — entails the loss of autonomy and therefore, in our culture, compromises one's status as a person. To not be a "person" is to be vulnerable; civil and social protections apply almost exclusively to persons. In fact, Engelhardt describes how the loss of the above abilities moves one from being a "person in the strict sense," to whom the full gamut of rights and protections applies, to being a person "in the social sense." Persons in the social sense find no intrinsic basis for protection and are accorded such rights only insofar as they are important to "full" persons or serve some socially useful function. If they are not or do not, the further they slip away from the norm, the more open they are to any sort of treatment, including the ultimate in abandonment, namely, "being killed painlessly at nonmalevolent whim."[15] Thus, it is not unreasonable to fear dependence, abandonment, and neglect under current cultural circumstances.

---

12. H. Tristram Engelhardt Jr., *The Foundations of Bioethics*, 2nd ed. (New York: Oxford University Press, 1996), p. 136.

13. Apart from discussions of Alzheimer's and other forms of dementia, there is little or no sense that aging impacts one's "possession of a sense of moral concern." In fact, the elderly are often described in terms that render them guardians of "morality" or spirituality.

14. Christiansen, "A Catholic Perspective," p. 406.

15. Engelhardt, *Foundations of Bioethics*, p. 146.

Memory or Remembering?

A recent move designed to temper the realities of dependency and stave off the threat of abandonment and neglect has been to relocate the center of the geriatric self not in rationality and autonomy but rather in "memory."

Indeed, memory has become one of the major motifs for giving meaning to the process of growing old. Whether it provides the basis for the recently developed pastorally or psychologically mediated therapeutic practice of "life review" or constitutes the elderly's specific contribution to society, the relationship between memory and aging is often depicted as follows:

> When we reach the "noon of life," the movement is toward the "twilight"; there is a turning inward. Our consciousness naturally reflects upon who we are, and we search for a vision of what we might become. Most of us are familiar with the proclivity of old people to tell stories about the past. . . . What a pity it is that so many of us are loath to "waste the time" to listen. . . . The story telling of the aging is a source for enriched memory and a stimulus for the imagination. . . . Another way to say this is that as we grow older the *time* we have (or appear to have) diminishes, but the *space* of our world should expand. Death comes closer and we can no longer think in terms of time measured in many years ahead, but we can gain more freedom to explore the space of our inner world. This is one way to describe a "second childhood," which is a bit like Paul Ricoeur's "second naivete." We move into what some have called a receptive mode of consciousness — as opposed to a mode of action — where images and free association within space take precedence over temporal, logical thinking, with its desire for prediction and control. We become like the little child, not in the literal foolishness of pretending to be one, but in the graceful wisdom of one who has recovered the capacity of wonder and surprise.[16]

Through memory, the elderly both have something to contribute to those who would only listen and find a place to explore their very selves in creative freedom.

16. Urban T. Holmes, "Worship and Aging: Memory and Repentance," in *Ministry with the Aging*, ed. William M. Clements (San Francisco: Harper and Row, 1991), pp. 96-97. One of my, shall we say, "older" colleagues, Father Jack McGrath, remarked upon reading this passage that "many, many older people *love* prediction and control." I think Father McGrath's response points to the possibility that many, many older people would not recognize themselves in the literature on aging. This leads one to speculate on how this professional discourse seeks to shape the elderly in specific normative ways, and to postulate what ends such formation may serve.

This rehabilitation of memory in the service of aging stems from a number of sources. Historical memory seems to be primarily the reserve of the elderly — thus, it is something of value that they, and they alone, possess. Phenomenologically, the turn to memory finds validation in stereotypes — the "proclivity of old people to tell stories about the past" or the sense that elders tend to "live in the past." Biologically, short-term recall seems to become less reliable as one grows old but long-term memory often seems to sharpen.

But can "memory" so construed, and the practices it engenders, transmute the distress of dependency or provide a new status for the elderly among the community that will deter the threat of abandonment and neglect? Can it provide an account that makes our continued care for the elderly intelligible? Unfortunately, I think it cannot. Memory as it functions in this discourse serves simply as another way to shore up the disintegrating self; it seeks to establish a new basis for value and identity, apart from job or family, rooted in the individual. And for many who grow old, this will simply be insufficient. To show how this is the case requires a display of how memory is constructed within this discourse. For that we turn, of course, to Augustine.

From Augustine to Alzheimer's

The classic starting point for contemporary understandings of memory is Augustine's *Confessions*.[17] In Book Ten, his reflections on memory span no fewer than thirteen chapters (chaps. 8-20). The conclusions that he reaches in the course of these meditations seem rather obvious, indicating their commonsense nature as well as their historic influence on millennia of Western thought. Augustine begins in chapter eight with a simple and straightforward observation, that memory is basically an archive — of images, knowledge, and experiences accumulated over a lifetime. It is "like a great field or a spacious palace," he notes, "a storehouse for countless images," a cloister, a vast sanctuary (X.8). This archive is definitely private, something within us, "an inner place" (X.9). But this description is not sufficient, he notes, for memory is surely more than merely a place; it is also an ability, a capacity. The idea of memory, then, implies not only the sum total of stored images but also the capacity to store and retrieve these images.

Augustine's study of memory continues in this vein, momentum building, and in chapter fourteen he makes a very important shift. Not only does

---

17. Augustine, *Confessions*, trans. R. S. Pine-Coffin (New York: Penguin, 1961). References will be given parenthetically within the text.

he render memory as an archival faculty merely possessed by an individual; memory becomes equated with the self:

> But the mind and the memory are one and the same. We even call the memory the mind. . . . Yet I do not understand the power of memory that is in myself, although without it I could not even speak of myself. . . . The power of the memory is great, O Lord. It is awe-inspiring in its profound and incalculable complexity. Yet it is my mind: it is my self (X.14, 16, 17).[18]

At this climax, two points become clear. First, memory is cognitive, an intellectual faculty and process, located *within* ourselves — "it is my mind." Second, "it is myself," the very essence of one's identity and being; or as Brian Horne notes, for Augustine "memory and personhood are co-terminous. . . . without memory the person cannot exist."[19]

This Augustinian position, that memory is internal, individual, a private storehouse of images and the ability to retrieve them, constitutive of self and identity, continues to powerfully dominate contemporary thought.[20] Richard Schaeffler, for example, reflecting on the memorial/anamnetic dimension of the Eucharist, attributes three powers to memory, one of which is

> to *discover ourselves* among our shifting experiences, so that we may construct, out of the abundance of stories we could tell, that one story of our own individual and social life that allows us to attribute that abundance of experiences to ourselves as their 'subjects.' This task is controlled by the idea of the 'self,' that is, by the conscious purpose of

18. David Keck observes that "Many, perhaps most, modern theologians follow Hume in his shift from talk of a soul to concentration on a 'self.' This 'self' becomes the referent of bundles of impressions, ideas, and thoughts which exhibit continuity over time in each person's own consciousness . . . " (*Forgetting Whose We Are: Alzheimer's Disease and the Love of God* [Nashville: Abingdon, 1996], p. 106). Given Augustine's reflections on memory, we might trace this back farther than Hume.

19. Brian L. Horne, "Person as Confession: Augustine of Hippo," in *Persons, Divine and Human*, ed. Christoph Schwobel and Colin E. Gunton (Edinburgh: T&T Clark, 1991), p. 71.

20. See, for example, K. Brynolf Lyon, "The Unwelcome Presence: The Practical Moral Intention of Remembering," *Encounter* 48, no. 1 (Winter 1987): 139; Keck, *Forgetting Whose We Are*, p. 126; Marjorie Proctor-Smith, "Liturgical Anamnesis and Women's Memory: 'Something Missing,'" *Worship* 61 (September 1987): 407-8; Dale M. Schlitt, "Temporality, Experience and Memory: Theological Reflections on Aging," *Eglise et Theologie* 16 (1985): 89; and Richard Schaeffler, "'Therefore We Remember . . .': The Connection between Remembrance and Hope in the Present of the Liturgical Celebration. Religious-Philosophical Reflections on a Religious Understanding of Time," in *The Meaning of the Liturgy*, ed. A. Haussling (Collegeville, Minn.: Liturgical Press, 1991), pp. 15-16.

discovering within our life-situations the one characteristic way in which we have appropriated the external circumstances and their changes as *our own story;* how, in an equally characteristic way, we may have failed in that task; or how we have lost ourselves in the flood of events and retrieved ourselves from it.[21]

Thus according to this account, memory is the vehicle through which I construct myself, through which I grasp my identity. It is the existential essence of the individual.

Reflections on memory and aging likewise reflect this standard account of memory. In Urban Holmes's earlier comments, for example, memory is found by turning inward to the space of our inner world. It is an intellectual process, an exercise of reflective consciousness, the function of which is to discover or construct our self and identity.

This way of construing memory vis à vis aging is troubling, however, in a number of ways. First, it may mask a latent focus on productivity as the locus of individual worth; pacifying a utilitarian calculus, those with memories have something to offer.[22] Second, as reflected in Holmes's comments, memory is situated as that activity particularly fitting to those who have no future. Dale Schlitt, likewise, in a reflection on aging and memory states: "Imperceptibly the threshold is crossed where one tends to locate one's primary point of reference no longer in the future or in those with whom one presently lives and works but in persons and events now recalled from the past."[23] But a third point is most problematic. If memory plays such an important role in the meaning of aging and is so crucial for personal identity, what do we make of the fact that as people age, memory is often precisely that which they lose? We are familiar with phrases like "she's not who she once was," "he's really no longer himself," and how those with diminished capacity are referred to as "shells of their former selves." Insofar as memory, premised as the foundation of the self which is internal and intellectual, recapitulates the terms of the liberal construction of the self that gives rise to the threats of dependence, abandonment, and neglect, it cannot withstand aging's ultimate threat.

Memory as remedy for the meaninglessness of aging fails most dramatically when faced with the dreaded loss of mental ability, captured most viv-

21. Schaeffler, "'Therefore We Remember,'" p. 20.

22. In other words, to caricature this position: the elderly no longer have anything to contribute to society *except* their memories or "wisdom," which, as a valuable commodity under a market model, can be traded for our continued support of them.

23. Schlitt, "Temporality, Experience, and Memory," p. 99. It is interesting that this observation occurs in a subsection entitled "The Aging from an Augustinian Perspective on Memory."

idly in the possibility of Alzheimer's disease. Not only does Alzheimer's entail the most radical sort of dependence over a period of years or decades; the victim's very self disintegrates before the eyes of those who care for and love him as he loses not only his abilities and personality but even his very memories. This radical loss of self no appeal to memory can salve. Consequently, caring for those with Alzheimer's becomes completely unintelligible.

This is precisely the issue taken up by David Keck in his compelling book *Forgetting Whose We Are: Alzheimer's Disease and the Love of God*.[24] Like Augustine, Keck finds memory to be awe-inspiring in its power and complexity, and key to individual identity. But at the same time, through caring for his mother as Alzheimer's disease deconstructs her self, he finds that the reality of the disease challenges deeply held convictions about memory and selfhood which further challenges theological beliefs grounded in this anthropology:

> Ontologically, what happens in Alzheimer's? What becomes of a person and her memories? Is there a metaphysical basis for the human person which this disease does not destroy? The human subject in many ways lies at the center of contemporary theological reflection; we are presumed to be rational, self-actualizing, and intentional. But can we be confident about theologies predicated on a self-conscious, decision-making subject when a person may live for over ten years without any subjecthood? . . . How is it possible to speak of a personal relationship with God, when there seems to be no person left? Does the Holy Spirit depend on a conscious subject in order to be present or to provide comfort to a person?[25]

The above perspectives on memory emerge from anthropological reflection — Augustine's reflections on the working of his own mind, philosophical reflection on the construction of one's own personal narrative, and ethnographic reflection on the behavior and opportunities of those who grow old. But Keck's questions raise theological issues and as such require a

24. As will be clear, I am deeply indebted to David Keck's remarkable reflections on memory in the second chapter of this exceptional book.

25. Keck, *Forgetting Whose We Are*, pp. 39-40. Rabbi Hershel Matt, a nursing home chaplain, casts this question in terms of the *imago dei*. Noting that traditionally the notion of creation-in-the-image refers to intellectual, rational, psychological, or spiritual human faculties, he asks: "What can be said, however, when mind itself falters and regresses, and when such mental capacities as reason, logic, memory, recognition, response, imagination, anticipation — all of them surely aspects of the 'image' — begin to deteriorate and function only feebly or intermittently?" ("Fading Image of God? Theological Reflections of a Nursing Home Chaplain," *Judaism* 36 [Winter 1987]: 78). His conclusion is that the image of God is indeed effaced.

theological starting point. A theological account of memory should begin with God's way of remembering, a thick description of which is found best, of course, in Scripture.

Memory Theologically Re-Read

In Scripture we find that God remembers. From the beginning, God's remembering emerges as radically different from human memory as described above. First, God's remembering is crucial for human existence. To be remembered by God is to be held in existence, to live. To be forgotten, on the other hand, means death: "'not to be remembered,'" Keck notes, "is 'not to exist.'. . . in Psalm 88, the person whom God has forgotten has no strength, is already in the grave, already in 'the regions dark and deep.'"[26]

But God's remembering is not simply the generic substrate of existence, a philosophical concept of 'being.' It is concrete, particular, pervasive.[27] To be remembered by God is to be healed, to have one's prayers heard and answered, and "to be assured of God's tender concern." Yahweh remembers specific individuals; God "remembered" Rachel (Gen. 30:22) and Hannah (1 Sam. 1:11, 19-20) and answered their prayers for children. The blinded Samson's strength is reborn when God answers his prayer to be remembered (Judg. 16:28-30). God remembers not only individuals but Israel as well, as God remembers the covenant (e.g., Gen. 9:16; 19:29; Lev. 26:42-43; Deut. 9:27; Ps. 104:8-10; 105:45; 110:4-5; Ezek. 16:60-63).[28]

Thus, a number of characteristics differentiate God's remembering from human memory. To begin with, it is cast as a verb rather than as a noun. Scripture rarely speaks of God's memory per se; God's memory is known only through God's acts. For God, therefore, remembering is not a cognitive, mental operation; rather, it entails efficacious, "providential, salvific activity."[29] As

---

26. Keck, *Forgetting Whose We Are*, p. 43. See also Proctor-Smith: "to be forgotten by God is to die; to be remembered by God is to live" ("Liturgical Anamnesis and Women's Memory," p. 412).

27. Merold Westphal's account of Christian memory likewise emphasizes this particularity: "Christian memory is radically different from Platonic recollection. . . . Christian memory opens itself to an historical event in all of its unique particularity. . . . The term *event* is appropriate here because it signifies that Christian memory resists the dissolution of the temporal and particular in the eternal and universal" ("Lest We Forget," *Perspectives* [February 1996]: 11).

28. Keck, *Forgetting Whose We Are*, pp. 43-48, and Proctor-Smith, "Liturgical Anamnesis and Women's Memory," p. 410.

29. Keck, *Forgetting Whose We Are*, p. 47.

such, while God may remember the past (or remember it not, an act character-ized as forgiveness), God's remembering primarily implies presence; when God remembers, God becomes present to individuals and to Israel. Conse-quently, God's remembering is other-oriented. We do not find God reviewing images in the divine mind in order to construct the divine "personal" identity; rather, God's acts of remembering, while contributing to God's identity, are primarily acts that constitute God's relationship with another. Thus, to speak of God's memory is not to speak first of identity but, as Keck notes, "to speak of God's fidelity."[30]

As relational, moreover, God's remembering calls forth a response.[31] As God faithfully remembers individuals, Israel, and the covenant, God likewise calls and expects Israel to faithfully remember as well. Keck notes, "after the great work of liberation wrought by God in the Exodus, itself a manifestation of God's faithful memory, it is Israel's duty to remember these deeds and to employ this communal memory as a spur to the fulfillment of the law."[32] Again, God does not want simple mental recall on the part of Israel; remem-bering entails action, namely, observance of the law, the remembering of God and others. "To remember God is a commandment," writes Keck, "but like-wise so is remembering human beings. 'Remember those who are in prison' (Heb. 13:3) and 'remember the poor' (Gal. 2:10)."[33] Such remembering on the part of Israel and the early church entails not mental recollection but rather concrete acts of presence and service.

In practicing the Law, the lives of the faithful become a tapestry of remem-bering. Although the memory of God's deeds and the observance of the Law are essential to who they are as a people, however, Israel knows that the root of its identity lies not in its own memory but in the acts through which God remem-bered the Israelites, liberated them, covenanted with them, and constituted them as a people. It is God's remembering, therefore, that confers identity.

But while it is characteristic of God to remember, it is characteristic of humanity to forget. Time and again, Israel forgets the Lord, in spite of the im-precations of the psalmists and prophets ("Do not forget the works of the Lord," Ps. 78:7), and forgets the widows, orphans, and strangers among them.

---

30. Keck, *Forgetting Whose We Are*, p. 45.

31. As Proctor-Smith notes: "the notion of remembrance found in the Hebrew Scriptures is dialogical, effective and concrete (or embodied). It is dialogical because it presumes a relation-ship between God and people; effective because the remembering calls forth a response, whether from God or from people; concrete because it involves specifics such as names, people, actions, and objects . . . " ("Liturgical Anamnesis and Women's Memory," p. 410).

32. Keck, *Forgetting Whose We Are*, p. 46.

33. Keck, *Forgetting Whose We Are*, p. 55.

Such forgetfulness of God and neighbor is equated with the descent into sin — either the sin of idolatry or the sin of injustice. Such forgetfulness of God and neighbor, time and again, sunders Israel's relation with God and precipitates its demise.

Yet although Israel and humanity forgets, God remains faithful. God continues to remember even when forgotten. This is the essence of the paschal mystery, God's penultimate act of remembering. Here, the character of God's remembering as faithful, life-giving, efficacious, other-oriented, relationship-constituting, and identity-conferring is seen in all its fullness. God remembers us to the point of assuming human flesh and living among us, suffering our forgetfulness in his very body, and in rising, forgiving — or remembering our sins no more. Through God's act of remembering in Jesus we are given life anew; our enslavement to the tyranny of existential forgottenness — death — is vanquished.

Our task is then very simple: "Do this in remembrance of me." Thus, at the center of the life of discipleship, itself a tapestry of remembering, we remember God's great act of remembering which confers our identity; we celebrate the Eucharist. This remembering is not simply recall of a past event but is instead *anamnetic*, "an effective remembering that makes something genuinely past to be present and active in the community today."[34] We experience God's great act of remembering as present.

With this presence, eucharistic remembrance transforms our identity as we become a member of the one who is remembering us, a member of the body of Christ. As Merold Westphal notes, looking at remembrance from the obverse:

> To forget . . . is to prevent the forgotten from shaping our thought, feeling, and action as it should. . . . When Jesus invites us to eat the bread and drink the wine "in remembrance of me" . . . here memory is not the ability to answer questions but *the openness to having our lives (trans)formed by what we attend to.*[35]

The key to this transformation is inherent in remembering itself. When we "remember," for Westphal, "the remembered event is to be renewed, or better, allowed to renew itself upon us in order that we may be renewed in a variety of senses that include regeneration and conversion."[36]

---

34. Elizabeth Johnson, *Friends of God and Prophets: A Feminist Theological Reading of the Communion of Saints* (New York: Continuum, 1998), p. 234.

35. Westphal, "Lest We Forget," p. 11.

36. Westphal, "Lest We Forget," p. 11.

As the elements are transformed into the body of Christ, eucharistic remembrance embeds our relationship with the divine, our renewed identities, in our very bodies. As our bodies become transformed by the events and Person we attend to, liturgical remembrance reveals that God remembers through the material, that the material world and indeed our very bodies — both individual and corporate — mediate God's grace. As Marjorie Proctor-Smith notes:

> Liturgical anamnesis involves not only remembering with the mind but also remembering with the body (individual and collective). More than the repetition of words, liturgical anamnesis involves the use of the body in gesture and movement, sometimes familiar, sometimes awkward. This bodiliness reminds us of the embodiment of divine activity in history, the Word made flesh. It also brings, experientially and dramatically, divine activity into the present, not only in time but in space. The human body and human community then are seen as the locus for this activity. This embodied remembering is found at the center of all Christian liturgy insofar as that liturgy remembers, and remembering celebrates, the paschal mystery of Jesus Christ crucified, dead, risen and present in the power of the Spirit.[37]

Through the Eucharist, our bodies shaped and transformed by God's remembering become enabled to mediate God's remembering to others, as we, through lives of discipleship, engage in concrete acts of remembering.

Theologically construed, therefore, the relationship between memory, selfhood, and identity emerges very differently from the Augustinian-based liberal account with which we began. It is not, primarily, that identity and the self reside in one's own personal recollection of one's own history; rather, identity is conferred through God's remembering of us and, correlatively, through our faithful remembering of God and each other. But it is clear that many of us are far more adept at forgetting than at remembering. The next question, then, is where do we learn how to remember? More specifically, where do we learn how to remember each other in the way that God remembers? Oddly enough, within the Christian community, one of the primary places we learn how to remember the living is where we learn to remember the dead — through that remarkable Christian practice of remembering, namely, the practice of funerals.[38]

37. Proctor-Smith, "Liturgical Anamnesis and Women's Memory," p. 409.
38. Other liturgical practices would be worth exploring in this regard, including the practice of reconciliation, the kiss of peace, the sacrament of anointing of the sick, prayers of petition, the litany of saints, and marriage.

Funerals and the Communion of Saints

That Christians hold funerals seems neither particularly remarkable nor unique. But what Christians do and proclaim in the course of funeral rites is rather extraordinary. For here Christians remember those whose minds and bodies have disintegrated in the most radical of ways, whose lives have certainly "changed but not ended." In doing so, funerals shape and train us to remember each other, particularly those whose minds and bodies have begun to diminish, those who grow old among us, whose lives likewise are changing but not ended. As they proclaim that the dead are indeed alive, the funeral rites remind us that what is determinative for our identity is not that we are selves but that we are saints. In doing so, they provide a radically different lens through which to see — and thereby remember — those among us who are isolated and marginalized. Finally, as we participate in the rites, we learn to remember as God remembers — as concrete, particular, active, other-oriented, present, eucharistic, embodied, life-giving, relationship-constituting, and reconciling. In order to display how the rites train and shape us to remember as God remembers, let us turn to the Roman Catholic *Order of Christian Funerals*.[39]

Remembering the Dead

Even the most superficial glance reveals that funerals embody God's way of remembering. No mere mental meditation or recollection of a person's life, funerals are concrete acts undertaken by the community, the body of Christ,

---

39. In this essay, I will refer only to the Roman Catholic funeral rites, given that this is the tradition out of which I work and with which I am most familiar. The rite can be found in the International Commission on English in the Liturgy, *Order of Christian Funerals: The Roman Ritual, Revised by Decree of the Second Vatican Ecumenical Council and Published by Authority of Pope Paul VI/Prepared by the International Commission on English in the Liturgy* (New York: Catholic Book Publishing, 1989). It is important to note, however, that the Roman Catholic rites, in their revised form, are quite similar to those used within other Christian denominations, especially insofar as the various rites retrieve early church practices and root their prayers in Scripture. See, for example, discussions of the Lutheran *Burial of the Dead* in H. P. V. Renner's "A Christian Rite of Burial; An Instrument of Pastoral Care," *Lutheran Theological Journal* 26 (May 1992): 72-77, and Eric E. Dyck, "*Lex Orandi;* a New *Lex Credendi:* 'The Burial of the Dead,' 1978 from an Historical Perspective," *Consensus* 18, no. 2 (1992): 63-73; of the Presbyterian rite in the 1993 *Book of Common Worship* in Stanley Hall, "Renewing the Rites of Death," *Insights* 110 (Fall 1994): 39-50; and of the Orthodox rite in Kallistos Ware, "'One Body in Christ': Death and the Communion of Saints," *Sorbornost* 3, no. 2 (1981): 179-91.

oriented toward particular individuals (both the deceased and those who mourn). Through the acts that comprise the various rites, the church challenges the contemporary existential credo: Christians do not die alone. Rather, death within the Christian tradition is an experience of ongoing, communal presence. Again and again in these rites, a world in which the living remember, accompany, and care for the dead is concretely rendered. Through a continuous set of rites and practices, the church maintains a constant and unbroken presence to those who are dying beyond the point of their burial.[40] This reflects the historic practice of the church of offering not only presence to the dying but also assistance to the dead on their journey to heaven. A powerful embodiment of presence and solidarity — the funeral procession — opens the liturgy, as the deceased is carried in by his or her family and friends, borne aloft, and set at the center of the community for the celebration. The community gathers not merely as a voluntary association of family, friends, and acquaintances but as persons tied together ontologically — as the *ecclesia*.

Moreover, funerals are eucharistic. Contrary to secular practice, the center and focus of the funeral liturgy is not primarily the deceased but rather Jesus Christ, the paschal mystery, celebrated in the Eucharist.[41] The prayers and

40. The rites begin before death with those contained in the *Pastoral Care of the Sick and Dying: Rites of Anointing and Viaticum*. Here, the community has been present to the dying person with prayer, the reading of Scripture, and communion or Eucharist; these rites end with the "Prayer at the Moment of Death." This process continues with the *Order of Christian Funerals*. Comprised of much more than the funeral liturgy itself, the *Order* circumscribes each moment between death and burial through a series of rites that span the days following death. These rites include the "Prayers after Death," the rite of "Gathering in the Presence of the Body," the "Vigil for the Deceased," the "Office for the Dead," the "Transfer of the Body to the Church," the rite of the "Reception of the Body at the Church," the "Funeral Liturgy" itself, the "Final Commendation," the "Procession to the Place of Committal," and the "Rite of Committal." These rites can be combined in a variety of ways. Thus, the one who has died is constantly in the company of family and friends, and, through their prayers and practices, in the company of the church. Importantly, those who mourn likewise remain in the presence of community and the deceased.

41. The pastoral notes to the rites stress this focus in their comments on the readings and homily, first noting that "in the celebration of the word at the funeral liturgy, the biblical readings may not be replaced by nonbiblical readings," although nonbiblical readings may supplement those from Scripture during prayer services with the family (no. 23). Furthermore, the notes remark: "A brief homily based on the readings is always given after the gospel reading at the funeral liturgy . . . but there is never to be a eulogy. Attentive to the grief of those present, the homilist should dwell on God's compassionate love and on the paschal mystery of the Lord. . . . The homilist should also help the members of the assembly to understand that the mystery of God's love and the mystery of Jesus' victorious death and resurrection were present in the life and death of the deceased and that these mysteries are active in their own lives as well" (no. 27). The rites do al-

readings of the liturgy, while giving voice to grief and lament, preach primarily the Good News of God's remembrance — of the forgiveness of sins wrought through the paschal mystery and of Christ's victory over death in the resurrection. Furthermore, in a funeral context, the Eucharist itself may take on new meaning for many, truly becoming "that sacrament of God's participation in our brokenness";[42] for although we proclaim the joy of the resurrection, as we repeat the words of institution Christ is present as the crucified. We are reminded that God is not distant from pain, suffering, lament, death, and grief but rather is especially and powerfully present in their midst.

As Christ's death encompasses the death of our companions, we have confidence that in Christ's body, they will find the promise of the resurrection. As eucharistic, Christian funerals are no gnostic practice; they are deeply embodied. The body of the deceased is central to the rites.[43] Over and again, the community exercises care with and for that body. Traditionally, the body has been washed, anointed, kissed, carried, sprinkled with holy water, and anointed.[44] But equally central to the structure of the funeral rites are other bodies — specifically, the body of Jesus crucified and risen and the members of the community as the body of Christ.

With bodies so juxtaposed, the rites locate our lives and death within the context of Christ's death and resurrection and display that this resurrection is the resurrection of the body. For Christians, this is not merely a wish rooted

---

low for eulogizing, however, after the Liturgy of the Eucharist has concluded: "a member or friend of the family may speak in remembrance of the deceased before the final commendation begins" (no. 170).

42. Nicholas Wolterstorff, *Lament for a Son* (Grand Rapids: Eerdmans, 1987), p. 39.

43. It is also in this context that the practice of cremation — which is now permitted within the Roman Catholic Church as long as the body of the deceased is present for the funeral liturgy — remains troubling for Christians. For perspectives on this issue see H. Richard Rutherford, "Honoring the Dead: Catholics and Cremation," *Worship* 64 (November 1990): 482-94, and Ware, "'One Body in Christ,'" p. 182.

44. Current rites limit the interaction with the body to sprinkling with holy water and incensing. Earlier practices included that of the bishop and all the faithful sharing with the deceased the kiss of peace (a practice continued in the Orthodox Church; see Ware, "'One Body in Christ,'" p. 181) and the anointing of the body after the funeral liturgy (see H. Richard Rutherford, *The Death of a Christian: The Rite of Funerals*, Studies in the Reformed Rites of the Catholic Church, vol. 7 [New York: Pueblo, 1980], p. 23). Robert Hoeffner critiques current funeral rites in "A Pastoral Evaluation of the Rite of Funerals," *Worship* 55 (November 1981): 482-99. He argues for a return to concrete acts of care for the body of the deceased by members of the community — including preparation of the body and vigils in the home. He suggests that our current distance from the bodies of the dead derives both from the abdication of the preparation of the corpse to funeral homes and from the death-denying attitude of contemporary culture.

in an archaic cosmology but rather a fundamental theological claim. It is a claim that our bodies are an integral part of who we are. The resurrection affirms that God will raise us to new life, "'Us' — not some disembodied spirits, but the full persons he knew, loved and saved."[45] It is a claim that God's grace is mediated through the material: in the incarnation, God became human flesh and dwelt among us; in the Passion, it was Christ's body that was crucified; in the Eucharist, Christ is truly present in the elements of bread and wine; as we partake of these elements, approaching the altar with our bodies, eating and drinking, we become the very body of Christ; and in the eschaton, it is this very materiality of creation that God will transform and glorify. So Christian practice believes that human bodies, even after death, mediate God's grace.

Funerals likewise remind us that God's remembering is life-giving and -sustaining. Again and again, the prayers of the rites invoke God's remembrance of the deceased, petitioning for concrete acts of presence and care. For example, among a multitude of entreaties, the prayers ask God to "have mercy on your servant" (no. 72), to "lead him/her over the waters of death" (no. 167), to "welcome him/her into the halls of the heavenly banquet" (no. 167), to forgive their sins, and to give them refreshment, rest, and peace. That the church believes that God can continue to remember in this way embodies the powerful conviction: through concrete acts of remembrance God continues to hold the one who has died in being. The one who has died is alive.

Remembering with the Angels and Martyrs

And he is not alone. Not only is God present to the one who has died, but the rite summons the hosts of heaven to accompany and welcome the dead: "May the angels lead you to paradise; May the martyrs come to welcome you and take you to the holy city, the new and eternal Jerusalem" (no. 176). The rites ask God to "admit him/her to the joyful company of your saints" (no. 164). The dead, we believe, are alive in the company or, better, the "communion of saints."

In popular parlance, the notion of the communion of saints seems primarily eschatological; it says something about what happens to people when they die. But, as Elizabeth Johnson demonstrates in her valuable retrieval of the doctrine in *Friends of God and Prophets: A Feminist Theological Reading of the Communion of Saints,* historically it is rather first and more centrally

---

45. John P. Meier, "Catholic Funerals in Light of Scripture," *Worship* 48 (April 1974): 212.

ecclesiological. The concept indicates as much — or more — about the nature of the church as it does about the nature of the afterlife.

The doctrine emerges out of Paul's use of the term "the saints" *(hagioi)*. For Paul, the term "saint" refers not primarily to the dead, nor primarily to individuals, nor even to morally or spiritually righteous exemplars, but rather to the community as a whole, a community made holy by the presence and activity of God.[46] As Johnson notes,

> The net effect of being part of this community is that all members are considered participants in the holy life of God. This comes about not because of a state of life they choose or a set of virtues they practice, not because of their innocence or perfection, but because of the gift of the Spirit who is given to all. The Spirit of life who raised Jesus from the dead is poured out on them and they are clothed with Christ, being transformed into the very image of Christ. As always, this is a gift freely given. Its effect is to create a community in grace. . . . Its extensive use in reference to the community of living Christians reflects the heat and vigor of their sense of the presence and action of God in their midst through the life, death, and resurrection of Jesus Christ, which leads to a sharing of physical and spiritual goods among themselves.[47]

Thus, the term "saint" is a theological and ecclesial claim. Through God's gracious action and vital, ongoing presence within the community, God has rendered those baptized into the church as "saints" and has rendered the church as a whole a "communion of saints." The term further indicates the scope of the church, confidently positing "a bond of companionship among living persons themselves who, though widely separated geographically, form one church community."[48]

Likewise, it confidently posits a bond of companionship between the living and the dead, a confidence rooted not in a naive realism or an archaic cosmology but in an ecclesial and sacramental ontology. The practical and theological foundation for the communion of saints is baptism and the Eucharist.

---

46. As Johnson notes, this is the term's most extensive meaning in the New Testament, occurring some sixty times. The term is multivalent as well, however, "referring on different occasions in the New Testament to the angels, to pious Jews who have already died, or to Christians who die under persecution. . . . In addition to the general notion of Israel as the holy people of God, some scholars believe that the specific background for [its referent to the Christian community as a whole] is found in late Jewish apocalyptic literature where 'the saints' describe the elect who will share in the blessings of the messianic age" (*Friends of God and Prophets*, p. 60).

47. Johnson, *Friends of God and Prophets*, p. 60.

48. Johnson, *Friends of God and Prophets*, p. 7.

Through baptism we become members of the church; through the Eucharist we become members of one body, the bonds of which death's destructive power cannot sever.

Thus, through the Eucharist, through the communion of holy things, not only are the living rendered a communion of saints, but insofar as death cannot separate us from the love of God and membership in the body of Christ, the dead remain with us, tied to us in one church, one body, one communion. As the *Order of Christian Funerals* affirms,

> In partaking in the body of Christ, all are given a foretaste of eternal life in Christ and are united with Christ, with each other, and with all the faithful, living and dead: "Because there is one bread, we who are many are one body, for we all partake of the one bread" (1 Corinthians 10:17). (no. 143)

Bonded together in communion, the living and dead continue to care for each other through practices of remembrance. The earliest evidence of Christian funerary practices indicates that prayer of the living for the dead has been considered part of appropriate care for the dead since the beginning. Early Christians offered prayers of praise and thanksgiving, prayed to accompany the deceased on their journeys, and asked God that the deceased would find rest. The church continues this prayer today. As eucharistic and anamnetic, through prayer we come into each other's presence in an active, embodied way, speaking concretely, going out of ourselves toward the other in a way that is creative, healing, life-giving, and salvific. Keck concurs:

> Such a prayer affirms that our responsibilities as caregivers do not cease. Prayer then is not just a mental act of memory and commemoration. It is a real work of the soul which links the living, the dead, and their God. It is a real work of caregiving. (We may add, that in the churches which believe in intercessory saints, caregiving prayer is offered both for the dead and by the dead — the deceased, too, are caregivers).[49]

The doctrine of the communion of saints echoes this belief that the deceased act as caregivers as well; they remain active in prayer in remembering the living. According to Johnson, with the practice of remembering and venerating the martyrs arose the practice of directly calling on them for prayers. Within this context, the martyrs were seen as partners, co-disciples, mutual

---

49. Keck, *Forgetting Whose We Are*, p. 145.

companions in Christ, reflecting a vigorous sense of continuing companionship between the dead and the living. Just as living members of the church
would pray for each other in their struggles to be faithful disciples, so the
martyrs were called upon for their prayers as "a specific way of evoking the
solidarity that existed between pilgrims on earth and those who had been
sealed with the victory of Christ. These latter were asked to participate in
Christ's continuing intercession and remember before God their brothers
and sisters who had not yet run the whole course."[50] This understanding of
the prayer of the dead was simply an extension of the ordinary Christian
practice of the church as communion, the practice of praying for others for
support and specific intentions. As Johnson notes:

> Scripture encourages persons to pray for all human beings and for
> specific needs and is replete with examples of people praying for each
> other. . . . Such prayer functions as a key way of expressing love and
> concern for others. . . . If living persons can and do ask each other for
> the encouragement of prayer, must that stop when persons die? . . .
> The saints in heaven . . . are with their companions on earth in one
> community of grace. [If so], then calling on a saint in heaven to "pray
> for us" is one particular, limited, concrete expression of this solidarity
> in the Spirit.[51]

Keck further observes, in reflecting imaginatively on the afterlife: "Indeed, we
may wonder if it is possible for someone to have experiences of God's presence and not desire to share them with others, just as the Triune God who is
self-communicating love seeks to share his love with his creation."[52] The dead

---

50. Johnson, *Friends of God and Prophets*, p. 78.

51. Johnson, *Friends of God and Prophets*, p. 132. For a wonderful reflection on the intersection of these practices in the Orthodox tradition, see Ware, "'One Body in Christ,'" pp. 188-91.
Mutual prayer is a fundamental relational practice of discipleship among the living; therefore,
construing the church as the communion of saints suggests mutual prayer between the living
and the dead. As Ware notes, "If, then, as members of a single family we are united by the bond
of mutual prayer, and if within this family there is no division between living and departed,
then it should surely be considered normal and natural that we pray for the departed, and ask
the saints to pray on our behalf. Whether alive or dead, we belong to the same family: therefore,
whether alive or dead, we pray for one another. Here on earth we pray for others: why should we
not continue to pray for them after their death? Do they cease to exist, that we should cease to
intercede for them? Here on earth we likewise request others to remember us in their prayers:
and since in the risen Christ the saints are not divided from us but belong still to the same family, why should we not continue to ask them for their intercessions?" ("'One Body in Christ,'"
p. 189).

52. Keck, *Forgetting Whose We Are*, p. 152.

pray for the living, we believe, because they are immersed in the joyous presence of God, which their souls shaped as self-communicating love cannot help but impart, but also because they remain disciples, wayfarers with us on the journey toward the kingdom.

One specific form of caregiving in particular is worth mentioning, namely, forgiveness and reconciliation. Given that central to God's remembering is the forgetting of our sin in reconciling us to himself, one of the concrete ways in which our remembering of the deceased is normed by God's prior act is as reconciliation. Bishop Kallistos Ware makes this point well:

> All too easily it can happen that we postpone seeking a reconciliation with someone whom we have alienated, and death intervenes before we have forgiven each other. In bitter remorse, we are tempted to say to ourselves: "Too late, too late, the chance has gone forever; there is nothing more to be done." But we are altogether mistaken, for it is *not* too late. On the contrary, we can go home this very day, and in our evening prayers we can speak directly to the dead friend from whom we were estranged. Using the same words that we would employ if they were still alive and we were meeting them face to face, we can ask their forgiveness and reaffirm our love. And from that very moment our mutual relationship will be changed.[53]

Thus, remembering as reconciliation can be a transformative, renewing, even conversional, practice of mutual caregiving. Moreover, it may take different forms. It might entail acting so as to foster reconciliation between the deceased and another person or to make practical amends for a wrong one committed against the deceased. And beyond prayer and reconciliation, acts of remembering might also include attending to the deceased's former responsibilities — for example, visiting the deceased's elderly parents; carrying on the work of those martyred; providing companionship to those who mourn the loss.

And so, the Christian practice of funerals boldly immerses us in a theological reality — one comprised of a vibrant community between the living and those diminished to the point of death, sustained by God's gracious remembering. Through the rites we discover that the deceased remain present with us in the communion of saints, engaged together with us in mutual practices of remembrance as care. And if this is true for the deceased, how much more is it the case for those visibly among us? In learning to remember

---

53. Kallistos Ware, "'Go Joyfully': The Mystery of Death and Resurrection," in *Beyond Death: Theological and Philosophical Reflections on Life after Death*, ed. Dan Cohn-Sherbok and Christopher Lewis (London: Macmillan, 1995), p. 38.

the dead and that we are remembered by them, we are simultaneously reoriented toward those among us, living but diminished. We learn to remember those who grow old.

Saints and Disciples: Remembering Those Who Grow Old

And so it turns out that making visits is a profoundly theological practice.[54] Through unassuming, everyday activities, ordinary folks in Sweetser, Indiana, engaged in an important mode of discipleship. They remembered the dead, through funerals and cemetery visits, and they remembered each other; they remembered those among them who had "grown old." In doing so, their lives gave witness to fundamentally different convictions about what it means to grow old and to what practices are appropriate for caring for the elderly among us.

Fundamental to these practices is a basic affirmation: that what is determinative for the elderly is not whether they qualify as "persons," nor their individual memory of their personal story, nor that they can share historical memories with others, but rather simply that they, as much as any other member of the body of Christ, are in fact "saints." To be clear, the term "saint" refers not to some degree of moral or spiritual perfection, implying that the elderly, because they have more time for spiritual introspection and prayer, are somehow closer to God. Indeed, as many age they seem to become the antithesis of our narrow notions of saints. Personal eccentricities magnify into embarrassing or frustrating obsessions; they become set in their ways, critical of innovation, cantankerous, loudly complaining of their loneliness and bodily afflictions. Moreover, little perfection or spiritual depth seems to be found in those who suffer dementia, who must be watched, fed, helped in the bathroom, and dressed, as hostility, obscenity, and irrational mutterings are

---

54. That visiting is a "practice" follows from Alasdair MacIntyre's well-known definition of "practice" in *After Virtue* (Notre Dame, Ind.: University of Notre Dame Press, 1981), p. 175. Visiting certainly is a "coherent and complex form of socially established cooperative human activity," as my great-grandmother's news network would attest. There are certainly goods internal to it, standards of excellence which define it and systematically form participants in the virtues. These might include friendship, hospitality, being present to the other, patience, and, often, fortitude. Unlike many activities advanced as practices (e.g., chess-playing), visiting is a locally embodied practice open to all and engaged in by regular folks (mostly women). That this is the case speaks not against its status as a practice but may instead provide a corrective against elitist, universalized, and competitive accounts of practices. That it is theological as well is apparent from Jesus' own life, the corporal works of mercy, and the prophetic and Pauline injunctions to remember the widows.

tolerated. What might it mean, then, to look anew at our aging neighbors — indeed, our parents — and see them as saints? It means that the Spirit of Life who raised Jesus from the dead has been poured out on them and has transformed them into the very image of Christ. It means that God remains present and active with them, among us, in a vital and vigorous way, so that among us there is a mutual sharing of physical and spiritual goods.

Now, in some ways, this may not seem like a terribly profound claim. But I would argue that it has profound implications both for how the elderly construe themselves and for how the Christian community understands the status of growing old. As the relationship among the members of the communion of saints is constituted by practices of remembrance as care, so it should be with regard to those who grow old. While it is difficult to specify such practices in too much detail apart from their display in a concrete community, the broad outlines of such an approach can be sketched.

Growing Old in Discipleship

Turning first to the elderly themselves, redescribing them as saints suggests that, even as they grow old, the elderly remain disciples. For those who grow old in Christian community, "retirement" is not an option. Just as death does not dispense one from continuing to follow the call to discipleship, the elderly, as members of the ecclesial community, remain called to a vocation, a ministry, to concrete practices of care modeled on God's remembering. They remain called equally to the practices of the corporal and spiritual works of mercy, to theological reflection, to prayer and worship, to liturgical ministry, to sharing the faith with the young, and to the promotion of social justice. The elderly minister to others in the community in a variety of ways, offering their historical memories, their example and wisdom, to those who seek to navigate paths they have already traversed — the struggles of marriage, child-rearing, or forgiveness and reconciliation. In continuing to follow the call of discipleship, they witness to the fact that identity is rooted not in employment or autonomous self-achievement, challenging the perspective of those of us preoccupied with these pursuits. Given the diversity and individuality among those who grow old, the vocations and ministries to which they are called will be as varied as for those at any other stage of life. The elderly, with the community, must continually discern how they can continue the work of discipleship as their circumstances change.[55] The com-

55. Marius L. Bressoud's moving and compelling reflection on his own "personal" spiritual

munity must likewise foster this call and welcome their gifts of ministry and service, especially in public sacramental ministries.[56] And as importantly, the church must discern the vocation of those who are diminished, those with Alzheimer's, for example, who seem to have nothing to offer. They remain, after all, saints.

Thus, the communion of saints not only "forges intergenerational bonds across time that sustain faith in strange new times and places."[57] In recasting the elderly as saints and disciples, the communion of saints forges intergenerational bonds among those in the community. It challenges those approaches to "religion and aging" which situate the elderly in a passive, receptive position, as primarily recipients of the ministrations of others.

Construing the elderly as saints and disciples likewise challenges another troubling tenet of contemporary discourse on aging. As Mary M. Knutsen comments, "A common and influential image of human development in aging is that of an upward and then downward curve centered on work and economic productivity and characterized by a 'mid-life crisis' (the beginning of the downward curve) and finding its final denouement in retirement."[58] As was noted earlier, those who are in the "twilight" of their lives are characterized as spending a greater proportion of their time reminiscing about the past, since the past is all they have in terms of either identity or what they have to offer.[59] Understanding the elderly as members of the communion of

---

journey in his "eighth decade" highlights this well. He finds that he is not merely called to a comfortable process of introspective personal reflection on his own spirituality but rather finds himself called to minister concretely, in a way he never would have anticipated, to a dying homeless man named Ramon. See Marius L. Bressoud, "A Slow Dying," *Second Opinion* 21, no. 1 (July 1995): 43-47.

56. This public, sacramental role is important to overcome the all too frequent marginalization of the elderly within their communities and to remind the church that without the elderly it is incomplete. This might mean, of course, that the "efficiency" of our public rituals may need to be sacrificed; the elderly may read the Scriptures more slowly as lectors; they may need assistance in distributing Communion and may take much longer than their crack, thirty-something counterpart. But their presence at the altar is crucial in challenging the fear of growing old and the devaluing of the elderly, outweighing the importance of completing Mass or worship in fifty-five minutes.

57. Johnson, *Friends of God and Prophets*, p. 85.

58. Mary M. Knutsen, "A Feminist Theology of Aging," in *Aging, Spirituality and Religion: A Handbook*, ed. Kimble et al., p. 466.

59. See, for example, the discussion of the practice of "life review" in David G. Hawkins, "Memory, Hold the Door," *Journal of Religion and Aging* 3, no. 3-4 (Spring-Summer 1987): 13-21, and Drew Christiansen, "Creative Social Responses to Aging," in *Aging*, ed. Cahill and Mieth, pp. 114-22. It is this construct of aging that fuels the ubiquitous practice of "life review," one which is "characterized by the progressive return to the consciousness of past experiences and,

saints, however, means, at minimum, that they have a future. While that future surely includes the experience of their own death, more importantly, it is a future that includes those who will remain behind. In that future, they will be reunited in a new and concrete way with those who have preceded them in death. And, although they may feel alone now, grieving the loss of their parents, spouse, siblings, and friends, the communion of saints reminds them that they are not — those who have gone before us remain with us.

Remembering As a Communal Practice

Given the realities of aging, however, the elderly are not only disciples but need to be ministered to as well. As disciples, we are called to remember as God remembers — as concrete, particular, active, other-oriented, present, eucharistic, embodied, life-giving, relationship-constituting, faithful, and reconciling. This challenges human tendencies to count good intentions or mental recollection as remembering or to value interactions with the elderly that are primarily self-oriented and controlling.

To remember is to act; thus, remembering the elderly will be embodied in concrete activities.[60] As often as these activities may be meaningful and enjoyable, they may also be onerous, boring, painful, unpleasant, constraining, and take valuable time away from our schedules and priorities. As Keck reminds us, "remembering, after all, takes time, and . . . entails distinct responsibilities."[61]

The most basic act of remembering, and fundamental to all others, is simply the act of being present. As Keck astutely observes, "As anyone in a nursing home will tell us, not only is it important to be remembered, it is also

---

particularly, the resurgence of unresolved conflicts" (Hawkins, p. 18, quoting Robert N. Butler, "Life Review Therapy," *Geriatrics* 8 [November 1974]: 165). As a therapeutic technique aimed at the maintenance and preservation of the elderly's "self-image," it is unclear what role "life review" has in an ecclesial or pastoral context; it might be more properly located, and therefore modified, as a component of an ongoing practice of reconciliation.

60. It could also be suggested that concrete activities and encounters are required to sustain our very ability to remember anyone or anything. Moreover, we will find as we engage in concrete activities of remembering with the elderly that they become much more a part of who we are. This, then, will indeed make their deaths more painful, but at the same time we will find that "remembering" them when they are gone has become second nature.

61. Keck, *Forgetting Whose We Are*, p. 58. For a realistic display of the fact that remembering (in this case, waiting on someone as he dies) takes time and challenges our desires for efficiency and control see Curtis W. Freeman, "What Shall We Do About Norman? An Experiment in Communal Discernment," *Christian Bioethics* 2, no. 1 (1996): 34-36.

crucial to be visited."[62] Those who have visited nursing homes know how valuable a commodity such visits are for the residents and how devastating it is for those whose children never come. Like God's remembering of us, our presence to the elderly as we remember them sustains them.

Beyond visiting, remembering takes as many forms as there are people who grow old. But certain common practices are important. Growing old invariably entails the loss of those who structure one's life — spouses, siblings, parents, friends. An important concrete act of remembering is that of consolation and ministry to the grieving in times of death. We are called to the sometimes uncomfortable task of encouraging the elderly to talk about one who has died and of being present and listening as they do so, as they cry, not just during a "legitimate" period of mourning but on an ongoing basis.

Beyond simply listening, the *Order of Christian Funerals* counsels continuous, concrete practices of care for those who mourn, extending to "act[s] of kindness, for example, assisting them with some of the routine tasks of daily living" (no. 10). Assistance with the mundane and everyday is no less crucial for the elderly, examples of which could multiply: "assistance in activities that are a routine part of living: shopping, cooking, cleaning, banking, and so on . . . nursing chores, such as bathing, grooming, and supervising medication . . . sharing social activities such as visiting, listening to stories, sharing feelings, and so on . . . and [facilitating] the authority competent adults exercise over fundamental aspects of their lives."[63]

All too often, these activities are assumed to be the sole responsibility of family members. As such, they can be overwhelming. The funeral rite, however, reminds us that remembering is a communal activity, that responsibility for remembering lies not only with family members but rather with the whole church. At minimum, dispersing the concrete, mundane tasks of care required to sustain the elderly makes the burden of doing so less onerous; but it also concretely renders the community as the body of Christ. As David Keck notes:

> Supporting this Herculean (or better, Samsonian) task of the caregivers is one of the ways in which non-caregivers can most clearly fulfill their call to join the body of Christ. In 1 Corinthians 12, Paul describes the diversity of the body's parts as a way of describing the different gifts of the Spirit and tasks of diverse Christians. So too can we see that those who come by for visits with caregivers, perhaps

62. Keck, *Forgetting Whose We Are*, p. 47.
63. Christiansen, "Creative Social Responses to Aging," p. 117.

bringing home-made soup, or who serve as part-time caregivers in their different roles help to form the body of Christ into which Christians are baptized. These seemingly simple tasks (which require so much effort and are not done frequently) help make us one.[64]

But remembering as a communal practice can encompass more than the mundane. A wonderful display of a community which took seriously this responsibility can be found in Curtis Freeman's essay "What Shall We Do About Norman?"[65] Freeman recounts how his parish, "Norman's church family," found themselves charged unexpectedly with the task of deciding whether Norman, a seventy-nine-year-old friend and member who suffered a heart attack and fell into a permanent vegetative state (PVS), should be sustained with medical treatment or allowed to die. A task generally reserved as almost sacred for family members or special appointees, proxy consent became proper to them not only because of their friendship but because of Norman's "identity as a member of the community of God's new creation which we witnessed in his Christian baptism on May 9, 1926."[66] As he was one of the saints among them, the community found that remembering Norman took the form not only of keeping vigil with him in the hospital as he lay dying but also of an extended and deliberative communal process of discernment and eventually decision-making.

Freeman's account of his community's care for Norman also reminds us that from baptism to death, the community assumes responsibility for the faith of its members. The central moral question became for them:

> How could we as a community of discernment assist Norman to live with integrity the life which he owned in baptism? . . . Even in a PVS Norman remained part of the community he joined in baptism, and he was still responsible for living his life in keeping with that baptismal pledge. Our role was to support and sustain him in those decisions which we understood to be consistent with faithful discipleship.[67]

Freeman's account renders the community as co-disciples, responsible not for helping its members to achieve the personal fulfillment of an autonomous self but rather for helping them to be faithful to the life embraced in baptism.

64. Keck, *Forgetting Whose We Are*, p. 137.

65. Freeman's description of the parish's discernment process, and his theological analysis, resonates with many of the points made in this section.

66. Freeman, "What Shall We Do About Norman?" p. 26.

67. Freeman, "What Shall We Do About Norman?" pp. 26, 30.

Keck takes this claim one step further, suggesting that an important task in remembering the elderly may be to assume the responsibility of believing for them. While this certainly defies understandings of faith that privilege individual rationality and autonomy, it gains credence within a framework of communal identity premised in the resurrection:

> Because the patient seems to lose all capacities of subjecthood, it is the work done by others for him which becomes crucial. As the community accepts the responsibility of believing for a newly-baptized infant, so too at the end of life does the church accept this task for those in end-stage dementia. . . . In light of Alzheimer's we come to recognize that we sometimes must do the believing for others. As we assume this heavy responsibility, we should consider that we have a particular responsibility not to underbelieve. That is, as we bear the fullness of a person through the last years of dementia, so too should we bear the abundance of the resurrection and God's work for us. Not everyone can bear this plenitude — either as a caregiver or a Christian — but, as caregivers strive to sustain the fullness of a person, so should the body of Christ seek to bear the fullness of his work.[68]

Thus, through concrete practices of remembering, the Christian community rescues the elderly — even those with Alzheimer's or those in a persistent vegetative state — from abandonment and neglect. It is in this context especially that failure to remember — or forgetting of the elderly — correlates with alienation and death, and thus becomes an act of sin. Forgetfulness sunders not only our relationship with God but also human relationships: "the adulterer forgets the spouse, the rich forget the poor, the friend forgets the friend. We forget the simplest acts of writing thank you and birthday cards. Perhaps we are too busy to remember."[69] For the elderly especially, "not to be remembered," to be forgotten, is a cause of deep pain and despair, sometimes even making them wish they no longer existed.

But we do forget. Perhaps we are too busy. The structures of aging, which remove the sick and elderly to places like nursing homes, facilitate our forgetfulness. Thus, crucial to practices of remembering are practices of forgiveness and reconciliation. In all the relationships entailed in this communion of saints, significant need remains for reconciliation: between the elderly and their companions who have died as well as between the elderly and those who comprise their communities. Remembering the elderly as an act

---

68. Keck, *Forgetting Whose We Are*, pp. 91, 134.
69. Keck, *Forgetting Whose We Are*, p. 58.

of presence will require the painful remembering of harms they have committed against us and we against them. To be a people capable of remembering as God remembers, we must remember our sins, committed in the past, as well as our ongoing failures, and in remembering seek forgiveness and reconciliation.

Such reconciliation will be not be easy, nor will it be superficial, simply therapeutic, or painless. The remembered acts of sin, failure, and harm in all their ugliness will renew themselves upon us, released from where they have festered. We will recognize them as part of our mutual identities; we will recognize that the past cannot be changed nor, in most instances, made right. On their own such acts would continue to sunder the very relationship for whose sake we remember them. Thus, reconciliation must be normed and made possible by the act of remembering which constitutes our unity, namely, the Eucharist. Only in this context, when the act of God's forgiveness in Jesus Christ likewise renews itself on us, can practices of reconciliation as remembrance be transformative.[70]

Not only does the Eucharist provide a context for enabling reconciliation, it also provides the center from which further liturgical practices of remembrance spring. The prayer of the community is a form of remembering that makes present and thereby unites those separated with the community. In the prayers of petition or intercession, the community prays for those who are sick and for those absent from the worship gathering. As the funeral liturgy attends to the grief that accompanies death, so the Christian community needs to attend to the fears, diminishment, and grief that accompany the losses and illnesses of aging, praying for the specific needs of those in their midst. Related sacramental activities, such as commissioning ministers to bring Communion to the sick and shut-ins and the practice of anointing of the sick, are further acts whereby the community as ecclesia makes itself present to those who are separated.

This eucharistic context suggests one final dimension of practices of remembering. As noted earlier with regard to the dead, an important part of the refusal to deny death is the attention to the body during the funeral rites — from the personal care of the bodies of the dead to the presence of the

---

70. As Westphal notes, such practices of reconciliation are not only individual but require communal repentance as well: "Those who stand in this perpetual need of revitalization and re-direction include not only the individual believers who make up the community of faith but the community itself as a corporate body. Remembrance involves personal and collective renewal at the same time" ("Lest We Forget," p. 11). In the context of communities who have marginalized the aging or who have sinned against an individual member, acts of reconciliation as practices of remembering would be indicated.

body at the funeral liturgy, the materiality of the eucharistic celebration, and the affirmation that resurrection is indeed bodily. Likewise, learning to read aging through the baptismal and eucharistic context of funerals helps to challenge cultural tendencies to deny the bodies of the elderly: to treat them as a medical problem to be solved, as undignified failures from the norm of which we should be ashamed, or, in a dualist modality, as separable from a brain-centered notion of personhood. These ways of situating aging bodies each suggest that real bodies might be expendable: if the "problems" they present cannot be solved with technology, if they compromise dignity individually defined, or if specific intellectual faculties become impaired.

Over against these constructs, the affirmation of the resurrection of the body situates aging bodies differently. The resurrection affirms that our bodies, our very materiality given to us in our creation, are integral to who we are as persons. Our bodies are members of the body of Christ, a capacity or character that aging cannot erase. God has entered into this very materiality and so, even in a diminished capacity, our bodies remain vehicles of God's grace. Contrary to accounts that construe aging bodies as falling away from the human norm, Mary Knutsen suggests that aging bodies be read rather as an actualization of the incarnation and paschal mystery:

> Bodies are the very medium of communion with God, with others, and with the earth — and so the medium of all joy. . . . At the center of God's own triune life [is] the incarnation of God in Jesus Christ, God "deep in the flesh" of bodily, finite, cruciform human life. For Christians, growth into the actuality of particular, finite bodies with age is an ever deepening journey into God "deep in the flesh" in Jesus Christ, an ever deepening actualization of our baptism into the corporeal and communal body of Christ. Hence aging and death need to be seen not just as part of the "downward slope" of human life but in light of the paschal mystery of Christ.[71]

That this light is the paschal mystery is important, for as crucial as the resurrection is in affirming the intrinsic value and importance of our bodies as they age, the crucified, suffering body of Christ cannot yet be dismissed. The embodied experience of growing old is often one of significant physical infirmity, illness, loss, and suffering, and the "fear of pain and suffering" could be added as a third to Drew Christiansen's twin fears of aging mentioned earlier (the fear of dependence and the fear of abandonment and neglect). The journey into actuality described by Knutsen is one in

---

71. Knutsen, "A Feminist Theology of Aging," p. 473.

which we enter increasingly into our finitude and the fallen nature of creation. Although we trust that our bodies will be taken up into the resurrection and ultimately transformed when creation is renewed, for now the diminishment and disintegration of our bodies — even unto death — must be seen "as intimately connected with sin, which crucified Christ and which violates and rips life with each other and God."[72] Thus, while such diminishment is not to be welcomed and can legitimately be addressed, neither is it to be escaped by eliminating or devaluing the bodies of the elderly. Situated within the paschal mystery, the elderly in their bodies, and we as we tend to them, meet Christ who suffers the depths of pain, suffering, sickness, and death.[73] Thus, the practices of remembering, especially those that entail particular attention to the bodies of the aging, take on new significance. Normed by the Eucharist, they take on a sacramental dimension in their own right.

Lord, for Your Faithful People, Life Is Changed, Not Ended

Thus we find that theological re-reading of memory, practiced through funerals and the communion of saints, challenges the dominant ideology of the self that so devastates us as we grow old. It challenges the ideology of personhood as comprised solely of rationality and autonomy. The communion of saints reminds us that dependence, or rather interdependence,[74] is not a developmental and alien challenge to the foundation of our person-

---

72. Knutsen, "A Feminist Theology of Aging," p. 474.

73. It is important to remain cautious when mapping suffering on to Christ's Passion. As Curtis Freeman aptly states, "The connection between the suffering of Christ and our own suffering is not an easy one to make. Nevertheless, when guided by the spiritual disciplines of worship, prayer, reading and ministry it is possible for the Christian to envision her pain as the sacramental *anamnesis* of the cross" ("Redeeming Love and Suicide: An 'Evangelical Catholic' Response to Amundsen," *Christian Bioethics* 1, no. 3 [December 1995]: 320, note 5; Freeman here cites Stanley Hauerwas, *Naming the Silences* [Grand Rapids: Eerdmans, 1990], pp. 86-89). Such a reading should be available in the community to those so habituated through practices of *askesis* (as were the martyrs) who are thereby capable of taking it upon themselves; when forced upon another, it becomes a weapon of torture. Richard, "Toward a Theology of Aging," and others also explore the relationship between the suffering of aging and the Passion through the concept of *kenosis*. See also Christiansen, "A Catholic Perspective."

74. The use of the term "interdependence" is not simply a matter of semantics but rather one of accuracy. The use of the language of "dependence" with regard to the elderly severs their present situation from the larger context of their overall life, which when viewed more broadly would reveal a complex tapestry of interdependence construed over a lifetime.

hood but rather is constitutive of Christian identity from the beginning.[75] At the same time, the reality of the communion of saints situates the elderly as equal partners in the body of Christ; without the elderly, the church is not complete.[76] Thus, abandonment and neglect of the elderly are not only unfortunate afflictions attendant upon aging; when present within Christian communities they stand as indictments of sinfulness and of the communities' failure to be the church.

Likewise this account challenges the ideology of memory, critiquing its continued privileging of a notion of the self individually construed. A theological reading of growing old locates identity not individually but rather communally. One's identity as a member of the body of Christ comes not as an individual achievement but rather as a gift, as God remembers us and makes us saints, participants in the holy life of the Trinity. Such an identity, such a foundation for who we are, the ravages of aging cannot efface, not even unto death.

What becomes important, then, is not so much that those who grow old can remember but rather that we, as a community, actively and concretely remember them. In so doing, we become a people of memory, faithful to God's way of sustaining his creation — a people for whom life will always change but never end. This my great-grandmother began to teach me when I was ten years old.[77]

75. More broadly speaking, such interdependence is likewise constitutive of human identity as well, if one affirms the conviction that humans are created in the *imago dei*. The image of God as Trinitarian suggests that identity is not located within an individual but rather is located in the spaces between myself and others, constructed through the relational actions of remembering that occur in those spaces. In short, my identity is comprised in my relationship with others. As Knutsen notes: "Within the life of the triune God, and among all created life in God, relationality generates each personal identity, and the personal identities thus generated in turn constitute and transform the dynamics of their relationality" ("A Feminist Theology of Aging, p. 471). Similarly see Freeman: "sacredness . . . is not an ontic category *within the self* but a dialogic notion *between the self and others*" ("What Shall We Do About Norman?" p. 24).

76. The reality of the communion of saints also reminds us that the church is equally comprised of others who may be marginalized or excluded from our communities — the disabled, the poor, the mentally ill, those of different racial or ethnic backgrounds — and likewise calls us to redefine their roles among us. Many of the reflections in this essay would apply equally to other constituencies.

77. That this essay exists is certainly a testimony to the communion of saints. It could not have been written without the material assistance of my Nonny and others who inspired me as I wrote; my colleagues Terrence W. Tilley, Sandra Yocum Mize, Michael Barnes, Dennis Doyle, Una Cadegan, James Heft, Jack McGrath, and Maureen Tilley who read earlier drafts of the essay; Stanley Hauerwas who called it into existence; and my friends who are gracious enough to remember me (even and especially when I'm not so good at remembering) and, in so doing, sustain my work and my life.

Contributors

David Aers is the James B. Duke Professor of English and Religious Studies in the English Department of Duke University.

David Cloutier is Assistant Professor of Theology at St. Benedict's College and St. John's University, Collegeville, Minnesota.

The Rev. Rowan A. Greer is Emeritus Professor at the Divinity School of Yale University.

Stanley Hauerwas is Gilbert T. Rowe Professor of Theological Ethics at the Divinity School, Duke University.

Judith C. Hays is Associate Research Professor in Psychiatry and Behavioral Sciences, and Senior Fellow in the Center for the Study of Aging and Human Development in the Duke University Medical Center.

Richard B. Hays is George Washington Ivey Professor of New Testament in the Divinity School of Duke University.

Shaun C. Henson is a graduate student, finishing his Ph.D. at Oxford University, England.

The Rev. Dr. L. Gregory Jones is the Dean of the Divinity School of Duke University.

The Rev. Susan Pendleton Jones is Director of Special Programs in the Divinity School of Duke University.

Prof. Patricia Beattie Jung is in the Department of Theology of Loyola University, Chicago.

The Rev. D. Stephen Long is Professor of Theology at Garrett Evangelical Theological Seminary, Evanston, Illinois.

M. Therese Lysaught is Professor of Theology and Ethics in the Department of Theology at the University of Dayton, Ohio.

Prof. David Matzko McCarthy is Chair of the Department of Theology at Mount St. Mary's College, Emmitsburg, Maryland.

Keith G. Meador, M.D., is Clinical Professor of Psychiatry and Behavioral Sciences in the Duke School of Medicine, and senior fellow in the Duke Aging Center. As Professor of the Practice of Pastoral Theology and Medicine in the Duke Divinity School, he is Director of the Program in Theology and Medicine.

Prof. Charles Pinches is in the Department of Theology and Religious Studies at the University of Scranton, Pennsylvania.

Joel James Shuman is Professor of Theology and Ethics at King's College, Wilkes-Barre, Pennsylvania.

Prof. Carole Bailey Stoneking is Chair of the Department of Religion at High Point College, North Carolina.

Laura Yordy is a Ph.D. student in the Graduate Program in Religion at Duke University.

Index

abandonment, 273, 299, 301

abortion, 22n.7, 186

Abraham, 6, 8-9, 10, 177

Aelred of Rievaulx, 175, 177-80, 183, 184

after-school programs, 199

age segregation, 37, 73, 128

age-rationing, 96-97

ageism, 83-84, 96-97, 117, 125

aging: ambiguity of, 270-73; cultural assumptions, 67; denial of, 69, 128; diversity of experiences, 118-27; gracefully, 127; "illness" of, 96; medicalization of, 116, 154-56; moral significance, 83; in New Testament terms, 4-5; "problem of," 67, 68, 69-70, 82; revaluing, 87; romantic views of, 117; theological reflection on, 89, 139-43; virtues of, 204-5, 208-21

aging industry, 88-89

alienation, 170

allegorical exegesis, 40

Allen, Jessie, 119, 122

Allen, Woody, 113

Alzheimer's disease, 97n.16, 106, 107, 115, 187, 196, 278, 293, 297

Ambrose, 24, 26-27, 28, 31, 146

Americans for Generation Equity, 84

Americans With Disabilities Act, 257

Anderson, Ray, 152n.1, 162, 165n.40

andropause, 125

Angel, Ronald and Jacqueline, 132n.8, 137, 139

angels, 286

Anna, 6-7, 177, 239

Apostolic Constitutions, 32

Aquinas, Thomas, 44, 93n.8, 147, 175, 180, 205, 223, 224, 251, 263

Arendt, Hannah, 154

Aristotle, 39, 44, 45, 93n.8, 175-76, 181, 263

Athanasius, 22, 35n.66

atheism, 186, 221n.9

Augustine, 20n.2, 21n.5, 30, 43, 45-46, 93n.8, 144-45; on Christian life, 37; on death, 23; on human ages, 39-40, 41; on memory, 275-76, 278; on music, 194; on resurrection, 25

Augustus, Emperor, 31

autonomy, 160, 172, 173, 175n.5, 178, 181, 232-35, 238, 241, 246, 248, 252-53, 257-58, 274, 297, 300

baby boomers, 235

Bacon, Roger, 48-49, 56

Bagnall, Roger, 3n.1

Balthasar, Hans Urs von, 254-55, 256

baptism, 25, 26, 148, 149, 163, 166, 196, 199, 200-201, 249-50, 253, 287-88; and dependence, 259; and memory, 296-97; and suffering, 255

Barer, Barbara M., 119

Barmen Declaration, 103

Barth, Karl, 102-3, 104, 140

Bartholomaeus, 38

Basil the Great, 23, 24, 27, 36